CAN BRITAIN SURVIVE?

CAN
BRITAIN
SURVIVE?

Edited by
EDWARD GOLDSMITH

Preface by E. J. Mishan

Tom Stacey

First published 1971 by
Tom Stacey Ltd, 28/9 Maiden Lane, London WC2E 7JP England

© 1971 Tom Stacey Ltd

SBN 85468 064 0

Printed in Great Britain
by Richard Clay (The Chaucer Press), Ltd, Bungay, Suffolk

CONTENTS

PREFACE

Dr E. J. Mishan

Professor of Economics, Washington University
Reader in Economics, London School of Economics

Plus ça change plus c'est la même chose – so runs the familiar refrain, at once
cynical and comforting. It is but half true, however. Much of what remains
unchanged from century to century are things that fall within the cycle of
life; birth, death, fear, love, hate, friendship, conflict, all the gamut of human
relationships; the search for beauty and meaning in life; the need for trust,
respect and a place of one's own; a love of pageant and ritual; a need for
worship and surrender. Again there appear to be certain immanent attitudes
in man testifying to something like a moral instinct. In all ages there is to be
found a contempt for cowardice and corruption and an admiration of
courage and integrity. While mores and customs change over space and time,
attributes such as these remain the common heritage of all cultures.

The things we are concerned with in this book, however, are the things that
change from generation to generation, sometimes indeed, from one decade to
another: population, literacy, wealth, technology, economic organization,
communications and transportation, and the consequences of such changes
on our physical environment and style of living. If today's doomsday prophets
– to employ the playful epithet used by our incorrigible progressives against
those alarmed at recent developments in the social and physical environment
– talk of unprecedented happenings they are clearly concerned with matters
falling in the latter category. And from the undeniable fact that there always
have been alarmists and Jeremiahs, one can extract very little comfort.
Cassandra, we do well to recall, was invariably right.

For more than two centuries men have distrusted machines. They were not
always wrong. The first half of the nineteenth century in Britain was a time of
acute distress, suffering and degradation for the labouring classes, men,
women and children. Whether such an epoch was a necessary condition for
the material improvement of later generations is doubtful. But whether or
not, it can be justified only on the immoral premise that the ends justify the
means. What is more pertinent, the industrial revolution that began in the
eighteenth century, or earlier, far from abating, is gathering momentum.
And this gathering momentum is now on a scale that has begun to fissure the
physical environment and to produce complex chains of ecological disruption.
The forebodings of the past may after all soon be vindicated.

The historian may also observe that for at least four centuries men have looked back wistfully to an earlier age and deplored the growing materialism and irreligion, the unnecessary bustle and change – from which observation one can deduce a great many things, but *not* that the present age is no more materialistic, no more irreligious or no faster-changing than any preceding epoch.

Indeed, one can go back further. Since the age of Chaucer historians have discovered – in poems, essays, sermons, plays, diaries and novels – a recurring nostalgia for the times when nature was more abundant, times more settled, communities more intimate and life more wholesome. In particular they will find a recurring sadness and dismay at the disappearance of green forests and the irreplaceable beauty of the English countryside. And if today conservationists inherit this mood of concern and deplore the rapid erosion, since the war, of coastline, woodland and much of our remaining scenic and historic heritage, one may legitimately infer that the concern of some people at the destruction of the rare and beautiful is an abiding characteristic of humanity. One cannot infer, however, that things have not changed, and changed for the worse in this respect: one cannot deny, that is, that the remaining area of accessible natural beauty per person is only a tiny fraction of what it was, say, in the eighteenth century.

A final variation on the same theme; the belief that the end of the world was drawing nigh was widely held at different times in human history. But from this historic fact there is no consolation. Only since the last war have men prised open Pandora's box, and have discovered technologies for destroying all life on earth many times over and in a variety of ghastly ways. Time, measured only in years, will disseminate this knowledge among smaller and less stable nations that are ruled over by adventurers and tyrants. From this prospect alone one may conclude that the chance of human life surviving the end of the century is not high. To annihilation from military mishap or irresponsibility must be added the possibility of extinction of the species from an uncontrollable epidemic (arising from man's organism being unable to adapt quickly enough to the new and more deadly viruses resulting from wholesale application of 'miracle' drugs), from an ecological calamity (arising from the inadvertent destruction of animal and insect life that preyed on the pests that consume men's harvests while the pests themselves became resistant to the chemical pesticides), and the possibility of a slower and more painful death from choking in the waste products of advancing technology.

It is, of course, possible to be too alarmist. But it is easier to be too complacent, or rather to continue being so. Since the war our political leaders have been so busy charting the course of GNP, continually making invidious comparisons with other countries' GNP's, formulating unlikely growth rates, vainly urging the workers on to feats of productivity and whipping up expectations of material plenty, that employees throughout industry have become hypersensitive to cost of living indices and to their position in the hierarchy of incomes – a development that is chiefly responsible for the wage-push inflation that politicians publicly lament and economists ignore. So preoccupied have our political masters become with playing at index numbers that they have failed to look around them and to observe the impressive growth of pollution – noise pollution, air pollution, water and soil pollution and above all the perverted development of towns, suburbs and villages, in the hopeless attempt to accommodate the rising flow of motorized traffic. Comparable phenomena in the United States, along with the rapid growth over the last two decades of annual rates of divorce, suicide, crime, violence, delinquency and drug taking, would suggest to an open mind that economic growth *per se* is not a panacea for all forms of social ill; indeed, that there are likely to be connecting links between levels of affluence and technological advance (at least under familiar conditions) and social maladjustment.

Notwithstanding failure of political leadership, the last five years or so have seen a public awakening to environmental problems. The vision of a frontier of unlimited material opportunity, and the prospect of an accelerated exploitation of natural resources implied by the conventional goal of self-sustaining economic growth, have begun to be widely challenged. This older vision of the role of economic man is giving way to a newer and a truer one. We are beginning to think of the world as a delicately balanced ecological phenomenon that occurred as some sort of miracle: a tiny, vulnerable and unique planet warmed and nourished by a dwarf star near the edge of one of a million galaxies, it is man's only haven in a vast, freezing, inhospitable and lifeless universe.

Ecological balance has been maintained and variety has flourished despite man's intervention for thousands of years. But the scale of that intervention has begun to grow rapidly over the last two centuries. Each successive decade up to the present has seen the scale of that intervention so enlarged that it is with difficulty that nature breathes and renews herself. Unless we can cope successfully within the next decade we may lose control of our civilization before the century is out.

True, we are beginning to take action, falteringly and indeed reluctantly. Too many of us are still in thrall to the nineteenth-century myth of endless progress, believing that somehow science and technology will themselves be able to save us in time from the dire consequences of widespread and indiscriminate application of their own products. Many an innocent layman takes comfort from the thought that there are thousands of scientific experts about

11

the place and vast government departments dedicated to poking their noses into everybody's business.

I wish I could subscribe to this touching faith, but I find it impossible to do so in the light of the facts and in the light of reason. The accumulation of radio-active dust, the recent history of Thalidomide, the reckless application of DDT, the spread of oil pollution, the poisoning of vast lakes, traffic-choked cities, the unbreathable air in built-up areas, testify neither to knowledge or wisdom. What is more, the men in political power, the men in charge of our great industries and research establishments, are not unduly perturbed. Their public statements reveal that for the most part they are deeply imbued with the nineteenth-century dogma of serving the social interest through unlimited economic expansion. If they have begun, dimly and belatedly, to perceive an environmental problem, they make use of it – as indeed they make use of the more traditional problems of society, associated with the aged, the sick and the poor – to update the relevance of the dogma of growth. We need to have *more* growth, they protest, not less if we are to tackle these urgent problems. All facts are grist to the growth mill. For where economic growth appears to have improved living conditions, there is obviously a case for more economic growth. And, wherever it appears to have made living conditions pretty hideous – why, more economic growth is needed to remove these untoward features!

Quite apart from the two-headed penny character of growthmen's arguments, the call today for faster economic growth to tackle environmental ills is disingenuous for at least three reasons.

First, that over the last ten years the type of industrial growth, in particular the growth of chemical products, plastics, automobiles and air travel, generates incomparably more pollution than is eliminated by private and public expenditures. What is more, economists anticipate much the same sort of growth over the next few years, whereas they do not anticipate any substantial increase in anti-pollution expenditure.

Secondly, if the government were indeed to commit itself to use a large proportion of the annual increment of GNP to combat pollution, the argument for pressing on with growth might take on plausibility. But the bulk of the annual increment of GNP goes at present in expenditures on technological hardware and software. In the United States, for instance, the annual growth of GNP is between $20 billion to $35 billion. What proportion of this increment is devoted to additional expenditure on anti-pollution measures? No one as yet knows the exact figure. But I should be surprised if it exceeds one-tenth of one per cent. And my guess is that the proportion for Britain is yet lower than that in the United States.

It is then up to those who use this argument to state the proportion of the increment of GNP that will be directed to attack pollution and environmental problems – else the public must continue to suspect that future expenditures on cleaning the environment will continue to fall far short of the pollution damage caused by the increment of GNP.

Thirdly, the 'need' for more GNP in order to do good in this and other ways is pure figment. True, economists have not yet been so bold as to produce from the statistics available that proportion of GNP which in reality goes only to making life more costly, or the rough proportions of GNP that could be classed as 'expendables', 'luxuries', 'near-garbage' and 'positively harmful'. But the broad trends are unmistakable. Granted that the average American was materially very comfortable about 1950 (producing then more *per capita* than we do today), we should hardly feel unjustified in sharing among the above arbitrary classes of goods a substantial fraction of the annual increment in GNP as between 1950 and 1970 – a total of some $200 billion would not, I think be an exaggeration. To talk then of the *need* for more resources before pollution, or social, problems can be effectively tackled is manifest nonsense. It is true only in the trivial sense which accepts as unalterable data all existing institutions, mechanisms and political programmes – accepts, among other things, the annual expenditure in the United States of $20 billion on the task of endlessly persuading consumers to buy more of a virtually unlimited assortment of goods that presses hard against the consumers' capacity to absorb them, an assortment ranging from plastic gew gaws to private planes, from liquor to extra automobiles, from electric bootbrushes to pornographic literature and entertainment.

Finally, and perhaps most relevant of all, very little increase in public expenditure is called for. What is called for is effective legislation that puts the burden of curbing pollution squarely on the shoulders of the pollutors. The outcome of such legislation would be a reallocation of resources away from pollutant-creating goods and towards investment in pollutant-preventive techniques.

Other examples could be given of that mixture of innocence, cussedness and cant which, interfused in solemn utterances of our unrepentent growthmen – who alas include, at present, the political leaders of both our major parties – serve to disarm and mislead the public into placing their hopes for a better world on more and faster economic growth. But this preface is not the place for them. Already I may have trespassed a little in availing myself of the courtesy of the editor to use the preface to articulate my impatience with the repeated and spurious arguments of growthmen.

Having said more than once that time is short, I shall not detain the reader further from dipping into the contents of this book. The chapters, most of them, are written by distinguished scholars in a number of special fields. They will go far to persuade him, as I have been persuaded, of the gravity of the ecological problem by providing information on its recent growth and present dimensions.

A larger, more informed and concerned public is necessary to bring pressure on governments to move away from their fixation with the policy of head-on economic growth towards a policy based on ecological stability and on a number of criteria of social welfare; to move, that is, from commitment to economic growth to a commitment to quality of life. This book, I believe, will make a distinct contribution towards realizing the goal of the editor of bringing just such a public into being.

INTRODUCTION

Edward Goldsmith

Editor, *The Ecologist*

Our experts predict a rosy future for the inhabitants of these isles. By the end of the century, they maintain, our standard of living will have just about doubled, everybody will be twice as rich and able to afford twice as many consumer goods and services. Many scientists, and in particular ecologists, are not happy about predictions of this sort. Some even doubt the desirability of attempting to achieve an increase in our standard of living at considerable cost to our social and physical environment. This would mean turning over much of our countryside to urban development, depriving wildlife of its natural habitat and destroying beautiful buildings to make way for factories and blocks of flats. It would mean, too, destroying rural life by forcing people to live in ever larger and uglier urban areas which do not provide suitable environments for them, and to which they would find it difficult to adapt. It would mean using up even more rapidly the world's limited stock of natural resources and polluting our rivers, seas, soil and air with the waste products of agriculture and industry.

Even if it were desirable to make such sacrifices on the altar of economic growth, it is by no means certain that this growth can be achieved. Economic growth, like all other forms of growth, cannot proceed indefinitely.

In order to gauge the economic future of this country and to determine what sort of growth is possible, we must first realize that from the economic point of view Britain is a factory that buys much of its food and practically all its raw materials abroad and transforms the latter into finished products, many of which must be exported to obtain the money necessary to finance further purchases of food and raw materials.

This mechanism has worked very well so far, well enough to provide the British people with a relatively high standard of living, but that is not to say it will continue to function indefinitely. It could only do so under very specific conditions. Firstly, food and raw materials must be available abroad and the people who produce them must be willing to part with them at a reasonable price. Secondly, we must retain the capacity to manufacture finished products better and more cheaply than our rivals, and thirdly, our customers must have both the capacity and the desire to buy these products from us. As will be shown in this book, it is unlikely that these conditions will always be satisfied; in fact, during the next thirty years they are less and less likely to be satisfied. If this is so, then our standard of living, rather than increase as our economists predict, is likely to fall and continue falling at an ever greater rate. The material on which this argument is based is presented in the twenty-two chapters that make up this book. Such information is readily available; much of it is contained in the report of the *Council on Environmental Quality* to President Nixon.[1]

It might be asked why this information is not generally taken into account by our economists and the politicians they advise. There are a number of possible explanations to this.

The first is simply that people have a built-in tendency to avoid facing disagreeable facts. If such facts are too disagreeable, and their acceptance would threaten people's mental equilibrium, they tend to be rejected, which may in fact be a very necessary adaptive mechanism. A clear example of this rejection appears in Alan Moorehead's *The Fatal Impact*.[2] When Captain Cook first sailed into Botany Bay, he saw a number of Australian aborigines going about their daily chores, digging for roots, picking berries and catching small animals. It is probable that these people had never seen more elaborate boats than their own dug-out canoes. Captain Cook's three-masted schooners must have been a truly spectacular sight. The aborigines might have been expected to crowd to the beach and gape in amazement, perhaps get down on their knees and worship the strangers as gods. Alternatively, they might have fled in total panic. However, they did none of these things. They simply went on with their normal activities as if nothing was amiss. Clearly to accept the presence, if not the possibility of the existence of these extraordinary monsters, was not compatible with the maintenance of their mental equilibrium.

They had no alternative but to refuse to do so and thus to reject such totally unacceptable information. But why was this information so unacceptable? It was in conflict with their basic cognitive structure or world-view, just as it would be with us if we suddenly saw a unicorn or flying elephant. Anthony Wallace in his book *Culture and Personality*[3] shows that people will do anything to preserve that system of beliefs which makes up their world-view and in terms of which their whole behaviour pattern must be understood. He refers to this as the Law of the Preservation of Cognitive Structure. It seems to apply equally well to that part of the world-view of an individual that distinguishes him from his fellows, as to that part that is common to all the members of his society. The reaction of the Australian aborigines to Captain Cook's ships is no different from ours when we refuse to look at unpleasant facts, such as those presented in this book. After all, we try to persuade ourselves, what can we do about them? 'I don't want to know,' is the usual response. Illustrations of this principle can be found in the behaviour of many primitive peoples. The efficacy of the magical rites performed

16

by rainmakers to induce rain is doubted by nobody. Such a belief persists because failure to produce rain will not be attributed to the inefficacy of the rituals, *but to some technical fault in their performance*, such as the presence of someone who has violated a taboo.

Even more illustrative is the behaviour of the head-hunting Jivaro Indians of Eastern Ecuador.[4] Their chief aim in life is to obtain an 'aroutam' soul, whose acquisition, as the result of a complex ritual, confers upon them in-vulnerability in war. This soul, after another ritual, leaves the body of its host. However, its power remains, ebbing away only very slowly. It is at this point that the Jivaro, who have just acquired and lost an aroutam soul, must join a killing party whose role it is to kill a member of some other tribe. This is an essential part of aroutam ritual, as it is only by repeated killings that one can replace the ebbing soul with a new one. Though they are supposed to have complete invulnerability, it occasionally occurs that the killing party is unsuccessful, and one of their members is killed in the attack. When this happens, the Jivaro are not led to revise their belief in the invulnerability conferred by the aroutam soul. On the contrary, the death is simply considered 'to be evidence that the deceased had already lost his aroutam soul without realizing it.'

On the other hand, the Jivaro are consistent enough in their belief to 'realize' that their killing expedition would have little success if their intended victim were protected by an aroutam soul. For instance,

> 'A man who has killed repeatedly, called Kakaram, or "powerful one", is rarely attacked because his enemies feel that the protection provided him by his constantly replaced souls would make any assassination attempt against him fruitless ...'

Thus, he is only attacked if the raiders believe that he has lost his aroutam soul. If they should fail to kill him, this would not cast any doubts as to the vulnerability of people who have been abandoned by their aroutam souls. On the contrary, failure would be attributed to the fact that ...

> 'the enemy still retained the soul, or had a second one in reserve.'

There is a tendency to laugh at such tales. Yet we ourselves are constantly doing the same thing. We are constantly reinterpreting data in such a way that it becomes reconcilable with the generalities of our cultural pattern.

Now, in our industrial society, one of the most basic of these is the ideal of progress which we associate, consciously or not, with economic growth and the corresponding increase in our standard of living. Unfortunately, it happens that the countries in which these associated processes have proceeded furthest, *i.e.* the United States, Japan, Great Britain, are those with the most serious social and ecological problems.

All the evidence presented in this book tends to show that progress is not necessarily the boon we think it is and that in any case it ceases to be desirable once a certain degree has been achieved.

This evidence, however, is psychologically unacceptable to most of us, and we find ourselves forced to seek to interpret the data on which it is based in such a way as to be led to different conclusions. Our plight, we try to persuade ourselves, is due to certain tendencies which may occasionally accompany economic growth, and hence progress, but which can easily be avoided if we take the necessary trouble. More education, a little law and order, for instance, will stop the continued growth of crime, delinquency, drug addiction, alcoholism and the other symptoms of social disintegration. A little pollution control here and there, and all the economic growth we want becomes reconcilable with the conservation of our environment. It is essential that we realize that in persuading ourselves that this is so, we are behaving exactly in the same way as the rainmaker and the Jivaro Indian headhunter.

However, even had we the courage to face facts, it is unlikely that we would make the maximum use of the social and ecological information to which I am referring. This is so for a number of methodological reasons. The first is simply that our learning is divided up into a host of watertight compartments. Our academics have become specialists concerned only with examining a very limited amount of data – that falling within their particular discipline. Unfortunately the world is not divided up in this manner. It developed as a single integrated process and as a result, it is a single, integrated system. Also, its parts are so closely inter-related that they cannot be examined *in vacuo* but only in accordance with their function within the system as a whole. Academics are not in a good position to make precise predictions, except in the artificial conditions of their laboratories. Economists are no exception to this rule and it is becoming increasingly evident that factors other than those falling within the scope of their particular discipline must be taken into account to make accurate predictions of economic currents. In this respect, the importance of sociological factors was emphasized by Polanyi.[5] A study of the economics of primitive societies led him to contest one of the basic principles of economics; that man would act to increase his material advantages. He wrote, 'The outstanding discovery of recent historical and anthropological research is that man's economy, as a rule, is submerged in his social relationships. He does not act so as to safeguard his individual interest in the possession of material goods; he acts so as to safeguard the social standing, his social claims, his social assets. He values material goods only in so far as they serve this end. Neither the process of production nor that of distribution is linked to specific economic interest attached to the possession of goods; but every single step in that process is geared to a number of social interests which eventually ensure that the required step be taken.

18

Introduction

These interests will be very different in a small hunting or fishing community from those of a vast despotic society, but in either case the economic system will be run on non-economic motives. The explanation in terms of survival is simple. Take the case of a tribal society. The individual's economic interest is rarely paramount, for the community keeps all its members from starving unless it is itself borne down by catastrophe, in which case interests are again threatened collectively, not individually. The maintenance of social ties, on the other hand, is crucial. First, because by disregarding the accepted code of honour, or generosity, the individual cuts himself off from the community and becomes an outcast; second, because, in the long run, all social obligations are reciprocal, and their fulfilment serves also the individual's give-and-take interests best. Such a situation must exert a continuous pressure on the individual to eliminate economic self-interest from his consciousness to the point of making him unable in many cases (but by no means all), even to comprehend the implications of his own actions in terms of such interest.' Weber, in his celebrated work *The Protestant Ethic and the Spirit of Capitalism*,[6] showed, with reference to the Industrial Revolution in Britain, that economic growth cannot be predicted by simply taking into account those variables that normally fall within the discipline of economics. They are much more of a sociological nature. He showed that the Industrial Revolution was largely the work of a single group of people with a common religion and a corresponding set of values. These were the Quakers and other non-conformists. They worked not just to make money but because working was an essential part of their religion. It was the only way of being virtuous, the only way of pleasing God. In more general terms, economic growth would only occur among people for whom it constituted a cultural ideal. It is thus the cultural pattern of a people more than the availability of capital, cheap money, low wages and other similar purely economic factors, that will determine the level of economic growth. Weber's thesis, as it has come to be called, has been made use of to explain many examples of economic growth in different parts of the world. In general it appears to explain them quite adequately. More recently Hagen in *The Theory of Social Change*[7] pushes Weber's analysis several steps further. Like Weber, Hagen maintains that economic growth occurs in a society for which it provides a cultural ideal. He says that a class of entrepreneurs is required, among whom this ideal is particularly pronounced. It must have been deprived of its normal behavioural outlet, which had hitherto provided it with its means of achieving the level of success and prestige that it was geared culturally to expect. In addition, this class must be sufficiently prestigious to be emulated by the rest of society so that a general capitalist ethic should reign. Hagen shows how economic growth in England during the Industrial Revolution, in Japan after the Meiji Revolution, in the Antioquia province of Colombia in the last thirty years and in a particular district of Indonesia, can be explained in terms of this thesis.

If the connection between sociology and economics is becoming apparent, that between ecology and economics has been established so far by very few writers. In the United States, the first economist of note to have underlined the relevance of ecological factors was Kenneth Boulding. He showed that our world is finite – it is nothing more than a 'spaceship' and it clearly cannot accommodate the unlimited economic growth to which our society is geared. In Britain, Dr E. J. Mishan in his well-known book *The Costs of Economic Growth*[8] has done more than anyone to shatter the ideal of economic growth. It is clear that to understand the process involved and its effect on the total environment, account must be taken of a vast amount of information that does not fall within the conventional field of economics. Ideally, one should build a complete inter-disciplinary model of the biosphere in order to establish how economic growth affects all its numerous and closely inter-related parts. What is certain is, that so long as the economist remains a specialist only capable of taking into account a restricted number of variables falling within the scope of his particular discipline, there is very little chance that his predictions will be sufficiently accurate to guide any major aspect of public policy. This brings us to yet another reason why economists may not have taken ecological factors into account. In order to make their predictions, they are quite happy to project current economic trends into the future. This is an application of the inductive method favoured by empiricist philosophy at present in fashion in Anglo-American academic circles.

According to this philosophy, the only way to predict the future is to base the prediction on what has happened in the past. This method may be satisfactory for making predictions in a highly stable environment in which discontinuities are unlikely to occur. However, as the environment becomes more unstable, more subtle means for making predictions are required.

In all cases, predictions are based on information, which must not be confused with data. Information is a measure of the organization of data. It is best regarded, as Kenneth Craik[9] was the first to show, as constituting a model of the relationship between the system and its environment, *i.e.* of the bigger system of which it is part. This model can only be an approximation of the latter since it can only take into account a finite number among the infinite number of factors involved. As a result, predictions can only be probable. They can never be certain, and this limitation must apply to even the most sophisticated scientific predictions. Their probability, however, can always be increased by the simple expedient of improving the model. This involves increasing the amount of relevant data, and its degree of organiza-

Introduction

tion, and also the rate at which it is detected and interpreted (ensuring in this way that predictions are based on the most up-to-date data).

Thus, in order to predict the economic future of this country, we must begin by collecting the maximum amount of relevant data, regardless of the discipline of which it is normally part. This must be organized in such a way as to show how they are inter-related, providing us with a dynamic model of Britain as a social and economic system.

That is what this book attempts to do. I am not suggesting we have gathered together sufficient data, nor that it has been organized sufficiently well to permit accurate predictions. What I do maintain is, that any predictions which do *not* take these data into account, nor the inter-relationships established between them, cannot be taken seriously.

A number of contributors to this book intend to form a permanent Committee that will attempt to build a model of Britain as it will be affected by social and ecological changes in the next thirty years or so. This model will be monitored in the light of all new developments and the public will be kept informed of its progress in the pages of *The Ecologist* magazine.

REFERENCES

1   COUNCIL ON ENVIRONMENTAL QUALITY. 1970. *First Report.* Washington.
2   MOOREHEAD, ALAN. 1966. *The Fatal Impact.* London: Hamish Hamilton.
3   WALLACE, ANTHONY. 1963. *Culture and Personality.* New York: Random Press.
4   HARNER, M. J. 1966. Jivaro Souls. In *America Anthropologist, 64* (2).
5   POLANYI, KARL. 1968. *Primitive, Archaic and Modern Economics.* New York: Doubleday.
6   WEBER, MAX. 1930. *The Protestant Ethic and the Spirit of Capitalism.* London: George Allen & Unwin.
7   HAGEN, E. E. 1964. *On the Theory of Social Change.* London: Tavistock.
8   MISHAN, E. J. 1967. *The Costs of Economic Growth.* London: Staples Press.
9   CRAIK, KENNETH. 1952. *The Nature of Explanation.* Cambridge: CUP.

PART ONE

Limits of Growth

1 LIMITS OF ECONOMIC GROWTH

Dr E. J. Mishan

Professor of Economics, University of Washington
Reader in Economics, London School of Economics

The popular image of the economist appears to be that of an apologist for the economic Establishment, a sort of intellectual descendant of Gradgrind, whose main occupation is that of scrutinizing the indices of employment, exports, interest rates and, of course, economic growth. By reference to such indices alone, it is thought, and quite impervious to the changing features of the world about him, he forms solemn judgments about the nation's prospects, and concludes either that the economy is sound – and, therefore, by extension, the state of the nation at large – or, much more frequently, that it is unsound.

That there are such people in our midst is certain. Some are the spokesmen of our great industries. Some are to be found among our financial journalists, highly skilled in this art of index economics and conditioned over time to rejoice at detecting an upturn in any economic indicator and to lament at detecting a downturn. Too many of such watchdogs are yet to be found among government ministers and senior officials. For there is no easier way to earn a reputation for prodigious common sense and no-nonsense realism than to be seen bustling about the country, bursting with the latest statistics, warning against complacency and exhorting the business community to greater feats of productivity.

But the economist, as scientist at least, has no commitment to objectives connected with economic growth. Some economists approve of such policies, some do not. But there is nothing in economic theory that can be adduced to support either growth or anti-growth.

It so happens, however, that a lively interest in what we now call the quality of life can be found in the writings of many of our great economists. John Stuart Mill is frequently quoted in the conservation literature, but apposite quotations could also be culled from the writings of a number of others, Marshall, Pigou, Keynes, Knight – to mention only those that spring to mind – who have inveighed against the mere pursuit of materialism in disregard of the social consequences. Indeed, in the last decade, and contrary to popular belief, a number of professional economists in this country and in the United States have been in the forefront of the battle against the mounting spillover effects of indiscriminate economic growth. And there is an increasing number, at present less vociferous, in close sympathy with the growing concern over the last few years at the noise, filth, congestion and environmental destruction that appears to follow inevitably in the wake of rapid economic growth. What is more, the economist has a distinct contribution to make. Compared with the contribution to be made by the ecologist, it is, perhaps, limited. But it is by no means parochial.

The economist can attempt to restore perspective, casting doubt on the need-to-grow thesis and on the significance of indices of national income; he can, by reference to economic concepts, promote an understanding of the social problems posed by pollution; he can examine the economics of the alternative solutions proposed. Let us consider each facet of this possible contribution in turn.

With the rapid growth in the popular channels of communication it is more true than ever that the sheer weight of reiteration, rather than the power of reason, influences the attitude of the public. A simple term such as growth potential is loaded with compulsion: it suggests that waste is incurred whenever we fail, as we invariably do, to realize this potential growth. It is a term apt to the technocratic approach, that envisages the country as some sort of vast power-house with every grown man and woman a potential unit of input to be harnessed to a generating system from which flows this vital stuff called industrial output. And since this stuff can, apparently, be measured statistically as Gross National Product (GNP) it follows that the more of it the better. Viewed as power-houses for the generation of GNP, some countries appear to perform better than Britain. It is then inferred that we must make every endeavour to catch up, otherwise we shall be left behind in the race. Once it is discovered that, say, America uses more engineers, or has more PhD's, per million of population than we do, the cry goes out that we *need* at least x per cent more engineers and y per cent more PhD's if we are to 'compete effectively in the modern world', or 'break into the twentieth century', – or any other journalistic cliché indicative of thrust or go-go.

And so we go on; steel output could, if we tried hard, rise to z million tons by 1980, as much *per capita* as the United States has now. In consequence, we *need* to expand steel capacity by w per cent per annum. With such 'needs of industry' to be met we shall require increased commercial transport. We shall therefore require more roads, more fuel imports and so on, in consequence of which we shall *need* to work harder in order to pay for these future needs. Thus, we progress from implicit choices to explicit imperatives.

It would be futile, of course, to suggest that we should be thinking of the possibilities of reducing the working day. How could we possibly hope to compete in world markets? What choice have we but to return to the treadmill.

This is a sad state for any nation to be in, and in an affluent society surpassingly strange. To have come this far into the twentieth century, with business economists interpreting the alleged increase in our national income as 'enrichment' or, more sagaciously, as 'an extension in the area of choice', and then to be told almost twice a day that we have no choice – that if we are to pay our way in the world we have to work harder! It is enough to tax the credulity of any being whose judgment has not yet been swept away by the torrents of exhortation.

But of course we have a choice, a wide range of choice. The so-called policy of economic growth, as popularly understood, is little more than a policy of drifting quickly, of snatching at any and every technological innovation that proves marketable with scant respect for the social consequences.

In the formulation of the ends of economic policy, the word *need* is not to be invoked. Markets do not need to be expanded – although of course, businessmen dearly *like* to see them expand, whether through a rise in *per capita* income or through a rise in domestic or immigrant population. And it is a sad and surprising fact that governments today have not yet weaned themselves from the habit of equating the 'needs' of industry with the well-being of society. Indeed, it is entirely possible so to arrange things as to produce fewer gadgets and to enjoy more leisure. Though blasphemous to utter, it is also possible to train fewer scientists and engineers without our perishing from the face of the earth. We might even enjoy life better. Nor do we need to capture markets in the hope of lowering costs, or to lower costs in the hope of capturing markets. We can quite rationally and deliberately choose to reduce our foreign trade and to produce smaller quantities of some goods, possibly at higher cost. We can decide to reduce the strains of competition and opt for an easier life. I do not argue that this is a better policy; only that such choices and many others can be translated into perfectly viable alternatives if ever the public is prepared to consider them.

The choice of a quieter economic life does, however, imply turning our backs on GNP or any other indicator of national product. I need hardly argue in this book that GNP is not to be viewed as a measure of gross national achievement. Neither is it, contrary to the impression conveyed by newspaper editorials, an index of civic virtue. On the contrary over the last

25

twenty years or so, it is probably the best index we have of gross national pollution.

What it purports to be is an indicator of what Professor Boulding (of Colorado, USA) has called 'throughput', an index of the resources we have destroyed during the year (allowance being made for some addition to the stock of capital). On a biased view (biased because technological innovation is ignored) the faster we consume the earth's resources, the higher the index of economic growth. Regarded as an index of social well-being, either on an aggregate or on a *per capita* basis, it is also perverse. Does anyone really believe that the average person or family in the United States is two and a half times as contented or 'fulfilled' as the average person or family in the United Kingdom? If we increase our leisure, GNP declines. If resources are directed to producing fewer goods and towards combating an increase in the incidence of crime and disease, there is no reduction in GNP.

Indeed, an increase in the numbers killed on the roads, an increase in the numbers dying from cancer, coronaries or nervous diseases, provides extra business for physicians and undertakers, and can contribute to raising GNP. A forest destroyed to produce the hundreds of tons of paper necessary for the American Sunday editions is a component of GNP. The spreading of concrete over acres of once beautiful countryside adds to the value of GNP. The destruction of historic buildings or parts of a hamlet in order to make room for a new road or supermarket takes its place as a positive item in GNP. The night flights that make some people's life a virtual nightmare are an essential component of GNP, as is the output of the industrial processes that daily pour their effluent into the air and into lakes and rivers. And so one could go on.

It is for such reasons that economists, particularly in the United States, are increasingly dissatisfied with the use of GNP as an index of anything save crude output. They are preparing to refine it by subtracting from it components that are effectively intermediate goods and not final goods, and by subtracting from it the incidental outputs of bads or pollutants. For instance, subtracting expenditures on internal and external defence that can better be regarded, not as final goods wanted for themselves, but simply resources spent in promoting the conditions necessary to production and consumption. Another example would be the removal from GNP of expenditures used up by workers, personnel and businessmen simply in commuting to work. When GNP is trimmed down to size in this way, it is surprising how unimpressive the progress over the past half century looks. They are proposing also to supplement it by other, more direct, indices of social welfare, such as those purporting to measure the incidence of crime, violence, divorce, drop-outs, drug-consumption, to mention just a few.

The economic approach to problems of pollution differs – in degree rather than in kind – from that of the ecological in that it is limited to the foreseeable and more tangible consequences of economic activity, in particular to those consequences to which money values can be assigned. Though this does indeed impose limits on what the economist can say, the mere fact that he can translate the effects of his proposals into sums of money assures him of a respectful hearing in a society such as ours, readily impressed by figures.

The principle on which the Western economist attributes values to the by-products of economic activities is no different from that used in evaluating goods in general. Accepting the dictum that each man knows his own interest best, he goes along with the attitudes and the existing tastes of the community. The value, then, he attributes to any good or new acquisition is the (maximum) sum a person is willing to pay for it; and to any bad, or loss of a good, the (minimum) sum a person is willing to accept as compensation for bearing it. Although this routine procedure, I am aware, must appear of limited relevance, if followed consistently it can lead to quite sensible proposals, as we shall see later. For a century at least, the economic concept of a spillover effect – the unintended by-products, good or bad, of otherwise legitimate economic activity (of which ecological consequences form the broadest class) – has exercised the minds of economists. In particular, since the war there has been a marked proliferation of economic literature on this subject, part empirical but mainly theoretical, and of uneven quality and relevance.

The reader may well wonder why it is that these developments have not, then, been brought more forcibly to the attention of the public. There can be more than one reason, and it is revealing to discuss some of them.

First, the professional economist has until very recently concentrated largely on spillover effects within an inter-industry context. The favoured examples are those spillovers produced by one industry or firm that fall on another industry or firm. These inter-firm or inter-industry spillover effects are easier to calculate than those suffered by the public at large, and schemes for adjustments are more feasible as between organized groups than as between an unorganized public, on the one hand, and the industries in general, or the users of their products, on the other.

Secondly, the professional economist, before the war at least, regarded these spillover effects as merely one among several factors – such as the degree of monopoly in industry, or the incidence of taxes and subsidies, or imperfect mobility and information – that stood in the way of an ideal solution to which, at any moment of time, the economy was moving. They were regarded more as one of the standard obstacles in the construction of quasi-mathematical optimum systems, rather than as an urgent social problem. And in economics, far more than in the physical sciences, immersion in pure theory is a sure way to lose all sense of proportion. No empirical restraints intrude and, more often than not, effects of the greatest social significance are cast down by the merest shadow of an improbable relationship.

Thirdly, there is the undoubted difficulty of measuring the damages suffered by the public at large. The additional cost of keeping one's clothes and person clean in a smoke-polluted area can be estimated without too much difficulty and added, along with such costs for all other persons, to the commercial costs of producing the good in question. The costs of water-pollution by one or more factories is also amenable to measurement wherever the authorities have estimates of the damages caused to other industries or to fishermen. But the major social afflictions such as industrial noise, dirt, stench, ugliness, urban sprawl and other features that jar the nerves, offend the sight or in general assault the senses and impair the health, are difficult to measure and to impute to their respective sources – which is, of course, no reason for treating them with resignation.

Finally, and perhaps most important of all, there are proponents of *laisser-faire* still at large who argue that nothing need be done. Given enough time and, presumably, enough forbearance, things will sort themselves out; that is to say, if the spillover is 'uneconomic' it will be eliminated sooner or later. And if it persists, the presumption is that, after all, it is not 'uneconomic'.

Let me illustate this line of reasoning by reference to a private airport. It may well be that the families residing in the neighbourhood could together raise a sum that is more than enough to compensate both the airport authorities for moving to another site and local businessmen anticipating profits from consequent development. But under existing institutions the initiative for bringing about such an arrangement is not available. Even if it were, the incidental costs of estimating and ensuring a fair contribution from each of some several score thousand families would be prohibitive. In the event, the potential economic improvement does not take place.

But then, says our *laisser-faire* friend, this result is just what it should be. For the costs of estimating and securing a fair contribution from all these families, the costs of negotiating with the airport authorities, the costs of legalizing such agreements and so on – call these *transactions costs* – are not imaginary costs; they are real costs; they use up scarce time and resources. And since transactions costs exceed the potential gain of moving the airport elsewhere, there is on balance a net loss in doing so.

But this inference is far from being conclusive. Indeed, a little reflection reveals the argument to be double-edged. For if existing laws were devised to protect the amenity of citizens, then all the costs incidental to a change (by mutual consent) in the *status quo* would have to be borne *not* (as at present) by the victims of spillover effects, but by the creators of spillover effects. Under such a law a wide range of activities from airline flights and automobile traffic, to chemical works and package tourism, would be drastically curbed –

and resources released for the production of other non-polluting goods and services.

In equity there is a strong case for such laws, and it is only the fact of their non-existence that poses for the community an artificial problem. For in the absence of such amenity legislation, not only do the costs of compensating the polluting industry fall on the victims but also the full *transactions costs*. If, on the other hand, anti-pollution measures are to be financed by the public, the proposal meets with political resistance. Taxpayers, it is pointed out, are not keen to have their burdens increased. Commissions are then set up by governments and local authorities, editorials are written calling for more research by scientists and industry, and so things continue much as before.

Clearly, if the responsibility for a range of pollutants, including noise, were instead put squarely on the shoulders of the perpetrators, the problem would be much more amenable. Industry would have an immediate incentive to discover the cheapest method of controlling its pollutants, since the alternative would be either to compensate all legitimate claimants or to close down. The burden, that is, would be shifted at once on to the industries responsible and any additional costs would, in time, be shifted on to those using the products of such industries.

I emphasize the case in equity, since the apparent dilemma – to have people lose sleep or to have the country lose money – arises, in the last resort from the government's quite cynical disregard of the physical and mental suffering caused by promoting traffic and other developments. The growth in night flights is only one of the more blatant instances in which, in our so-called affluent society, large numbers of innocent people are made to suffer so that others have additional opportunities to pursue profits and pleasure.

This situation, however, did not affront the conscience of our socialist ministers, and there is no inkling that it causes any pangs to existing ministers of the Crown. I shall be impertinent enough to suggest that if the nightly slumbers of the members of the front bench, or of their children, were persistently disturbed by aircraft noise we should get immediate action. But while it is only others that suffer, the law protecting the airlines continues. Priority is given to technology and commercialism; not to considerations of right or of social justice.

The pre-condition, then, both of social justice and of good economic allocation is a radical alteration of our existing laws, the aim being to safeguard the citizen from the torments inflicted on him by the processes and products of the new technology. The Age calls for a charter of amenity rights, and on moral grounds at least, the case for such a charter is more powerful than that for the existing laws on property rights.

At all events, once such amenity legislation is accepted, the various proposals put forward by economists fall easily into place, or else become superfluous. Pollutant-creating industries will then have a choice of compensating claimants, of curbing outputs, of fitting anti-pollution devices or of joining in comprehensive schemes involving the recycling of waste materials. The latter method of dealing with pollutants appears, at present, to be one of the most economic, and once the law provides the incentive to industrial research into new ways of dealing with pollutants, we can look forward to further development of such techniques. In the United States, a number of economists have devised sophisticated mathematical programming models and in a number of cases have fitted estimates to them, in order to discover the minimum costs of meeting a variety of alternative water-purification targets in river basins.

A secondary and supplementary proposal which might be unnecessary once strong anti-disamenity laws became an essential part of our heritage, merits attention as an immediate and practical measure. The State alone is in a position to promote social welfare by taking the initiative in providing separate areas for those for whom quiet, clean air and pleasant environment are highly valued. This can be done without prejudice to the interests of others who care less about them. Indeed, now that science has succeeded in launching humanity into the supersonic era, it is of the utmost urgency that governments everywhere be prevailed upon to set aside large areas free at least of aerial disturbance. The longer the delay, the greater becomes the apparent dependence of the economy upon such flights; the more industrial operations become re-scheduled to new timetables, the further the process of integrating airline flights with other means of transport and the more massive the build-up of vested interests and expectations.

If reservations were set aside in the United States as a matter of justice for the American Indians who wanted no part of the society of the white man, a similar justice is surely due to the citizen who wishes to opt out of at least some of the features of technological society. For it is surely an injustice to compel noise-sensitive people to put up with arbitrary and continual noise-bombardment – though it is practically unavoidable in the absence of noise-free zones. Such zones are in any case prerequisite to experiments in a variety of separate areas offering wider choice to the citizen in respect of environmental quality.

REFERENCES

KNEESE, A. R. 1971. Background for the economic analysis of environmental pollution. In *Swedish Economic Journal*, March.
KNEESE, A. V. and s. c. SMITH (Ed.). 1966. *Water research; economic analysis; water management, evaluation problems*. Washington: Resources for the Future, Inc.

Limits of Economic Growth

KRUTILLA, J. V. 1967. Conservation reconsidered. In *The American Economic Review*, September.

MISHAN, E. J. 1967. *The Costs of Economic Growth*. London: Staples Press.

MISHAN, E. J. 1971. The postwar literature on externalities. In *The Journal of Economic Literature*, March.

2 LIMITS OF DEMOGRAPHIC GROWTH

Robert Allen

Deputy Editor, *The Ecologist*

It is the year 2371. The population of the world is 6 million million. That of England and Wales is something over 500 million – its density is lower than most countries, only 3,366 people to the square kilometre, the same as Singapore today. The only scraps of greenery are a few moth-eaten parks in Wales and the Pennines, and two dozen National Nature Reserves and Sites of Special Scientific Interest heavily guarded by officers of the Nature Conservancy. Like everybody else in the world, we eat single-celled marine organisms. No food is grown on land as there isn't enough room, and meat-eating was eliminated 150 years ago. The present population can be maintained only because the algae are capable of maximum efficiency (8 per cent conversion of solar radiation). Mirrors are being put into orbit to maximize the input of solar energy. A population of 15 million million is predicted for 50 years time and everybody is grimly optimistic.

Preposterous? Ecologically and socially, no doubt; mathematically, no. Assuming Britain's population continues to grow at the rate of 0·6 per cent a year (giving it a doubling time of 117 years) and that of the world as a whole at 1·9 per cent (a doubling time of 37 years), then in 400 years time that is what the figures will be.

Professor J. H. Fremlin, who first sketched this scenario in an article for the *New Scientist*,[1] suggests that world population could continue to grow for yet another 400 years – up to 12,000 million million people – by when the problem of dissipating waste heat (long more important than the acquisition of energy) will have become insurmountable. In making these predictions Professor Fremlin considers only the earth's physical limits, and he makes some crucial assumptions. These are that there will be world-wide co-operation in the application of food technology, that a technology will be developed that is 100 per cent efficient, and that it will be subtle and flexible enough to resist the tendency of all ecosystems to become complex, to diversify at the species level. Because well before 2371 there will be room enough only for man and his algae.

My own opinion is that the population of England and Wales will be nowhere near 500 million in the year 2371. Political and ecological forces will reduce world population long before it reaches absolute physical limits.

Limits of Demographic Growth

My purpose in indulging this fantasy is to demonstrate how close we are to obliging later generations to lead highly restricted lives, even if current growth rates were to decline slightly. Provided that we can develop the technology to mitigate any ecological backlash, we are committing our descendants to (among many other things) a diet of algae. Perhaps they will adapt to it, they might grow quite to like it, but what right have we to do this?

What right – and for what possible reason? There is no need for us to condone perpetual growth, even if it were possible, and there are plenty of other courses we can take. It would not be difficult to stabilize Britain's population at 60 million by the year 2000, and thereafter a decline of 0·6 per cent a year (the same rate as the increase today) would be by no means impossible. If this decline were maintained, then a population of 10 million could be achieved by about the year 2300.

500 million or 50 million, 100 million or 10 million – as a society we have the choice and we cannot avoid it. If we ignore it, if we opt for inaction because the choice is so difficult, we *choose* for ourselves and our children a life progressively deprived of other choices, of all the different freedoms which constitute what we know as personal liberty. Furthermore, by choosing to do nothing, we choose famine, disease and war as regulators of our population rather than more humane socio-economic methods. These methods, and the relationship of choice to the idea of an optimum population for Britain, will be considered later on in this chapter. Meanwhile I would like to consider some of our expectations for the year 2000.

There are 56 million people in Britain today. Most (49 million) live in England and Wales. It is an unusually high population, the result of a highly abnormal growth rate. It took about 10,000 years for Britain to achieve her first million, and another 1,000 for the next nine to come along. By 1800 the population was 10 million. Since then it has taken us only 170 years to add a further 46 million, so that in 1·5 per cent of the total period we have more than quadrupled our population. In the middle of the nineteenth century the excess of births over deaths was about 250,000 a year. This rose steeply until by the end of the century it was almost 400,000 a year. It dropped sharply in the 1930s to around 100,000, but has since climbed so that it is again well over 250,000 a year. Thus although the rate of increase of 100 years ago has been halved (then 1 per cent, now 0·6 per cent), the absolute increase (the actual number of extra people we have to deal with) has not dropped at all.

In England and Wales there are more than 320 people to each square kilometre of land, a density exceeded only in the Netherlands (375) and Taiwan (365), if we exclude small depressed islands like Mauritius (415) and city-states like Monaco (16,107) or Hong Kong (3,708). Even if we take the United Kingdom as a whole, its density (226 per sq. km.) is exceeded by only

C

five other countries: Japan (270), Korea (302), Lebanon (242), Belgium (314) and West Germany (233).

In 1969 Miss Jean Thompson, the Chief Statistician at the General Register Office, told a meeting of biologists and social scientists on *The Optimum Population for Britain*[2] that the current projection for the year 2000 was a population of 66 million. Three principal assumptions lay behind this projection: (1) during the next 30 years more people will reach middle age (although many do already) but our chances of reaching a greater age will not be significantly improved; this assumption allowed for 'further benefits to be reaped from existing medical knowledge, and for the effects of further steady advance not only in medical knowledge and techniques but in its application', but not for any possible breakthrough; (2) the influence of migration will be slight and that as today there will be a small net outward flow; (3) the average family size will be 2·5. What are we to make of these three assumptions?

The life expectancy of a middle-aged man has risen by only three years since 1841. The principal causes of the three afflictions largely responsible for this disappointing increase – cancer, heart disease and other degenerative diseases – seem to be malnutrition (too much food of the wrong sort, especially carbohydrates and saturated fatty acids) and stress. This combination is likely to remain with us and to grow both in diversity of symptoms and in intensity as we become even more urbanized and seek to cut still more corners in our food production. So perhaps we might see a slight drop in expectancy. Miss Thompson is probably right to ignore the possibility of a breakthrough in medical knowledge, indeed I think she is over-sanguine in expecting further steady advance. We are unable to provide the hospitals and doctors we need for our present population, while some of our priorities are plain silly, as Sir Alan Parkes[3] has pointed out: we spend £6,000 per patient for a kidney transplant 'when 2,500 women die every year in the United Kingdom from cervical cancer, the early diagnosis of which by the cervical smear technique is so vitally important and so inadequately provided for'. We should not dismiss the possibility that the decline in the death rate will level off, perhaps be reversed, well before 2000.

At the moment there are 32,900 *less* immigrants a year than emigrants. Immigration is subject to more and more stringent restrictions, a trend which is likely to continue. Emigration will doubtless remain as popular as it is (if not more so) for as long as life in the old country is not as pleasant as it should be and opportunity is greater in less crowded lands. Migration is thus unlikely materially to affect the size of Britain's population in the year 2000, though it is an important topic and I shall return to it later on.

About 100 years ago the average family size in England and Wales began to drop. It went from over 6 in 1860 to under 6 (1870), just over 4 (1895), 3

Limits of Demographic Growth

(1910), 2·5 (1920), to just over 2 in 1940. During the 1930s 44 per cent of all families in Britain had either no children or only one, and by the 1960s this proportion had fallen to 27 per cent. Today, Miss Thompson[2] reports, 'there has been a distinct (upward) swing to the 2- and 3-child families and also an increase in the families with 4 children'. The reasons for the long drop and for the slow rise during the last 30 years are problematical and opinions differ considerably. We do not know why the birth rate has risen from below replacement level (as it was in the 1930s, when it was assumed that this was a characteristic of heavily industrialized, densely populated countries – it isn't) to well above it. Perhaps a family size of three or four children is a function of affluence; it is interesting to note that the proportion of people who think that four or more children per family is the ideal number is 23 per cent in Britain but 41 per cent in the United States. May we relate these percentages directly to differences in standard of living? Do the expectations of affluence include four children as well as two cars, colour television, a deep freeze and holidays twice a year? If so we should expect family size to keep on growing as long as people's rising expectations in terms of goods and services are reasonably satisfied. Perhaps, therefore, if the promises of the politicians are to be believed, we shall see an average family size of three between now and 2000.

Miss Thompson's principal assumptions, few and conservative as they are, have been shown, I hope, to be reasonable. Perhaps she errs on the side of, I will not say optimism, in suggesting that the death rate will decline slightly; but then she might also be optimistic in suggesting that the birth rate will not rise. Perhaps these 'errors' will cancel each other out. It doesn't matter, for the difference will only be a few million. More important is that Miss Thompson commits herself to a population of at least 60+ million: 'The age structure of the present population, with its relatively large numbers of children and young adults, means that it looks inevitable that (barring natural catastrophes) the size of the population of Great Britain will surpass 60 million even if fertility should, from now on, drop to replacement level and mortality show no further improvement.'

Can we afford to bar 'natural catastrophes'? I doubt it. There are so many possible catastrophes, or discontinuities as Paul Ehrlich[4] mockingly calls them, that just by the laws of chance it won't be long before we suffer at least one. No organism can indefinitely increase its numbers – at some point a catastrophe occurs and the population crashes. In our case such a catastrophe may be war, pestilence, famine or an explosion of social and psychic distress. It must not be forgotten that Britain is a part of world-wide economic, political and ecological networks. We depend on the rest of the world for half our food and for much of the raw materials we convert into manufactured goods to pay for it. This dependency will certainly not diminish. At the present rate of increase, our standard of living will have doubled by the year 2000, when the demand for goods and services (and hence on resources) of one person will be the equivalent of that of two today. It might help to remind us of this projected level of consumption (and of waste) if we were to refer to a population in 29 years time not of 66 million but of 132 million!

At the same time the population of the rest of the world is also growing, and it is estimated that – again, barring natural catastrophes – it will soar from the present 3,600 million to almost 7,000 million at the end of the century. All these extra people, like us, will be entertaining rising expectations of the good material life. It is unlikely that the 'underdeveloped' world, which accounts for two-thirds of today's population and probably over four-fifths of it in 2000, will continue to tolerate a situation in which an entrenched minority consumes most of the world's protein, raw materials and energy. We cannot expect them to so generously assist our 'development' at the expense of theirs. In addition we will face ever fiercer competition from North America, Japan and the rest of Europe for those essential resources which, if not entirely depleted in 29 years time will be exceedingly scarce.

It should not be difficult to predict the consequences of ever more people with more 'needs' (real and artificial) going after fewer resources? At home there will be social upheaval, while abroad war, both nuclear and conventional will be an obvious diversion.

As for pestilence, with both population and demand increasing so as seriously to strain our present water sources, it would not be unduly alarmist to predict a water-borne epidemic or two during the next couple of decades. René Dubos[5] thinks that even if chemical pollution of water, air and food is kept at a low enough level to cause neither death nor offence to our already blunted senses, over a period of time the result will be 'a great variety of delayed pathological manifestations'. These could well appear in the near future, and a population so weakened would be highly vulnerable to alien viruses circulating by courtesy of the international airlines from one overcrowded land to another.

We cannot precisely identify whatever misfortune will befall us (misfortunes tend to be clearly identifiable only when they are upon us), nor can we predict when it will occur. It is possible – human ingenuity being what it is – that we will be able to support a much larger population and still prevent demographically significant disasters. But it would be a tragedy if our capacity for innovation were restricted to the treadmill of averting one crisis after another, rather than significantly improving the quality of our lives. Besides, as Paul Errington remarks,[6] 'the idea that adaptable mankind may be able to adapt to a new, crowded, tightly integrated, superlatively artificialised way of living still does not answer questions as to why this way of living should be a goal so desired, so worthy of attainment. Surely, we have what it takes to fill the earth with people to its habitable limits, but why must we if we can possibly avoid it?' Is it possible that we are prepared to suffer anything rather than control our populations?

Professor Ivor Mills has eloquently testified to this country's soaring rate of attempted suicide and to growing violence among young people. He asks if this is not a sign of social strain and concludes that the quality of life in Britain 'is already suffering as a result of the population pressure in an affluent society'. Affluent though we may be we cannot even house ourselves adequately. The 1970 *Report of the Department of Health and Social Security* shows that the number of people in emergency accommodation rose from

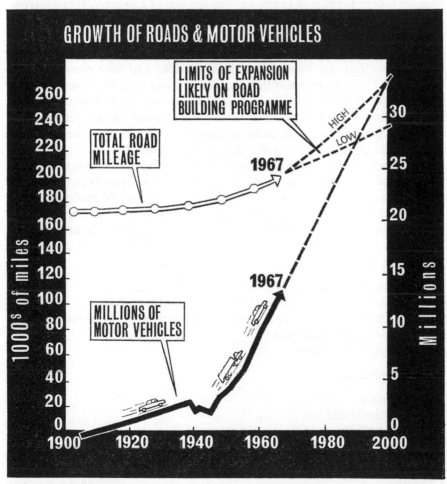

Fig. 1. Growth of roads and motor vehicles projected AD 1900–2000. Based on data from Basic Road Statistics – 1968 published by the British Road Federation.

10,176 in 1967 to 20,820 in 1969, while the *Greve Report* claims that in London alone 7,600 people are homeless, and an additional million people live in rented accommodation so bad as to qualify them as homeless.

The Peak National Park is suffering from erosion by tourists, and the time is not far off when access to beauty spots will have to be severely restricted. The 10,816,100 cars on the roads in Britain in 1968 will have risen to 20,100,000 by 1980, and 27,800,000 by 2000 – when even with a greatly expanded road-building programme it is most unlikely that there will be room enough to make them worth the driving (see fig. 1).

By the year 2000 we will have to build ten more towns the size of Birmingham, or twenty the size of Leeds, or fifty the size of Coventry. It is sobering to reflect on these urban proliferations in the light of Newcastle Planning Committee's study of the socio-medical differences between districts. In the words of Claire and W. M. S. Russell (Chapter 19), the study showed that the 'sharpest contrast was between the most crowded and least crowded third of the city. The most crowded third produced more than five times as many offences against the person, more than four times as many larcenies, seven times as many people on probation, three times as much juvenile delinquency, more than five times as many cases of neglect of children, five times as much venereal disease, and 43 per cent more prenatal deaths.'

Paul Ehrlich[4] defines overpopulation as 'the situation where human numbers are pressing on human values'. That point has now been passed. At the conference on the *Optimum Population for Britain*[7] 90 per cent of the delegates considered that the optimum has already been exceeded, though only two were brave enough to hazard what that optimum might be. L. R. Taylor has outlined what the conference meant by 'optimum'. 'An optimum population,' he writes, 'should seek to maximize:

1   the vigour and potential of individuals;
2   the currently acceptable pattern of social organization;
3   the realization of cultural goals which were listed as moral, political and aesthetic standards;
4   real output per head.

It should minimize:

1   pollution,
2   nutritional and
3   social stress.

To do this it must be less than the carrying capacity of the environment and hence *capable of being indefinitely maintained.*'

At the moment we can support a population well in excess of the carrying capacity of the land because various countries like Canada, the United States,

Limits of Demographic Growth

New Zealand and Australia can sell us their surplus grain and protein, while countries within the underdeveloped world sell us (far too cheaply) oil-seed and fish, which they cannot afford to be without, so that we can fatten our own animals and gorge ourselves with cheap excess protein. How long can we depend on our developed suppliers, and how shall we compete when demand for their surplus increases, as it must? And how can we justify our continued feeding off underdeveloped countries, at the expense of their health and survival, merely because they have been persuaded that by industrializing they will join Europe, Japan and North America in the technological paradise?

We depend on imports for 50 per cent of our food supply, and to maintain this proportion we must increase agricultural productivity by 80 per cent by the end of the century. 'Productivity', of course, is a euphemism for through-put, since output can never be greater than input, this input being vast quantities of pesticides and over-simple fertilizers in the case of cereals, and of antibiotics in the case of livestock – as well as machinery in both cases – none of which contributes to the long-term fertility of the soil, as L. B. Powell points out in Chapter 7.

Obviously this situation cannot be maintained indefinitely. Our population must fall by at least half before we can hope to feed ourselves both well and for a long time. Thus a population of 20 million should be our long-term goal – say in 200 years time. If many 'developing' countries still wanted to abandon their traditions for the new technology – if they wanted to have a significantly higher standard of living, then we would have to have a lower one. How much lower is impossible to tell at the moment, but the smaller our population the more choice we would have in the matter. Once a population is at a level that can be indefinitely maintained, then it has much greater freedom to concentrate on all that makes life worth living.

How could we achieve a population of 20 million by the year 2171? Our first task will be to stabilize it, and a conservative realistic goal in this respect would be 60 million at the year 2000. The maximum family size consistent with stability is 2·1 children (this is the replacement number, the extra 0·1 accounts for deaths before the age of 50). But as we have seen even if family sizes are reduced to 2·1, our population is still due to rise well above 60 million by the end of the century. So in the first instance an emigration policy is required.

Emigration is not a solution to the problems of overpopulation. George Kuriyan[8] has pointed out that 'if 150 million Indians are to be transported (from India to Australia), say, within a year, the rate of transport would mount up to approximately 3 millions per week – a figure which may take up something more than the entire shipping facilities of the world'. In our case, however, it will be a useful short-term device. Edward Goldsmith[9] has proposed a package deal with Australia and Canada, two of the few countries in this world with plenty of space. If only 300,000 extra people emigrated to those countries every year from now until the end of the century, Britain will be less crowded by 8,700,000 people. In return for this emigration agreement (we of course would have to offer special incentives) and for special trading rights and long-term options (both countries are rich in mineral resources, fossil fuels and food), Britain would abandon its efforts to join the Common Market.

One advantage of our not joining the Common Market would be that we would no longer be obliged to permit the free movement of labour within the Community. International movement of labour is incompatible with a policy of population control, and of course a government that is going out of its way to encourage emigration would be grossly inconsistent if it permitted immigration. Immigration should be halted completely, irrespective of colour and origins.

Once population has been stabilized then a policy of decline can be initiated. It has been argued that a declining population leaves a burdensome number of aged dependents on society. But population growth produces just as unfavourable an age composition. If a population is declining at 0·6 per cent a year, then there will be more old people to support than if it were stationary, but there will be fewer infants. Conversely, if it is increasing at this rate (as ours is), then there will be correspondingly less old people to support, but more children. Population growth also absorbs capital. 'A population growing one per cent per year,' writes Joseph Spengler,[10] 'absorbs capital amounting to something like 4 per cent of national income.' By the same token a shrinking population releases capital and allows a higher *per capita* product.

How can we stabilize our population? Tough legislation and soft persuasion are both out of the question. Limiting families to no more than two children by statute and/or licensing would be almost impossible to enforce, and of course extremely easy to evade. As for voluntary co-operation, an appeal to conscience, this is undesirable for two reasons: (1) people will not suffer deprivation voluntarily if they think the next man isn't playing the game, and generally he won't be; (2) ultimately we would bring about the extinction of conscience, or as C. G. Darwin has it, *Homo contracipiens* will be superseded by *Homo progenitivus*.

What is needed is, in Garrett Hardin's words,[11] 'mutual coercion, mutually agreed upon'. It will be objected by some that a society has no right to interfere with such a fundamental freedom as choosing the size of one's family. A United Nations statement of 1967[12] is often quoted with approval: 'The Universal Declaration of Human Rights describes the family as the natural and fundamental unit of society. It follows that any choice and decision with regard to the size of the family must irrevocably rest with the family itself,

40

and cannot be made by anyone else.' But Douglas Houghton[13] argues that 'just as marriage and divorce is not a purely personal and private matter, just as abortion isn't either, so the procreation of children is not a purely private matter. The more we do jointly with the State – or the community – the greater our social obligations.' I would add that just as a responsible parent will limit the number of children he brings into the world to those he can feed, clothe and bring up properly, so a responsible society will ensure that its numbers do not exceed its capacity to give fulfilment to its members.

In the past, governments have often tried to stimulate population growth by banning or discouraging contraception and by offering incentives and penalties. In the same way governments can encourage population decline. The alternative, after all, is much less palatable. The example of Ireland is a classic: in the late seventeenth century the population of Ireland was about 2 million. Then came the revolutionary potato, and it grew rapidly to 8 million by 1845. That was the year of the great potato famine when 2 million died and another 2 million emigrated. The remaining 4 million learned a sharp lesson, and despite Catholicism, the population today is less than 3 million.

Societies in equilibrium, principally those of hunter-gatherers and of certain slash-and-burn cultivators, have always determined family size by social convention, assisted by devices to inhibit or mitigate the effects of fertility. By definition those populations that have intuitively recognized their optimum size do not grow. One that is growing, however, is not necessarily below the optimum. It has often exceeded it, but because recognition of the optimum can be intuitive no longer, any semblance of a control mechanism is lost. Such is the case with us, and our task must be to devise artificial socio-economic methods to limit family size.

We could start by:

1   Establishing a National Population Service to (a) publicize the relationship between a growing population and the deteriorating quality of life; (b) provide comprehensive advice on contraception and free contraceptives. The cost of such a service would be more than offset by savings in social and welfare services – childcare, education, housing, *etc*. At the moment, according to Simms and Medawar,[13] out of 250 Local Health Authorities, 39 give a full family planning service, 129 a partial service and the rest not at all.
2   Acting on Aubrey Manning's suggestion[14] that 'since every birth costs us over £200 in direct grants and care (we should offer) a similar amount or rather more as a bounty for submitting to sterilisation.' We should also make abortion easier to obtain.
3   Discouraging reproduction by (a) abolishing family allowances, and replacing them with a graduated scale of taxation; (b) imposing a

luxury tax on nappies, baby foods, *etc.*; (*c*) giving equality of opportunity to women. Measures (*a*) and (*b*) will alarm many as they will directly affect children. I do not believe that a really effective programme can do otherwise. Parents are responsible for their children, and the only way of encouraging them to be more responsible is by showing them that if they aren't their children will suffer.

4   Educating children in birth control, and directing research grants towards population control.

What are the advantages of a population of 20 million? We must first discard the notion that a smaller population means an end to prosperity. GNP is a very inadequate index of well-being and I hesitate to use it to make a point. But since many economists and politicians endow it with an almost magical significance, I will relent. According to the International Bank of Reconstruction and Development, of the fourteen countries with a higher *per capita* GNP than the United Kingdom ($1,620), only two (United States $3,520 and West Germany $1,700) have higher populations, and only two (West Germany and Belgium $1,630) have higher population densities. If our population were 20 million, then only two more countries (France $1,730 and Canada $2,240) would have higher populations, and three more (Switzerland $2,250, Luxembourg $1,920 and Denmark $1,830) would have higher densities. And still Australia (population 12·2 million, density 2/sq. km.) and Sweden (population 8 million, density 17/sq. km.) would trail far behind us – yet they enjoy *per capita* GNPs of $1,840 and $2,270 respectively.

If our goal is the accumulation of goods and the proliferation of sophisticated services, then population control will help us reach it. For while our numbers increase, we shall have to concentrate our efforts much more on mere survival, and much less on luxury. A reduced population, however, will mean more for each one of us, and still more for our children.

If we value above all else our mobility, our freedom to go where we like and live where we like, then again population control is essential. Already traffic jams, flight and train delays, the tyranny of the parking meter and the heavy hand of planning restrictions are common everyday experiences. They illustrate a most important axiom: the more people there are in a given area, the less their freedom to do as they wish.

If we desire that we and our children enjoy fresh air, pure water, a variegated landscape in which man and the rest of nature work not in conflict but in harmony – in short an environment that will bring fulfilment – then population control is a prerequisite. We do not have these things now; we shall never have them unless we act wisely and quickly.

We can have a population of 20 million or 200 million. Which is it to be? We have the choice – will we make it, or will we delegate to disaster?

Limits of Demographic Growth

REFERENCES

1   FREMLIN, J. H. 1964. How many people can the world support? In *New Scientist*, *415*.
2   THOMPSON, J. H. 1970. The growth phenomenon. In TAYLOR, L. R. 1970. (Below.)
3   PARKES, A. S. 1970. The doctor's dilemma. In TAYLOR, L. R. 1970. (Below.)
4   EHRLICH, PAUL R. 1970. Pollution control or Hobson's Choice. In TAYLOR, L. R. 1970. (Below.)
5   DUBOS, RENE. 1969. The human environment. In *Science Journal*, *5A* (4). 1970. The limits of adaptability. In DE BELL, GARRETT. *The Environmental Handbook*. New York: Ballantyne/Friends of the Earth.
6   ERRINGTON, PAUL L. 1962. Of man and the lower Animals. In *The Yale Review*, *51* (3): Reprinted in SHEPARD, PAUL, and DANIEL MCKINLEY. 1969. *The Subversive Science*. Boston: Houghton Mifflin.
7   TAYLOR, L. R. (Ed.). 1970. *The Optimum Population for Britain*. London and New York: Academic Press.
8   KURYAN, GEORGE. 1962. The population of India: a geographical analysis. In *Population Review*, *6*.
9   GOLDSMITH, EDWARD. 1970. The stable society – can we achieve it? In *The Ecologist*, *1* (6).
10 SPRINGLER, JOSEPH. 1962. Population and freedom. In *Population Review*, *6* (2).
11 HARDIN, GARRETT. 1968. The tragedy of the commons. In *Science*, *162*.
12 UNITED NATIONS. 1970. *Statistical Yearbook 1969*. New York.
13 HOUGHTON, A. L. N. D. 1970. The Legislation barrier. In TAYLOR, L. R. 1970. (Above.)
14 SIMMS, M. and J. MEDAWAR. 1970. How much pressure on the individual? In TAYLOR, L. R. 1970. (Above.)
15 MANNING, AUBREY. 1970. No standing room. In *The Ecologist*, *1* (1).

3 LIMITS OF GROWTH IN NATURAL SYSTEMS

Edward Goldsmith

Editor, *The Ecologist*

The first stage in the study of any aspect of the world we live in is to gather together all the relevant material. During this stage, researchers are invariably struck by the amazing diversity of nature. During the second stage this material is organized, at which point researchers are equally struck by the surprising similarities underlying much of this diversity. It is during this stage that science really begins.

Though the process is well advanced within specific disciplines, there has been little attempt, until recently, to discover what there is really in common between things at present falling within the domain of different disciplines, such as molecules, cells, biological organisms, societies and business enterprises. Most scientists today, reared on empiricist philosophy, would in fact refuse to admit that anything more than a vague analogy could possibly obtain between things that appear so very different. This is not the view, however, of those involved in the new field of 'general systems' who prefer to regard these things as different specialized instances of a basic organization which they call a system.

A system is defined as something made up of parts in dynamic inter-relationship with each other. I prefer to regard it as an autonomous unit of behaviour – which, by its very nature, must be made up of such parts. Systems, however different they may appear, have a basic structure in common. All are bound by the same set of laws, which they must observe as rigorously as the law of gravity and those of thermodynamics. The great value of general systems theory is that by determining what systems have in common, it becomes possible to develop a general theory of behaviour, or a unified science, which enables one to examine our biosphere as a whole and determine the total effect on it of any local change. This is necessary if science is to serve the true interests of mankind.

In this chapter, I shall make use of general systems theory to determine what are the principles governing growth in systems. I shall attempt to show that growth like all other aspects of systems, is bound by rigorous laws from which there is no escape – and that these laws must apply equally well to the growth of complex systems, such as human societies and business enterprises, as to that of the much simpler systems studied by chemists and biologists.

Limits of Growth in Natural Systems

A SYSTEM AS A NEGENTROPY MACHINE. The second law of thermodynamics states that our world is running down or moving towards disorder or 'entropy'. In spite of this tendency, order, or *negentropy* (negative entropy), has been increasing over the last few thousand million years, during which time complex and highly ordered systems have developed, which we call living things. It is convenient to regard a system as an organization specifically designed to increase order, or negentropy. A system receives an input of low-order resources and transforms them into a high-order output. During this transformation waste is generated. However, so long as the reduction of order of that amount of input that has been transformed into waste is less than the increase in order of that amount of input that has been transformed into output, then the system's order, or negentropy, will have increased. Let us consider the conditions in which this process can occur.

VERTICAL STRUCTURE. One of the basic conditions of order is that the parts of a system should be closely linked together. In every different type of system, a different set of bonds assures this linkage. Thus the bonds holding together an atom are very different from those holding together a cell or a human family. However, their function is the same, and they have limited extendability. This means that they cannot stretch to include things that are too distant from each other. This sets a limit to the size of a system and when this limit is reached, it can only grow by associating with others to form a new type of system held together by a new set of bonds. When this occurs, a new 'level of organization' is said to have been attained. It is at this point that atoms join to form a molecule, that molecules join to form a cell and that cells join to form a biological organism. There is every reason to suppose that the same principle applies to more complex systems such as human societies. Individuals can be joined together to form a family and families can be linked together to form a small community. However, it is as impossible to create a society out of a whole lot of individuals, who are not organized into families and communities, as it is to form a biological organism out of atoms that are not organized into molecules and cells, *i.e.* a system must display its correct structure.

Cancer is an example of the growth of tissue which no longer displays its correct structure. A modern city is an example of the same principle at the level of a society. Demographic and economic growth tends to destroy the essential structure of a society, by tending towards ever-increasing urbanization and the development of ever-larger social and economic units. The fact that, with growing economic units, people tend to live ever further from their work also means that the bonds linking them with their neighbours become minimal – housing estates can never make sound and stable communities.

As we advance to more complex systems, the bonds become more sophisti-

45

cated and take longer to develop. Those holding together a family are an obvious example, *a fortiori* those that hold together a community. Economic growth invariably means increased mobility. People are no longer treated as members of a community or of a specific culture, but simply as units of labour that can be shifted around in accordance with the demands of industry. This prevents people from living together long enough for the necessary bonds to develop. The social disorder and its various manifestations measured in terms of crime, delinquency, alcoholism, drug addiction, mental disease, *etc*, resulting from the erosion of these bonds must set a limit to the desirability and feasibility of growth.

HORIZONTAL STRUCTURES. A system must also have an optimum horizontal structure, *i.e.* a correct ratio must be maintained between the differentiated parts of a biological organism as between the different skills required in a business enterprise. Assuming that all the parts of the system can be quantified, we can then formulate the essential principle of all systems, which we can refer to as the law of optimum value. There must be an optimum value for every part of the system, which is determined by that of the other parts. To allow one of these values to increase without reference to the others, is to destroy the essential structure of the system, and bring about its breakdown. So if we regard the United Kingdom as a system, there is an optimum population at any given moment. There is also an optimum number of houses, an optimum number of cars, an optimum standard of living, an optimum differential between the wages paid to different people; there is an optimum longevity and even an optimum amount of social deviation. It must follow that there is no conceivable variable whose value can be increased or decreased indefinitely without bringing about the breakdown of the system. Economic growth is no exception to this rule. It cannot possibly be regarded as desirable *per se* but only in accordance with its effect on the other variables in terms of which we describe our social and ecological system.

SELECTION: HOW THE STRUCTURE IS MAINTAINED. The growth of each part of a system, in other words, must satisfy the requirements of the system as a whole. This is ensured by the fact that all the parts of a system are closely connected by feedback loops and that it is the system as a whole that must trigger off the sub-system's behavioural responses. In fact the environment can be regarded as selecting the required response from among all those which the system is capable of providing. Thus within a biological organism, a cell comes into being with a full complement of hereditary material rendering it capable of performing any function within the organism. Slowly, however, it will become specialized in fulfilling a specific function as part of the liver or the intestine, for instance. It is in response to the requirements of

Limits of Growth in Natural Systems

its environment that it has developed to fulfil a very small range of the functions it was initially capable of. Its development, in fact, can be regarded as being selected by the environment from among all those it could originally perform. The behaviour of populations obeys the same principle. The environment selects those genetic features of the population that are adaptive to it, to the exclusion of those that are not. In fact, natural selection rather than being a unique principle, is a specialized instance of a very general one. In a polymorphous ant colony the same is also true. Only two types of egg are produced: male and female. The female is capable of giving rise to different types of ants and the actual distribution of those types is determined by environmental selection. In a human society it is clear how in ideal conditions environmental requirements will determine the number of people who should be trained in the different trades and professions.

Environmental selection is clearly essential in a system whose correct horizontal structure is to be respected. It is only in this way that its output remains differentiated so as to correspond qualitively and quantitively to the requirements of the larger system of which it is part. When growth develops too quickly, however, the parts are no longer selected by the environment. They no longer develop to fulfil specific environmental requirements. They are therefore no longer differentiated. Growth proceeds by multiplication rather than by differentiation, and the system's essential horizontal structure must break down.

An example is to be found in the field of education. If selection were allowed to occur normally, the correct ratio between the different specialists made available by the educational system corresponding to the economic, social and ecological demand for them, would be maintained. As it is, we are producing a vast quantity of young people with specialized knowledge in obscure branches of learning for whom there is unlikely to be any demand. In this way we are methodically creating unintegrated parts that must of necessity rebel against a system in which they have no place.

As economic growth proceeds, so the educative process, *i.e.* the process whereby members of our society are differentiated culturally to fulfil specific functions within it, is becoming ever more chaotic. Information is transmitted less by the family and the small community, and more by the state, and by whoever directs communications media. In this way, it becomes less designed to enable people to fulfil their essential differentiated functions as members of their family and of their small community.

Education, too, is foisted on people in a totally indiscriminate way with no regard for their intellectual capacity, nor for the sort of society which they will inhabit. For instance, people living in agricultural or pastoral tribal societies are being provided with an education designed to enable them to fulfil functions within an economy totally alien to their own, and one which, simply on the basis of the approaching world shortage of raw materials, they cannot conceivably aspire to achieve. The basic mechanism of environmental selection is breaking down more and more and the ever-growing chaos associated with the uncontrolled proliferation of culturally undifferentiated people must set a further limit to economic growth.

THE DESTRUCTION OF CULTURAL CONSTRAINTS. Order can be defined as the influence of the whole over the parts. It is also defined as limitation of choice, for the greater the influence of the whole over the parts, the greater must be the constraints imposed on them to ensure that they behave in a way that will further the interests of the whole.

Every system owes its existence to the operation of a specific set of constraints. As it increases order so as to increase its ability to face a given challenge, there is an increase in the constraints applied, and hence a reduction in the range of choices open to the parts of the system. As the system develops and achieves new levels of organization, *e.g.* as molecules join together to form cells, or as families join together to form small communities, and small communities to form larger ones, new constraints are imposed. Each system possesses an organization of information to which I shall refer as a 'cybernism' which constitutes a model of the environment and at the same time provides the system with a goal-structure and its corresponding constraints. A culture, *i.e.* that set of beliefs cherished by an ordered society, constitutes its 'cybernism', in terms of which it interprets environmental data and mediates responses to them. We can best understand a culture as a control-mechanism that applies the constraints ensuring that each member of the society behaves as a differentiated part of it. Once these constraints are no longer operative, the society will distintegrate. One of the implications of this principle which we might not be too happy to accept is that permissiveness can only be regarded as the inevitable sign of social disintegration. Permissiveness appears to be a natural concomitant of social and economic growth. It is the result of the breakdown of those ethical codes associated with the culture of small, relatively isolated communities. Permissiveness is inextricably linked with the other symptoms of social disorder.

CONSERVATION OF THE ENVIRONMENT. It is essential to realize that a system must provide the ideal environment for its parts, since the only reason the parts were developed was to fulfil specific differentiated functions within it.

People are part of a family system, which is, in turn, part of a social system which in its turn is part of a vaster ecological one. One must therefore regard people as having been developed (phylogenetically and culturally) to fulfil specific functions within their family, society and ecosystem, and one must assume that it is in fulfilling these functions that they obtain maximum satisfaction.

For them to do this, they must be provided with the appropriate information, and also with the correct environment, or rather, one whose characteristics are maintained within the required parameters.

When these conditions obtain, people will behave in that way which favours the survival or increased homeostasis of the system they belong to. However, if the latter does not provide the optimum environment, or if the information is not appropriate, then they will behave in a way which will tend to lead to the system's disintegration.

It is for this reason that a stable society requires little or no government, while the more unstable it becomes, the greater the need for autocracy in all its forms.

Unfortunately, what constitutes a satisfactory environment for human beings has never been properly determined. Clearly, the external environment must have certain basic features such as the availability of food, water and air, but the presence of the physical necessities of life alone does not suffice to create a satisfactory environment. Man also needs a satisfactory social environment which involves the maintenance of the correct social structure. He needs a family, a small community, probably a larger one, and he certainly needs enemies. If he is not provided with them he tends to invent them. In this way, when the Comanche Indians were put on reservations they simply invented a host of evil spirits to replace the enemies of which they had been deprived.

Man has other requirements for which his environment must also cater. He has a sense of aesthetics. He cannot adapt readily to living in the grey, monotonous surroundings of our urban conglomerations. He cannot work up any enthusiasm for conserving an environment made up of chaotic complexes of concrete blocks or bleak fields mutilated by pylons, factories and housing estates. These, however, are the inevitable concomitants of economic growth. It must be true that to create such an environment specifically for the purpose of increasing society's 'standard of living' is to sacrifice its long-term stability in the interests of acquiring dubious short-term benefits.

SELF-REGULATION. The environment selects the response that it requires. This selection process will establish an equilibrium situation between the sub-system and the system. However, this equilibrium can be established with varying degrees of homeostasis. The mechanism that ensures that the response satisfies the requirements of the sub-system as well as the system by tending towards their maximum homeostasis, is referred to as a control mechanism. It is basically the same in all systems. It involves detecting data from the system, transducting it into the correct informational medium made use of by the sub-system's cybernism (brain, gene-pool, *etc*) and interpreting them within the model of the system that this cybernism constitutes. The corresponding response must be the only one reconcilable with the particular interpretation of the situation. This mechanism of self-regulation must be a feature of all stable systems. It is the only way to ensure that a system's response to its environment, *i.e.* to the larger system of which it is a part, corresponds to the requirements of both the former and the latter – requirements which it learns to satisfy ever better as its control-mechanism becomes more perfected. It is in fact the only way to ensure that a system conserves its environment.

The relationship between the individuals making up a human family and the family itself provide an excellent illustration of how this mechanism of self-regulation achieves the requisite stability of the systems involved. A woman satisfies her basic biological and psychological requirements best by fulfilling her functions as a wife and a mother within her family unit. A man satisfies his basic requirements best by fulfilling his functions as a husband and a father. In other words, behaviour that satisfies the requirements of the sub-systems is also that required to ensure the stability of the system – in this case the family. The system is thus totally self-regulating.

There are many ways in which the family can break down as we have already seen. When this occurs, its members automatically seek substitute satisfactions. The husband may take a mistress for instance. This may provide him with satisfaction, but it will not contribute towards the stability of his family unit. The self-regulating mechanism will have been impaired. He may also take to drink and to drugs as substitute satisfactions. These, however, will tend to reduce his capacity for fulfilling his essential functions within the family unit, and the self-regulatory mechanisms will be further impaired. It is only when these mechanisms have broken down and the family ceases to be capable of self-regulation that outside forces or 'asystemic' controls are required to look after its members.

In such a situation, only help from the community can permit the family, or what is left of it, to survive at all, for it has ceased to be self-regulating.

This help, though it may appear to alleviate the suffering of the members of the disintegrating family, will in fact favour its further disintegration by reducing the need for responsible behaviour on the part of the father. This must be true of all asystemic or external controls, including those introduced by modern technology. By destroying natural self-regulating mechanisms, they must further contribute to the system's disintegration, thereby increasing the need for further asystemic controls.

Limits of Growth in Natural Systems

INTEGRITY. A system, as we have seen, has an optimum structure, no surplus capacity and the parts are all differentiated. It is an integral whole, and the destruction of any of its parts can lead to total breakdown.

This is a point which has rarely been taken into account at a cultural level. Colonialist powers have constantly interfered in the most irresponsible way with the cultures of the societies they controlled. Missionaries and colonial administrators have tampered with the delicately adjusted cultural systems of highly stable and ecologically sound societies which they regarded as 'primitive' or 'barbarous' and in most instances brought about their breakdown. The consequences for the inhabitants of these societies has been disastrous. They usually become rootless members of a depressed proletariat in the shanty-towns we are thereby methodically creating. The consequences for the ecosystem as a whole have been equally disastrous. By reducing order as well as cultural variety or complexity, we have seriously reduced the stability or homeostasis of the world's human population.

MULTI-ETHNIC SOCIETIES. It is not surprising that systems which are sufficiently differentiated, such as biological organisms and societies, will tend to develop mechanisms that will enable them to exclude foreign bodies likely to menace their integrity. At the biological level, such devices are known as rejection mechanisms. Experience with organ transplants has revealed that to suppress these mechanisms is to increase one hundredfold the patient's susceptibility to cancer, *i.e.* to the anarchic proliferation of cells. Mechanisms of this kind are essential at all levels of organization. Of the 3,000 simple societies so far examined by anthropologists, all appear to have laws of exogamy and endogamy. Marriage is forbidden within a restricted family circle, but also outside the cultural group, the object being to avoid cultural hybridization and hence the production of sub-systems that are differentiated parts neither of one system nor of another. What is today regarded as prejudice against people of different ethnic groups is a normal and necessary feature of human cultural behaviour, and is absent only among members of a cultural system already far along the road to disintegration. The notion of the universal brotherhood of man is therefore totally incompatible with the systemic approach to human cultural systems. It is as absurd as the notion that the cells, making up a vast number of different biological organisms, can be shuffled and still give rise to viable biological systems. Economic growth is leading to increased mobility. Industrial countries tend to develop labour shortages and to import labour from elsewhere. In this way quite large ethnic minorities are being built up in many countries. In addition, economic development is tending towards the development of ever-larger political units, which often embrace ethnic groups with little in common with each other. All this is creating a very unstable situation, one which can only lead to civil wars and to the massacre of minorities singled out as scapegoats when inevitable economic and social crises occur.

RESOURCES. A system cannot be regarded as stable unless there is a guarantee that the resources on which it depends will always be available. The only way it can ensure this is to live off the interest and not the capital of available resources. In the highly stable societies of our hunter-gatherer ancestors, this was the case, as in the example of the Plains Indians. They lived off the vast herds of buffalo and pronghorns without causing any reduction in the herds' numbers. Their consumption of non-renewable resources, such as metals, was minimal and timber provided them with all the fuel they required. To satisfy this essential requirement, it is clear that populations must be kept low, as must their standard of living measured in terms of their consumption of non-renewable resources. Once we start living off our capital, it is a matter of time before we exhaust it and our economic system grinds to a halt. The greater the economic growth, and our corresponding dependence on these resources, the more dramatic this eventual collapse must be – this is made possible by a philosophy that teaches that man is part of nature rather than above it. Primitive people do not regard the possession of a soul, for instance, as a prerogative of man distinguishing him from all other creatures. All have a soul, and often the primitive hunter will pray to that of the animal he is about to kill, explaining the necessity for the crime he will commit. Seldom, too, will he kill more than he strictly requires. Indeed, it is said in Southern Africa that the bees do not sting the bushman because they known he will take only the amount of honey he requires, never more.

DISPOSAL OF WASTE. A system can only remain stable if the larger system of which it is but a differentiated part is capable of absorbing its waste products at the rate at which they are being produced. If it grows too quickly and becomes too big, then it will produce more than the larger system is capable of absorbing. It will then be steadily reducing the order of the larger system by replacing its highly differentiated parts with waste or random parts. By destroying the environment in this way, a system is simply spelling its own doom, as it cannot survive in an environment made up of random parts, *i.e.* displaying total entropy. Needless to say, our society is moving in just this direction. Much of our pollution control equipment, rather than provide a means of getting rid of waste, serves merely to shift it, and it cannot be long before the global problem of waste disposal presents an insuperable barrier to further economic growth.

POLLUTION. Toxic substances can be generated in any system, mainly but not entirely in the form of waste products. Let us not forget that a system is developed phylogenetically (and culturally in the case of society) as an adaptive response to a specific environment. If the latter is changed sufficiently radically, *i.e.* if those qualitative parameters within which a system is designed to function are no longer respected, then it can no longer survive. Industrialization is bringing about a radical transformation of our environment at an ever-increasing rate. It is but a question of time before the accumulation of insecticides, detergents, radioactive wastes and carbon-dioxide and heat from the burning of fossil fuels so transforms our world that it ceases to provide a suitable environment for complex forms of life.

COMPLEXITY. If there is a tendency for systems to become more and more complex, it is because complexity renders them more stable. Another way of looking at complexity is in terms of variety, assuming that the variants do not occur at random, but together constitute an integrated system – though in the case of a population or gene-pool, the degree of integration is not very high. The greater the variety, the greater the system's ability to deal with improbable changes. Serious disruption of its basic structure also becomes less likely.

A reduction in variety, or a simplification of a system, will thus lead to a reduction in stability. It is worth noting that the destruction of the numerous cultures of primitive people throughout the world, and the absorption of their cultures, has produced a radical and dangerous simplification at the cultural level of organization – reducing our stability and rendering our species vulnerable to changes or accidents that would normally affect only a small section of it. In agriculture, monoculture is a drastic simplification of plant life. The use of antibiotics and insecticides causes drastic simplifications, in that it involves replacing complex controls that normally keep insects in check by crude and indiscriminate killers.

Technological processes, when used to replace natural ones, are further simplifications. In all these cases, stability is being reduced and vulnerability increased. We are forced to accept the unpleasant fact that practically all man's efforts today are tending towards the simplification of the total ecosystem and leading to our ever-greater vulnerability to environmental changes. As this drastic simplification of our biosphere proceeds, so there must be a corresponding probability of the occurrence of plagues and epidemics of all sorts. This sets a further limit to economic growth, for a time must eventually come when they become ecologically and socially intolerable.

SYSTEMIC ADAPTATION. To understand what is wrong with asystemic control, one must understand that during the normal process of feedback development, each individual response is selected not to satisfy a single environmental requirement but a whole set of environmental requirements;

to maintain, in fact, the balanced structure of the larger system, of which the system concerned is but a differentiated part. *Vis-à-vis* each individual requirement, the response must therefore be a compromise. For instance, nature does not aim at breeding strains of wheat with maximum yields, as we do. A high yield is only one of the system's countless requirements. As a result, the strains of wheat devised by nature are adaptive, and those designed by us are not. Whereas self-regulating systems tend towards increased stability, ours, on the contrary, tends towards increased instability, because every time we 'solve' one problem, we are, by the same token, creating others. Take the following example.

Due to a faulty diet, people in Britain have developed a new pattern of diseases (see Robert Waller, Chapter 9). Among these is tooth decay. This has got so bad in Britain that there are now some 17 million people with no teeth at all. The correct remedy is clearly to return to a healthier diet. This, however, would mean closing down a large number of food factories and returning to a sounder, non-industrial agriculture. It would mean putting a lot of people out of their jobs, cutting down profits, increasing the price of food, reducing the GNP and the standard of living. Nevertheless it is clearly what should be done. However, since we are not willing to do it, we must find some gimmick for getting rid of some of the more obvious symptoms of the diseases we have created. This gimmick is fluoridation of drinking water. In this way, tooth decay can be reduced. However, this does not prevent the other side-effects of a faulty diet, such as diabetes, heart and kidney disease. In fact all that has happened is that our diet has been rendered that much more tolerable, which means that we are less likely than ever to do anything about changing it. This is true of most technological devices. By helping to render more tolerable the symptoms of the pathological situation we have brought about, modern technology serves only to perpetuate it. The techno-logical devices developed to control pollution are no exception to this rule. If we succeed in developing filters that prevent all air pollution from the exhaust of motor-cars, we will simply have eradicated one of the many symptoms of the pathological situation created by the preposterous prolifera-tion of these machines. By rendering them that much more tolerable we would then be better capable of supporting the noise they make, the destruc-tion of our towns and countryside with the roads required to accommodate them, and the highly undesirable level of economic centralization that they effect. Technology is introducing positive feedback into the increasingly un-stable system that our world is becoming, thereby rendering it even *more* unstable.

ASYSTEMIC REGULATION. Asystemic controls have the further disadvantage of rendering the functioning of our environment dependant on human efforts and ingenuity. A so-called controlled environment, the technologist's dream, is one in which all the self-regulating mechanisms of our biosphere have been replaced by the externally regulated asystemic mechanisms of our technosphere. In such conditions, we would have to depend for our drinking water on desalination plants and sewage works, for our food supply on factory farms and processing factories and for the very air we breathe on vast plants to filter noxious gases out of the atmosphere. Have our technocrats ever bothered to think of the almost unbelievable vulnerability of such a society? An industrial dispute, an act of sabotage, a technical failure, a shortage of some key resource would deprive us of the basic necessities of life.

The recent sewage strike revealed this vulnerability of a society depending too heavily on technology for its survival. Clearly there must be a limit to the extent to which external controls can be allowed to replace self-regulating ones, and to which the technosphere can be allowed to replace the biosphere.

CONCLUSION. By using general systems theory, it is possible to indicate a large number of limits to the desirability and feasibility of growth in all systems. Such limits must apply equally well to growth in technologically based human social systems.

To suppose that technology can permit permanent growth is to refuse to face basic scientific facts. It can indeed enable growth to proceed temporarily beyond these limits, but only at the cost of increasing the instability of the social and ecological systems of which we are part, and with that instability, the likelihood and the severity of the cataclysm that must eventually restore a stable situation.

REFERENCES

VON BERTALANFFY, L. 1962. General systems theory: a critical review. In *General Systems*, VII.

BONNER, J. T. 1955. *Cells and Societies*. Oxford: OUP.

CRAIK, KENNETH. 1952. *The Nature of Explanation*. Cambridge: CUP.

HARLOW, H. F. and M. KUENNE. 1962. Social deprivation in monkeys. In *Scientific American*, November.

HEARN, LAFCADIO. 1904. *Japan: an attempt at interpretation*. New York: Macmillan.

LINTON, RALPH. 1965. *The Study of Man*. London: Peter Owen.

MAIR, LUCY. 1962. *Primitive Government*. Harmondsworth: Penguin Books.

MURDOCK, G. P. 1965. *Social Structure*. New York: Macmillan.

OPLER, M. 1959. *Culture and Mental Health*. New York: Macmillan.

WADDINGTON, C. H. 1957. *The Strategy of the Genes*. London: George Allen & Unwin.

WALLACE, A. F. C. 1963. *Culture and Personality*. New York: Random House.

PART TWO

Food

4 WORLD FOOD PROBLEM

Michael Allaby

Editor, *SPAN*
Associate Editor, *The Ecologist*

The future of Britain is connected with that of the rest of the world. Any small island which imports more than half of its food and whose economic survival depends on trade is an integral part of a world community. Life in these islands has been influenced by events overseas for the whole of its history and in the last three centuries British industrial development has been made possible by the availability of imported raw materials and export markets for manufactured goods. Any realistic appraisal of life in this country at any time in the foreseeable future must take account of what is happening in the rest of the world.

By far the largest part of the world, in terms both of area and of population, is poorer than Britain, and the gap is widening. It is generally accepted that the world population is rising exponentially. The problems of the latter part of the century will be concerned with population in relation to resources. As competition for what is available increases, life in Britain is bound to be affected.

The population explosion is not distributed evenly. In 1965 the economically developed countries of Europe, the USSR, North America and Japan had somewhat more than 1,000 million inhabitants. A further 800 million lived in the communist countries of Asia. Some 1,500 million lived in the less developed countries. By 1985 the population of the rich countries will probably have increased by 25 per cent, while that of the poor countries will have increased by 60 per cent.[1] Thus, of every 100 additional people born between 1965 and 1985, 85 will live in the poor countries. The first problem will be to feed them. Unless it can be solved, all other problems are irrelevant.

This increase in population alone calls for an increase in food supplies by 1985 of 80 per cent. This assumes, however, that *per capita* incomes will not rise in the developing countries. If they do, then the food demand may increase by 140 per cent.[2]

This is the world food problem and it is this that the largest of the United Nations agencies, the Food and Agriculture Organization, was created to solve. In August 1969 FAO published its *Indicative World Plan* for agricultural development (IWP). Work on the IWP began after the First World Food Congress held in 1963 as part of FAO's Freedom from Hunger Campaign.

The IWP postulates a population increase of 2·6 per cent per year, which, combined with the increased income which it also assumes, will call for an increase in food supplies of 3·9 per cent per year. From 1956 to 1966 food production rose by 2·7 per cent per year. If the difference between production and demand were to be met from imports, the cost to the developing countries would be US $26,000 million by 1985, and more if prices were to rise above their 1962 level. Since the Third World found great difficulty in meeting its $3,000 million food import bill in 1962, it is not unreasonable to conclude that food production must be increased in the countries where the demand is to be met. People must be able to feed themselves.

This is only one reason for increasing the productivity of agriculture in the developing countries. In some, frustration at the slow rise in food production has led to rapid industrialization, in an attempt to by-pass agriculture altogether in the quest for an economic 'take-off'. This has worked where there have been rich oil or mineral deposits, but elsewhere it has created far more problems than it has solved. Factory industry is often not labour-intensive and provides few jobs. If investment is diverted from agriculture to pay for it, there is an increase in unemployment and a consequent reduction in demand for industrial products, combined with a reduction of the rate of increase of food production. The flow of raw materials into industry slows, exports flag, while food imports rise. The balance of trade swings heavily into the red. With less money coming into the country a vicious spiral is created and the situation gets worse and worse. A sound agriculture is vital to all subsequent economic development.

The need, therefore, is for agriculture to provide the additional food that will be required in the years to come, to earn and save foreign exchange and to provide a large part of the additional employment that will be needed, while at the same time providing still more employment outside agriculture itself in the 'agro-allied' industries.

When we talk of agriculture we are talking mainly of cereal production. It is cereals which provide the staple foods and the feedstuffs for livestock. If agricultural production is to be increased the necessary first step will be an increase in cereal production. Not only are cereals of prime economic importance, they are also psychologically important. Even we, urbanized and sophisticated as we are, still call bread 'the staff of life'. The IWP therefore devotes a great deal of attention to ways in which cereal production may be increased.

There are two possible lines of approach. Existing farmland may be cultivated more intensively, or new, 'virgin' lands may be brought into production. The IWP opts unequivocally for the former. There is much to be done to improve standards of husbandry in existing farmed areas, and to bring new land under the plough would divert scanty investment and spread it too thinly over projects which would be expensive, slow and uncertain.

In any case, the amount of new land which could be ploughed up is limited. In India all the land available to agriculture is in use and at the present rate of expansion into marginal land there will be no virgin land left in the world by 1985.[3]

Curiously, the intensification of existing farms would bring more employment, rather than the reverse, since there is considerable under-employment in rural areas where more people live on the land than can usefully be employed on it. They are unable to leave because of a lack of alternative employment elsewhere. The intensification of farms would find work for many of them.

Although cereal production is regarded as the essential first step in overcoming the world food problem, the most serious aspect of the problem is what is called the 'protein gap'. The daily requirement of protein varies from one country to another, but averages about 48·4 grams per person.[4] At the present time this is supplied in developing countries mainly from vegetable sources. In India, for example, in 1963, of a total protein consumption of 50·1 grams per day, only 6·4 grams were of animal protein. In Mauritius, in the same year, of a total of 49·1 grams per day, 13·4 were animal protein. This pattern is general throughout the Far East, Near East and Africa.[5] The amount of protein available remains fairly constant from year to year and therefore, although the 1963 average consumption is above the minimum requirement, production is rising more slowly than demand. The simplest first solution may be to increase the protein content of cereal crops by introducing new, high-protein varieties. An increase of a few grams in the protein content of rice would at one stroke improve considerably the protein/calorie balance and eliminate much of the protein deficiency in Asia.[6] Other high-protein vegetable crops may also be introduced, such as soya, and then, with a secure cereal base to provide concentrate feeds, livestock may be introduced to increase the availability of animal protein.

Thus the IWP argues that the first need is to increase cereal production on existing farms. How shall that be done? The answer is deceptively simple: by the introduction of new 'high-yielding' cereal varieties. These are a series of hybrids which are highly responsive to heavy fertilizer applications.

Traditional tropical cereal varieties are long-stemmed. If inputs of fertilizer and water are increased the result is a heavier ear which the stem cannot support. The plant falls, or 'lodges' and cannot be harvested. The new varieties, developed first in Mexico and then in the Philippines, are short-stemmed. They also mature quickly so that up to three crops a year may be taken from the same land. IR8, the new 'miracle' rice, has a performance which varies from country to country, but the highest recorded yield, in the Quezon Province of the Philippines, was 10,000 lb per acre, as against the local varieties' 1,330 lb.[7] The recorded results are impressive and it is understandable that high hopes should be entertained for a new breed of plant which promises so much. It is understandable that the FAO should take the new hybrids as the cornerstone for its entire plan and the basis for what has come to be known as The Green Revolution. Unhappily, the cornerstone may be unsound.

IR8 requires 70–90 lb of fertilizer per acre. Indeed, the IWP defines the high-yielding varieties as those which can give a linear response to up to at least 90 lb per acre.[8] If two crops are to be grown in a year this means 140–180 lb per acre and for three crops, which is considered possible IR8, 210–270 lb. This rate of fertilizer application is not high by European or American standards, but in 1962 the fertilizer consumption in Latin America averaged 10·6 lb per acre and this was higher than the figures for Africa south of the Sahara, the Near East, N.W. Africa or the Far East. It seems that if IR8 is to succeed, ways will have to be found of increasing fertilizer availability throughout the entire Third World so that each farmer has access to up to twenty-seven times the fertilizer he uses at present. Where is this fertilizer to come from? How will it be paid for? Domestic production of fertilizers is growing, impressively says the IWP, so that by 1966 the developing countries were producing 50 per cent of their requirements. This is nothing like enough. It is the policy of FAO to urge the governments of developed countries to make fertilizers available as part of their aid. It has not happened. Asked whether he would name the countries which are not co-operating with FAO in its fertilizer programme, the Director-General, Mr A. H. Boerma, said that none of the developed countries are doing so. So it seems that there will be a major fertilizer shortage.

Let us assume, however, that fertilizer becomes available. The effectiveness of fertilizers depends on the structure of the soils on which they are used. Many, though not all, of the soils in the Third World are badly depleted and seriously eroded. Experience in the developed countries which use large quantities of fertilizers has shown that much of the fertilizer applied to a soil with a poor structure drains away. It ends in the local water supply where it may cause eutrophication problems, killing the fish and, eventually, rendering the water unusable. At the same time there is some evidence that even given a

60

good soil with a sound structure, repeated application of heavy fertilizer dressings will damage the structure,[9] so reducing the effectiveness of the fertilizer itself and undermining the fertility of the land. It is highly probable that over a number of years the use of fertilizer on the scale demanded by the new cereal hybrids would cause damage to the soil and pollution of the environment.[10] It is also likely that applications would need to become heavier as, with declining structures, more of the fertilizer was lost. Demand for fertilizer would grow from 90 lb per acre to an unpredictable high level if yields were to be maintained.

The introduction on a large scale of any new plant variety will cause changes in the ecology of the area which may result in an increase of crop pests, weeds and disease. To some extent this is inevitable and we must live with it. The new hybrids, however, are more than usually vulnerable to pests and disease. This may be due in part to the intensity with which they are grown and perhaps, too, to the high degree of specialization involved in breeding for one quality alone which upsets the homeostasis of the organism. Whatever the reason, there will be an increase in the use of insecticides, herbicides and fungicides.[11] In the period 1962–4, 20 per cent of the world's pesticides were used in the developing countries, on some 70 per cent of the world's farmland. Again, it is the policy of FAO to urge the developed countries to make the pesticides available. Again, the developed countries have failed to do so. There will be a shortage here, too.

Nevertheless, let us persist and assume that the miracle worker who gave us the rice can also give us the fertilizers and pesticides we will need to grow it. It is in the developed countries that most of the experience of the use of chemical sprays has been gained and it is in these countries that it is coming to be recognized that their effectiveness is limited, because pest species develop immunity to them, and that the cost to the environment and possibly to the health of Man, is too high to be borne. Whereas pests can develop immunity, it seems that we cannot. A growing number of countries is either banning the use of some of the more popular pesticides, including DDT, or severely restricting their use. DDT and BHC are the cheapest pesticides; they have little immediate danger for the user, although we know little of the long-term effects and farmworkers in Britain who have been exposed to them for a number of years have complained of impotence. However, the crop protection programme for the new varieties is almost certain to centre on them. It is inevitable that there will be problems from pollution, there are likely to be serious pest, weed and disease outbreaks because of the disturbance of ecological balances, and as resistance to the chemicals develops there will be an almost irresistible temptation to move on to other, more sophisticated and more toxic compounds, which will aggravate the situation still further.

Never mind, at least we will be feeding people, even if we are destroying their soils and poisoning them to do it. But for how long can we go on feeding them?

Fertilizers, pesticides and their production and transportation, as well as farm mechanization, all depend on petroleum. It has been calculated that the world reserves of petroleum will last for some 70 years at current rates of consumption. This may be a conservative estimate. Hugh Montefiore reckons 31·7 years at current rates of consumption.[12] If the demand from developing countries grows as they intensify their agriculture, their demand for petroleum will grow also and the life expectancy of the world reserves may be reduced to something like 50 years. It is true that as resources of non-renewable materials become exhausted the developed countries, too, will have to make radical changes in their way of life, but they are stronger and better able to change. It seems a little unfair to launch the developing countries on an industrial and technological path which is based on a commodity which we know is running out.

There are two other main requirements for the new hybrids: irrigation and, to quote the IWP, 'a continued flow of suitable new varieties, resistant to the major pests and diseases, and capable of high yields in response to the application of modern farming technology. This implies both a multi-disciplinary breeding and research programme to produce and test the varieties; and a well-organized multiplication and distribution programme to ensure that quality seed is available to the farmers in adequate quantity'.[13] In other words, a constant supply of seed. This is unusual. Farmers retain seed from one harvest to sow for the next season. The IWP does not say so, but the probable reason is that the new hybrids are genetically unstable. After a limited number of generations they may revert to the old varieties. When this begins to happen crops will contain a mixture of old and new. Since the old varieties are long-stemmed they will shade their neighbours and since they require lower inputs they will be more likely to proliferate. Yields will be depressed.

In the end, the decisive limiting factor may be the large amount of water which will be required. Irrigation on this scale will produce violent ecological changes whose results are largely unpredictable, although we may expect a lowering of water tables, particularly in dry areas, a reduction in the water available for other uses, and an increase in water pollution. The strain on water resources may be intolerable. There is only so much water on the planet and only a certain proportion of it is fresh. In spite of years of research the cost of desalination of sea-water is almost prohibitively high for developed countries, let alone developing ones. There may be insufficient water.

Still, if we can find the fertilizer and the pesticides and the water and the seed and the people don't mind what we are doing to the soil, we can feed them. The consumers do not seem overjoyed with IR8. It becomes soggy when it is cooked and it has chalky spots.[4] One of the effects of its introduction has been to force up prices of the traditional, and preferred, varieties. This raises the whole question of the biological, nutritive value of the new hybrids. It would be interesting to conduct feeding trials with them. In the case of IR8 we know that the protein content is 5–7 per cent, compared with 7–9 per cent in traditional varieties.[3]

The picture we are left with is far from satisfactory. The entire FAO plan for short and middle term is based on the new hybrids. If we consider only 1975 and 1985, as the IWP does, the programme may be just feasible. However, if the new varieties are introduced on the scale proposed, and if they are to be grown, as they must be grown, with very heavy fertilizer applications and elaborate spray programmes in order to produce two or even three crops per season, then it is more than likely that by the 1990s the developing countries will be paying dearly for their short-term success in terms of damage to their environment and further depletion of their soils. They will have taken three steps forward and four back.

In June 1970 the FAO held its Second World Food Congress in the Netherlands Congress Centre at The Hague. The aim of the Congress was to point the way to decisions and actions which are necessary if hunger and malnutrition are to be abolished in the Third World. In the view of many of the delegates and even more of the Press, the Congress was a non-event. Its weakness, and the feeling of hopelessness that it generated, was probably due to the widespread acceptance by most of those who spoke of the validity of the Green Revolution concept and an unwillingness to face up to the problems.

For even before the appearance of the wider ecological difficulties which the introduction of the new varieties may produce, other problems have appeared. The first of these has been the social one of adjusting local situations so as to ensure that all sections of the community benefit from the increased income the new cereals may bring. A society may be stable and secure, but nevertheless exist at a low economic level which could be improved. If outside factors are introduced, however, the effect must be to create imbalances. Unless these are allowed for, the end result may be a situation worse than that which prevailed at the start.

There have been riots in India, which resulted in the death of a number of agricultural workers, caused by the introduction of blackleg labour by a landlord unwilling to pay higher wages for the harvesting of an increased yield of one of the new hybrids and so share the profit among those it was meant to reach.

The extent to which these social problems are real depends on how far the Green Revolution has spread. The new hybrids require high fertilizer, pesticide and irrigation inputs which can be made available only by the developed countries. This is not happening and Mr Boerma has said he is not optimistic about FAO's ability to achieve its aims in the present climate of world political opinion.

This is a serious admission. The aim of FAO is to feed the population of the major part of the world up to 1985. If it fails the immediate effect will be a general increase in food prices. The poor will go hungry, the oppressed will be repressed even more severely. We may expect to see increasing social unrest, revolution and localized warfare, possibly leading to widespread famine.

The sober fact is that the Green Revolution is in trouble. It has run into local political and social problems, it is hindered by wider political and economic difficulties and its success could bring ecological problems of unpredictable magnitude.

The Congress was divided into two main sections. The first dealt with the broad aims of FAO. The second concerned itself with the implementation and realization of those aims. On most mornings there was a plenary session at which a major issue was discussed by a panel with contributions and questions from the floor. In the afternoon eight Commissions met to consider particular aspects in more detail. It was in the Commissions that the Congress was to be seen at its worst. The platitudes rolled forth and the grinding of axes was heard as delegates, given the floor to ask questions, made long speeches.

The plenary sessions were a little less boring. The one held to discuss population growth was particularly relevant. After all, even if we accept that it is possible for the planet to continue to support its present population, and this is a controversial matter, it is clearly necessary to stabilize it at some level. There are demographers who point out that an exponential population increase in any species will lead to its collapse and there is no reason to suppose homo sapiens has procured the repeal of a well-known biological law. There were no neo-Malthusians at The Hague. The session was presided over by Miss Mercedes Concepción, Chairman of the UN Population Commission. Delegates heard an eloquent statement from Dr S. Chandrasekhar, Minister of State for Health, Family Planning and Urban Development, Government of India. He pointed out that India's annual population increase of 13 million is equivalent to a nation the size of Holland. In spite of all India's efforts to increase food production, the situation continues to deteriorate. 'Man must realize that he is just one member, albeit the most important, of Nature's large and interdependent fellowship of all living organisms, and that only by learning to live in humility and harmony with all else that lives can he ensure his own survival.' Dr Chandrasekhar argued that family planning should be regarded as a rewarding investment for the development of human resources. India is one country which accepts the need for population control and seeks to introduce it.

Miss Concepción placed the Green Revolution in its proper perspective. At best it can only buy time, she said, and there may be an employment–

World Food Problem

population crisis in the seventies to take the place of the food–population crisis of the sixties.

The session proceeded quietly, members of the panel making moderate appeals for a solution to what they saw as man's most pressing problem. Several questions were asked from the floor, and answered. Then Professor J. de Castro, author of *The Geography of Hunger*, exploded into a microphone. There is too much talk of the population explosion, he said. He attacked America's nuclear defence programme which costs $200 million a year. He said no one had shown that hunger is caused by over-population, pointing out that the population of Africa is lower than that of Europe. Malthus, he said, was unscientific, because he believed population growth was a constant, whereas it is governed by many factors.

His violent outburst was cheered and Professor de Castro left shortly afterwards, without waiting to hear the rest of the discussion. FAO had reached the centre of the problem and it seems there is no answer. Although many people believe there can be no long-term solution to any of the environmental problems facing mankind unless populations are stabilized, this view is not accepted by a large number of developing countries.

The following morning was given over to environmental conversation. The most forthright speaker was Dr Makoto Numata, Professor of Botany and Ecology at Chiba University, Japan. He warned of the mutagenic effects of certain common pollutants and foresaw the annihilation of man if the degradation of the environment continues. Even this session, dealing with a vital and, one would have thought, uncontroversial, issue, was inconclusive and the general atmosphere suggested a disturbing degree of complacency. The best hope for developing countries was that they should learn from the experience of the developed countries and try not to repeat their mistakes. It would have been difficult in that place and at that time to suggest a second look at the direction in which the Third World is being encouraged to move and that the developed countries might profit from a reconsideration of the bases of their own civilization.

Perhaps if the Congress had been more controversial, if those who care deeply about the future of mankind had spoken out, more would have been achieved. As it was the panels were polite, moderate and ignored.

Outside the meetings there was another mood. It was particularly evident at the New Earth Village, a converted army camp on the other side of the city, where several hundred young people from all over the world had gathered at the invitation of Mr Boerma. They came as citizens, delegates in their own right, with full status. In the Village, and among some of the delegates who said little in the meetings, the view was that the problems of the world are too profound to be solved by technological tricks. The young people accepted the need for a far more radical approach. Disillusioned with the Congress, they

E

held their own meetings and invited speakers, including Mr Boerma and Lord Ritchie-Calder, to meet them. The future of the world will soon be in the hands of these young men and women. In their village there was hope, an eagerness to discuss all the issues and a willingness to hear all points of view.

That was in June. In October the FAO issued a series of background papers to mark the occasion of its 25th anniversary. One of them began with this paragraph: 'The world's nutrition authorities are worried. For the past 25 years they have been trying to bring people more and better food through the Food and Agriculture Organization of the United Nations. But in spite of their efforts, the protein gap in developing countries is increasing. By 1985 the world is expected to be 3·6 million tons short of animal protein – more than the amount consumed in 1962 in the Common Market countries or in Black Africa, Latin America and the Near East together.'

The paper goes on to point out that in 1969, for the first time in 12 years, world food production fell because of a cut-back in the developed countries.

The world food problem is still with us. The Congress may have failed, but this does not invalidate the work which FAO is doing. It cannot be held responsible for the views of individual delegates and even the IWP was produced only tentatively, as a starting-point for discussion. The Organization is fortunate to be led by a Director-General who is able to inspire confidence among delegates, journalists and young people alike.

The outlook is gloomy, but it is not quite pitch-dark. A satisfactory solution to the world food problem may be less spectacular than the Green Revolution. There may be no magic, no miracles, but there is some hope.

Let us look again at the problem itself. There are people who neither grow enough to feed themselves, nor earn enough foreign exchange to buy food grown elsewhere, so they go hungry. In the short term they need food; in the long term they need an economy strong enough to support them. The mistake is to attempt a short-term solution to a long-term problem.

How are people to be fed over the next few years? It is interesting to note here that the problem in the developing countries is the exact opposite of that in the developed ones. In parts of Western Europe, including Britain, farmers have been demonstrating in the streets because their incomes have fallen. As their governments have urged them to grow more and more food, so prices have fallen. Now they complain of dumping and demand tariffs and import controls to protect themselves. In fact, they have over-produced, glutted their markets, and ways must be found to deal with their surpluses. If they were to be encouraged to maintain high levels of production and their surpluses were bought by their own governments for distribution in the developing countries as aid, there would be sufficient food for the interim years while the developing countries increased their own production. With the immediate pressure of hunger removed this could happen more gradually.

World Food Problem

Even now more food is produced in the developing countries than reaches the consumer. Wastage after harvest, from insects, bacteria, moulds and rodents, could be reduced by the provision of better storage facilities. In India, the protein available amounts to 71·5 grams per person per day, whereas consumption is around 51 grams.[4] It has been estimated that in 1964 the wastage of food grains in India amounted to 47·3 per cent of the harvest.[14] In Nigeria 46 per cent of sorghum is lost and 41 per cent of the cowpea crop; In Sierra Leone, 41 per cent of the rice crop and 14 per cent of the maize; in tropical Africa 30 per cent of all crops.[4] Not only is food lost, but other food is contaminated. Eczema, mange, asthma and a number of allergies are all caused by grain-pest larvae and there are all the diseases transmitted by rats. It is possible to reduce this waste by relatively simple measures. A 4-inch-high parapet all around a warehouse will keep out rodents. Sacks can be treated to repel insects. Better drying of grain prevents moulds and fungi and better storage bins can be constructed at low cost from plastics.[3] A halving of this wastage might increase the food available by up to 20 per cent.

Some farmers are more efficient than others and some types of farming are more productive than others. When considering ways of increasing production it may be profitable to examine the methods of the more successful and extend them. In many parts of the world, particularly in Latin America, the peasant produces most of the food crops for internal consumption, but he does so in small areas of the poorest land, since the best land is owned by estates whose productivity is low. In Chile, for example, 40·8 per cent of all agricultural families are peasants, yet they own only 7·4 per cent of the farmland. From it they produce 20 per cent of the country's total agricultural output. In Brazil 23·5 per cent of the agricultural population are peasants and they own 6·5 per cent of the land, from which they produce 21·3 per cent of the total output.[15] Paradoxically a considerable increase in overall production might be achieved by land reforms which would allow the landless agricultural families – 49·7 per cent in Chile, 61·9 per cent in Brazil – to own land held at present by the estates and to farm it as peasants.

A soundly based agriculture will require livestock. Animals are also required to increase the availability of high-quality protein. The IWP, solving the problem instantly again, suggests poultry and pigs, where these are permitted, farmed along modern 'industrial' lines.[16] Additional protein may also be obtained from game animals, particularly in Africa, although problems exist because indigenous livestock is adapted to its own environment but can act as a reservoir for diseases and pests to which it is immune but introduced stock is not.[17]

Attractive though modern intensive livestock units may be from the point of view of rapid production, they require heavy capital investment, they can be operated only with the aid of sophisticated veterinary services and access to drugs, they produce food about whose quality there are growing doubts and they cause serious pollution problems in disposing of their effluents. They contribute nothing to the land and may even deplete it by taking grains and returning nothing. In areas where land is not available for more extensive stock-rearing a case can, perhaps, be made for them, but in most developing countries this is not so. It would be better to improve local breeds and adjust stocking rates to develop a livestock husbandry allied to arable farming which centuries of experience have taught us enhances the fertility of the soil. The main difficulty may be the provision of feed during the interim period while cereal production is increasing. This may be overcome by supplementing rations with feeds containing single cell proteins (s.c.p.). Factories for the production of s.c.p. are in operation in several countries and the USSR is reported to have produced a million tons in 1970.[18] The process is based on a fungal or bacterial fermentation on a nutrient base of petroleum or starch.

All this is very well, but what, in fact, will happen? The lessons are simple. Populations are increasing faster than food supply, resources are diminishing, the rich countries are taking far more than their fair share of what is available and are giving little or no help to those less fortunate than themselves. The gulf can be bridged only if the rich are willing to consume less and if rich and poor alike can learn to control their numbers. The rich must be prepared to provide aid which actually helps those it should help; all too often aid programmes are 'possible' only if they are profitable for industry in the donor countries.

The lessons are simple, but it is unlikely that they have been learned, or can be learned, by those in power in the world today. It is just as possible that the young, who are more closely in touch with one another than with their parents, may have learned at least some of them. The future lies with them. If they fail, or forget, or if they come to power too late, nature will provide Malthusian solutions: famine, pestilence and war. From these no country will be able to hide: the dogs of war will know no frontiers.

World Food Problem

REFERENCES

1   PROVISIONAL INDICATIVE WORLD PLAN FOR AGRICULTURE (IWP). 1969. Vol. 3, p. 6, para 25. Rome.
2   IWP. 1969. Vol. 1, p. 12, para 14. Rome.
3   BORGSTROM, GEORG. 1969. *Too Many*. London: Macmillan.
4   PARPIA, H. A. P. 1969. Waste and the protein gap. In *Ceres*, September/October.
5   FAO. 1966. *The State of Food and Agriculture*. Rome: FAO.
6   IWP. 1969. Vol. 3, p. 34, para 144.
7   ZU LOWENSTEIN, HUBERTUS. 1969. The story of a sophisticated breed. In *Ceres*.
8   IWP. 1969. Vol. 1, p. 95, para 55.
9   WALLER, ROBERT. 1970. Modern husbandry and soil deterioration. In *New Scientist*, February 5.
10 WALTERS, A. H. 1970. Nitrates in soil, plants and animals. In *Journal of the Soil Association*, July.
11 IWP. 1969. Vol. 1, p. 209, para 113.
12 MONTEFIORE, HUGH. 1969. *The Question Mark*. London: Collins.
13 IWP. 1969. Vol. 1, para 80 (ii).
14 TAINSH, A. RAMSAY. 1965. Waste not, want not. In *Journal of the Soil Association*, April.
15 PEARSE, ANDREW. 1969. Subsistence farming is far from dead. In *Ceres*, July/August.
16 IWP. 1969. Vol. 3, p. 35, para 151.
17 IWP. 1969. Vol. 1, p. 264, para 92.
18 WALTERS, A. H. 1969. Whither farming in the year 2000? In *Journal of the Soil Association*, April.

5 DETERIORATING SOIL

L. B. Powell

Agricultural Journalist

Enormous advances in mechanization, the massive application of synthetic fertilizers, herbicides and pesticides and new plant varieties have given British agriculture a record in productivity second to none in the world. But this increased efficiency has been bought at a high price. Evidence accumulates to force home the fact that the soil on which we depend for so much of our food will not tolerate the unremitting exploitation which has been brought about by ever-increasing economic pressures.

By cutting back profit margins in order to compel farmers to increase their output, successive governments have caused agriculture to realize on its capital – the acquired fertility of the land, built up by centuries of wise husbandry. It is as if the soil were being mined – and lest the proponents of industrial farming remain intoxicated by their short-term achievements it should be remembered that mining always ends in abandonment.

The postwar record of productivity in British farming betters that of most manufacturing industries. During the last two decades the increase in overall production has been estimated at no less than 35 per cent. In 1946, the year before the Agriculture Act which established the annual price review system, the average yield of wheat in the United Kingdom was 19·1 cwt per acre. By 1968/9 it had risen to 28·2 cwt.

Barley showed a similar increase, from 17·8 to 27·4 cwt. Oats went up from 16·3 to 25·4 cwt, potatoes from 7·1 to 9·8 cwt and sugar beet from 10·5 to 15·1 cwt.

Cattle and calves increased from 9,629,000 in 1946 to 12,374,000 in 1969. Pig numbers soared from 1,955,000 in 1946 to 7,078,000 in 1969. Sheep and lambs went up from 20,358,000 to 26,604,000 and poultry from 67,117,000 to 127,220,000.

As with crops, yields of milk and eggs showed big increases. The average yield of dairy cows rose from 544 to 815 gallons, while new hybrid breeds of hens meant a rise in the average number of eggs per hen from 108 to 211.

These figures are the more striking in view of the decline in manpower and loss of farmland. The total labour force was 976,000 in 1946. It was more than halved by 1969. There are various estimates of the rate at which farmland is taken for urban development, but the figure most quoted is 50,000 acres a

70

Deteriorating Soil

year, which means that in 8 years an area the size of Nottinghamshire goes out of farming use. Professor W. Ellison of the Department of Agriculture, University of Wales, who produced an official paper for the Department of Education and Science on the multiple use of land, concluded that a further 50,000 acres a year were being taken for other non-agricultural uses, such as forestry, reservoirs, *etc.*

Draught power on the land shows dramatic changes. In 1946 there were 436,000 farm horses at work. By 1960 the number was down to 46,000 and for the years since no figures are available. (It may be noted in passing that there is a profitable revival in the breeding of shire horses.) The war boosted the number of tractors to 180,000 but in 1969 there were 420,000 – nearly one for every farmworker. All other kinds of machinery showed big increases.

Looked at quantitatively, it is an imposing record, justifying the claim that in terms of output per man and per acre British agriculture is more efficient than that of most countries. By providing just over 50 per cent by value of our total food requirements it has been a major factor in saving us from national bankruptcy.

But grim and forbidding signs have appeared in this picture of progress. Efficiency is more than a matter of increased yields. The economists, technologists and chemists have been leaving nature out of account and nature is retaliating.

The pressures exerted so relentlessly upon farming since the 1947 Act have taken toll of the most basic resource of all – the soil. Much of Britain's farmland is now debilitated to a serious degree. It is becoming worn out. The notion that the soil is an inert mass which needs only a constant plastering with chemicals to give increasing yields, is one of the tragic follies of the twentieth century and it has been encouraged by government policy.

Thus yields have begun to decline, in some cases very substantially. Crop diseases and the ravages of pests, far from having been conquered, have increased over wide areas. Among farmers of the older generation, familiar with the traditional practices of good husbandry, there has long been deep misgiving, a realization that sooner or later the techniques of high-pressure industrialized farming would have to be called into question.

That time is with us now. Warnings that it was at hand multiplied in recent years. In a paper given to the London Farmers' Club in 1967 one of our most prominent farmers, Mr H. R. Fell, drew attention to the deterioration in husbandry standards and the effects it was having on the soil. In 1969, prompted by disquieting reports from various parts of the country, the National Farmers' Union of England and Wales set up a committee to probe those problems of soil structure and texture that were most alarming.

With an organization reaching down to parish level wherever farming is carried on, the NFU is uniquely fitted to investigate matters of this kind, and it soon became evident that trouble was widespread. During the autumn of 1968 and the spring of 1969 exceptionally bad weather over much of the country brought into greater prominence the adverse effects modern farming practices were having on the soil and the ability of water to drain through surface layers.

In December 1969 Mr Cledwyn Hughes, then Minister of Agriculture, called upon the Agricultural Advisory Council to undertake an inquiry into soil fertility and soil structure as a matter of urgency, and a group of specialists, headed by Mr Nigel Strutt, was appointed for the purpose.

The group's terms of reference were: 'To advise whether, and if so, the extent to which present practices are having adverse effects on soil fertility and soil structure; whether it considers the National Agricultural Advisory Service has all the information necessary to advise on methods of preventing any such damage or remedying it after it has taken place; and whether any further steps are necessary to get this advice across to farmers.'

The survey was not confined to areas where signs of deterioration were most clearly to be seen. Soil profiles were taken throughout the country, and evidence was submitted by many individual farmers and various organizations. Giving evidence for the Soil Association, Douglas Campbell, the Association's research farm director, helped to keep the inquiry down to earth by emptying a bag of soil from Haughley's organic section on to the table during one session, declaring, 'This is what it is all about.'

The evidence submitted officially by the NFU emphasized the wide-ranging extent of soil deterioration. 'There is no doubt,' it said, 'that real problems exist in most parts of the country, and that these are considered as arising from the systems of cropping and cultivation which have been practised.'

And the Union went to the root of the matter when it observed, 'Farming practice and soil husbandry are determined, to an increasing extent, by current financial considerations, and full recognition must be given both to the economic causes of the present situation and to the changes that must be made to correct it.'

One of the most disturbing features of the report made by the group was that it showed a serious decline in the organic content of soil in many areas, sometimes to as low as 3 per cent. This means a drastic loss of that essential soil constituent, humus, and of trace elements that are just as necessary for healthy plant growth as are nitrogen, potassium and phosphorus – the trinity upon which the empires of the synthetic fertilizer manufacturers have been built.

It is worth while to consider more closely what the highly complex colloidal substance which we call humus really is, and what it does, bearing in mind that humus is the latin word for soil.

Deteriorating Soil

To quote the late Sir Albert Howard, 'Humus is a complex residue of partly oxidized vegetable and animal matter together with the substances synthesized by fungi and bacteria which break down these wastes'.

He went on, 'This humus also helps to provide the cement which enables the minute soil particles to aggregate into larger compound particles and so maintain the pore space. If soil is deficient in humus, the volume of pore space is reduced; the aeration of the soil is impeded; there is insufficient organic matter for the soil population; the machinery of the soil runs down; the supply of oxygen, water, and dissolved salts needed by the root hairs is reduced; the synthesis of carbohydrates and proteins in the green leaf proceeds at a lower tempo; and growth is affected.'

The beginning of this deficiency in organic matter goes back to what Mr W. Emrys Jones, director of the new Agricultural Advisory and Development Service, has described as 'the agro-chemical' era in British agriculture, when the traditional practice of returning farmyard manure to the land gave way to widespread use of artificial fertilizers, accompanied by extensive use of new herbicides and pesticides, the toxic effects of some of which persist for many months in the soil.

The chemical fertilizers possessed great though superficial advantages. In compound form their analysis was known. They were clean, easy to store and distribute. Above all, their use was subsidized by a nation which twice within a lifetime had been confronted with the prospect of military defeat by starvation and was therefore concerned only to increase the quantity of home-produced food so that quality soon came to be forgotten.

A pronounced feature of the agro-chemical phase has been the application of continually higher rates of nitrogen per acre in spring and early autumn, necessitating the use of heavy machinery. Immense pressure was, and still is, exerted by the fertilizer manufacturers to increase the use of nitrogen on farms. Millions of pounds have been spent in promoting its use, with press advertising, field demonstrations and advisory visits to farms, while the National Agricultural Advisory Service added its own persuasive influence to the campaign.

Closely linked to the pursuit of higher gross margins and the development of more intensive livestock systems, the nitrogen campaign has continued despite the risk of nitrate poisoning of crops and livestock and the risk of pollution by leached out nitrate of streams, rivers and lakes. The toxic effects of high nitrate levels was the subject of an extensive survey by Mr Harry Walters, consultant associate lecturer at the Department of Applied Biology and Food Science at the Borough Polytechnic, London, published in the *Journal of the Soil Association* (vol. 16, no. 3), which points the moral that the health of soil, plants, animals and humans is indivisible.

The rise of intensive livestock systems with poultry, pigs and cattle (there are signs that sheep will follow also) has meant vast accumulations of manure and acute problems of disposal. In an age ridden with statistics the amount of excreta deposited annually per bird and animal is known more or less precisely, and basing his calculation on the Ministry of Agriculture's June census a year or so ago, a NAAS worker reckoned that about 121 million tons of manure were produced annually: enough to cover the M1 up to Nottingham a mile high or the Isle of Wight a foot deep. Instead of being returned to the land, a high proportion of this is wasted, some of it through discharge into public sewers.

It was formerly thought that only a few hundred farms were connected to public sewers throughout the entire country, but the NFU, giving evidence to the Working Party on Sewage Disposal (Ministry of Housing and Local Government) said it appeared, from information they were receiving from members, local authorities and consultant engineers, that there could be as many as 10,000, many of which had been connected several decades ago and concerning which no records had been taken.

Intensive livestock systems may have an acceptable place in modern farming when buildings are adequate and there is enough land for the disposal of dung. When this is not so and heavier stocking is resorted to on pastures in the hope of reducing unit costs of production and meeting the challenge of poor returns, the effects on pastures can be disastrous.

Emrys Jones has described the most extreme example of intensive stocking he saw, on a farm in Montgomeryshire, where seventy-five cows were being kept on 36 acres of heavily fertilized grass. The fields, he said, were literally disintegrating, and cows were pulling the soil away in lumps as big as pancakes.

The great increase in barley production which we noted above has largely been achieved at the expense of grass, the best conserver of soil structure and texture. On this the NFU evidence was illuminating. Between 1960 and 1967 there was a reduction of 350,000 acres of permanent grassland, and in the same period there was an even greater reduction in temporary grass, or leys, amounting to some 570,000 acres. Along with this reversion from grass the old and well-proven practice of fallowing was abandoned and is now seen on very few farms.

The need for a substantial return to grass is one indication of the survey, but, as Emrys Jones has pointed out, this will not be easy on the clay soils of the Midlands, which he describes as having been thrashed and pounded by heavy machinery year after year; and there will be the financial problem of reintroducing herds and flocks in place of corn, potatoes and other arable crops.

It is foreseeable also that there will have to be a large-scale revival of planting trees as shelter belts and the restoration of hedgerows – not least in the

Deteriorating Soil

fenlands where the blowing of soils long ago gave warning of nature's retaliation for the removal of natural cover.

Hedgerow removal is an emotive subject often debated and it is as well to keep a sense of perspective in this matter. There has occasionally been a good case for some streamlining of the traditional patchwork quilt of a field system which derived from days when the horse was king, and small mixed farming was widely practised. But in addition to their prime purpose as stockproof boundaries, hedgerows are a source of timber and humus; they afford shelter to stock and mitigate the consequences of wind and water erosion. The tundras of Essex and East Anglia and the featureless fields of parts of the Midlands bear witness to the fact that destruction has gone too far and has contributed to soil deterioration.

In this we have followed the ancient English practice of appointing a committee and forgetting its findings. Public concern over hedgerow destruction led to the appointment of the Merthyr Committee as long ago as 1953. After taking evidence from over forty organizations the committee published its report two years later and said:

> 'We think that erosion is now a sufficiently important risk on a number of individual farms and fields to merit the attention of the landowners and farmers concerned ... If, owing to modern farming methods, the traditional hedge is to disappear, much of our heritage of wild flora would disappear with it. We think that the considerable loss to botanists, schools, rambling clubs and lovers of the countryside would be a calamity.'

The Merthyr Committee's main recommendation was that all concerned with land ownership should be encouraged to co-operate in maintaining and, where practicable, increasing the number of trees of the hedgerow and farm type, and to accept such measures as may be expedient. It further recommended an official campaign of education on the cultivation of hedgerow and farm timber, and that courses on hedgerow cultivation and management should be given at agricultural colleges and farm institutes.

How many of the latter do have courses of this kind? It would be interesting to know. The facts are that the rate of destruction has accelerated since the Merthyr Committee reported. It has been aided and abetted by grants and the encouragement given to farm amalgamations. As for management, the mechanical trimmer, which doesn't differentiate between hedgerow plants and valuable saplings, is now widely used, and the craftsman whose laying of a hedge can be a joy to behold is now a rare figure in the countryside.

Eight years after the Merthyr Committee reported, *Agriculture*, the journal of the MAFF which is not addicted to extreme statements, stated:

'Hedgerows have been a feature of the English countryside for about 200 years. If their present rate of destruction is not checked it is likely that they will soon cease to be a feature at all.'

It was further stated that in some parts of the country between a tenth and a fifth of the hedgerows had disappeared during the previous 20 years. These statements may have been too pessimistic but they nevertheless indicated the extent of the problem.

We have to thank the Nature Conservancy for the most extensive modern survey of hedgerow destruction. This lasted four years, was spread over forty-six counties and covered 1,230 miles. Aerial photos, maps and observations on foot were employed, and it was found that hedgerow loss had occurred in 78 of the 81 transects surveyed. The worst sample was in Huntingdonshire, where 70·8 miles of hedgerow in 7 miles in 1945 had been reduced to only 20 miles by 1965.

In Devonshire, the most hedgerowed county in Britain, destruction was estimated to be proceeding at the rate of 10 miles a year a few years ago: a rate which will be greatly accelerated when the new motorway to the west is under construction. A new look at the whole question of hedgerow removal has become urgently necessary, and we may well have to follow the example of West Germany where, following extensive destruction in the prewar years, a substantial policy of replanting hedgerows is now being carried out.

The weight of machinery used on the land has of course increased enormously, and ironically the ill-effects of this are seen where large slurry tanks have to be used, in unsuitable conditions, on land where intensive livestock systems are practised.

On this aspect the NFU stressed again the effect of economic pressures, pointing out that cultivations have become an urgent task that must often be undertaken in unfavourable weather. 'Farmers are unhappy,' said the Union, 'that they can no longer restrict land work to ideal conditions, so that timeliness in cultivations is now an ideal rather than a practice. The evidence we have received stresses that these factors form the major cause in the formation of unrecognized soil pans and the final breakdown of the structure.'

While the soil survey report was in preparation Emrys Jones expressed the view that a massive new drainage campaign would be needed if the desired rate of agricultural expansion is to be achieved. The evidence of the NFU substantiated this, pointing out that the rate of installing drains had not kept pace with the need to replace old systems. 'Many old drainage systems are now past their useful life,' it was stated, 'and comprehensive redraining is necessary. Maintenance has not been kept up owing to shortage of labour, and many counties have reported that the general condition of drainage systems leaves a lot to be desired.'

Deteriorating Soil

The soil report raises urgent questions, upon the answers to which the well-being of the nation will very largely depend. It is a challenge to the Ministry of Agriculture to get its priorities right. Will it induce the government to finance the extensive new drainage scheme that is called for? This could be done for a fraction of the expenditure that has gone on the Concorde project and would be an infinitely better investment. Will the cost–price squeeze which has pressed so heavily upon farmers and growers for so long be reversed so as to bring about a return to good husbandry?

And will there be also another massive campaign to advance the municipal composting of town wastes, which could provide vast quantities of organic matter for farms, market gardens and orchards and at the same time confer some much needed relief in rate burdens? Ominous increases in these are threatened as the outcome of the council workers recent strike which was in itself a dramatic indictment of our obsolete methods of sewage disposal. The number of municipalities who have gone over to composting has steadily increased in recent years, and there is some impressive evidence of the beneficial effects the disposal of their composts is having on the land, a conspicuous example being Jersey. More research is needed on the techniques of municipal composting and this is something the Agricultural Research Council ought to sponsor. The University of Birmingham is already doing important work in this connection but a great deal more is needed.

There are lessons in the technological revolution in agriculture which have been little heeded so far, but which the soil report will help to bring home. They are briefly that we must substitute an organic economy for the industrial economy that has begun to dominate farming, and that we must relate human biological needs to natural biological resources. Nature, we must learn, can be cultivated, but will resist attempts at subjugation.

To sum up, let us turn back the pages of history a few years, to days before Darwin's famous work on *The Formation of Vegetable Mould* appeared, and before Liebig's chemical conception of soil fertility began to hold its enormous sway. Many organic farmers will know the story, for it is a classic of its kind, and the moral is in no way invalidated by the fact that it derives from long ago.

George Sheffield divided his farm in northern Ohio into four tracts of 40 acres each. At the centre was a great barn and barnyard covering 2 acres. Broad swinging gates gave access to each of the four sides, and located in the four corners of the yard were stacks of straw, on permanent platforms raised about 6 feet above the ground. Beneath these stacks stock had good shelter in winter and fed on straw through partitions in the logs supporting the stacks, when they were not feeding in the barn itself. Plenty of straw was also thrown down for bedding.

The centre of the barnyard was occupied by a compost pit 100 feet long,

50 feet wide and about 2 feet deep. Manure from the barn was cleared each morning and conveyed to the pit in baskets conveyed on overhead cables. From a creek beside the barnyard water was piped for the stock and supplied when needed to the compost pit. Cattle, sheep, pigs and fowls had free run of the yard, and at intervals its contents were harrowed to the pit and distributed in an even layer, to be topped with a covering of fine clay. The compost pit served as a nursery for the breeding of untold millions of earthworms. Before spring ploughing began there was a generous 'seeding' of the fields with earthworms and their capsules from the pit, so that a permanent earthworm population was maintained, to perform their life-work of digesting organic material and depositing it on the surface in the form of highly homogenized soil rich in humus and soluble plant food. Throughout 60 and more years George Sheffield did not have a crop failure. He was renowned far and wide for the health of his stock and the excellence of his crops, the surplus of which commanded high prices for seed purposes. His system is fully described by his grandson, T. J. Barrett, in his book *Harnessing the Earthworm* (Faber and Faber, 1949).

REFERENCES

HOWARD, ALBERT. 1940. *An Agricultural Testament*. Oxford: OUP.
JONES, EMRYS. 1970. Address to *The Dorset Farming and Wildlife Conference*, July 25–26.
MOORE, N. W. 1967. The biotic effects of public pressures on the environment. In *Monk's Wood Experimental Station Third Scientific Staff Symposium*, March 20–21.
NATIONAL FARMERS UNION. 1970. The British Farmer. In *Journal of the NFU*, August 22.

6 DIMINISHING RETURNS ON PESTICIDES

Environment Staff Report

The effectiveness of pest control with modern insecticides is being seriously eroded by the response of insect species to the chemical attack. Reports from all over the world indicate that chemical pest control is approaching a state of crisis that could have far-reaching economic, political and social consequences.

The results of the initial use of DDT were truly spectacular. During the Second World War, DDT was credited with stemming a potentially serious outbreak of typhus in Europe. After the war, DDT and its relatives, and later some of the cyclodienes (dieldrin, aldrin, *etc*) were used with considerable success in lowering the incidence of many insect-borne diseases throughout the world. In agriculture they afforded crop protection to a degree that had never before been achieved. So promising were the early accomplishments of these poisons that the Swiss chemist, Paul Mueller, discoverer of the insecticidal properties of DDT, was awarded a Nobel Prize in 1948.

It wasn't long, however, before it became obvious that the powerful new synthetic killers were not the complete answer to insect control. In 1946[1] some populations of houseflies were reported to be resistant to DDT. By 1948 the list of pest species showing resistance to the new organic insecticides had grown to 12. By 1957 the list jumped to 76 and since then has been steadily increasing; a total of 224 pest insects are now resistant to one or more of the modern insecticides. Among these are 97 insects of public health or veterinary importance and 127 insects which attack field crops, forest crops or stored products.

Oddly, the increasing failure of some of these chemicals is almost entirely due to the characteristic which once made them the most talked about agricultural tool since the combine – their deadly effect on insects.

Resistance to insecticides can be defined as the ability of an insect to escape death from a dose of poison that would have been lethal to one of its recent ancestors. The mechanisms by which this can happen are diverse and complex, ranging from behavioural changes which allow an insect to avoid a poison, to the most serious and most widespread kind of resistance, the occurrence of genes which produce enzymes that can destroy, or detoxify, the poison.

Behavioural avoidance has been observed in some malaria control programmes. Mosquitoes which normally inhabit human living quarters become irritated by the DDT sprayed walls and are driven outside. Those that are not driven out are killed, and a strain of outdoor-dwelling mosquitoes is developed. Such avoidance of pesticides has developed in mosquitoes in Java, Mexico and Panama.[2] Selection of genes which produce detoxifying enzymes is a far more common occurrence and has been extensively studied. In some cases (as in the much-studied fruit fly) the exact location on the chromosomes of the genes for resistance are known.

Resistance appears when those members of a population that are susceptible to the poison are killed, leaving only those insects which are in some way tolerant of the poison. This is a classic example of selection, the 'survival of the fittest' first described by Darwin. Resistance for the most part tends to be quite specific. For example, selection for DDT resistance produces insects tolerant of DDT and its relatives, such as methoxychlor and DDD, but not to other kinds of chlorinated hydrocarbons such as the cyclodienes (dieldrin, aldrin, endrin, *etc*). Resistance to all the major classes of modern insecticides – DDT and its relatives, cyclodienes, organophosphates and carbamates – has been found in insects.

The characteristics of most pest control programmes are ideal for the appearance of resistance. Such programmes aim to kill a high percentage of the target insect, treat as large an area as possible and repeat the treatment as many times as necessary to prevent return of the insect pest. When these conditions are met – and they often are – resistance can develop quickly, for all susceptible insects are kept out of a large area for enough time to allow the few resistant individuals to multiply and establish themselves. The salt marsh sandfly developed resistance to dieldrin after only three applications of one pound per acre. The resistant insects were also less susceptible to heptachlor, chlordane and gamma BHC. Insects with more than one generation per year and a high reproductive rate adapt most quickly to insecticides.

Resistance is not the only troublesome problem encountered when broad-spectrum insecticides are used in crop protection. Another problem is becoming more and more serious as the persistent pesticides are replaced by non-persistent but more toxic materials; the resurgence of pest populations in treated areas. In recent years the use of chlorinated hydrocarbons on many crops has been curtailed, either because the pests they were used on have become resistant or because tighter restrictions have been placed on their use by the Food and Drug Administration. Consequently, a greater reliance has been placed on the more potent, less persistent, organophosphates. But this is only a temporary solution. After spraying with one of the powerful, non-selective organophosphates, fields are nearly devoid of insects, including the natural enemies of pests. Then, because of the speed with which these chemi-

Diminishing Returns on Pesticides

cals are broken down and disappear, pests from neighbouring fields can reinvade and build up very quickly, without natural enemies to slow their population growth. The result is that the interval between treatments becomes shorter, fulfilling one of the conditions under which resistant populations are selected. Another condition is met by the selection of an organophosphate – a high percentage of kill. This assures that only resistant insects can survive and then multiply freely. When resistance begins to appear it can sometimes be met by increasing the dosage applied to the crop. In fact this is often done when it is known that the pest is resistant to another class of insecticide and changing materials will do little good.

Still another problem of increasing importance and one which has occurred on nearly all crops where pesticides have been used is known as the pest 'trade-off'. All agricultural ecosystems harbour numerous insects that never reach significant numbers because their populations are kept under control by a variety of natural enemies. The intrusion of a pesticide into these eco-systems for the control of a particular pest can so upset this natural balance that one or more non-pests can become pests, thus trading one pest for another. 'Trade-offs' have occurred with such regularity that many current pest-control recommendations allow for the control of such normally bio-logically suppressed species. Thus, the list of insect pests is growing rather than diminishing.

The problems created by the use of broad-spectrum pesticides are being demonstrated dramatically in various parts of this country. Cotton producers in the lower Rio Grande Valley of Texas are having serious difficulty con-trolling two of the most serious pests of cotton, the cotton bollworm and its close relative the tobacco budworm. Tests conducted at Texas A&M Univer-sity in 1965[3] show that bollworm populations in that year were more than 30,000 times more resistant to DDT than they were in 1960.

At the same time it was revealed that bollworms were thirteen times more resistant to endrin, four times more resistant to Sevin, 21 times more resistant to a mixture of Strobane-DDT and eleven times more resistant to a mixture of toxaphene-DDT. When these studies were made in 1965, methyl parathion, a potent organophosphate, was still giving adequate control of bollworm populations and, although concern was great, it was not an emergency situation. However, in 1968, massive spraying of parathion in the valley did little to inhibit the highest tobacco budworm populations ever recorded. Dr P. L. Adkisson, Chairman of the Department of Entomology at Texas A&M,[4] in assessing the situation, stated that the worms were nearly immune to appli-cations of parathion. So disturbing was this that Dr Adkisson told a group of cotton growers that if they wanted to stay in business they would have to stop relying on chemical poisons to control pests in their fields.

A similar situation is found in Louisiana where some of the largest amounts of pesticides have been used on cotton. In some areas as much as 1·6 lb of endrin and 24 lb of a toxaphene-DDT mixture have been used per acre of cotton during a single growing season. Since 1963 even more exotic mixtures have come into favour, the most popular of which has been 2 lb of toxaphene plus 1 lb of DDT and ¼ lb of methyl parathion.

For generations, cotton insect control in Louisiana was aimed at the boll weevil. When chlorinated hydrocarbons like DDT appeared, these were directed to the same target. In 1955 it was recognized that the weevil had become resistant to chlorinated hydrocarbon compounds, however, and a drastic shift to the use of organophosphates was required. Since that time a significant change in the pest status of at least three species has taken place. Although the boll weevil still remains the key pest, two species of bollworms that were only occasional pests now appear regularly in the cotton fields in such numbers that entomologists sometimes consider them to be more important than the boll weevil. According to Dr L. D. Newsom, Chairman of the Department of Entomology at Louisiana State University, spider mites, virtually unknown before the new chemicals were used, are now classified as serious pests in Louisiana. In some areas of the cotton belt,[5] as in Texas and California, there are populations of bollworms and spider mites that can no longer be controlled by any currently available insecticide.

The list of insecticides to which pests are becoming resistant is growing faster than new chemicals are produced. Eighteen pests of cotton in the United States have shown resistance to chlorinated hydrocarbons, and eight of those have also shown resistance to organophosphates. Two species, the cotton bollworm and the tobacco budworm, have shown resistance to all four classes of synthetic pesticides.

The production and marketing of new chemicals of increased toxicity is no answer to the problem. However, when resistance becomes a serious problem, farmers eagerly accept any new material in the hope that it will save them from crop failure. Such was the case with Azodrin, which was offered to cotton farmers as a cure for losses suffered from damage by the cotton bollworm and lygus bug. In California alone over a million acres of cotton were sprayed with Azodrin in 1967, and the results were far from satisfactory. Aside from the massive wildlife losses caused by the use of Azodrin, it is highly questionable whether its use was effective in preventing losses from insect damage. University of California entomologists who had studied the poison before its use in the State were so disenchanted that they warned growers in their 1968 cotton-pest-control bulletin against its use. In this case the problem was resurgence. When used early or in midseason, it so disrupted the existing complex of natural enemies that late season populations of the bollworms were allowed to build up to destructive levels. This required further treatments which added considerably and maybe unnecessarily to the

Diminishing Returns on Pesticides

growers' pesticide bill,[6] with no real evidence that it paid for itself in increased yields.

Both the amounts of pesticides used and the cost to farmers are increasing,[7] as shown by the production and sales figures for the years 1962 to 1967. During that period US pesticide production jumped from 729 million lb in 1962 to over 1 billion lb in 1967. Production in 1967 increased 3·6 per cent over the previous year, but the dollar value of 1967 pesticide production was 25·6 per cent greater than in 1966. Some of the increase in usage is caused by an increase in the total number of acres treated, but in some states where problems are serious, there has been a sharp increase in the amount of material used per acre. In Arizona,[8] which has kept good records and is a major cotton-growing state, pesticide use nearly tripled between 1965 and 1967. Total chlorinated hydrocarbons increased from 2 million lb in 1965 to 6 million lb in 1967. (Arizona has since instituted a temporary ban on DDT, but use of other chemicals remains high.) Organophosphates increased from 463,400 lb in 1965 to 1·8 million lb in 1967. A significant percentage of this increase can be attributed to the fact that pest species are increasing and are becoming more difficult to kill. So far, agriculture in the United States has managed to avert a complete crop failure due to depredations by insects, but we seem to be approaching the kind of disaster Dr Adkisson spoke about in Texas.

Some of the underdeveloped countries which have tried to increase agricultural production through the use of modern pesticides have been less fortunate. *Environment* (January–February, 1969) detailed some of the disastrous results of the massive use of pesticides in Peru and elsewhere.

In Peru[9] the cotton industry suffered a complete collapse in 1956, largely because of the massive use of synthetic organic pesticides. In 1943, before the introduction of the new poisons, Peruvian cotton growers in the fertile Cañete Valley harvested an average of 406 lb of cotton per acre. In 1949 the first chlorinated hydrocarbons were widely used for insect control and yields increased to a record 649 lb per acre in 1954. But then the trouble began. The list of pest species had grown from seven to thirteen and several pests had become resistant to DDT and BHC. By 1965 the yield in the valley had dropped to 296 lb per acre. In the worst years, 15–25 applications of various pesticides, either alone or in mixtures, were used to control harmful insects, but, because of resistance, no effective control was achieved.

The result was that a completely new pest-control programme was devised in which more cultural and biological control methods were instituted, and less reliance was placed on synthetic poisons. By 1960 the Cañete Valley situation was remedied to such an extent that a record yield of 923 lb per acre was harvested.

Some of the most serious problems are now being encountered in the cotton-producing areas of Central America, especially in Nicaragua, where cotton represents 46 per cent of total export earnings. For the past several years cotton production has been declining from the record production of 568,000 bales during the 1964–5 season. Production for the 1967–8 season was about 425,000 bales, approximately 30 per cent lower than the 1964–5 season. This failure has been attributed principally to the inability of growers to control overwhelming insect populations. Some growers were unable to pay off loans from banks and credit from suppliers, and others went out of business entirely. The drop in production coupled with the lower world prices paid for cotton during the past few years is seriously threatening the political and economic stability of Nicaragua.

Other countries have had their principal crop threatened by resistance. In Ghana, where the principal export crop is cocoa, there was a serious crop failure in 1961.[10] The main insect pest, the cocoa caspid, had developed resistance to lindane, the pesticide generally used for control. Egyptian cotton growers suffered severe losses in 1961 when cotton leaf worm developed resistance to toxaphene, upon which complete reliance for control had been placed. Other pesticides were brought in, but in 1966 another severe loss occurred – the leaf worm populations had become resistant to endrin and parathion. More potent insecticides such as Azodrin and Cyolane are now being used. The cost of these materials is considerably higher, and how they will fare in the future is open to question.

Public health officials the world over are also having their problems with resistance. During the global campaign to eradicate malaria,[11] a total of 35 species of anopheline mosquitoes developed resistance, 34 of them to cyclodiene insecticides, and twelve to DDT. In Greece, Egypt, Java, the area around the Persian Gulf and in Central America, mosquito populations have been found that are resistant to both kinds of chemicals. In Central America, one species, *Anopheles ablimanus*, a carrier of the most serious kind of malaria, has also shown an increased tolerance to malathion. If a strong resistance to organophosphorous compounds develops, as it appears to be doing, only one class of pesticide, the carbamates, will be left to control this mosquito – and no one can predict how long they will be useful.

Genetic studies have shown some interesting patterns of resistance development. For example, the mosquito which carries yellow fever develops *both* DDT and cyclodiene resistance when treated with *either* of these chemicals. In other cases, such as with the stable fly in North America, no resistance to DDT has ever developed, while the same species in Europe has developed a strong resistance.

DDT resistance usually spreads through populations very slowly because the first resistant strains that appear apparently do not compete as effectively as non-resistant strains. It takes several generations for selection to develop

Diminishing Returns on Pesticides

strains that are both competitive and resistant. However, once this takes place, such strains are spread quickly through the population. On the other hand, resistance to cyclodienes spreads very rapidly because the genes for resistance do not seem to diminish competiveness at all. The peak of irony seems to be reached in eastern Canada where the cyclodiene-resistant forms of the cabbage maggot live twice as long and produce twice as many eggs as do their non-resistant cousins.

It has now been 23 years since the first resistant houseflies were discovered in Sweden, and the list of resistant species and the chemicals to which insects are developing resistance continues to grow. The measures so far employed to combat resistance, such as increasing dosages or substituting other classes or compounds, have shown little promise either because they become too expensive or because pests ultimately develop another kind of resistance. Even some of the more exotic chemicals, such as chemosterilants, have been shown to have diminishing effects under laboratory conditions. It seems that both agriculture and public health will inevitably encounter more situations like the complete breakdown of cotton production in the Cañete Valley of Peru and the recurrence of malaria-carrying mosquitoes in Central America.

The development of resistance can never be completely avoided as long as pesticides are used, and it is very unlikely that they will be completely abandoned, given the kinds of agriculture now being practised in most of the world. However, it is possible to reduce the problem by using these chemicals wisely and sparingly. Not only will this practice postpone resistance and reduce resurgence problems, but it will cut down on the increasing pollution of our air, water and soils. That this can be done while still producing crops efficiently has been clearly demonstrated. The work of A. D. Pickett in apple orchards in Nova Scotia is a good example.[12]

By judiciously using less toxic and more selective insecticides and carefully timing their application, Dr Pickett and his associates were able to reduce the number of damaged apples at harvest time. True, when DDT and parathion were eliminated from the spray schedules the amount of insect damage increased at first, but then it gradually decreased when the natural enemy complex was allowed to become re established. Injury caused by the codling moth, the most important pest of apples, was reduced from 30·8 per cent in 1948 to 4·1 per cent in 1958 and remains at about that level today.

Sometimes a simple farming technique can have a tremendous effect on the balance between pest populations and their natural enemies. In California, mowing large continuous acreages of alfalfa was shown to be a damaging practice as far as the balance between the spotted alfalfa aphid and its natural enemies were concerned. A technique was developed in which fields were harvested in strips. This allowed the crop to mature at various times through the season, always providing a refuge in which natural enemies could maintain relatively high populations. A comparison of natural enemy populations was made between fields in which strip-cutting was practised and those where regular harvesting methods were used.[13] In the strip-cut fields parasites and predators of the aphid averaged 56 per square foot compared to 14 per square foot in the regularly harvested fields. Although this practice is a simple one, it can significantly affect the number of spray treatments needed to control the aphid.

In another case, again in California, Dr R. L. Doutt, an entomologist at the University of California, demonstrated how important it is to study the ecology of both pests and their natural enemies. Several years ago the grape leafhopper developed resistance to organophosphate materials. Increased numbers of treatments at higher doses failed to give satisfactory control. An appeal was made to the University by several grower associations for help in solving their problem. A large research project to establish an integrated control programme was undertaken in 1961.

One of the first things discovered was that the leafhopper was under heavy attack by a tiny wasp, *Anagrus*, during part of the season. Unfortunately, the protection afforded by the wasp did not come early enough in the season to prevent the leafhopper from causing damage to the young grape leaves. The reason for this was soon discovered. The wasps do not remain in the vineyards throughout the winter, but instead seek out blackberry vines where they attack a related but different leafhopper. At times the blackberries are scarce and at long distances from the grapes. Furthermore, blackberry vines are considered to be weeds and are usually killed with herbicides. In the spring when the young grape leaves are attacked by the leafhopper, the wasps are too slow getting back to the vineyards to effect good control. Experimental plantings of blackberries are now being made in vineyards and they show great promise of keeping high populations of the wasp within striking distance of the leafhopper populations. At the same time new and more selective chemicals that will not interfere with this programme are being evaluated for use on other grape pests.

These are only a few cases in which an understanding of ecological principles has helped reduce the amount of pesticides applied to a crop. There are many more. In the past, as long as a cheap, effective chemical was available, the dollars and health protection gained appeared to outweigh the cost to the environment. Now, as farmers, foresters and public health officials evaluate the use of synthetic poisons, they must face the fact that effectiveness of the chemicals in terms of crop and health protection is diminishing and at the same time their cost, both in dollars and ecological disruption, is rising.

Diminishing Returns on Pesticides

INSECT PESTS RESISTANT TO MODERN PESTICIDES

+ Resistant   − No resistance developed

	DDT and relatives	Cyclodienes and relatives	Organo-phosphates	Carba-mates
MOTHS				
Tobacco budworm	+	+	+	+
Tobacco hornworm	+			
Cabbage moth	+	−	−	−
Cabbage looper	+	−	+	−
Coddling moth	+	−	−	−
Oriental fruit moth	+	−	−	−
Cotton bollworm	+	−	−	−
Pink bollworm	+	−	−	−
Argyrotaenia velutinana	+	−	−	−
Potato tuber moth	+	+	−	−
Protoparce sexta	−	+	−	−
Euxoa detersa		+		
E. messoria	−	+	−	−
Chilo suppressalis	−	+	+	−
Ephestia cautella	−	−	+	−
Epiphyas postvittana	+	−	+	−
Plodia interpunctella	−	−	+	−
Diatria saccharalis	−	+	−	−
Alabama agrillacea	−	+	−	−
Spodoptera litteralis	−	+	+	−
Estigmene acraea	−	+	−	−
Bucculatrix thurberiella	−	+	−	−
Aeneolamia varia	−	+	−	−
FLIES (NOT MOSQUITOES)				
Euxesta notata	−	+	−	−
Hylemia liturata	−	+	−	−
H. platura	−	+	−	−
H. brassicae	−	+	−	−
H. floralis	−	+	−	−
H. antiqua	−	+	−	−
H. arambourgi	−	+	−	−
Merodon equestris	−	+	−	−
Psila rosae	−	+	−	−
Dasyneura pyri	−	−	+	−

	DDT and relatives	Cyclodienes and relatives	Organo-phosphates	Carba-mates
Tryporyza incertula	−	−	+	−
House fly	+	+	+	−
Chrysomyia putoria	+	+	+	−
Glyptotendipes paripes	−	+	+	−
Chironomus zealandicus	−	+	−	−
Haematobia irritans	−	+	+	−
Phaenicia cuprina	−	+	+	−
P. sericata	−	+	−	−
Stomoxys calcitraus	+	+	−	−
Psychoda alternata	+	+	−	−
Leptocera hirtula	+	+	−	−
Culicoides furens	−	+	−	−
Hippelates collusor	−	+	−	−
Fannia canicularis	+	−	−	−
Phormia terraenovae	+	−	−	−
Simulium aokii	+	−	−	−
S. venustum	+	−	−	−
Drosophila melanogaster	+	−	−	−
D. virilis	+	−	−	−
Leptoconops kerteszii	+	−	−	−
Chaoborus astictopus	+	−	−	−
LICE				
Pediculus corporis	+	+	−	−
Linognathus vituli	+	−	−	−
Haematopinus eurysternus	+	−	−	−
Bovicola limbata	−	+	−	−
B. caprae	−	+	−	−
FLEAS				
Zenopsylla cheopis	+	+	−	−
Z. astia	+	+	−	−
Pulex irritans	+	+	−	−
Ctenocephalides canis	+	+	−	−
C. felis	+	+	−	−
TICKS				
Boophilus microplus	+	+	+	−
B. decoloratus	+	+	−	−

Diminishing Returns on Pesticides

	DDT and relatives	Cyclodienes and relatives	Organo-phosphates	Carba-mates
Amblyomma americana	−	+	−	−
Rhipicephalus sanguineus	−	+	−	−
R. evertsi	−	+	−	−
R. appendiculatus	−	+	−	−
Dermacenter variabilis	+	+	−	−
COCKROACHES				
Blatella germanica	+	+	+	−
B. orientalis	−	+	−	−
BEDBUGS				
Cimex leticularis	+	+	+	−
C. hemipterus	+	+	−	−
MOSQUITOES				
Aedes aegypti	+	+	−	−
A. sollicitans	+	+	−	−
A. taeniorhynchus	+	+	+	−
A. nigromaculis	+	+	+	−
A. melanimon	+	+	+	−
A. dorsalis	−	−	+	−
A. cantator	+	+	−	−
A. atropalpus	+	−	−	−
A. cantans	+	−	−	−
A. albopictus	+	−	−	−
A. vittatus	+	−	−	−
A. vexans	+	−	−	−
Anopheles sacharovi	+	+	−	−
A. sundaicus	+	+	−	−
A. stephensi	+	+	−	−
A. subpictus	+	+	−	
A. albimanus	+	+	−	−
A. pharoensis	+	+	−	−
A. quadrimaculatus	+	+	−	−
A. annularis	+	+	−	−
A. culicifacies	+	+	−	−
A. albitarsis	+	+	−	−
A. nunez-tovaria	+	−	−	−
A. aconitus	+	+	−	−

	DDT and relatives	Cyclodienes and relatives	Organo-phosphates	Carba-mates
A. gambiae	−	+	−	−
A. coustani	−	+	−	−
A. pulcherrimus	−	+	−	−
A. pseudopunctipennis	−	+	−	−
A. aquasalis	−	+	−	−
A. vagus	−	+	−	−
A. barbirostris	−	+	−	−
A. sergenti	−	+	−	−
A. fluviatilis	−	+	−	−
A. splendidius	−	+	−	−
A. m. flavirostris	−	+	−	−
A. labranchiae	−	+	−	−
A. strodei	−	+	−	−
A. triannulatus	−	+	−	−
A. neomaculipalpus	−	+	−	−
A. crucians	−	+	−	−
A. filipinae	−	+	−	−
A. l. atroparvus	−	+	−	−
A. maculipennis	−	+	−	−
A. messeae	−	+	−	−
A. rangeli	−	+	−	−
A. philippinenis	−	+	−	−
A. funestus	−	+	−	−
Psorophora confinnis	−	+	−	−
P. discolor	−	+	−	−
Culex quinquefaciatus	+	+	+	−
C. pipiens	+	+	−	−
C. tarsalis	+	+	+	−
C. coronator	+	−	−	−
C. tritaeniorhynchus	+	+	−	−
C. peus	+	−	−	−
C. salinarius	+	−	−	−
C. erythrothorax	+	−	−	−
COLEOPTERA (BEETLES)				
Leptinotarsa decemlineata	+	+	−	−
Epitrix cucumeris	+	−	−	−
Anthonomus grandis	−	+	−	−
Lema oryzae	−	+	−	−

Diminishing Returns on Pesticides

	DDT and relatives	Cyclodienes and relatives	Organo-phosphates	Carba-mates
Lissor hoptrus oryzophilus	—	+	—	—
Conoderus fallii	—	+	—	—
C. vespertinus	—	+	—	—
Limonius californicus	—	+	—	—
Diabrotica virgifera	—	+	—	—
D. balteata	—	+	—	—
D. longicornis	—	+	—	—
D. undecimpunctata	—	+	—	—
Graphognathus leucoloma	—	+	—	—
Hypera postica				

HEMIPTERA (BUGS AND APHIDS)

	DDT and relatives	Cyclodienes and relatives	Organo-phosphates	Carba-mates
Typhlocyba pomaria	+	—	—	—
Myzus persicae	+	—	+	—
Erythroneura lawsoniana	+	—	+	—
E. variabilis	+	—	—	—
E. elegantula	+	—	—	—
E. elegantula	—	—	+	—
Dysdercus peruvianus	—	+	—	—
Psallus serialus	—	+	—	—
Aphis gossypii	—	+	—	—
A. pomi	—	—	+	—
Delphacodes striatella	—	+	—	—
Leptocoris varicornis	—	+	—	—
Scotinophora lurida	—	+	—	—
M. cerasi	—	—	+	—
Sapaphis pyri	—	—	+	—
S. plantaginis	—	—	+	—
Therioaphis maculata	—	—	+	—
Chromaphis juglandicola	—	—	+	—
Phorodon humult	—	—	+	—
Toxoptera graminum	—	—	+	—
Nephotettix cincticeps	—	—	+	—
Blissus leucopterus	—	—	+	—

ACARINA (MITES)

	DDT and relatives	Cyclodienes and relatives	Organo-phosphates	Carba-mates
Tetranychus urticae			+	—
T. cinnabarinus			+	—
T. tumidis			+	—

	DDT and relatives	Cyclodienes and relatives	Organo-phosphates	Carba-mates
T. mcdanieli			+	−
T. schoenei			+	−
T. candadenis			+	−
T. atlanticus, T. pacificus			+	−
Panonychus ulmi			+	−
P. citri			+	−
Vasates schlechtendali			+	−
Aculus cornutus			+	−
Byrobia praetiosa			+	−

Compiled from A. W. A. Brown, *Insecticide Resistance Comes of Age*, Bulletin of the Entomological Society of America, Vol. 14, No. 1, pp. 3–9, 1968.

REFERENCES

1 BROWN, A. W. A. 1968. Insecticide resistance comes of age. In *Bulletin of the Entomological Society of America, 14* (1).

2 MATTINGLY, P. F. 1968. Mosquito behaviour in relation to disease eradication programs. In *Annual Review of Entomology, 7*.

3 ADKINSON, P. L. and S. J. NEMEC. 1966. Comparative effectiveness of certain insecticides for killing bollworms and tobacco budworms. In *Publication B-1048, Texas Agriculture Experiment Station, Texas A & M University.*

4 UPI. 1968. *Press release, McCallen, Texas,* January 20.

5 NEWSOM, L. D. 1968. Some ecological implications of two decades of use of synthetic organic insecticides for control of agricultural pests in Louisiana. In *Conference on the Ecological Implications of International Development, Airlie House, Virginia,* December.

6 SHEA, K. P. 1968. Cotton and Chemicals. In *Scientist and Citizen, 10* (9).

7 USDA. 1968. *The Pesticide Review,* December.

8 ANGUS, R. C., C. H. READER and C. C. ROAN. 1968. Pesticide use in Arizona. In *Progressive Agriculture in Arizona, 20* (5).

9 BOZA-BARDUCCI, T. 1968. Ecological consequences of pesticides used for the control of cotton insects in the Canete valley, Peru. In *Conference on the Ecological aspects of International Development.* (See above.)

10 SMITH, R. F. and H. C. REYNOLDS. 1968. Effects of manipulation of cotton agroecosystems on insect pest populations. In *Conference on Ecological Aspects.* (See above.)

11 BROWN. 1968. (See above.)

12 SCHLINGER, E. I. and E. J. DIETRICK. 1960. Biological control of insects aided by strip-farming alfafa in experimental program. In *California Agriculture, 14* and *15.*

92

7 DISAPPEARING HEDGEROWS

Michael Allaby

Editor, *SPAN*
Associate Editor, *The Ecologist*

In the West Country fields are small and you don't notice that the hedges are going – at least their absence is less apparent than in the traditionally more open parts of East Anglia, where pathetic attempts to imitate American methods for the sake of the 'big wheat country' touch send combine harvesters sailing out three or four abreast across the diminutive prairie which stretches hedgeless to the horizon in every direction.

Farming in this country has changed, is changing, and nobody doubts it. It is becoming more industrialized, more conscious of efficiency along shop-floor lines. It uses larger machines and fewer people. Labour costs have been rising and the drift away from rural areas has created labour shortages. The economic reasons for the disappearance of the hedges are complex and to the farmer, in the short term at least, convincing. But there are serious considerations both agronomic and ecological which should be taken into account before we let them go.

A traditional stockfarmer who grazes his animals out of doors might have 150 acres divided into fifteen fields of 10 acres each. This means he will have about $4\frac{1}{2}$ miles of hedgerow of which $2\frac{1}{4}$ miles mark the boundary of his farm. To maintain these by the cheapest method, mechanical clipping, costs 30p a chain a year. If he wishes to have his hedges laid in the traditional manner, this will cost him about £6 per chain every 10 years, or 50p a chain a year. Few hedges are laid except in areas where the hunt is strong. Such a farmer may be tempted to remove some of his internal hedges, say 880 yards, leaving the boundary hedges intact. The hedges he removes he will replace with a wire fence. This will leave him with 4 miles to maintain. The cost of removing the half mile will be £4 a chain – £160. He will save the cost of clipping, which will amount to £12 a year, but the fence will cost £10 a year to maintain and at 30p a yard it will have cost him £264 to erect. He will be out of pocket.

However, if his fields are under 40 acres in size and he wishes to grow arable crops as well as keeping his stock, he will have difficulty in manoeuvring his farm machines. So he may consider removing internal hedgerows without replacing them. Not only will he save the cost of maintenance and achieve more efficient use of machinery, but for every mile of hedgerow he grubs up he will gain an acre of land for cropping, which could bring him in

93

£44 a year. Now the picture begins to look rather different. If he adds together the saving on maintenance and the increase in his cropping area he will find he can expect a 23 per cent return each year on the capital he invested on removing the hedge.

He may go further. He may find that his return on his arable crops is so much greater than that from his stock that he decides to sell the animals. Now he will need no hedges to retain or shelter them. Even if his fields are already 40 acres each he will be tempted to remove the remaining hedges to save the cost of maintaining them. The gain in crop acreage and the saving in maintenance will pay for the cost of removal in a few years.

Add to these figures the fact that provided he can convince the Ministry of Agriculture that the changes he proposes are in the best interest of his farming system he can receive a 25 per cent grant for removing the hedgerows and if he needs to replace any of them with fences he may possibly be entitled to a further grant for this. As the poultry moves into battery and deep litter houses and the cattle into intensive yards it is not difficult to see where the hedges have gone.

It may seem from this that hedges have had their day, that their usefulness to agriculture is ended, and many farmers would agree that this is so. They assume that stockless arable farming is here to stay, but is it? The best pre-server of soil fertility is the grass ley and it may be that in years to come there will be a return to mixed farming with animals kept out of doors. Already the intensive livestock units are experiencing difficulties which may eventually make them uneconomic. If this should happen we may wish we had retained our hedges.

Even in the short term this is not the whole story. A hedge will help to control drainage and its removal may mean field drains must be laid. It provides shelter from the wind for the soil and crops as well as for stock, so that for a distance on the lea side of a hedge equal to twice the height of the hedge wind speed is reduced to zero and for a distance equal to twelve times the height of the hedge it is halved. In the sheltered area moisture is conserved in the upper layers of the soil and the soil temperature is higher. This can be a mixed blessing. In the case of corn crops it may cause uneven ripening, though with other crops this is less likely to be a problem. If the crop is grass there may be a good early bite which will be valuable to the stockfarmer whose winter feed supplies are running low. The increased yield of grass may be as high as 20 per cent, though with other crops the figure may be lower. The figure of 20 per cent is critical, for this is the minimum crop increase which is required to pay for the maintenance of the hedge and so make it an immediate economic advantage.

The removal of hedges may cause other problems. Each year in parts of East Anglia and the east Midlands, there are soil blows. From March 16–20

Disappearing Hedgerows

1968, wind speed across the fens rose to above 20 knots with gusts of over 40 knots. Snow-ploughs were called out to clear the topsoil from the roads and dykes were filled to the brim. The immediate cost to farmers amounted to up to £25 an acre in lost seed and fertilizer. Admittedly, this was a particularly severe example and farmers in the area had to go back to 1955 and 1941 to recall blows like it. But every year for at least a few hours wind speed rises above 33 knots and a little more topsoil is lost.

There are three areas of Britain which are susceptible to large-scale blows: the fens, the Breck on the border of Norfolk and Suffolk and the light, sandy soil on the border of Lincolnshire. The peat fens lose about one inch of topsoil a year, but seven-eighths of this is due to oxidation of the organic matter in the peat.

The one-eighth of an inch lost through wind erosion may sound trivial, but it is being lost from the most fertile soil in Britain and it is not replaceable, because the highly organic nature of the peat makes it impossible for the soil to renew itself from the parent rock. A century of careless farming could destroy a level of fertility that has been built up over millennia.

The Brecklands are very similar topographically to Schleswig-Holstein, the German Land, which stretches from the Elbe to the Danish border, bounded on the west by the North Sea and on the east by the Baltic. The highest ground is only about 90 metres above sea level and much of the area is at 30 metres or less. In places it lies below sea level. Roughly one-third of the land area is low lying marsh and fen.

The planting of hedges in Schleswig-Holstein began around 1800, at about the time of the Enclosure Acts which gave Britain its characteristic landscape. In the 1870s to '90s co-operatives were established which required their members to plant hedges in proportion to the area of their farms. Banks gave good loans for hedge planting. In the 1930s German farming went 'economic' and it was decided, centrally, that hedges and windbreaks were unnecessary. Many of them were removed.

The policy had its opponents. Probably the most notable was Professor Alwin Seifert, the designer of the first Autobahnen, who visited Schleswig-Holstein for the first time in 1934 and saw what was happening. From then on he campaigned against the agricultural economists in Berlin. Twenty years later it was acknowledged that he had been right.

Between 1954 and 1967, over 3,800 km. (2,425 miles) of shelter were planted. In 1957 an area on the Danish border was being planted with windbreaks, some form of shelter was planned for the whole of the western fenlands and more substantial protection was planned for some of the higher ground. At the same time the Ministry proposed to remove some hedges from the over-protected areas. The situation for the farmer now is that he may not remove any hedge or windbreak without the express permission of the government and this is granted usually only if he proposes to replant a similar length elsewhere. The aim is that there shall be not less than 80 metres per hectare (33½ yards per acre) anywhere in the Land.

The effect of hedges on crop yields in Schleswig-Holstein was measured between 1933 and 1943 and an increased yield was found in direct proportion to the amount of cover. Remembering that it is an increased yield of 20 per

EFFECT OF HEDGES ON CROP YIELDS IN SCHLESWIG-HOLSTEIN

Hedge length	*metres hectare* 20	30	40	50	60	70	80
	% increase in crop yield						
Winter wheat	5·0	6·7	10	15	19	26	35
Winter rye	3·6	5·1	7·2	9·5	12	14	17
Maincrop potatoes	5·0	7·3	10	13	15	17	20

cent which makes a hedge economic in this country, it would seem that under similar conditions to those in Schleswig-Holstein hedges will benefit winter wheat and, to a lesser extent, potatoes. If other crops were considered the advantage might be even more apparent. Schleswig-Holstein conditions will be found in any flat, exposed area of land with a light soil.

Agronomic arguments are not likely to impress the town-dweller. While he is willing to concede that farmers must make a living he finds it difficult to think of the countryside as a shop floor. Of course, he is right. The countryside is required to do far more than produce food and there may be situations in which other factors must override purely economic considerations.

We may care about wildlife, for example, and believe that it should be protected. From this point of view hedges are vital. Wildlife needs cover and ecologically hedges are very similar to woodland edge, which is one of the richest habitats. An acre of woodland may contain two pairs of blackbirds; an acre of hedge may contain forty pairs. Hedges form pathways from one small area of wilderness to another, a network linking together the larger habitats throughout the country. If these links are broken the larger areas will become isolated. Fauna living in them will adapt to the particular environment and should there be any change in that environment they may be wiped out. The loss of much of our wild flora and fauna is one price we may have to pay for more 'efficient' farming.

The richness and diversity of British landscape, the patchwork fields, the trees and hedges, are an attraction to tourists. This is a direct economic benefit which could and should be calculated. Would Americans be willing to travel up to 5,000 miles to see a prairie?

The pattern of the countryside is determined by the farmers on the basis

Disappearing Hedgerows

of the short-term economics of their industry. If society as a whole wishes its landscape to be managed differently, if it wishes factors other than agronomic ones to be taken into consideration, then it is up to society to make known its demands and to encourage the farmer to provide the countryside it wants. If the economics of farming obstruct this, then the economics should be changed. A grant for the maintenance of hedges, for example, would reduce the 5,000-mile annual loss. If boundary and roadside hedges were to be considered separately from internal hedgerows it might be possible for local authorities to contribute to their upkeep.

What we must not do is make demands upon the farmer that he is not able to meet. It is senseless to ask him to put himself out of business by burdening him with costs which will bankrupt him. The countryside belongs to all of us, is of value to all of us. It is up to us to see that it is possible for those who manage it to do so in the best interests of everyone. There is not much time. It will not be many years before the whole of East Anglia becomes one vast prairie. Action to save our hedges and trees is in the best interests of farming for in all probability a farm that looks good is good.

8 FACTORY FARMING

Ruth Harrison

Author of *Animal Machines*

Can man survive in the year 2000? A fatalistic question which does not really get us anywhere, for survival by itself is surely not enough. Survival must be worthwhile and for that man must surely have a sense of continuity, a harmonious environment and the health with which to enjoy it. He must be able to feel proud of his heritage and anxious to pass it on undiminished. And for this it is necessary to think hundreds of years ahead even if planning can only be carried out piecemeal.

A characteristic of farming methods during the thousands of years when the human race was expanding at a controllable pace was that they were self-perpetuating – in broad principle what was taken out of the soil was, in one way or another, put back into it and the soil continued to produce.

The Industrial Revolution, however, brought in its train new modes of thought in which immediate material gain became paramount and this new attitude spread to farming, if more slowly than in other spheres. It was partly ignorance but also partly greed that resulted in the ravaging of virgin prairie soils by concentration on one-crop agriculture. The Industrial Revolution also brought with it the chemist and the use of fertilizers and man began to tread the slippery downward road of taking more out of the soil than it could bear, making up the deficiency with the application of fertilizers. He is still treading this road and so far, taking things by and large, he has managed to maintain and even increase production from the soil, and he will be able to continue doing this for many years to come. But not forever, and not at a continually expanding pace.

'There is a running battle between pests and diseases on the one hand and scientists on the other,' comments the recent report on soil fertility, and adds, 'It is undeniable that specialization in cropping has made it more difficult for scientists always to be on the winning side.' A similar battle has for years existed over the disease problem with livestock.

Once man felt he could safely ignore the self-regenerating process which had been the feature of earlier farming practices he turned his attention to modifying livestock farming in the same way. Intensification of output has been a natural evolvement but factory farming has not. Let us be absolutely clear about the difference between intensive farming and factory farming. It

Factory Farming

is all too often assumed that they are one and the same thing and that consequently the whole of livestock farming is under criticism. This is not so.

The intensive farmer uses technology with discrimination; he takes advantage of increasing knowledge and research to achieve greater productivity from his land by better management, fertilization, feeding and breeding, *but without significantly changing the pattern of life his animals lead*. Intensive methods in this context cover outdoor as well as indoor methods.

The factory farmer aims at a maximum turnover of capital with a minimum of effort and *through the introduction of a new system*. He makes use of all that technology has to offer him and his main criterion is immediate profitability. Psychiatrist Dr David Cooper has described these systems, in their most stringent forms, as 'characterized by extreme restriction of freedom, enforced uniformity of experience, the submission of life processes to automatic controlling devices and inflexible time-scheduling ... and running through all this the rigid and violent suppression of the natural.'

GROWTH OF FACTORY FARMING. The individual farmer has been under increasing economic pressure; on his limited acreage he has had to increase the scale of his operations to meet rising costs. The trend towards permanently housed animals, and increased stocking rates has been due to this individual need rather than to any overall national shortage of land. While it is true that we lose some 50,000 acres of cultivated farmland a year to urbanization and industry – and tragic that it is so often best-quality farmland – it is out of a United Kingdom total of more than 30 million acres of rough grazing.

If we were, indeed, so short of land that it became necessary to pack animals shoulder to shoulder in buildings we would have to switch to growing vegetable protein to feed direct to people, for although we save space by confining the animals in this way they still have to be fed. Further, we rely on imported feedingstuffs for them (as was brought home with some force during the recent dock strike) and some of this food comes from countries with a serious food shortage of their own.

Grassland is being used at only a fraction of its potential because there has been a tendency for agricultural support to favour the man who confines his animals in buildings. Agricultural economist J. R. Bellerby goes into this in some detail in the book *Factory Farming* distributed by the British Association. He points out that 'about two-thirds of the agricultural gross rent is paid by those who graze their stock ... meanwhile those who pay virtually no rent in rearing livestock are directly and indirectly subsidized to an extent which places them in the position of an "infant industry". In a period of up to ten years, up to and including the year of the estimates for 1968/9, substantial sums, reaching a total of £800 million or more, have been

99

assigned to subsidies of particular benefit to those who have reared animals indoors.'

A third and important factor has been the development, and promotion by high-powered salesmanship, of buildings and equipment, of electrical and mechanical appliances covering such things as lighting, ventilation and automatic feeding, watering and slurry removal. There has been an enormous investment in research into new feed compounds and into genetic breeding towards increased productivity. There has also been competition from the pharmaceutical firms with insecticides, growth promoters, antibiotics and therapeutic drugs. There may have been a direct saving in labour on the farm but proliferation of jobs for the boys behind the scene has been almost endless. This research has undoubtedly led to increased productivity in agriculture from improvements in housing, breeding, feeding and labour-saving devices. It is relevant to ask whether it is not the results of the research which have led to increased productivity rather than permanent close confinement of animals in buildings? And whether, where these results have been applied to more traditional methods, haven't they proved just as efficient?

When one considers these factors, along with high-powered advertising, official advice and social pressures on farmers not to be 'old-fashioned', it comes as something of a surprise to find that only a minority of farmers use extreme methods, and very often these are not farmers at all but business interests who have entered the farming industry. For example, although 86·8 per cent of laying hens are kept in battery cages they are in the hands of only 21 per cent of commercial egg producers. A minority of producers with very large holdings can thus cause suffering on a very large scale.

Factory farming. Emotive words? Maybe, but for an emotive situation. Many millions of animals especially in western Europe and other highly developed countries now eke out their existence in dim buildings and so closely confined that they have difficulty even in grooming themselves.

Is it worth while? Are these 'biological factories' producing healthy food? Are they feeding the hungry? Necessary because of increasing populations? Beneficial to the environment or even to agriculture itself?

THE WORLD'S HUNGRY. The reasons for people going hungry in many parts of the world are complex. They can be due to social and biological as well as economic causes and cannot be measured out solely in terms of shortage of calories. That half the people of the world go hungry may be due to the inefficiency of their agricultural methods, in which an absence of water conservation, poor storage and distribution play their part. The reasons for this are again complex but contributing factors have been poverty, apathy and ignorance. Factory methods, devised for capital intensive, labour-saving situations, have no place in developing countries which have little capital but

100

a vast labour force in desperate need of employment. Despite this, commercial interests, intent on their own gain, are pushing their battery cages and broiler birds by high-pressure salesmanship in every corner of the earth.

It is now generally recognized that the only effective way to help developing countries is to help them to help themselves and that this can best be done by methods basic to the fertility, and hence the output, of their soil. These are the methods recommended by FAO and by responsible bodies such as OXFAM; irrigation schemes, tree breaks, improvement of crops and pastures, and in livestock by better feeding and breeding, and by control of disease. Where there is actual hunger, vegetable protein is not only cheaper to produce but cheaper and easier to transport. It is wheat the Americans send to India not their surplus broiler chickens from Georgia. For the same reason the emphasis in US agriculture is moving gradually from beef to soya beans.

Millions of pounds of research work is under way to produce 'textured steaks' derived from protein processed from vegetables, carbohydrates, wood, leaves, algae or petroleum. These genuine factory 'meats' will eventually replace the tasteless broiler chickens, barley beef, pork and veal, and at a fraction of their cost – if the problem of palatability can be overcome. Already in the States they are said to have taken between 2 per cent and 3 per cent of the market. Within the next thirty years it seems likely that those farmers who make gods of efficiency at any cost will discover that it is at their own cost. But the market will probably settle into a butter/margarine situation. These foods will take their place alongside a gourmet market demanding quality food reared by more natural and healthy methods. These new proteins are only a palliative, not an answer, and where they are processed from minerals are helping to use up one of the world's resources in shortest supply. Meanwhile the textured proteins are actually helping factory farming by providing a cheap protein for livestock who are not so fussy about taste.

CONSUMER HEALTH. Although genetic breeding has resulted in birds and animals which convert food more efficiently, it has also resulted in less hardy animals with decreased resistance to disease. Permanent close confinement in buildings and heavy stocking rates also militate against health. It has been queried whether the circulatory system in an animal which has been denied exercise is able to respond adequately to the extra demands placed upon it by disease and, in spite of all the research into new vaccines and drugs, disease outbreaks in these buildings seem inevitably to reach epidemic proportions. One has only to mention Marek's, fowl pest, infectious bronchitis, diseases which cost the industry many millions of pounds a year.

Where animals are kept in hundreds or even thousands there can be very little individual attention and the practice has grown of adding antibiotics to feedingstuffs as a routine measure, not only as a prophylactic but also as a

101

growth promoter. This has led over the years to resistance in organisms of the gut to the antibiotic used. Further, this resistance can] be passed from one bacterium to another and multiple resistance can develop against all known antibiotics. In certain circumstances this resistance has been passed on from animals to man. A large percentage of the ever-increasing reported incidents of food poisoning each year have been traced back to abattoirs, poultry-packing stations and farms of origin. It is almost beyond belief that agriculture should have allowed the routine use of chloramphenicol, our only weapon against typhoid. The Swann Committee, set up to investigate the use of antibiotics in agriculture, recommended in its *Report* of 1969 the withdrawal of chloramphenicol except in rare cases of therapy, and also that no antibiotic be used as a feed additive if it were used in either human or animal therapy. A first step, but one cannot help thinking rather wistfully that a ban on the routine use of any antibiotic in feedingstuffs would have resulted in an immediate improvement in management and a reversion to better systems.

It is impossible to mention all the additives used but two more deserve a brief word. Arsenical compounds are used as growth promoters in pig and poultry feeds and spot checks have revealed residues above approved levels. A public analyst recently did checks in four or five abattoirs and found arsenic in pigs' livers in varying amounts up to 30 ppm, whereas the regulation limit is 1 ppm. Stilboestrol is still used to fatten 'barley beef' steers although its use has been considered sufficiently hazardous for it to have been banned in every other European country.

Very little work has come to light on differences in nutritional quality of food produced under different systems. The little which has reveals why.

For example, tests on eggs have shown significantly less B_{12} in battery eggs compared with strawyard eggs. The biochemists report (to Animal Defence Society for whom they carried out the tests) states: 'The most dramatic difference is in the figures for vitamin B_{12} (anti pernicious anaemia factor). This is serious especially for vegetarians.' A comparison of meat from broiler chickens with that from free-range chickens, carried out by the Ministry of Agriculture, showed significant loss of thiamine in the broiler birds. In one regimen a third was lost, in another a half. Initial work has shown that there is only half as much iron in 'white veal' as in veal from normally reared calves, a result to be expected since 'white veal' calves are fed an iron-deficient milk substitute to keep their flesh pale.

Significant loss of individual factors alter the balance in food. It has been argued, wrongly I suspect, that this is of no importance to lavishly fed people. But a far more serious question is arising, that of a change of composition in some factors. Dr Michael Crawford and other nutritionists have found a change in the proportion of saturated to unsaturated fats in wild and domestically fed animals. Dr Hugh Sinclair has commented that this is still further accentuated as between grazing and stall-fed animals. Both scientists point to a change in farm systems as being the cause. Dr Crawford comments (*Lancet*, 17 December 1969): 'As the high-saturated fat, low-quality product appears specific to the modern intensive systems and does not apply to any other animal system, it could not have applied to the food practices of recent history, let alone prehistory,' and Dr Sinclair stated on a television programme: '... these bullocks are eating their natural food at the present time, namely grass. But during the winter they would be stall-fed and would produce more saturated fat on them. The same is true for pigs ... the broiler chicken has largely saturated fat as compared with the free-ranging chicken, and the same is true of the battery egg as compared with eggs from a free-ranging hen. So that the more we feed animals on their less natural foods the more we produce saturated fat in their bodies and therefore in our own bodies.' Dr Sinclair believes that these abnormally large quantities of hard (saturated) fat are causing the epidemic of coronary disease in man.

It is tempting to make the cynical comment that people will get the food they deserve if they are not willing to pay a little more and make a little more fuss. But in fact this is not strictly true. For it is only by labelling that the public can make known its preferences, and labelling of food as to all chemical additives and methods of production has been rejected as being too complicated to enforce. The townsman has little chance of being really discriminating but the rash of shops selling 'free range' and 'farm fresh eggs' shows that he does try.

AMENITIES. It is not only man's health which is at stake. There is degeneration of the countryside to which he turns for refreshment and revitalization.

BUILDINGS. Subject to certain provisos a farmer can build up to 5,000 square feet without seeking planning permission. This he can continue to do at 2-yearly intervals. Alternatively he can seek permission to develop, can appeal on a refusal and if the appeal is dismissed can claim compensation. Planning authorities are becoming increasingly wary of granting unqualified permission, but in many areas the damage is already done and sites are covered with row upon long row of buildings, sometimes with silo-type food hoppers at the head of each, indistinguishable from a monotonously designed factory or munitions dump. Most amenity societies have confined their concern to this visual spoilation of the countryside but there are other important issues.

NUISANCE. There is nothing to stop farmers building adjacent to residential property and in these cases nuisance from mice, rats and flies is almost inevitable and most difficult to overcome. Battery houses form an ideal breeding ground for flies. The birds, who would otherwise deal with the problem themselves, are prevented from doing so and flies breed in comparative peace. So we create a health hazard, since flies carry disease from dung to human food, which can only be kept in check by the highest standards of management. Too often lethal doses of insecticide are used to cover up management inefficiency, insecticide which finds its way eventually on to the land or into our water supplies.

These food factories create other nuisances. An unremitting noise twenty-four hours a day from the automated equipment; an unremitting smell from the enormous output of effluent.

EFFLUENT. I said earlier that the soil used to be self-regenerating. One of the reasons for this was the ploughing back of animal droppings, a principal source of fertilizer. It is one of the biggest indictments against factory-farming methods that this erstwhile beneficial process has been turned into a mammoth problem.

Often animals and birds are kept on slatted or wire floors and droppings are collected into slurry tanks below them. There is a very real danger of a build up of noxious gases which, if ventilation is inadequate, can cause mortality to both livestock and their human attendants. Added to this, where slurry is sprayed on to fields after storage in tanks it can create nuisance by smell, especially in hot weather.

At one time it was possible to discharge effluent into rivers and waterways, but in 1961 this became an offence and permission had to be sought from Water Boards. Strong effluent discharged direct into waterways causes loss of oxygen, death of insects and fish, plant flora are drastically affected and finally the watercourse becomes putrid.

Manure is sometimes discharged into public sewers. When one considers that a sewage disposal unit for 24,000 hens is equal to that for 4,000 people not only the size of the problem but the absurdity of the wastage is apparent. Where the facility is available farmers may now be charged for it, and the charge can be prohibitive.

Over the last few years methods of drying effluent have been developed to make it into an odourless fertilizer. But this process has run into problems and much suffering has been caused in the vicinity from the smell. Factories of this nature have had to be closed by local authorities receiving too many complaints. There has been talk of dumping effluent out to sea.

SOCIAL COSTING. How often have we been assured that we *can* have cleaner air, less noise, better quality food, better landscaping and so on and so on, but that it will cost a little more? This is largely costing which can be fairly accurately measured. But it is very rarely pointed out that against this there is the social costing which is less easily measured but every bit as important. Have it now – pay later, is one of the slogans of modern society and this, in many ways, is what conservation is all about.

How does one cost the joy of a beautiful and varied landscape, the pleasure of seeing animals in the fields? How does one cost relief from flies, rats, noise, smell and distress caused to so many people living alongside these units? It is easier, but by no means easy, to assess the benefits of healthy food, healthy soil and healthy attitudes in relation to the amount we have to pay to rectify the results of poor food and unhealthy soil, but these are long-term factors and it is always easier for governments to meet crises as and when they arise and to make piecemeal regulations to deal with them.

TO SUM UP. Some of our present farming systems, known as factory farming, are ethically unacceptable to a large sector of the community, are producing less-balanced, less-nutritious food with possible hazards from additives used. The methods are contributing to nuisance in the countryside, to loss of fertility and to loss of amenity. Further, they do not contribute one iota to feeding the world's hungry. On balance they may do the reverse by absorbing a disproportionate amount of available resources on luxury food appropriate primarily to overfed, highly developed countries.

Piecemeal measures which have been taken so far have only made the situation worse by a refusal to face the real issues involved. For example, chickens have been too closely confined indoors. This has led to disease, counteracted not by less close confinement but by mass medication. It has led to 'vice' which again has not been counteracted by a change in the system but by cutting back the beak to prevent damage or by keeping the birds in darkness so that they cannot see to peck.

So we fall from one crisis to the next because we are afraid of admitting that we may have overdone things in the first place and of taking any really positive steps.

But there is nothing absolute, nothing inexorable about the situation. The impetus of extreme methods has been strengthened by artificial causes rather than by natural needs. If we feel that they are not in our long-term interest they can still be changed; we do have a choice.

It saddens me when otherwise humane people condone suffering in animals on the grounds that it is necessary because increasing human populations have to be fed, without querying the morality of ever-increasing human populations. Will not the degrading of every other form of life lead in the end to man's own degradation?

It is profitless to fool ourselves that we can exist without exploitation but it is part of our ethics to differentiate between what is essential and what is avoidable, and where do we draw the line? Most farmers, as I have shown, draw the line far short of immobilization of their stock, and commercial interests are increasingly putting effort into improvement of more traditional systems. I would like to see far more urgent research into this form of improvement for herein lies the only real progress. We need systems which do not deprive the animal of the exercise of inherited behaviour patterns, that do not deprive the soil of organic manuring without which long-term fertility is lost, systems which maintain the precious amenity value of a rich and varied landscape.

It would be unfair to ask the farmer to provide all this at his own expense. We must as a community decide which systems are biologically and ethically acceptable and then as a community make sure that the farmer is adequately recompensed for using these systems on our behalf. I have shown that it has been of short-term financial advantage to the farmer to take his stock off the and and confine them in buildings. The long-term advantage is not proved. The social disadvantages, in my opinion, *are* proved and we can reverse the financial situation so easily and immediately by rechannelling funds from factory farming to the improvement and use of grassland for grazing stock. In making this simple administrative change we shall, at the same time, contribute to the amenity value of a varied and pleasant landscape with animals once more to be seen in the fields.

Our ultimate survival depends on our ability to live in harmony with our environment, to work with nature rather than in spite of it. Because food production increases steadily in pace with population increase it may be thought that it can go on increasing indefinitely. A little thought will show that this is not so. The land we have available on our globe is of finite extent and this earth of ours will produce only an optimum amount of food to support a finite population. The optimum balance will, furthermore, only be maintained in conditions in which constant regeneration, the availability of nutrients for the soil, of water and so on, is possible. Though it is outside the scope of this article, it can be said that farming the sea as an adjunct to the land has equally finite limits – there are not other continuing sources of food for *homo sapiens*.

REFERENCES

ANIMAL DEFENCE SOCIETY. 1969. Survey of eggs. In *Annual Report*.
BELLERBY, J. R. (Ed.) 1970. *Factory Farming*. London: British Association for the Advancement of Science.
COOPER, DAVID. 1966. The effect on man himself. In *Factory Farming*. (See above.)

CRAWFORD, M. A. 1968. Fatty acid ratios in free-living and domestic animals. In *The Lancet*, June 22.

HARRISON, RUTH. 1964. *Animal Machines*. London: Vincent Stuart.

HMSO. 1969. *Joint Committee on the use of Antibiotics Animal Husbandry and Veterinary Medicine*. Cmnd 4190.

HMSO. 1965. *Report of the Technical Committee to enquire into the Welfare of Animals kept under Intensive Livestock Husbandry Systems*. Cmnd 2836.

PUBLIC HEALTH OFFICERS. 1966. *Report of a Working Party in Chester on Public Health problems of Intensive Farming*.

VIPOND et al. 1964. Some difference in the composition of broiler and free-range Chickens. In *Proceedings of Nutrition Society, 23*, xxxviii.

9 DECLINE OF NUTRITIONAL QUALITY

Robert Waller

Editor, *Journal of the Soil Association*

According to the official figures a middle-aged man can expect to live about 3 years longer than his counterpart in 1841. Over a period of more than a 100 years, this shows a negligible advance. In a paper given to the Royal Society of Health in 1967 Dr R. Logan, Director of Medical Care Research Unit, summarized the hazards for middle-aged men as follows:

1 in 4 will suffer from chronic bronchitis; 1 in 5 will develop coronary heart disease; 1 in 12 a peptic ulcer; 1 in 4 cancer, of which 1 in 30 will be cancer of the lung; 1 in 12 will be admitted to a general hospital each year; 1 in 300 will be admitted to a psychiatric hospital each year. A similar picture for women can be summarized by saying that 1 in 4 will be regularly attending a GP with a chronic disease; 1 in 8 will die of diabetes. Dr Logan also stated that sickness absence has doubled since the war. In their early sixties 13 per cent of men are incapacitated through illness.

Coronary heart disease; peptic ulcer; cancer; diabetes. A new pattern of disease is being observed in Western Europe. The infectious epidemic diseases brought down the expectation of life for everyone in the past. In this century they have been brought under control. How is it, then, that the expectation of life for the middle-aged has increased by such a meagre amount? The explanation is that the new diseases strike mainly in the second half of life: they are known as degenerative diseases. Doctors refer to the 'twenty years abuse', meaning we can abuse our natural good health for 20 years or so before the effects catch up on us, which brings us to the age of about forty-five. But it should also be noted with alarm that America reports an increase in cancer among children which not so long ago was unknown.

While these diseases continue to increase at their present rate, the expectation of life for those over forty-five will fall. Must the second half of life have its particular forms of illness? Are we facing up to this problem?

Research done by Mr A. Elliot-Smith, formerly senior surgeon at the Radcliffe Hospital, Oxford, shows that there were only five cases of appendicitis at the hospital between 1895 and 1905. There are now over 500 cases every year. Stomach ulcers were not recorded before 1890. Yet in the last war 23,500 men were discharged from the army with them over a period of 30 months (1939–41). These ulcers were not due to army life or army cooking;

most of the recruits brought their ulcers with them. When Mr Elliot-Smith examined the records of six separate London hospitals from 1925 to 1929, he found a dramatic rise in ulcers over this period.

Mr Elliot-Smith had worked in Africa and had noticed among unsophisticated native peoples the absence of diseases most prevalent in this country. Back in Oxford, he undertook his research to establish whether these diseases were newcomers or if they had always been present. He not only discovered that they were new but that their incidence rose with the change in the national diet due to the new industrial processes of refining sugar and flour.

Several other doctors and surgeons who had worked among primitive peoples noted the same difference in the pattern of diseases and they all suspected that diet must play a part in the causation of the 'civilized' diseases.

For example, Surgeon Captain Cleave noticed that Africans who ate Western food developed the new Western diseases, while those who were still eating their traditional foods did not. This view has been supported by Mr D. P. Burkitt, a distinguished surgeon now of the Medical Research Council, celebrated for his work relating diseases to different regions of Africa. Cleave worked with a South African doctor, G. D. Campbell, comparing the hospital records in Western food areas with those in less sophisticated ones: they found that the Western diseases included far more than appendicitis and ulcers; they extended to diabetes, obesity, coronary thrombosis, dental decay, varicose veins, diverticulitis, constipation and several infections of the bowels probably related to constipation. Support for this view comes from many other medical authorities working in areas where traditional diets are being superseded by Western diets.

The most obvious difference in the diet between the two groups is that Western diets have white sugar and bread, processed, packaged and synthetic, while the older peasant diets are based on unrefined cereals, fruit and sugar. This is what is called wholefood by the diet reformers, since little or nothing has been removed from the grain and the sugar cane.

Cleave, Campbell and Painter (a surgeon at the Manor House Hospital, London) noticed that in war-time when these refined foods were rationed and/or the extraction of nutrients and bran from bread had been limited by law, these diseases declined, only to shoot up again when the restraints were removed. Today we eat ten times more sugar per head than we did in the eighteenth century.

In the process of refining flour for white bread very little of the original nutritive value of the grain is left. It is said by some nutritionists that this does not matter because these nutrients can be obtained by eating a varied diet. On the other hand, this means that we may have to eat too much to get adequate nutrition. Obesity due to overeating is also a disease of our time. More important than that, however, is that the bran, which is removed, should serve the function of stimulating the movement of the bowels. This may not be a nutritive function but it cures the white man's ailment of constipation at no cost. Recent experiments by Mr Painter at his hospital, where he has fed bran to all his patients, has had remarkable results in restoring their health. Mr Painter has succeeded in introducing wholemeal bread into the hospital diet.

It has been shown that food takes six to eight times longer to pass through the intestine in Western countries than in parts of Africa and India, where the staple diet is wholefood.

THE SACCHARINE DISEASE. Carbohydrate as starch is digested and absorbed as sugar in the body. Refined flour is almost pure starch so we add it to our refined sugar consumption. Since the increasing consumption of carbo-hydrates and refined sugar can be so closely associated with the new diseases, Cleave and his collaborators have given a group of them one name, as described in their book *Diabetes, Coronary Thrombosis and the Saccharine Disease*.[1] Saccharine rhymes with Rhine to distinguish it from the sweetener.

If a relationship has in fact been established between dietary habits based upon excess of sugar (saccharine) in the body it should not be necessary to await an understanding of how this causes disease before attempting preven-tion.

As these diseases are the result of abstracting from the 'whole' food, we are faced with a new outbreak of deficiency diseases. So one calls to mind the challenges faced by medical science in the past in curing such dietary deficiency diseases as scurvy, beriberi and rickets. The results were easily discernible and the diseases responded quickly to the correct treatment. The new kind of dietary deficiency disease caused by these concentrated incomplete foods builds up slowly over half a lifetime and then manifests itself in this wide variety of degenerative diseases both acute and chronic.

SUGAR, FATS OR BOTH? Dr Hugh Sinclair of Magdalen College, Oxford, a nutritionist, has for a long time incriminated some animals fats as a major cause of degenerative diseases. He illustrates his argument with lung cancer. Lung cancer is now associated with smoking; but in Spain and Japan, where smoking is as common as in our own country, lung cancer hardly exists. So there must be another factor: Dr Sinclair believes it is the saturated fatty acids in animal fats.

There are two kinds of fatty acids, one essential – the unsaturated fatty acids – and one not essential, the saturated fatty acids. The essential ones are not made in the body and have to be taken in through food. They tend to be unstable in the air and turn rancid, so the manufacturers have found a means of changing their chemistry by saturating them. Here, then, we have another

110

source of deficiency. A deficiency of essential fatty acids will weaken the membranes of our body cells, which serve to protect the cells from invasion and penetration by alien bodies likely to damage them.

Dr Sinclair has done experimental work which he claims shows that modern high energy feeding of pigs also destroys the essential fatty acids in their bodies. In a letter to *The Lancet* (12 December 1969) he has been supported in this view by Michael Crawford of the Nuffield Institute of Comparative Medicine. Crawford said, 'People have always eaten some fat, but only the modern "high-energy" feed systems produce large amounts of saturated and mono-unsaturated short-chain fats.' He goes on to argue that in modern factory farming methods 'Fat seems to replace functional tissue. We have examined 14 different wild herbivorous species, and have been unable to find any signs of such gross infiltration, which prompts the question of whether such lipid (fat) deposition is pathological.'

This fat is mainly the inessential fat and is not found on animals able to choose their own food by free-ranging grazing.

Crawford believes that simply to stop eating sugar is not enough: we need also to have the right amount of essential fatty acids in order to build up the arteries of our body with proper structural constituents.

As Crawford says in his letter, an attempt at prevention by rebuilding the damaged arteries through the right diet should be simple enough. 'But,' he says, 'from a practical standpoint it would be difficult in so far as it touches on almost every aspect of modern food technology.'

We may add here that not only is the feeding of the animals indicted in modern agricultural methods but the feeding of the plants as well. For the plants on which we and animals feed are also fed by fertilizers and the modern practice is to concentrate these in the same way as flour and sugar are concentrated by extracting essential elements. This has been studied by Michael Blake in his book *Concentrated Incomplete Fertilizers*.[2] There is no place here to discuss it but the principle is the same. Nitrogen is concentrated at the expense of other important plant nutrients which unbalances both the soil and the metabolism of the plant.

To sum up. What is alarming about the present health situation is that the rules of good health – fresh air, fresh food, adequate exercise and a temperate attitude of mind – which have been handed down from generation to generation – are being put out of reach of the individual who chooses to follow them. We are becoming aware of the dangers that arise from the pollution and contamination of the environment: but threatening as these are, they are no more dangerous than the changes in the composition of our food as a result of technological advances.

REFERENCES

1   CLEAVE, T. L. and G. D. CAMPBELL. 1969. *Diabetes, Coronary Thrombosis and the Saccharine Disease*. Bristol: John Wright and Sons Ltd.
2   BLAKE, MICHAEL. 1967. *Concentrated Incomplete Fertilizers*. London: Crosby Lockwood.

10 PROSPECTS FOR BRITISH AGRICULTURE

Robert Waller

Editor, *Journal of the Soil Association*

To project current trends into the future and to argue that farming in the twenty-first century will simply be an intensification of farming in 1970 is not difficult. It has been done by many experts. It is hard to believe, however, that discontinuities will not occur to modify if not reverse this trend. One can illustrate the absurdity of indiscriminately projecting current trends into the future by drawing an analogy with literature. How do you answer the question: What will the novel be like in AD 2000? It clearly depends on countless factors that must all be taken into consideration if our prediction is to be at all accurate. It depends in fact on what sort of a society we are likely to have at that time. In a stable, self-governing society, the novelist is valued as an artist, in a capitalist society, the novelist is above all a business-man writing a saleable product for the mass market, while in a Communist society he is first and foremost a propagandist exploiting themes issued to him by the party leaders. In these latter two types of society, art is either unprofitable or subversive. A true artist is driven into isolation and is regarded as a crank, a sort of outcast living on the periphery of society and imbued with none of its accepted values. Surprisingly enough with agriculture this situation is very similar. Good husbandry does not pay and those who persist in it to satisfy their conscience are universally regarded as cranks. They are also regarded as subversive because they threaten what has become the orthodox husbandry – intensive agriculture, designed specially to satisfy the short-term demands of mass society. The farmer, like the author, has thus been transformed into a technician who receives directives from the outside. His only responsibility in these conditions is to make farming pay, but only too often at the expense of the soil, the health of his animals and the nutri-tional quality of his produce. The pressures towards intensification of agri-culture are indeed very considerable. The high rate of interest on borrowed capital compels the young farmer to follow the general pattern.

The whole framework of prices, grants, subsidies and incentives within which he will be working will also favour intensification. It developed basically within the 1947 Agricultural Act. This well-intentioned Act was designed to shield the farmer against the forces of the free market by fixing prices and subsidies that would assure him a reasonable livelihood. In practice it has had the opposite effect, as farm prices have simply not kept up with the prices of manufactured goods. In 1956 the Act was amended to ensure that net farm income should not fall in any year by more than $2\frac{1}{2}$ per cent. But every year inflation has exceeded this figure so that the farmer's income has lagged ever farther behind that achieved in other industries. As a result, the farmer, just in order to survive, has had to make use of every device, however unsound, for increasing the yield of his crops and the profit he can make on his stock. The irony is that, rather than regard these devices as necessary evils, the government has been led by its agricultural experts to consider them as real improvements. The public too has fallen under this delusion and the extraordinary 'efficiency' of British farming has come to be regarded by all as an important national achievement. The government, inebriated by the apparent success of its policies, has been led to encourage intensification in all its forms.

For instance, subsidies are granted to farmers for uprooting hedgerows to make fields of over 100 acres, a practice we know to be contrary to our long-term interests (see Michael Allaby, *Our Disappearing Hedgerows*, Chapter 7). Subsidies are granted to encourage the use of artificial fertilizers, though not of organic manure whose use is thereby openly discouraged. On both counts this is contrary to our long-term interests (see L. B. Powell, *Our Deteriorating Soil*, Chapter 5). Thus it has become official policy to subject our long-term interests to the short-term considerations of providing profits for industry and cheap food for the nation. The question is, can this process go on indefinitely? Undoubtedly it cannot, and for obvious reasons.

Soil deterioration caused by the excessive use of fertilizers and the heavy machines in use on poor soil structure is taking place at an ever more frightening rate. The Ministry of Agriculture's Committee on Soil Structure and Fertility has written a report on this subject, and delay in its publication led to charges that it shirked exposure of the ill-effects of its own policies. Resistance to pesticides is steadily building up in more and more insect pests. Already more than 200 are immune to DDT. There are growing signs that by reducing natural controls, pesticides are actually reducing food production too by creating the conditions for epidemics of some pests, and these conditions might well become irreversible (see *Diminishing Returns*, Chapter 6). Pesticides are also killing off wildlife, especially predators at the end of food chains, and traces of the more persistent varieties of toxic chemicals are to be found in every form of life in the most remote parts of the world. The average man in this country now carries more than two parts per million of DDT in his fatty tissue. The adverse effects of DDT and related chemicals to human health, especially under conditions of stress, are becoming better known; it remains to determine just what levels we can tolerate (see *Pollution of Wildlife*, Chapter 16).

Prospects for British Agriculture

Nitrates from artificial fertilizers tend to run off into rivers causing over fertilization of the vegetation (*eutrophication*); this will gradually make them unfit for fish life by reducing the available oxygen. Nitrates can be transformed into nitrites by the appropriate bacteria. These are a serious threat to our drinking water and especially dangerous to babies.

Factory farmers are experiencing ever greater difficulties in disposing of the vast quantities of manure produced by their animals indoors. For the most part they have no land to put it on, so it ends up in rivers, causing further eutrophication. At the same time disposal can be so costly that it threatens the very survival of such enterprises.

The use of many antibiotics essential to protect factory farm animals from epidemics (to which they are particularly vulnerable by reason of the dense conditions in which they live) has been condemned by the Swann Committee. Its recommendations have not yet been implemented but as the use of antibiotics in stock-raising can lead to immunity to them when used to combat diseases affecting humans, it hardly seems credible that the government can defer action very much longer. Indeed, the pollution problems associated with intensive agriculture are so serious that Dr Mellanby, Director of the Monk's Wood Experimental Research Station of the Nature Conservancy, considers that it would be better to import most of our food from abroad. Conservationist pressure will increase during the next decade: people will object more and more to large areas of our landscape being turned into a treeless prairie, to our rivers becoming biological deserts, to the extermination of rare species of birds, in fact to a general reduction in the quality of life in order to increase short-term agricultural productivity.

There is also likely to be an ever-increasing dislike of the dullness and tastelessness of food produced in this manner. One might well see a vogue for organically produced food simply because it tastes better, and one can also foresee mounting opposition to the use of the countless additives used in processed food, which will be required in ever greater proportions in the range of new synthetic foods soon to be marketed.

Few of these factors appear to be taken into account in the predictions of our experts, who anticipate no end to the intensification of British agriculture and its consequent increase in productivity. However, if they were to take all these factors into account, a very different picture would emerge. Each one of the different technologies used to increase intensification is subject to the fundamental law of diminishing returns. Slowly the countless disadvantages resulting from each new input of machinery, fertilizer, pesticides, *etc*, will begin to outweigh their initial advantages. This process must render each further increment of growth achieved by these means progressively less profitable, until such time as negative returns set in.

Moreover, when it finally becomes apparent to the government and its experts that their agricultural policy has been so misguided, the food-producing capacity of the land will have deteriorated so much that it will take a long time to restore it by a return to sounder methods of husbandry. The sooner we return to such methods, the easier the transition will be.

What are these methods and how can we introduce them? In answering this we must realize that the only type of agriculture that can last is one that is ecologically sound. Intensive agriculture could only work in the long run if it could get round basic ecological laws, which it clearly cannot – farmers are bound by these as they are by the laws of physics and chemistry. For example, the cycle of growth has first a production phase and then one of decomposition, during which the plant residues are returned to the soil for composting so as to provide humus and nutrients for the next crop. Present-day farming practice treats this second phase as unnecessary, because it is unprofitable. Instead it seeks to replace it by the use of artificial fertilizers. Whether profitable or not, the composting process is an ecological necessity. By obstructing it, we destroy the topsoil – an inch of which takes hundreds of years to produce. The object of good husbandry should be to intensify the composting process in the topsoil so that it is capable of producing the crops we require while at the same time retaining its fertility and structure. Fertilizers feed the plants but they do not contribute to the soil structure. This is also a living system, a very complex one, made up of thousands of millions of different micro-organisms, all in close inter-relationship with each other, and requiring food and suitable living conditions like any other living things. The British fertilizer policy concentrates on three major nutrients – nitrogen, phosphate and potash (NPK). These are unnaturally intensified, especially nitrogen, and unbalance the nutrient and mineral ratios on which all the living organisms, including the plant roots depend for ionic inter-change, *i.e.* feeding.

Firstly, people should be returned to the land. In Britain today there are less than 400,000 people working on the land, half as many as there were 20 years ago and the numbers are still decreasing. We tend to consider this a great achievement, as output per man is increasing at the same rate. Of course this is a sheer illusion, as many of the people who are no longer working in the fields are now employed in factories making pesticides, fertilizers and agricultural machinery. They are thus still involved in the production of food.

We have noted the ecological damage caused by technological substitutes for labour, but what is equally important is that they will not be available indefinitely. One day the raw materials required for the manufacture of the machinery, and the fuel it uses, will run out. (Incidentally, 1 ton of nitrogen fertilizer requires 5 tons of oil to produce it.) If we allow intensification to go on until this situation overtakes us, there will be no trained people to take over. In addition to this, the social advantages of reconstituting rural life are essential to a healthy nation. Small rural communities are the backbone of a stable society and cannot be dispensed with. As people flock to the cities and further overcrowd them, social disorder will increase until it becomes un-manageable. If we want a sound and healthy agriculture together with a vigorous and stable society, we must clearly reverse all these trends which have no justification other than to satisfy short-term economic ends, and which ignore social and ecological necessities.

If one of the essential requirements is people, another is the small family farm or the farm run by working partners. These could probably work together within a producers' co-operative marketing organization rather than a marketing organization dominated from the top by vast integrated financial combines. Governments must work out prices, incentives, grants, *etc*, to favour good husbandry and the smaller unit farm. It will be essential to guarantee a good livelihood to the mixed farm by such means as a grazing subsidy which should take the place of, or at least counterbalance, the subsidy on fertilizers. The wages of the farmworker must be brought up to the same level as the industrial worker to maintain more men on the land. the community as a whole must share the cost of conserving the beauty of the landscape within the pattern of agriculture, for while this benefits the public it is often unprofitable to the farmer.

All this can be done, *if we wish to do it*. The relative costs involved have never been estimated, but there would be a lot on the credit side, including the savings from less pollution and contamination. The big industries argue that to put more men back on the land and to cut down the chemical and machine aids is simply regression, a return to peasantry. We are told, for example, that the small farm is finished and must give way to the large farm with its greater economies of scale. Nevertheless, food production per acre is often higher on small farms than on large ones, even though the profit is not. Government policy, it would seem, is not aimed at increasing production but at forcing out of production so-called unprofitable farms whatever the loss in output or in the quality of the product.

In Cornwall the average output for holdings of less than 50 acres is twice that of the national average. These are mostly small, mixed farms. Between 1960 and 1967, 700 of these farms were lost through farm amalgamations and 382 full-time workers, their wives and children, left the land. In 1945 there were 17,500 employed in Cornish farming: in 1967 it had fallen to 8,500. Most of these people were forced off the land by government policy. In farming today neither excellence nor high output per acre (it is output per acre not output per man that matters to the community) is enough to guaran-tee survival. There is an immense gap between the just reward for efficient hard work and what the farmer receives. This is because profit is not related to optimum output – that is the output consistent with continuous soil fertility – or to quality, but to the scale of operation. A dairy farmer with fifty cows that produce 1,000 gallons per lactation and an average profit of £100 per cow is not so well off as a farmer who has a hundred and fifty cows that produce 700 gallons per lactation and a profit of £60 per cow. Yet from the national point of view, the smaller unit makes the bigger contribution. Government policy, therefore, contradicts its own stated aims of greater production and increased self-sufficiency in food.

According to the NFU Farm Accounts scheme average net outputs per acre (1965) in £s were –

AVERAGE NET OUTPUT PER ACRE (1965) NFU *Farm Accounts Scheme*

ACREAGE	Mainly arable	Arable mixed	Mainly dairying	Dairying mixed	Mainly livestock	Livestock mixed
0–50	70	76	53	56	50	50
51–150	51	43	40	40	25	34
151–300	44	40	36	35	22	30
Over 300	41	37	36	38	13	27

in £s

AVERAGE PROFITS		
ACREAGE	1965	
	£	
0–50	599	
51–150	965	
151–300	1,381	
Over 300	2,386	

These tables show that it is scale of operation that creates profit and not output. Since farmers require profits to stay in business they are compelled to increase their scale of production, which usually means employing mass production methods. In most other industries this has already happened; it is 'progress', and most people cannot see why agriculture should not progress in the same way. At present the major profits of agriculture do not go to the farmers but to the industrial enterprises associated with it. The history of Danish farming shows that no matter what tremendous efforts are made by the small farmer under the present system, the benefits will go elsewhere. Although productivity per labour unit in Denmark increased two and a half times from 1950 to 1966, the wretchedly low returns led to a strike in 1961 when the return on capital was only 0·5 per cent. This was in part due to the low world prices for primary products which benefits the big manufacturing nations at the expense of those which provide the essential raw materials. The example of Denmark shows that even a highly efficient Western nation that depends primarily upon small farms for its existence cannot stand up to these pressures, for between 1939 and 1966 manpower on Danish farms dropped from 309,000 to 58,000. In England and Wales since 1954 farmers' net incomes have fallen by 10 per cent (while all other incomes have risen by 56 per cent), and farmers indebtedness to banks has more than doubled. Forcing the small farmer off the land despite his high productivity is an example of wealth accumulating while men and their families fade from the scene. The contradictory nature of government policy is shown by the fact that there is now one agricultural adviser to every nineteen farmers – which works out at £96 million or £320 per annum per farmer. If the government policy is to produce fewer farmers, why more advisers? From these simple examples, we can see that government attitudes to farming finances are upside down. Since the Industrial Revolution agriculture has been displaced from its rightful place as the basic industry to which all others should be related in respect of profits, wages, prices and capital investment. Is it not on food and quality of food that we all depend for our survival and our health?

With the exhaustion of raw materials through the ever-increasing expansion of the industrial machine, the economic disparity between agriculture and other industries will begin to even out. Obviously, if raw materials become scarce, the pace of mass production will have to slow down and the scale of operations will shrink, until it becomes nearer to that of agriculture and in some cases below it. Agriculture depends upon the use of renewable resources, while many industries depend upon resources that are extracted from the earth and whose stock is strictly limited. Any government capable of foreseeing this, will give priority to agriculture as the industry with the most certain survival value. It will also recognize that the landscape which is a national heritage is, nevertheless, for the most part the creation of agriculture, so that every means must be used to bring town and country together in maintaining it. Methods of husbandry must be preferred that make the maximum contribution to the development of our society as a whole and to the continuous fertility of the soil. These two aims are surprisingly interdependant as Sir George Stapledon showed in his book *Human Ecology*. This policy of applying the principles of human ecology to agriculture would not be incompatible with profits and output, on the contrary, in the long term, it must be the only way of guaranteeing them.

But, as I said at the beginning of the chapter, if we are to have a sound and durable agriculture in the year 2000, this will depend upon a revolution in our culture as a whole – a human ecological revolution. If the momentum of our industrial civilization is not arrested, the collapse of our society is inevitable. The decision rests with us all.

REFERENCES

BLAKE, MICHAEL. 1970. *Down to Earth. Real principles for fertiliser practice.* London: Crosby Lockwood.

BORGSTRÖM, GEORG. 1969. *Too Many.* New York: Collier/Macmillan.

FRENCH, MARY. 1969. *The Worm in the Wheat.* London: J. Baker.

HMSO. 1968. *A Century of Agricultural Statistics.* 1866–1966.

NICOL, HUGH. 1967. *The Limits of Man.* London: Constable.

STAPLEDON, GEORGE. 1971 (2nd edition). *Human Ecology.* London: Charles Knight.

TAYLOR, L. R. (Ed.). 1970. *The Optimum Population for Britain.* London and New York: Academic Press.

KNUDSEN, P. H. (Ed.). 1967. *Agriculture in Denmark – a survey of Structure and Development, compiled by the Council of Denmark.* London: Land Books.

WALTERS, HARRY. 1969. Whither farming in the year 2000? *Soil Association Journal, April.*

PART THREE

Diminishing Resources

11 MINERALS

Preston Cloud

Professor of Biogeology
University of California at Santa Barbara

The rapid deterioration of our environment, that we are experiencing today, can be attributed to two associated causes: the exponential growth of human populations, and their consumption and waste of the earth's material resources. Among these I include food, pure water, clean air, space and non-renewable minerals. However much informed estimates of these resources vary, they must all agree that there is some annual harvest of food that cannot be exceeded on a sustained basis, some maximal quantity of each mineral and chemical that can be extracted and kept in circulation.

Data available on the ultimately accessible and extractable reserves of most mineral resources are not yet good enough to say what the ultimate limits may be, but they do cast some sobering shadows.

It is axiomatic that nothing can expand infinitely on our finite spaceship earth. Mineral resources are finite, because, for all practical purposes, the formation and differentiation of the earth is complete. The useful elements available to us, moreover, comprise only a fraction of the total world-mass, and of this minute quantity, much has not been located, and much is un-recoverable by any known technology.

Copper will illustrate the problem. It is a metal which is neither very abundant nor in immediate jeopardy. Its abundance in the earth's crust averages about 55 parts per million, which is a lot of copper. However, of that amount, probably no more than a billion or two tons is recoverable, and of this about 210 million tons is represented by ore reserves not known. It will be difficult, therefore, even if we discover these and work lower grades, to increase copper

121

production by as much as ten times our present reserves. If we allow for increasing population and for expected end-of-century demands, it becomes clear that a limit must be reached within another couple of generations. The continuing availability of copper will then depend largely on the recycling of already mined metal. It is inevitable that the same must ultimately be true of all other metals.

Mineral resources are products of millions of years of earth history, and different mineral deposits are localized in different geochemical provinces. Since new deposits do not form fast enough to replace those mined, they are non-renewable. Mines bear no second crop. As new discoveries decrease, there is only retreat to ever lower grades, imports, substitutes, synthetics, recycling and eventually, exhaustion.

No part of the earth is self-sufficient in all critical metals. North America, for instance, is rich in molybdenum but poor in tin, tungsten and manganese. Asia is rich in tin, tungsten and manganese, but poor in molybdenum. Most of the world's essential chromium and gold comes from South Africa. Cuba and New Caledonia possess about half the world's known reserves of nickel. Most cobalt is in the Congo Republic, Cuba, New Caledonia and parts of Asia. The world's mercury supply is essentially limited to Spain, Italy, Yugoslavia and parts of China and the USSR. The iron deposits of the world, basic to industrial development, are concentrated in particular old sedimentary belts of the continental cores.

As industrial nations use up their own supplies they turn increasingly to recycled metals and to foreign sources. Today all industrial nations except perhaps the USSR are net importers of most of the metals and ores on which their economy depends.

The United States, by far the world's largest consumer, although with only 6 per cent of its land area and people, depends increasingly on foreign sources. Among many other mineral commodities, it imports most of its manganese, chrome, cobalt, tin and bauxite. It extensively supplements its lead, zinc and tungsten from foreign sources. Its dependence on foreign petroleum, iron-ore and copper grows annually. Except for bulk non-metallic materials like coal and phosphate, it is currently self-sufficient only in magnesium, molybdenum and a few other metals. Even its readily accessible reserves of ordinary construction materials, like sand and gravel, are dwindling as the cities consume them and expand over them. Can such levels of consumption be extended world-wide, or even long maintained in the United States without population control?

At what point, moreover, does exportation of resources by developing countries begin to prejudice their prospects of eventual industrialization? What kind of social and political turmoil will arise when these nations discover that exportation has handicapped their chances for development? Is

122

Minerals

universal industrialization inevitable, impossible or even desirable – and if not desirable how can its limitation be harmoniously achieved?

Considering the demands for resources and their finite supply, eventual depletion is probably inescapable. But what is the time-scale and real magnitude of the problem, and what can we do to defer the final confrontation with it?

Unfortunately, reliable estimates of ultimate reserves for most minerals are not available. Economic factors, including mining, extractive technology and transportation are key factors in establishing whether a particular type and grade of mineral concentrate at a particular place is or can be an ore. As we know also that new reserves will be discovered by geological exploration or be created by technological innovation, and that both population and *per capita* demands are bound to go on increasing for some time, we have to cope with many variables in estimating the lifetime of metals. These variables, however, tend to balance one another out, so that we can roughly estimate the apparent lifetime of secure reserves for the twenty best-known commodities. Graphs of such lifetimes (see table) show that platinum, zinc, gold and lead are in very short supply. Only eleven of the twenty world-lifetimes and four for the United States persist beyond the end of the century. Present commercial deposits of silver, tin, uranium, natural gas and crude oil will be pressing their limits by then. By the year 2042, which is only as far into the future as the invention of the aeroplane and the discovery of radioactivity are into the past, we can count on only eight of the twenty commodities for the world and maybe three for the United States – molybdenum, perhaps iron and coal (as well as, of course, magnesium, bromine and salt from the sea). Even if assured reserves could be tripled, or multiplied by ten, we would still be in trouble, for, in addition to the estimate that United States requirements for metals and energy in the year 2000 will be four and a half times present demands, world demands, if raised to the *per capita* level of the United States, would then be about thirty times greater.

What can be done to prolong the availability of the most critical resources?

One partial but often overestimated escape hatch is nuclear energy. The promises of breeder reactors and controlled nuclear fusion are threefold. First, they could provide almost 'limitless' energy for the next few thousand years, permitting the 'fossil fuels' (petroleum, coal, natural gas, tar sands, oil shales) to be conserved, as they should be, for the manufacture of petrochemicals, plastic and other synthetics, and for essential liquid fuels. Second, vastly increased cheap power will bring new non-commercial mineral resources to the market place by lowering the costs of transportation and beneficiation at the mine. Third, we could apply energy to extract dispersed metals from low-grade sources. Although records show little correlation between mineral production and energy input as such, the threat of resource scarcity requires that all possibilities be explored. Hence we should investigate the potentialities of nuclear fracturing of sparsely metalliferous rock in place. But this would create the problem of containing the radioactive wastes – of

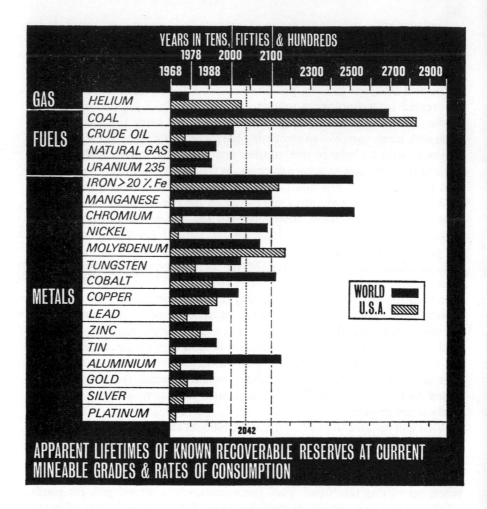

APPARENT LIFETIMES OF KNOWN RECOVERABLE RESERVES AT CURRENT MINEABLE GRADES & RATES OF CONSUMPTION

keeping them out of contact with humans and other organisms and out of the product. Thus the third promise of nuclear energy – drastically lowering the grade of mineable rock – is a very uncertain quantity.

Substitution and synthesis through technological innovation are other ways of stretching mineral supplies. Various metals can substitute for one another, and plastics for some metals. Aluminium already substitutes for copper in many roles, as copper and nickel now replace silver in coinage. Synthetic crystals come increasingly into use. Other substitutes can be created if price is not a consideration. But the production of plastics consumes petroleum and coal. Metals in general cannot be synthesized at temperatures attainable on a sustained and large-scale outside exploding stars, and other elements have unique properties which exclude substitution. Substitution and synthesis must still be exploited to the limit, but we must recognize that they are insufficient, either alone or in combination with nuclear energy, to overcome the limitations of natural supply for ever.

A more promising means of extending the lifetime of resources is to improve the technology of new discovery. We must turn increasingly to geochemical methods that can assist in discovering ore deposits that lie beneath a cover of younger rocks or sediments – including the array of now remote-sensing devices that is becoming available for trial as a spin-off from the space programme.

Although major new mineral discoveries have been made in recent years, and will be made in the future, none of them means that we can relax the search for more. The discovery of a new, perhaps 10 billion-barrel oilfield at Prudhoe Bay on the North Slope of Alaska, during the summer of 1968, is one of the increasingly rare discoveries of major new oilfields, of which probably few remain to be found – particularly outside of remote regions and the continental shelves.

In considering the discovery of new sources of earth materials, we have focused so far on the land-surfaces of the earth. What about the sea? In 1964, it accounted for about 10 per cent of the value of minerals recovered. However, if the theory of sea-floor spreading is correct, the floor of the ocean beyond the continent slope will be a poor place to look for useful minerals. To consider as an important mineral resource the interesting but thinly dispersed manganese crusts and nodules of the deep sea floor is to risk falling into the sort of trap which led post-First World War Germany to imagine she might repay her war debts by extracting gold from sea-water. The nickel, cobalt and copper in these nodules continues to attract industrial interest, but their recovery and metallurgy pose problems of enormous magnitude. The best that can be said of them at this time, therefore, is that their potential remains to be evaluated.

Far more likely as a source of marine minerals are the submerged areas that belong geologically to the continents. Exploration for new mineral resources from the sea should be concentrated here. About 17 per cent of the world's petroleum and natural gas is now produced offshore and more will come. Other mineral products likely to be recovered from the sea-floor in substantial quantities include heavy metal deposits formed on beaches and in streams along the coast. Submarine deposits will be limited to heavy products like gold, tin and diamonds, and in general to depths of 130 metres or less. They will not go far towards solving the problem of other materials in short supply.

When other inescapable limitations are taken into account, moreover, it becomes apparent that the sea, although it must be a prime target for continued intensive research, offers no panacea for resource shortages.

It has been suggested that we may one day export people to other planets or import resources from them. However, even assuming that a habitable planet is available with accessible mineable resources, the impracticability of colonizing or of importing industrially significant quantities of materials from other planets is illustrated by a computation made by Garrett Hardin for the cost of colonizing the moon. He calculates that if four-fifths of the current GNP of the United States were devoted to that project it would take us a year to export one day's increase of world population at present growth rates. The import problem is of the same dimensions.

The facts reviewed here make it clear that there is no easy way out. But there is a way. We must limit populations, limit *per capita* consumption among the already affluent, and introduce sensible conservation measures, including the recycling of wastes and scrap and the recovery and storage of essential by-products such as the helium in natural gas. And, of course, we must also accelerate geological research, exploration and the search for the technological innovations which will make it possible to recover and utilize larger fractions of the earth's mineral resources with minimal harm to the environment.

Although we must continue to meet the inevitable demands of a growing world population, as well as increasing *per capita* consumption among the currently deprived, much of the metal that is now lost through dispersal and burial can be retrieved. The only inevitable losses are those from oxidation and friction, and even these can be limited by a determined policy to reduce waste and encourage recycling. Provident use of our resources, including our human resources, implies sensible economies in the use of materials and energy. We must recycle as much as practicable, and preserve for later use essential materials that are unwanted or deleterious by-products of other operations.

But there are as yet few signs that the magnitude of the problem has been recognized. Prompt and effective action is needed.

REFERENCES

BOULDING, K. E. 1966. The economics of the coming spaceship earth. In *Environmental quality in a growing economy* (Ed. Jarrett). New York: Johns Hopkins Press, Resources for the Future.

FLAWN, P. T. 1966. *Mineral Resources*. New York: Rand McNally & Co.

HARDIN, GARRETT. 1959. Interstellar migration and the population problem. In *Journal of Heredity, 50*.

NATIONAL ACADEMY OF SCIENCE COMMITTEE ON RESOURCES AND MAN. 1969. *Resources and Man*. New York: W. H. Freeman & Co.

SAINSBURY, C. L. 1969. Tin resources of the world. In *U.S. Geological Survey, Bulletin, 1301*.

12 ENERGY

Peter Bunyard

Science Editor, *World Medicine*
Associate Editor, *The Ecologist*

Man is indulging in a fantastic energy extravaganza which is totally transforming his way of life. Politicians, economists, industrialists and many scientists view this way of life, with satisfaction: to them it means affluence and a booming economy. Like P. J. Searby of the UK Atomic Energy Authority, who states in *Atom* (1969, *157*, 286), 'Energy provides the power to progress ... with a sufficiency of energy properly applied a people can rise from subsistence level to the highest standard of living ...', they obviously feel that the benefits of man's new-found affluence far outweigh the disadvantages.

But not everyone is so easily captivated by the power vested in a few billion tons of coal, oil or uranium ore, and a growing number of thinking people see the increasing profligate exploitation of energy as being one of the greatest potential threats to survival that man has ever faced. There are growing fears for example as to what might happen to our climate and other meteorological processes should we continue consuming energy at an ever accelerating pace. Dr David Berkowitz, in *Science* (1970, *169*, 426) points out that we are already releasing a substantial amount of energy into the environment – it adds up to approximately $\frac{1}{2500}$ of the total solar radiation balance at the earth's surface, a balance which goes into heating air, evaporating water and driving meteorological processes. If the population grows at the rate forecast and consumes energy at the rate some scientists and economists would like, he sees a time within the next century when man could be releasing energy into the environment at a rate equivalent to $\frac{1}{20}$ of the solar radiation balance with incalculable effects, he adds, on the atmosphere and the world's climate.

In the light of this kind of projection the United States' needs by the year 2000 have a sort of horror-fiction ring about them. The energy release to the environment from North America alone in 30 years' time is expected to exceed 190 million BTU per year (4 BTU are equivalent to 1 kilo-calorie), much of which will be released in the Boston–Washington megalopolis area. There will obviously have to be some hard rethinking about energy trends, for three engineers, R. T. Jaske, J. F. Fletcher and K. R. Wise from the Battelle Memorial Institute, Richland, Washington, have estimated that energy release into the environment will amount to as much as 50 per cent of the total solar radiation striking the area. Water is also closely linked with energy requirements, not only to turn the turbines but also to cool the plant. Engineers estimate that if the United States power requirements were met as currently projected for 1980 – just 10 years away – then up to one-third of all the water flowing in that vast nation's rivers and lakes will be necessary for cooling. (*The Ecologist*, August 1970.)

But even if the environmental problems facing mankind were not so momentous, would there always be sufficient energy on tap for as long as man cared to exploit it?

The average person in Britain, as elsewhere in the developed nations, takes his supplies of energy very much for granted. He is not concerned how petrol got into the garage pumps, nor how at the flick of a switch he can get his electric shaver to work. Neither is he concerned about the future and whether his own personal demands for energy are going to be met. For the most part he believes implicitly that the technologists will solve all the problems.

From this point of view he has many people working for him. There are thousands of geologists and engineers now concerned with finding 'adequate supplies of energy in suitable forms, of acceptable quality and at reasonable costs and prices ...' (Organization for Economic Co-operation and Development, *Energy Policy*, 1966). But a renowned expert, Dr King Hubbert, sees this great quest for energy as a flash in the pan and he claims in *Resources and Man* (National Academy of Sciences, Washington, DC, 1969) that 'the period of rapid population and industrial growth that has prevailed during the last few centuries, instead of being the normal order of things and capable of continuance into the indefinite future, is actually one of the most abnormal phases of human history ...' (see fig. 1).

Most experts more or less agree about how long the fossil fuels are going to last. Dr Albert Parker, for example, states in *Fuel* (1970, *49*, 289) that the coals and lignites that can be mined economically should be sufficient for a good 500 years at the present rates of production and there should be sufficient quantities of petroleum oil to last beyond the year 2000.

This is an extraordinary state of affairs; the fossil fuels have taken some 600 million years to form by geological processes, and here we are, less than a few hundred years after their first being exploited, somewhat self-congratulatory because we have a few hundred years' supplies left. But the real significance of the figures becomes apparent when we look at the recent consumption of the fossil fuels. Coal for example has been mined for about 800 years, and yet one-half of the coal produced during that period has been mined during the last 30 years. The figures are even more dramatic for petroleum – half of the world's cumulative production of this fuel has taken place during the 1960s.

But man, like an inveterate gambler, is clutching at any straw to sustain his

I

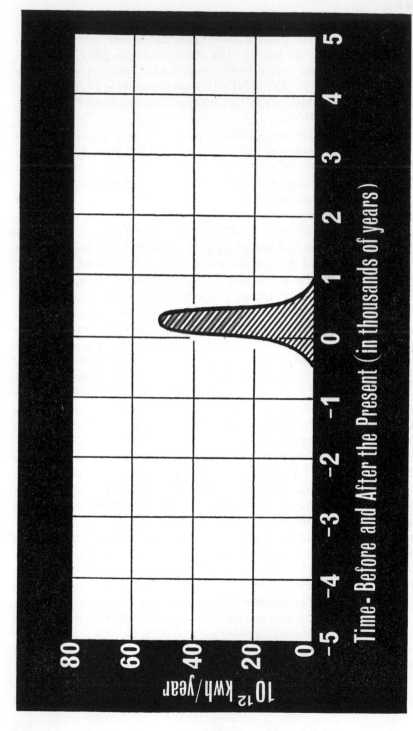

Fig. 1. Period of exploitation of fossil fuels, seen as a proportion of a ten thousand year period of human history. (From HUBBERT, 1962, Figure 54, p. 91.)

profligacy, and one of these straws – nuclear energy – has the eye-catching potential of a titanic. A lot is expected of it and Mr P. J. Searby in *Atom* suggests that by the year 2000 it may be providing one-quarter of the world's energy requirements, and of course much more energy will be consumed then than now. Whether Mr Searby's forecasts are right is a different matter; Britain for example prides itself on being in the forefront of the technology and despite the investment in North Sea Gas, was hoping to have between one-quarter and a third of her electricity generated by nuclear power in the late 1970s. Yet there have been some recent setbacks, particularly delays in construction and tremendous increases in capital cost, and according to Adrian Hamilton (*Financial Times*, 6 August 1970), by 1975 nuclear energy will only be providing 11·5 per cent of Britain's total output of electricity.

Similar difficulties have afflicted the United States and they too are behind in their nuclear energy programme. They are also having to face an entirely new problem – that of growing hostility towards nuclear reactors by an increasingly aware public. All in all these factors have caused a certain disenchantment with nuclear energy, and the power utilities, having ordered thirty-one nuclear plants in 1967, only ordered seven last year; since then there have been several cancellations.

People in Britain are also becoming aware of the dangers of radiation, and there has been some simmering at the UK AEA's request to quadruple the discharge of radioactive substances into the Irish Sea from Windscale. Also recently several councils including Kidderminster Borough Council and Droitwich rural district council have objected to the CEGB's plan to build a nuclear power station or indeed any power station at Stourport-on-Severn, and they appear to have won their case.

The councils in question were worried about the risk to a relatively large population which would be living within two miles of the reactor by 1980. They were also concerned at the loss of 'visual amenities' in the area, and at the local effects of the vapour discharged from the cooling towers: for up to 10 million gallons of water, abstracted from the River Severn, would be lost to the atmosphere each day. This vapour, says the Meteorological Office, could cause nearby houses to suffer a 'very light intermittent drizzle or mist' and houses farther away would feel the 'major effect of the plume itself … on otherwise pleasant sunny days'.

On the Continent a spate of nuclear power stations are in the offing; indeed some forty nuclear power stations are planned or under construction in the Rhine catchment area alone (*New Scientist*, 6 August 1970). Elsewhere too, nuclear plants are being planned and built and the demands for uranium fuel are beginning to rise rapidly. According to Dr Hubbert a very tight situation in uranium supply at anywhere near current prices is likely to develop within the next two decades and, he claims, unless the breeder-reactor programme can be got underway soon, 'the entire episode of nuclear energy will be short-lived'.

Breeder-reactors could be the answer because unlike the conventional consumer reactor they create as much fuel as they burn. But they are intrinsically more dangerous than even the largest of the consumer reactors. They operate at much higher temperatures; to be economic they need to be loaded with large amounts of uranium-235 or plutonium; and in general they use sodium as a coolant – a substance which explodes violently with water even at room temperatures. Although the technology is advancing fast, no breeder-reactors have yet been commissioned as power plants to feed the national electricity grid.

The other hope is from nuclear fusion, but this has yet to be achieved in a controlled fashion.

Thus in a very short time man has expended huge capital resources in energy and unless he is lucky with his technology he may find himself facing the next century more or less bankrupt. Undoubtedly he will always have recourse to other forms of power production – solar energy, the tides, water and wind power, geothermal power, but these sources of power although extremely useful can only supply a very small proportion of man's present demands for energy. Palmer Putnam in *Energy in the Future* (Macmillan, London, 1954) sees the plausible input from all these sources added together at costs no higher than twice those in the 1950s coming to between 5 and 10 $\times$ 10^{18} BTU over a total period of 100 years. The possible demand for energy over that period of time could well run into fifty times that amount.

The crisis is already looming, for the big cities with their very heavy dependence on power have already begun in some instances to outrun their supplies. The black-outs and brown-outs in the United States tell their own story, and according to *Time* (10 August 1970) during the recent devastating smog that enshrouded the major cities of the north-east, Con Ed – the New York State power utility – had to dole out up to 7,245 MW of electricity in the peak consumption hours, with the safety margin only a few hundred megawatts above this. For once customers were asked to unplug everything from air conditions, lights to escalators.

But even if the electric power utilities did expand to meet all possible future demands they would soon find themselves not only polluting the environment with enormous quantities of waste, including carbon dioxide, sulphur dioxide and possibly krypton-85 among other radioactive substances, but they would soon run out of pure physical space, for the power plant with its transmission lines and transformers encompasses a large area of land. Indeed, it would not take many doublings of the demand for electricity before people would find themselves ousted from the land by pylons and all the other paraphernalia of the power industry (*Environment*, March 1970).

132

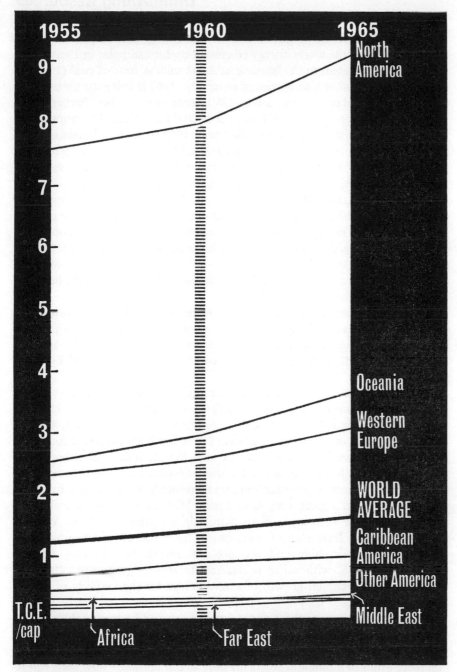

Fig. 2. Total consumption of energy per head (TCE/cap), measured in thousands of kilo-watt hours per annum, showing proportionately greater use in an industrial society. (From P. J. SEARBY, *Atom*, November 1969.)

Not that there are any signs at present that energy consumption is likely to go down. Take the world energy consumption for example; in 1950 it was reckoned as equivalent to the burning of 2,642 million tons of coal (1 ton of coal gives off 7 million kilocalories of energy), in 1967 it had gone up to 6,004 million tons of coal equivalent, and by 1980, according to Albert Parker (*Fuel*, 1970) it could be up to 8,000 million tons of coal equivalent. The population in the meantime went from 2,517 millions in 1950 to 3,420 millions in 1967 and will probably be in the region of 4,000 millions by 1980. So, while the population would have increased approximately 1·6 times in 30 years the world's energy consumption would have increased over three times – double that of the population. The greatest demand at present is for electricity: for example in 1960 the UK's *per capita* consumption was 2,600 K wh *per annum*, and in 1967 it had risen to 3,796 K wh *per annum*. India's *per capita* consumption for these two years was 46 and 81 K wh *per annum*, and the United States' 4,698 and 6,612 K wh *per annum* (kilowatt-hours.) Projections for 1980 indicate that the United States' *per capita* consumption of electricity may be up to 11,500 K wh *per annum* (see fig. 2).

A great many power stations will have to be built over the next few years to provide this hungry planet with power; power that has enabled Britain for example to increase its numbers of vehicles on the roads from some 400,000 in 1914 to more than 18 million now, with 26 million projected by 1980 (Parker, A.).

Everyone realizes that the present phenomenal expansion of the world's population must one day cease but very few people have considered why it is that the population explosion is such a contemporary phenomenon. Palmer Putnam suggests that the most significant factor has been the transition from illiterate subsistence farming to what he calls literate industrial–urban farm patterns. But what he emphasizes is that this transition has to be accompanied by an increase in energy consumption and therefore 'a great increase in world population without a great increase in demand for energy is not plausible'.

But we are now running into an extremely awkward situation. We are running out as we have seen of some of our main sources of minerals such as copper, lead, tin, zinc and the precious metals (see Preston Cloud, Chapter 11) which, with other substances in short supply, are extremely important for the capital growth of a nation and for the viability of its industrial processes.

What will happen when the industrial nations can no longer lay their hands on the raw materials that have become so essential for their existence? How for example can a nation as heavily populated as Britain survive when its industries grind to a halt and it has nothing to sell abroad – how then will it pay for imports of food? Equally important, what will happen to agriculture when the farmer can no longer afford chemical fertilizers, insecticides, anti-

134

biotics, fuel to run machinery or feeding stuffs for his livestock? What of productivity then?

It does not need much stretch of the imagination to see that terrible chaos lies ahead unless Britain and the other industrial nations turn their backs on their policies of unmitigated growth and expansion. Yet, judging by the exhortations of their leaders for greater productivity and by their obsession with growth, there are few signs that any of these nations are coming to terms with the future. Instead the population expands inexorably, people clamour for a greater and greater share of the dwindling profits, like a laval stream the raw effluent of industry flows ever more profusely into the environment, and the swollen numbers of the poor and deprived see less and less of the promised land.

No solution is simple, but the present blind faith in progress and in the power of a growing gross national product are obviously leading us to an abrupt dead-end. Yet when we think how much we have to depend on energy – for travelling, for heating our homes and running the household gadgetry, for making the nine to five office job possible, for communications – any thought of cutting down on energy consumption may seem out of the question.

But how much energy do we really need, and what is the price we are paying for it? Has anyone counted the cost of the poisoned air, water and land; has anyone measured the disastrous effect on our health and sanity of the noise, squalor and fumes that beleaguer us when we venture out into the street and to an increasing extent in our home?

Not that these are the only side-effects – there are many others which are impossible to measure, including the destruction of peoples and their cultures, and of a bewildering array of animal species. Some of us have begun to realize that the equation does not balance up: what man gains through the consumption of more and more energy he loses a thousand times over in other ways. And soon there will be no going back; for man will have sold himself out.

13 WATER

Dr F. N. Steele

Administrator, Scientific Civil Service
Environmental Researcher

It is popular to regard the year 2000 as some kind of watershed in the lives of men, and while we are so engaged in forecasting the problems that will confront us in that year of the magic numbers, we tend to ignore, or pass over, the problems that are confronting us now. Problems which if not tackled very soon will grow by the end of the century to such proportions and reach such complexity that they will be beyond man's powers to repair both in terms of technology and cost. Even taking the present rate of utilization of the Earth's resources and without making any allowance for an increase in demand, we can easily visualize that many of these resources will be so costly as to place them, before the end of the century, beyond the reach of any but the richest nations. Rather than the developing nations sharing the standard of living of, for example, the United States, they will be forced to sell their raw materials even to maintain the standards of living they have today. Even water, that most vital resource, will cost much more by 2000, indeed it is highly likely that its price will be significantly increased by the end of this decade.

It seems inconceivable that water could ever become a scarce resource when 71 per cent of the Earth's surface is covered by it, but the fact is that the world is threatened by a serious water shortage which, if nothing is done about it soon, could become acuter by the end of the century. Why should this be the case when the amount available on this planet has probably not altered much over the last million years or so? The answer lies in the way it is distributed (unevenly so that it is not necessarily found where it is most needed), in the demand which is spiralling due to the rapid population increase and the requirements of technology, and in man's misuse of it through waste and pollution.

From the earliest times communities have sprung up and grown along river banks, the rivers providing the vital water and at the other extreme a convenient means of disposing of wastes. Until the arrival of the Industrial Revolution the rivers could by and large quite easily cope with the demands Man made upon them, but with the explosion of population and industry in the last 100 years or so, the rivers have been quite unable to meet Man's requirements. In the industrialized countries in particular Man has to look

Water

farther and farther afield to satisfy his needs. Reservoirs must be built, often sited many miles from the towns and cities they serve, and frequently the groundwater must be tapped. Frequently, too, the most densely populated areas are to be found in the driest places. For example in the south-east of England, one of the most overcrowded parts of Britain, the natural evaporation of water from the land can in the summer months exceed the rainfall, and indeed London without groundwater and its reservoirs would be faced with water starvation. Even in those areas where there is an abundant rainfall, such as parts of north-west England and southern Scotland, there is a growing danger of a water famine. It is not surprising, therefore, to come to the conclusion that water shortages, now more commonly associated with the arid regions of the Earth will in the future, unless action is taken to prevent them, be commonplace in areas which have abundant rainfall, and will seriously affect the industrial nations.

Water is essential to industry and the quantities used are staggering. 4,400 gallons of water are required to make one ton of steel, 350 gallons to make 1 gallon of beer, 800 gallons to make 1 ton of cement and 20,000 gallons to make 1 ton of paper. Of the 8,740,000 million gallons of water authorized for use in the United Kingdom for the year ending 30 September 1969, no less than 4,857,000 million gallons were used by the Central Electricity Generating Board alone for cooling and steam raising. Although most of this water is recycled, much more will have to be conserved if industrial civilization is not to be brought to a halt. Indeed, it may be the shortage of water that could bring this about and not the shortage of other resources or the breakdown of social structures. The situation could be particularly serious for the smaller highly industrialized nations such as Japan and the United Kingdom, both of which incidentally have a natural abundance of water but both of which waste millions of tons each year, but while such countries will be the first to feel the effects of a water shortage, the larger countries will not be too far behind. The United States is at present moving into a position where water will be at a premium. It is estimated that in the 10 years from 1970 to 1980, the total water demand (domestic and industrial) in urban areas will increase by 30 per cent; 16 per cent of this will be required to take account of population growth at the current demand rate, 11 per cent for the increased demand by the original population and 2 per cent for the increased demand of the additional population. By 2000 America's needs will have trebled, Britain's doubled and taking the world as a whole, four times as much water will be required. As Man advances, his thirst for water rockets. In the developing countries a man might get by on $2\frac{1}{2}$ gallons a day, but a Londoner needs 33 gallons for his domestic use and in some cities of the United States the citizens cannot do with less than 55 gallons.

Water shortages on a wide scale will be very prevalent long before the end of the century. It is quite possible that severe shortages will be hitting British and American industry by 1980, and some people believe that unless the problem is tackled now, by 1980 the position will have reached the point of no return. Can the problem be solved? If we tackle it now, it can.

Firstly we must understand the problem in its entirety, we must know where we get our water from and to do this we need a thorough understanding of the hydrological cycle. This, for brevity's sake, is the circulation of water between ocean, atmosphere and land surface. The sun's energy evaporates oceanic water, acting rather like a huge still, and this 'fresh' water is taken up in the atmospheric machine and is eventually precipitated as rain, snow and hail. Of the proportion of this that falls on the land, some is locked up in permanent snowfields or glaciers or runs back to the sea down the rivers, some finds its way into the more porous strata of the continental rocks, and some is re-evaporated off the land by the energy of the sun. Areas covered in forests or jungle retain the moisture better than those covered with other types of vegetation, but all land covered by plants retains its water content much better than areas of barren rock, sand and concrete. Any interference with the natural water regime obviously bodes ill. The current craze for deforestation is an obvious threat and even the building of dams and reservoirs for the very purpose of water catchment can have an adverse effect. Some of the practices currently in common use actually impair the efficiency of the catchment system. One practice which is thought to improve efficiency has in fact the very opposite effect; this is the stripping of the hillsides around a reservoir of their trees, and in some instances all vegetation, replacing these with concrete slopes. This arose from a belief that the water would run quickly into the reservoir without taking in a load of soil and vegetation debris, but what was ignored was the fact that water was lost, particularly at times of comparatively low precipitation by evaporation off the concrete. What was further ignored was that vegetation itself conserves water and also because of the relatively higher humidity in a vegetated area evaporation is reduced from the surface water in the reservoir.

The siting of dams and reservoirs brings other problems. Since the Second World War perhaps the most notorious has been the building of the Aswan Dam in Egypt. No doubt the idea behind this dam was to enhance the welfare of the Egyptians, though it seems that prestige considerations were rather high up on the list of priorities. Very little thought must have been given to the ecological and medical aspects of siting a dam across the Nile. Within a few years of the dam's completion, a valuable fishery in the Lower Nile Delta has been destroyed, depriving thousands of people of their livelihood. The fertility of the Nile valley itself has been reduced, so much so that part of the power generated by the dam has to be used in preparing artificial fertilizers to replace those that were once brought down by the Nile itself.

138

Water

The Nile, which for thousands of years sustained an advanced civilization, has in a matter of less than a decade been destroyed by twentieth-century Man.

However, the growing demand for water makes the building of reservoirs imperative – water storage is an important aspect of the conservation of the resource – but these alone will never be sufficient. The water we have will have to be used over and over again and drastic attempts made to cut down wastage and pollution. Urban areas are particularly wasteful of water. Much of the storm water runs straight off the ground through the drainage system, very often down common pipes with sewage, and is contaminated by the time it gets into the rivers. What doesn't run off is directly evaporated into the air, whether this be through solar energy or the energy coming from the man-made power plants within the buildings. Modern agricultural methods are wasteful of water, again much of it runs off the land and is frequently contaminated by artificial fertilizers and pesticides. But so much of our water is wasted by ourselves in the home. In countries where water has been up until now plentiful it has been taken completely for granted, an inexhaustible supply at the turn of a tap. Before water was available on tap the average British domestic consumer used 5 gallons a day, now he wastes 4 gallons a day purely because of dripping taps and burst pipes, and he uses far more than he really needs. Water is cheap, a mere $17\frac{1}{2}$p per 1000 gallons for the domestic user in Britain. Compare, for example, his opposite number in Kuwait who has to pay £1·50 for the same quantity and treats water with the respect it deserves. Metering is an obvious deterrent to this type of wastage. A survey of 136 American towns and cities with populations exceeding 25,000 showed that the overall daily consumption (all uses) per head where 10 per cent of the supplies were metered was 143 gallons but when 50 per cent of the supplies were metered this fell to 58 gallons. A salutary example.

Closely married to waste is pollution which is really part of wastage because polluted water frequently cannot be used for industrial purposes and may be dangerous to domestic users. It can also be a threat to the food supply by being a hazard to domestic animals, to fish in rivers and lakes and ultimately in estuaries and coastal waters. Pollution has become one of the major problems of the latter half of the twentieth century and has particularly affected water supply in the latter half of the 1960s. Many of the rivers of the industrial nations of the northern hemisphere have been referred to as 'open sewers' with a great deal of justification. A 1958 Ministry of Housing and Local Government Survey of Britain's rivers showed that 1,278 miles, $6\frac{1}{2}$ per cent of the total river length of England and Wales, were grossly polluted and 4,144 miles, 20 per cent of the total, needed improvement. The Institution of Water Engineers, in a 1970 report, estimate that 'nearly as much as a quarter of the England and Wales water supply is drawn from sources that are frequently or continuously polluted in degrees varying from

139

slight to dangerous, and a further quarter from sources liable to sudden pollution, varying from slight to severe'. One of the most badly polluted river systems is the Trent and its tributaries, particularly the Tame which drains Birmingham and other West Midland towns; these are so polluted that many people believe that they can never be cleaned. Severe pollution problems are found in the Coln, Calder, Ouse, Lee, Tyne and Humber and Mersey river systems to name but a few. The situation is the same in many of the great rivers of the industrialized world, the Seine, the Rhine – which has been called the longest sewer in Europe – and many of the American rivers. The Great Lakes, vast stores of valuable freshwater, are being seriously threatened; Lake Erie is devoid of aquatic life and Lakes Michigan and Superior are heading in the same direction.

By far the biggest culprit in freshwater pollution is sewage, domestic and farm, which if untreated makes very great demands on the oxygen dissolved in the water on which aquatic life depends and which helps to keep the water 'fresh'. Although more and more effort is being made to increase sewage treatment facilities, the amount of untreated sewage being pumped into our rivers represents a serious threat to our water supplies. But sewage is only one of the pollutants, the industrial effluents add many more. Treatment of these is vital particularly when we consider that if it were not for returned effluents many rivers would not flow at all in dry weather. Taking the Trent as an example again, the amount of water abstracted is about twenty times the natural dry-weather flow of the river and about twice its average flow. It is estimated that the contribution of effluents to the dry-weather flow of this river will triple by the year 2000. A similar situation is found in the Calder, Mersey Weaver and Lee river systems. In fact there are instances where the water requirements of a factory exceed the natural dry-weather flow of a river and this in effect means that the whole river flows through the factory and there is also some reverse flow in the adjacent river channel upstream from the discharge point. Such examples show vividly the extent of Man's impact on a natural system and his responsibility for what he does to it. Already many public water supplies depend heavily on the extraction of returned effluents. In the London area we have the well-quoted example of a cup of fresh water from a tap having been through seven or eight other persons previously. What will be the position by the year 2000 when the population of the south-east of England will have risen from 20 millions to 28 millions with a projected doubling of the demand for water? And this is just one area. Unless pollution is minimized, more and more water recycled and more efficient methods of water catchment and regulation devised, the situation could become very serious. Accepting therefore that this must be done, there is a pressing need for considerably more detailed planning and control than currently exists and also for much increased charges for water.

Water

In Britain one of the biggest stumbling blocks to achieving the necessary planning is the fragmentation of the present system of water distribution and control. There are 29 River Authorities and 500 Water Undertakings. The former are responsible for the catchment areas of the major river systems in the British Isles and each one has wide powers for controlling rivers and water resources, for land drainage, prevention of pollution and the control of fisheries, and they are also responsible for estimating demands for water at least 20 years ahead and for planning the resources to meet those demands. The Water Undertakings, which can either be public authorities or statutory companies, are responsible for the supply of water in urban or rural areas. What the River Authorities are not currently responsible for are the sewage disposal systems and there is no comparable planning activity for the systems required as a consequence of the provision of water. Yet such systems cannot be divorced from one another. The *Report of the British Government's Working Party on Sewage Disposal* puts the point very strongly, 'Not only is the disposal the consequence of the abstraction, but the quantity, quality and location of disposal may well be related to another abstraction within the river system. The two operations of abstraction and return to the river are in practice inextricably linked; they are part of the overall river system.' Even with the Water Resources Board which is above the River Authorities and Water Undertakings and which is the national planning authority for water, Britain lacks an overall water control system to take into account all the aspects of water resource conservation and exploitation. Such a system must be set up. Under such a regime the water resource could be planned and distributed on a truly national scale. It should have executive powers not only to control the utilization of the water but to ensure that the resource is not misused or polluted. It would also fix the cost of water to industry and to the individual domestic user. For whether we like it or not we are going to pay more for our water and the psychological barrier which currently prevents government or local government from charging a realistic price to the consumer must go. There is a belief prevalent in our society, and I suspect in most Western countries, that we have as much a right to clean water as we have to clean air. As we have neither, since we have all been party to the pollution of both, we have to pay to clean it up, and we have to pay for the wastage. In addition we must pay for the distribution, an item that is frequently forgotten by those that maintain that water should be free.

The three aspects of the water-scarcity problem – demand, wastage and pollution – will have to be tackled on a national scale. Its cost and complexity forces this upon us. In this sense we in Britain are fortunate, for continental countries may have to tackle it intergovernmentally, a more delicate task. Even if we solve most of the wastage and pollution problems, we cannot overlook the fact that the demand will always present the major problem.

At the present rate of world population increase, freshwater availability will be inadequate to meet demand at some point in the future, and other sources of freshwater will have to be explored. Indeed some countries are already extracting freshwater from sea-water to meet their 1970 demands. Kuwait for example relies heavily on desalination and while it cannot be denied that this has brought great benefits to that country, which incidentally can afford to pay for it, the prospect of world-wide desalination brings its own problems – thermal pollution, the power requirements (and let us not forget that even nuclear power has its disadvantages).

Even if the population stabilized at present-day numbers, or a little more, the supply would still be outstripped by demand if every country aspired to a standard of living comparable to, for example, the United States. But on current observations even the United States will be feeling the pinch and this well before the end of the century. By the end of the century many of the now 'rich' nations will be in the same boat and far from being able to help those who are less endowed with wealth and technical know-how, they themselves will be pressed to the utmost of their ability to keep going. For all the water there is on the planet Earth, it is perhaps as well to remember that only 2 per cent of it is available to us as freshwater, 1 per cent is locked in the ice and snows of the polar regions and the other 97 per cent forms that vast and important controller of our climate, the ocean. And therefore we have to plan not only that this 2 per cent is used rationally but also that our population, and its level of consumption, do not exceed what the resource can sustain.

REFERENCES

AD HOC GROUP ON GOVERNMENTAL RESPONSIBILITY FOR THE NATURAL ENVIRONMENT. 1969. Governmental responsibility for the natural environment. In *Report presented to the Standing Committee of 'The Countryside in 1970'*.

BOURNE, ARTHUR G. *Pollute and be Damned!* London: J. M. Dent. To be published.

CENTRAL ADVISORY WATER COMMITTEE. 1962. *Reports of the Sub-Committee on the Growing Demand for Water. First report 1959; second report 1960; final report 1962.*

MINISTRY OF HOUSING AND LOCAL GOVERNMENT. 1970. *Final Report of the Technical Committee on Storm Overflows and the Disposal of Storm Sewage.*

MINISTRY OF TECHNOLOGY. 1968. Water pollution research, 1968. *Report of the Water Pollution Research Laboratory Steering Committee.*

WATER POLLUTION RESEARCH LABORATORY. 1965. Effects of polluting discharges on the Thames Estuary. In *Report of the Water Pollution Research Laboratory.*

WATER RESOURCES BOARD. 1970. Water Resources Act, 1963. In *Sixth Annual Report of the Water Resources Board for the year ending 30 September 1969.*

WATER RESOURCES BOARD and THE SCOTTISH DEVELOPMENT DEPARTMENT. 1968. *The Surface Water Yearbook of Great Britain, 1964–65.*

142

PART FOUR

Pollution

14 POLLUTION OF THE AIR

Dr Eric S. Albone

Research Associate, *Centre for Biology of Natural Systems,
Washington University, St Louis, Missouri.*

A year ago a man walked on the moon. Here was a measure of our time, inspiring and futile, cut out by cash and courage for the television sets of the world. But it was a crucial event, for here man stood outside his world and knew his oneness with a precious, living lump of rock set in a bleak infinity. Here was an experience different from that of generations of explorers struggling over the Earth's hostile hide in search of new lands and new fortunes. Here was a world grown small and fragile in the shadow of man's power.

From a relentless arrogance towards a world we still seem to believe was created for our benefit, and from a determination to exploit all we find with uncompromising thoroughness, has flowed the stream of achievements of which we are justly proud. Such attitudes, which Lynn White sees rooted in our half-forgotten theological past, are now by their very success and power threatening us with destruction. Their value has passed. Man must learn to replace harmony for aggression, or die. René Dubos has put it this way. 'In order to survive, mankind will have to develop what might be called a steady state society.' The transition implies momentous consequences for all aspects of our life and thought. But unless there is transition, our tenancy of this planet is limited.

Man's capacity today to kill and to communicate, to reproduce and to foul with his biological and technological excreta is global and therefore of dimensions critical to his survival. The problem is one of the scale of man's power, and pollution presents one facet of that impending problem, one manifestation of man's mindless might.

Let us here look at one kind of pollution, the physical and biological

143

aspects of the pollution of the air, remembering that in reality our environ-ment is an integrated whole and that a consideration of the air environment in isolation is not strictly valid. And if we wish to look to the future, let us mainly look to the present rather than lose ourselves in fantasy, for the present is where the future is born.

'Pollution' is not a scientific term, implying as it does a value judgment. It presents a convenient label but not a convenient starting-point. Rather it is necessary first to develop understandings of the nature of the many complex processes occuring in the environment. Judgments follow, for although on some occasions pollution will be evident to all, at others it will be illusory and at still others it may be hidden to casual examination.

So, what of the air environment? Each day each of us breathes his way through about 3,000 gallons of air composed, if dry and clean, of 78·09 per cent by volume of nitrogen and 20·94 per cent oxygen. The remainder is mainly argon and carbon dioxide. In practice, water vapour is also present to an extent varying from 1 to 3 per cent. Approximately one half the weight of the atmosphere lies below an altitude of 18,000 feet and 1 per cent above 100,000 feet. The composition and dominant chemical processes of the atmosphere differ from the troposphere, which extends from the ground to 39,000 feet at mid-latitudes, in the abundance of shorter wavelength radiation leading to a chemistry based on the photolysis of oxygen molecules to atomic oxygen. One consequence is the maintenance of an ozone layer which serves to shield the earth's surface from dangerous radiation. But even these remote heights feel man's impact. It is said that by flying for one hour at these altitudes, a super-sonic transport consumes 66 tons of fuel and casts out 83 tons of water, 72 tons of carbon dioxide and 4 tons each of carbon monoxide and nitric oxide. If such flights become common, the consequences are unclear. Anxiety has been voiced that the water vapour produced at elevations where natural water concentrations are low could have significant effects on the energy balance of the entire planet, and also that the vital ozone layer could be disrupted. But lacking sufficient background knowledge we can only advance an informed guess.

Into this thin envelope of air we pour our gaseous wastes. Carbon dioxide is produced in massive quantities, but this is not usually considered a pollutant. With water, it is the ultimate product of combustion. Of the major gases considered pollutants, the United States in 1965 released an estimated 72 million tons of carbon monoxide, 26 million tons of sulphur oxides, 19 million tons of hydrocarbons, 13 million tons of nitrogen oxides and 12 million tons of 'particles', together with a plethora of other materials lesser in quantity but not necessarily in significance. Future trends are uncertain, but if one recalls the astonishingly rapid and violent explosion in technology which this century has seen, one could be very pessimistic. On this point, the Spilhaus

Pollution of the Air

Report in America projected with regard to sulphur dioxide emissions that on the basis of 'severe but realistic controls . . . a 75 per cent increase by 1980 and a further 75 per cent increase by 2000' will occur, and John Middleton, US National Air Pollution Control Administration Commissioner, has written that 'by 1990 our potential to emit sulphur oxides could hit 95 million tons – and again our calculations may well prove on the conservative side'. What happens in America will surely be paralleled in Britain. Certainly the problem will continue to grow under the fragmentary yet relentless impulse of our dangerously narrow economic concern.

To put meaning into these numbers, various understandings are required. Firstly we need to know something about the diffusion, transformation and fate of the substances we add to air. This requires a knowledge of the location, nature and extent of emission sources and understandings derived from meteorology and atmospheric chemistry together with the support derived from an extensive monotoring programme of the ambient air. In all these areas we are weak. A second kind of understanding we require concerns the effects of materials added to the air at the concentrations and in the mixtures actually encountered. We may expect effects on man's health, on his possessions (through corrosion and soiling), on the plants he grows for food and decoration, and on the total web of life of which he is part. Effects on a global scale are to be expected and the less easily quantified consequences such as personal discomfort caused by odour and the psychological weight of dismal surroundings also have a place.

Only when such understandings are being developed can we hope to discuss pollution rationally. Then we shall begin to be aware of the real costs of our comforts in the modern world, and we shall become impatient with such statements as 'The Generating Board has been searching for years for a way of removing sulphur dioxide formed by the burning of fossil fuels without increasing the cost of electricity' (*Daily Telegraph*). We shall realize the real cost of dirty electricity.

The environment is a dynamic system and our gaseous wastes are unlikely to remain unchanged in it. If they were to, global air pollutant levels would slowly and inevitably rise. In fact, with the dearth of information we have, we probably wouldn't notice the early stages of this process anyway. We also have rather little information on the nature and extent of the various processes removing pollutants from the atmosphere, the natural pollutant sinks. We are unsure of the atmospheric fate of carbon monoxide (although we can guess) and of methane, although the possibility of oxidation in the stratosphere has been discussed. Usually we have not worried about such problems and have trusted that pollutants will be diluted by the winds and then forgotten.

But we cannot always trust the weather to be our friend. The December 1952 killer smog of London depended for its ferocity on the weather. It impelled Londoners to light fires to keep warm and then trapped the smoke in the damp atmosphere. Last summer (1969), the American mid-West experienced smog for several days and smog alerts were announced in Chicago and St Louis as stagnant air settled over the region and populations suffocated in their own fumes. In fact US government meteorologists (ESSA) regularly examine meteorological charts and issue high pollution warnings as such atmospheric conditions develop over a region. Los Angeles provides a notorious example of unfavourable climate. Pollutants from this heavily populated area concentrate in a stagnant atmosphere and, in the California sun, undergo photochemical transformations which are even now not fully understood. Most significant in Los Angeles are the oxides of nitrogen and hydro-carbons derived from Los Angeles County's 4 million cars. This accumulates in an atmosphere in which low winds and the surrounding mountains limit horizontal dispersion, and thermal inversion (which lies over the area some 320 days of the year) limits vertical dispersion. The outcome is a whole range of new pollutants, the oxidants, formed in the atmosphere itself. Best known are ozone and peroxyacetyl nitrate (PAN). An average oxidant level of 0·15 ppm or more for an hour is considered evidence of serious photochemical smog. Los Angeles experienced such smog on 29 per cent of the 714 days of 1964 and 1965 for which good records exist. This phenomenon, unknown before 1945, is now extending to other major cities of the world. It exacts a severe toll, the total cost of which has not been computed. Here are some elements of the cost. Oxidants produce severe eye and respiratory irritation and one study has revealed a general relationship between oxidant levels and the athletic performance of schoolchildren in Los Angeles. Materials are attacked, especially rubber, and plants are damaged. In 1954 the damage to crops from Los Angeles air pollution was even then estimated at $3 million per year. One estimate of the total agricultural damage in the United States resulting from air pollution has put the cost at $500 million per year. It is possibly greater. Nobody really knows. Today we have reports of smog killing nearly a million trees in a National Forest on the mountains 60 miles from Los Angeles.

But that is America, not Britain, we confidently say. Such things do not happen here. And certainly the British scene differs from the American. Sometimes it is better, sometimes worse. Conditions are not nearly so conducive to the formation of photochemical smog in Britain as in Los Angeles. But recall that there is neither extensive nor systematic monitoring of the air for oxidants in Britain, so our optimism has little base apart from supposition, albeit seemingly reasonable supposition in the case of oxidants. In this context, it is interesting to recall recent reports from Porton concerning an unexpected bactericidal component of ordinary air. It is conjectured that this component has an origin similar to Los Angeles smog, but this time 'made in Britain'.

Pollution of the Air

Apart from some measurements in London, we do not examine the composition of our atmosphere very thoroughly. The Ministry of Technology through its Warren Spring Laboratory has been conducting a very extensive National Survey of Smoke and Sulphur Dioxide for some years. By September 1969, 1189 daily sampling instruments were in use. This excellent study has resulted in the publication of a listing of geographical 'black areas' in Britain. It has also detected a very encouraging downward trend in ground-level sulphur dioxide and smoke levels in the country as a whole in recent years, especially following the Clean Air Act of 1956. But this limited success is grounds for more action rather than less, especially in the face of the bureaucratic farce in which shortages of smokeless fuel have now dictated a policy of *suspension* of smokeless zones. But the Ministry of Technology survey measures *only* smoke and sulphur dioxide. This is not adequate. Nitrogen oxides and oxidants should be added to the list, especially in view of the Porton reports. And a much more general approach to assessing air quality should be initiated. A report of the 1967 WHO symposium on the health effects of air pollution contains these remarkable statements: 'In the concentrations found in the air, none of the known pollutants would be expected to have serious effects on health ... some *unknown* substance is therefore responsible for the correlation between airway resistance and air pollution during the winter.' That is how much we understand the environment.

We need to be on the lookout for unusual or unexpected pollutants which can cause serious damage even following brief exposure at low concentrations. This form of pollution is most easily overlooked. An example is the damage observed to cut its way through the centre of St Louis last year following the chance release of quite a small quantity of defoliant. Defoliant is manufactured in the area. The effect on plant life could be mapped, but it required a trained scientist with an interest in the community to draw the observations together, and such persons are not often available.

ACID RAIN. But sometimes quite ordinary pollutants fox us. Consider the fact that Sweden's rain has become more acidic in the 60s. One theory is that the sulphur dioxide emissions from Britain and other European countries are to blame. Are they? We don't know. Since 1957 the pH (a measure of acidity, the acidity increasing the lower the pH) of rain over Britain has averaged pH 5·0. But, in Sweden, median values have been slowly dropping from pH 4·8 in the period 1957–61 to pH 4·5 in the years 1962–6. Isolated reports of rain of astonishing acidity exist. This phenomenon is not confined to Sweden. In 1958 precipitation of pH less 5·0 was limited to parts of the Netherlands. By 1962 rain of that acidity extended over areas of central Europe and in the Netherlands rain of acidity below pH 4·0 was encountered. It is pointless to debate who or what is to blame. We do not have any conclusive evidence.

147

For example, we do not have much information how much pollution we 'export' on the winds. An airborne spectroscopic technique developed in America would be valuable here, but it is unlikely to be applied. So far our one ground-level directional smoke and sulphur dioxide pollutant monitoring station on the Norfolk coast indicates that we 'export' just a little more than we 'import'. But one station is not enough to begin to assess the situation. And still people debate Sweden's rain. It seems that we are determined to fight the 'Fight Against Pollution' over unknown terrain. There is the frightening–amusing quotation of one of our lost leaders, Austin N. Heller, Commissioner of Air Resources, New York, that 'by reducing sharply the ambient sulphur dioxide levels, we could be increasing photochemical reactions . . . or smog'. I don't suppose anyone knows enough about any particular atmosphere to say whether or not this is so. But we do know the fight is world-wide. The Swedish rain situation indicates that. We know it too from the detection of pesticide residues (DDT, dieldrin, BHC, heptachlor epoxide) in the tissues of the animals of Antarctica, even if the concentrations are low. Pesticides have never been used in that entire continent. We know it too from the carbon dioxide affair.

Carbon dioxide with water is the ultimate major product of combustion. It is non-toxic and a natural constituent of the air. It appears quite harmless. But *global* carbon dioxide levels are rising. They have risen from 296 ppm in 1900 to 318 ppm today. The US President's Science Advisory Committee Report of 1965 entitled *Restoring the Quality of Our Environment* states that, as a result of the 'vast geophysical experiment' man is unwittingly conducting, 'by the year 2000 the increase in atmospheric carbon dioxide will be close to 25 per cent. This may be sufficient to produce measurable and perhaps marked changes in climate, and will almost certainly cause significant changes in the temperature and other properties of the stratosphere.' The root of the matter is that the carbon dioxide build-up, which through man's agency has been too rapid for the slow-acting natural sinks such as the ocean to respond, may perturb the globe's energy balance, for carbon dioxide, while allowing the sun's radiation to reach the earth in its usual way, has the property of trapping the longer wavelength radiation the earth re-irradiates back into space, thus tending to an overall global temperature rise. This might even eventually cause some melting of the polar ice-caps with an accompanying change in sea level. It seems, however, that this may not happen. The total situation is much more complicated. Not only carbon dioxide but also atmospheric water and dust levels (the dust level itself being partly the result of man's activity) together with factors depending on the sun's own activity, determine the Earth's temperature. In fact, global temperatures which had been rising, have, since 1940, been declining a little. The crucial point in all this is that *man is now acting in ignorance on a scale of global consequence*. Further it seems

148

practically impossible that he would be able to regulate his production of carbon dioxide anyway.

Even with smogs and smoke and sulphuric acid droplets in urban air, to see pollution in perspective, it must be recognized that man is not alone in pouring chemicals into the air. Estimates are that 80 per cent of the sulphur dioxide in the air of the whole world at any time derives from the natural sulphur cycle in which hydrogen sulphide is evolved by decaying organic matter. There is too a natural region rich in sulphate particles extending round the globe at altitudes just above the tropopause. Large expanses of vegetation evolve considerable quantities of organic materials. Even the reactive hydrocarbon isoprene has been thus identified. But man is unique in the rapidity and extent to which he is conducting his blind environmental experiments. A medley of pollutants marks his crowded communities. An American study shows that the level of lead in rain in a given locality is well correlated with the sales of leaded petrol in that location. In two cities, the level of lead in rain was twice the maximum allowed by US Public Health Service standards for drinking water. In this context, it is cheering to read in the 1968 Rothamsted Report that 'in most industrial countries, burning (sulphur containing) fuels put enough sulphur in the air and rain to provide for crops'.

Pollution of the environment by small quantities of metals is a vast subject, not fully explored. Metals can pollute the environment in various ways and can have serious effects on health. Lead has been much discussed, but it possibly exerts indirect effects. Very low lead levels occur in our cities as the result of using leaded petrol. Certain experiments also reveal that the lung's resistance to infection may also be lowered by exposure to small quantities of lead. Cadmium is linked with hypertension and a whole spectrum of other metals also exert their effects. NAPCA Behavioural Toxicology Unit at Cincinnati is looking at the way pollutants affect brain function. Carbon monoxide lead and ozone are under investigation, for although it has been said that carbon monoxide in the environment seldom results in blood carboxyhaemoglobin levels much in excess of those experienced by smokers, these levels could be of significance on our roads where any reduction in driver performance and perception could be critical. Metals in the environment might also play an important part in the chemical transformations of other pollutants. Thus manganese and iron speed the production of sulphuric acid from sulphur dioxide. Again more needs to be known concerning the full range of such catalysis.

In this sea of uncertainty, it is difficult to know where we stand with regard to the consequences of air pollution for our health. The 1970 Report for the Royal College of Physicians *Air Pollution and Health* does state that 'Britain has the highest death rate in the world for chronic lung disease in middle-aged men' and that 'men working in London had worse bronchitis and poorer function of the lung than those in either Bergen (Norway) or the cities of the eastern seaboard of the United States' taking men of similar age and smoking habits. It remains difficult to assess the precise impact of pollution on health because of the variability of susceptibility and exposure among the population and because of the importance of synergistic effects, that is, of combinations of effects acting together to create an enhanced total effect. The private (and therefore of less public concern) 'pollution' of tobacco smoking adds a further complication. As Lambert and Reid recently stated in the *Lancet*, 'The dominant influence of smoking on chronic lung disease is now well recognized,' yet air pollution effects are documented. Most dramatic was the London smog of 5–9 December 1952, responsible for an estimated 3,500–4,000 deaths. Increased deaths were notable among lung (especially bronchitis) and heart diseases especially in old people. Under less dramatic circumstances, Carnow has documented an increase in acute morbidity from respiratory disease in patients with bronchopulmonary disease in association with increased ambient sulphur dioxide levels in Chicago. Another survey published in 1969, comparing human lung tissue obtained at post-mortem from long-time residents of heavily polluted St Louis with similar tissue from Winnipeg where high pollution and stagnant atmospheric conditions are far less common, revealed a marked deterioration of the lung in the more polluted city. This effect was not accounted for on the basis of smoking history alone. For example, 'of the smokers, there were four times as many cases of severe emphysema in St Louis residents as was observed in Winnipeg'. This assessment was made on the basis of lung tissue examination.

This brief discussion of air pollution has touched lightly on only some of many aspects of the subject. Corrosion of metals and stonework, the discoloration of paints, the soiling and disintegration of fabrics, the effects on crops of pollutants where 'hidden' effects are sometimes as important as visible damage to foliage (hidden effects include reduction in growth rate of the plant), none of these have been discussed. Nor has the role of pollution in contributing to haze and mist nor the implications of pollution for ecology. As the 1969 American Chemical Society Report states, 'the relationship of air contaminants to the ecology, the aggregate of living things as they exist together in nature, is very nearly a total mystery'. We are increasingly learning the importance of odour in determining behaviour patterns of animals and the study of pheromones is in its infancy. The range of the implications of pollution is further suggested by one report suggesting that certain air pollutants possibly stimulate the growth of *Haemophilus influenzae*, a bacterium significant in relation to chronic bronchial disease.

But in all things, it is apparent that we are only beginning to understand what we are doing to our environment. Knowledge is scarce and the situation is serious. There is so much we need to know before we can begin to live in our

Pollution of the Air

world intelligently. The pressures are on. It is time to act now. But action means commitment and that means money. In the 105th Annual Report of the Chief Alkali Inspector (1968) we have been told that, with regard to air pollution control in England and Wales, money spent by scheduled industrial works in capital costs since 1958 had amounted to £150 million and that the latest year's working costs had been £39 million. Good, but not nearly enough for pollution is still with us and its costs are rising. It is significant that we in Britain must go back 16 years for the most recent general authoritative assessment of the costs exacted by air pollution on all of us. In 1954 the Beaver Committee on Air Pollution concluded that in Great Britain 'air pollution is costing as much as £250 million a year in direct costs and loss of efficiency'. One estimate has put today's figure considerably higher.

If we take up the economist's lens, we must beware its limitations. Conclusions cannot be better than assumptions and only in the simplest cases can the costs of air pollution be reduced meaningfully to neat bureaucratic figures in a ledger. By what algebra does one estimate the money worth of a living lung, the value of the equilibrium of the environment or the cash equivalent of surroundings that are not sordid? The *Beaver Committee Report* admitted these weaknesses thus, 'Our estimate is confined to those items which it is possible to measure in terms of money. We therefore have not attempted to include the effects on health (except in so far as reduced working efficiency is concerned), the possible higher death rate, the loss of amenity and a whole series of social consequences. Nor have we attempted to put a price on the unpaid labour of housewives whose work is substantially increased in smoky areas.' But *these* include the really important categories of cost, cost to health, to environment and to society. And apart from this, it is quite impossible to begin to assess the total cost of pollution *in any terms* when the available scientific understanding of what is happening in the environment is so limited. We are not surprised that the Chief Alkali Inspector should report (1969) that 'the conclusion has been reached, rather sadly, that meaningful cost/benefit cannot be achieved'. But, be sure the cost of polluted air is high. As yet we do not fully know how high.

Balanced action on pollution is urgently needed for the good of all. Clearly one of the first items of expenditure must be to pay for a closer watch on the environment. The mobilization of science in this service of the community is as essential as is the need to make freely available to public scrutiny and debate the objective scientific findings so generated. That handful of dedicated scientists who today work to guard our environment require massive support. In America, the National Air Pollution Control Administration has just recommended that by 1974 air pollution control manpower be increased three-fold. In Britain, the need cannot be less. Indeed, a new scale of priorities is demanded.

Pollution is exacting a rising, silent price which all of us pay. Too often we have been content to risk the irreplaceable capital of health and environment for cheap financial gain. Recycling, the recovery of wastes, the use of clean processes and similar solutions are often economically unattractive to the polluter.

There exist those minds which are dominated by the balance sheet. It is a myopia which in some measure is common to all of us. Some is evident in the Chief Alkali Inspector's cruel jibe, 'we see no rush by the alleged sufferers to finance the prevention of pollution at source, when on the face of it, there should be a phenomenal return for the outlay'.

Table 1 ESTIMATES OF AIR POLLUTION IN THE UNITED KINGDOM

Estimates of Pollution by Smoke and Oxides of Sulphur in Million Metric Tonnes from the Main Uses of Primary Forms of Energy in the United Kingdom in the Year 1969–70

(*one metric tonne = 0·9842 long ton*)

Estimates prepared by ALBERT PARKER, CBE, DSC

Figures for quantities of forms of energy were derived from the Digest of Energy Statistics 1969–70 of the Ministry of Technology

Form of energy and class of consumer	Quantity of energy	Quantity of pollutant
SMOKE		
Coal		
Domestic, including miners' coal	22·0	0·70
Railways	0·2	small
Industrial and miscellaneous, including collieries	27·8	0·08
	50·0	0·78
SULPHUR OXIDES		
Coke (excluding consumption in gas works and blast furnaces)		
Domestic, including other manufactured solid smokeless fuels	6·1	0·13
Industrial and miscellaneous	5·6	0·13
	11·7	0·26

Pollution of the Air

Form of energy and class of consumer	Quantity of energy	Quantity of pollutant
Coal		
Domestic, including miners' coal	22·0	0·56
Electricity power stations	77·1	2·20
Railways	0·2	small
Collieries	2·0	0·06
Industrial and miscellaneous	25·8	0·74
Coke ovens	25·7	0·08
Gas supply industry	7·0	0·05
Low temperature carbonization plants	2·4	small
Manufactured fuel plants	1·4	small
	163·6	3·69
Oil		
Domestic	2·7	0·01
Industrial and commercial	48·0	2·20
Gas supply industry	5·6	small
Road transport	18·3	0·06
Railways	1·1	0·01
Marine craft (inland)	1·1	0·03
	76·8	2·31
OVERALL TOTAL		6·26
Hydro-electricity (coal equivalent)	2·0	
Nuclear-electricity (coal equivalent)	10·7	
Natural gas (coal equivalent)	8·4	
TOTAL coal equivalent, including oil at 1 tonne = 1·7 tonnes of coal and including petroleum gases	322·7	

Table 2 ESTIMATES OF POLLUTANTS FROM ROAD VEHICLES IN THE UNITED KINGDOM IN THE YEAR 1969–70 IN MILLION TONNES

The estimated quantity of carbon monoxide discharged into the air from the other industrial and domestic uses of all fuels in the year 1969–70 is about 10 million tonnes including about 4 million tonnes from domestic heating appliances. These discharges are above ground level whereas the discharges from road vehicles are at ground level.

GRIT AND DUST. In the absence of numerous measurements of the discharges of grit and dust from each of the various uses of solid fuels it is possible to make only rough estimates of the total quantity discharged into the air of the United Kingdom. My estimate is that in the year 1969–70 the total amount was in the region of 0·55 million tonnes with somewhat more than one-half from electricity power stations, one-third from the industrial uses of coal and coke and one-sixth from domestic fires. In addition there are discharges of considerable quantities of grit and dust from various industrial processes, including cement works and iron and steel works for example. The total quantity discharged from these various special processes in the year 1969–70 was probably in the region of 0·5 million tonnes.

Consumption of motor spirit 13·45 million tonnes
Consumption of derv fuel   4·87 million tonnes

Pollutant	Petrol engines	Diesel engines
Carbon monoxide	6·3	0·10
Hydrocarbons	0·32	0·020
Aldehydes	0·01	0·003
Oxides of nitrogen	0·22	0·06
Oxides of sulphur	0·025	0·04

REFERENCES

AGRICULTURAL RESEARCH COUNCIL. 1967. *The effects of air pollution on plants and soil.* London: HMSO.

THE AMERICA CHEMICAL SOCIETY. 1969. Cleaning our environment; the chemical basis for action. Report of the *American Chemical Society*, Washington DC.

COMMITTEE OF THE ROYAL COLLEGE OF PHYSICIANS. 1970. *Air pollution and health.* London: Pitman Medical and Scientific Publishing Co. Ltd.

MINISTRY OF TECHNOLOGY. 1967. Investigation of atmospheric pollution, 1958–66, being the *32nd Report of the Warren Spring Laboratory.*

NATIONAL SOCIETY FOR CLEAN AIR. 1971. *Clean Air Yearbook.* Brighton: National Society for Clean Air, 134/7 North St., Brighton.

15 POLLUTION BY RADIOACTIVITY

Peter Bunyard

Science Editor, *World Medicine*
Associate Editor, *The Ecologist*

Slowly, insidiously, the levels of man-made radiation will be rising over the next decades as man commits himself further to the use of nuclear energy. Some of this radiation will be discharged from nuclear reactors which are springing up one after the other in both industrial and developing nations. Some will result from fall-out of nuclear devices that have been used in grand engineering adventures such as the blasting out of new harbours and of gigantic shipping canals. The rest – outside of a nuclear war potentially the most significant – may burst upon the hapless environment through an accident. The chances are that some time, somewhere, a nuclear reactor and its container structure will be breached by an explosion: or that a sealed tank full of seething radioactive waste to be entombed far from man's dwelling-places will get ruptured. The consequences in either case could be a radioactive cloud several hundreds of times more lethal than that which settled upon Hiroshima or Nagasaki.

These predictions may sound alarmist and more than a little exaggerated. Yet we know that the nuclear reactors in existence are silently discharging small quantities of radioactive waste into the environment and are even as at Windscale in Cumberland stepping up their effluent production by as much as a factor of four. We know that Russia and the United States are continuing with their underground tests and that the US Atomic Energy Commission (AEC) is committed to 'Plowshare' – the peaceful uses of nuclear devices. And we know of some accidents that have already happened.

Windscale is one famous example where in 1957 the number one pile went 'critical' and during the last-ditch attempts to suppress it, vented more radioactive waste than had fallen on Hiroshima after the bomb. Luckily for both the nuclear power industry in Britain and for the local inhabitants around Windscale the radioactivity was swiftly carried upwards into the atmosphere where it was diluted to relatively harmless levels. The United States too has suffered a lot of accidents, perhaps none so terrifying as that which happened to the Enrico Fermi breeder reactor in 1966. This reactor went so 'critical' as to make the authorities fear for the safety of more than $1\frac{1}{2}$ million people living in Detroit.

So far the total discharge of radioactive wastes into the environment – including the fall-out from bombs exploded in the atmosphere – does not add up to much after its dispersal, for by far the largest proportion of these man-made wastes are bottled up in 'impregnable' containers. For these reasons the great majority of radiation experts feel that the small increments in radioactive levels anticipated over the next few years will be of little consequence. Indeed, they point out that man is naturally subject to much higher levels of background radiation; from cosmic radiation for example and from naturally occurring radionuclides contained in the soil.

But are the experts right – can we really discount these additions to our background radiation? Several facts must be borne in mind. Firstly, the evolution of life, including man, has not taken place haphazardly; the environmental conditions at any one time and place have been critical for the type of ecosystem generated and radiation as a major cause of genetic mutations (some of them undoubtedly useful in the long run) has been one of these conditions. Increasing the levels of radiation by any degree could conceivably upset the subtle mechanisms by which life sustains itself. Secondly, the fission products from nuclear plants are a million to a billion times more toxic per unit weight – in terms of visible damage – than any other industrially known materials. Thirdly, some of these fission products like plutonium-239 have very long half-lives and once formed they are going to be around for a big chunk of man's future – assuming he has one.

Despite these facts the radiation experts are virtually unanimous on what they consider to be the working levels of radiation to which man can expose himself without apparent far-reaching consequences either to him or to his successors. All of mankind is therefore in the hands of these experts who through such organizations as the International Commission on Radiobiological Protection (ICRP) have established that the general population should not be exposed to more than 0·17 rem a year above natural background radiation – the rem being a measure of the biological effect of different types of radiation. This level of radiation, which adds up to 5 rem over 30 years, is unquestionably small and people living in Kerala, India, or in Guarapary, a Brazilian coastal town, both of which have high background radiation from high concentrations in the soil of naturally occurring radionuclides such as thorium, will be subjected to more radiation over an equivalent period of time.

Nevertheless initial studies carried out by the AEC on the inhabitants of Guarapary show that they contain a statistically significant increase in chromosome aberrations, and many radiation biologists are now realizing that any radiation – just one single alpha particle produced by the decay of a radium atom for example – is hazardous. Indeed, experiments have shown that the numbers of white cells in the body are depressed for a time and that

156

Pollution by Radioactivity

some detectable abnormalities are caused such as two nuclei in a cell instead of the normal single nucleus.

Radiation is now known to induce all types of cancer and not just certain ones such as leukaemia, and it is conceivable that given time – perhaps as much as 25 years – a cancer will originate from a very low dose of radiation. Because of this possibility two nuclear scientists from the AEC's Lawrence Radiation Laboratory in California, believe the present Federal Radiation Guide of 0·17 rem above the background to be too high by a factor of 10 at least. Dr John F. Goffman and Dr Arthur G. Tamplin have predicted that if everyone in the United States received this additional amount of radiation each year from birth, the death rate by the age of thirty would increase by 5 per cent.

Other radiation scientists feel that these two AEC scientists have exaggerated the issue. Studies of populations that have been exposed to fall-out, the survivors of Hiroshima and of Nagasaki for example, and the Marshall Islanders who were exposed to fall-out during the Pacific Tests, do not show anything like the effects, say the critics, that Goffman and Tamplin would predict from the dosages of radiation received. But we are now coming to realize that all the studies of populations that have been exposed to fall-out are inadequate on one count in particular – while focusing on the more conspicuous aspects of heavy radiation they have neglected to look at the effects of *low-dose* radiation on a sufficiently large number of people.

It costs a lot of money to look for minuscule changes, and the returns after intensive work are very small. For the same reasons studies in the cloistered surroundings of the laboratory of the effects of low-dose radiation on experimental animals have also been extremely limited.

But there is one survey of a human population which indicates a possible strong link between very low-dose natural radiation and congenital malformations. This survey painstakingly carried out by Dr John T. Gentry and his colleagues shows that the incidence of these malformations in New York State is significantly increased in those areas where the underlying rock formation contains high amounts of naturally occurring radionuclides such as thorium-232.

In New York State the radiation is emitted from three areas; from the igneous bedrock of the Hudson valley and Adirondack mountains; from river valleys in the Allegheny Plateau, and from recessional moraine areas with igneous or black shale bedrock left as glacial deposits as the ice sheets of prehistoric times advanced and retreated.

Dr Gentry classified any townships or cities falling within these three areas as *probable* and those falling outside as *unlikely*. He then looked at birth certificates of children born in New York State exclusive of the City in the years 1948–55 for any record of congenital malformations. He also studied

157

the death certificates of any children who had died before the age of five.

The incidence of congenital malformations in the *probable* areas was always higher than in the *unlikely* ones, and within the *probable* areas was higher in rural than in urban ones. In the same way children of fathers who had rural occupations such as farming in the *probable* areas showed a higher incidence of congenital malformations than those of fathers with jobs in the towns, whereas no such difference was apparent in the *unlikely* areas.

The pattern was maintained when the water supply was looked into; children of parents who used wells and springs in the *probable* areas had a higher incidence of malformations than those children of people using large surfaces of water such as rivers and lakes. In other words the closer the contact the parents had with the radioactive source the more likely were their children to be born with congenital malformations. It is difficult to explain away these results in terms of such factors as socio-economic ones or differences in medical treatment; the populations from the two areas – the *probables* and *unlikelies* – are just too comparable. Nor can altitude – bringing with it such physiological burdens as a more rarefied air and a generally more extreme climate – be the complete answer, even in the Adirondacks, which in parts exceed 3,000 feet, for much of the data was compiled for populations living nearer sea level.

One phenomenon, in particular, has largely been overlooked by radiation scientists; the unbelievable capacity of living organisms to concentrate certain highly diffused radionuclides. Norman Lansdell, for example, in his book *The Atom and the Energy Revolution*, reports a study of the Columbia River in the western United States in which the radioactivity is seen to accumulate progressively up the food chain in a remarkable and alarming way. The water itself contained very low concentrations of radioactive substances. But the radioactivity of the river plankton was 2,000 times greater; the radioactivity of the fish and ducks feeding on the plankton was 15,000 and 40,000 times greater respectively; the radioactivity of young swallows fed by their parents on insects caught in the river was 500,000 times greater, and the radioactivity of the egg yolks of water-birds was more than a million times greater.

Man himself is very much part of the food-chain and measurements of zinc-65 in the same area around the Columbia River showed that while the water contained only twenty-five thousandths of a picocurie (a billionth of a curie) per gram of this radionuclide, an average-sized man drinking milk and eating meat from the area could contain more than 4,000 picocuries. The zinc-65 is produced in a reactor when zinc components are bombarded with neutrons – the particles released from decaying uranium-235. But zinc-65 is just one of many radioactive substances produced during the normal running of a reactor, and some of these radionuclides – iodine-131, for example, are

158

Pollution by Radioactivity

potentially more dangerous for they accumulate in specific regions of the body, like the thyroid gland.

Dr Robert Pendleton, radiation biologist at the University of Utah, has reported what can happen as a result of fall-out of iodine-131, which in fact is a fast-decaying radio-isotope with a half-life of around 8 days. What is particularly disturbing in this story was the Federal Radiation Council's lack of concern.

On 7 July 1962, the day after the 100-kiloton 'Sedan Shot' had been exploded at its Nevada test site, Dr Pendleton and a group of students, were some 20 miles south-east of Salt Lake City measuring the background radiation near various rock formations.

A large dust cloud appeared on the horizon: 'Not,' remarks Dr Pendleton 'an unusual event in Utah during the summer.' But when the cloud reached them the radiation level shot up to 2 milliroentgens per hour – some hundred times higher than background.

Two days later the gross activity in the air had risen to 900 picocuries per metre and 8 days later samples of milk contained more than 2,000 picocuries of iodine-131 per litre. Dr Pendleton had suggested to the Utah State Department of Health that the contaminated milk be used for making cheese or be powdered or condensed so as to give the radioactive iodine time to decay and prevent the public being exposed, but his plea was rejected by the Federal Radiation Council.

During July contamination of milk samples taken from all over the State rose to a peak and then fell off. Nevertheless an individual drinking a litre a day of milk from one of the more contaminated sources could have taken in a total dose of up to 800,000 picocuries and, says Dr Pendleton: 'it is evident that a considerable fraction of Utah residents exceeded the current yearly protection guide for iodine-131 of 36,500 picocuries'.

Doctor Pendleton was particularly worried about children under 2 years of age because of the sensitivity of their thyroids to any irradiation. At that time there were about 53,000 children of this age group in Utah alone. If any of these got a full dose of the contaminating iodine-131 it would mean a total thyroid dose of 14 rad. The permissible dosage at the present time is reckoned at 0·6 rad in a year.

Dr Pendleton's concern appears to have been vindicated; now – more than 20 years since bomb testing began – public health figures for the State show an increase in thyroid disease among children and young adults. Even more startling is the increase in children dying between the ages of five and fourteen with congenital malformations.

Because Utah gets more than its fair share of fall-out from the Nevada bombs, whether tested in the atmosphere or underground, Dr Pendleton has suggested that the State should have been selected for studying the effects of low-dose radiation. 'Yet,' he says, 'though we pressed for large-scale studies to follow up these children only 2,000 in one place and perhaps 2,000 in another were examined. To follow up such low doses of radiation some 20,000 children at least should have been studied – but the objection was that it would cost a lot of money. In fact, for just a fraction of the cost of one of those large weapons we continually detonate we could have had some answers to essential questions about the hazards of low dose radiation.'

Despite a fundamental lack of knowledge about the effects of low-dose radiation the AEC continues to press ahead with its Plowshare Program. Already the Commission envisages using nuclear explosions to blast holes underground to stimulate natural gas production and for gigantic civil engineering projects such as boring out a sea-level canal in Central America to replace the Panama Canal.

In December 1967 the AEC launched its 'Gasbuggy' experiment in New Mexico to see how much natural gas could be produced. The gas was produced all right, but according to reports, as well as being contaminated with krypton-85 and carbon-14 it was excessively contaminated with tritium. All these radionuclides are known to be taken up by biological systems. Krypton, though an inert gas, is absorbed into fatty tissue, and both carbon and hydrogen (of which tritium is an isotope) pass through all the metabolic pathways of living organisms, including those concerned with synthesis of DNA – the organisms' hereditary material.

Yet, in the face of the unknown hazards of boosting environmental radioactivity, the AEC are still thinking of going ahead with the *Rulison Project* to create a large natural gas source under Rifle, Colorado. The AEC proposes to supply the contaminated gas, mixed with uncontaminated gas from other sources, to the public. The underground explosions may also cause groundwater to become contaminated with radioactive substances, and there is more and more documented evidence that 'faults' are appearing in geological strata many miles away from the blast. One explosion for example has set up disturbances in Denver which has never before suffered an earth-quake.

Dr Edward Martell, who is now with the National Centre for Atmospheric Research in Boulder, Colorado, is highly critical of the Plowshare Program and is fearful of the consequences should a sea-canal be blasted out in Central America.

Problems of fall-out aside, it is difficult, he points out, to predict with sufficient accuracy the effects of an underground explosion. 'Sulky', for example, was a 0·1-kiloton explosion at a depth of 90 feet in Basalt and most of the ejecta material fell back into the crater giving rise to a small mound with a central depression. 'Palanquin' on the other hand, a 4-kiloton explosion

160

Pollution by Radioactivity

at 280 feet in hard volcanic rock, erupted through the surface and the fireball pushed up through the void.

While the refractory radionuclides were more or less contained with Sulky a large fraction of them escaped into the atmosphere with Palanquin. The experts estimate that if nuclear cratering is to be effective and not too deep or shallow then up to 10 per cent of the radiation will unavoidably escape into the atmosphere.

Fall-out in Central America would be particularly hazardous, says Dr Martell. The annual rainfall is high, sometimes registering 400 inches and more. The winds too are very complex; easterlies predominate between 5,000 and 30,000 feet, westerlies between 30,000 and 55,000 feet and easterlies again higher still. The surface winds vary in their directions.

If fission devices were used many of the radionuclides, such as strontium-90, caesium-137 and iodine-131 would be biologically active. If, however, a clean Plowshare device were used, involving 99 per cent fusion and only 1 per cent fission, the hundred-fold increase in fission products would be largely offset by massive tritium production. And the dangers of tritium for living organisms are now being realized more and more.

While the canal was blasted out and for some time afterwards local populations would have to be evacuated. Some of these would include frontier settlers and primitive Indians such as the Cuna Indians who since time immemorial have made their living there. Such a disruption of the environment would seem to be not only indefensible but unnecessary.

Dr Martell has vividly described the canal blasting. 'The ejecta lip,' he says, 'will form a thick unsightly layer of radioactive mud and rock in a swathe several times as wide as the canal. Throwout and air blast will extend the devastation by flattening forests and structures for miles around in each direction. Seismic and acoustic waves generated by the nuclear blasts will produce unpredictable levels of damage up to distances of tens to even hundreds of miles. And there will be a serious concentration of some radionuclides in the terrestrial and marine biosphere in nearby downwind and downstream areas.' That man can still propose using nuclear devices to blast obstacles out of his way seems utterly crazy. But we must not forget that nuclear reactors with none of the drama and noise of the nuclear devices are also generating unbelievable quantities of radioactive waste. The AEC estimates that by the end of the century 800,000 cubic feet of solid waste will require 700 acres of abandoned salt mines for storage. To take one radioisotope in particular – strontium-90 – and make these figures more real, it is estimated that if nuclear power grows in the United States at the rate predicted there will be 6 billion curies of strontium-90 by the year 2000, and we know that a human can die from absorbing less than one curie of strontium-90.

We are hearing spine-chilling tales about some of the storage problems of these radioactive wastes. For example, nine tanks have failed out of 183 tanks located in Washington, South Carolina and Idaho and the contents have had to be put into new tanks.

These failures have occurred after less than 20 years and yet the contents of the tanks are utterly lethal for thousands of years. In addition the tanks have to be kept cool, otherwise they will burst from the rising temperature and pressure of the contents. Can we hope to keep these tanks safe for a millennium – and not only from our own mishandling but also from natural phenomena such as earthquakes?

Getting the radioactive wastes out of the reactors and into 'safe' storage requires a number of highly complicated processes. Dr David E. Lilienthal, formerly chairman of the US AEC and once an advocate for power from nuclear reactors, now looks upon the nuclear energy programme of the United States with alarm and dread. He has stated how 'these huge quantities of radioactive wastes must somehow be removed from the reactors, must – without mishap – be put into containers that will never rupture; then these vast quantities of poisonous stuff must be moved either to a burial ground or to reprocessing and concentration plants, handled again, and disposed of, by burial or otherwise, with the risk of human error at every step.'

The US AEC has come under very sharp attack in the past year for its nuclear energy policies and various authors including Richard Curtis and Elizabeth Hogan (*The Perils of the Peaceful Atom*) have revealed all kinds of terrifying and unsavoury facts about nuclear power and reactors in the United States. In Britain and Europe, on the other hand, the public has accepted the nuclear industry without much question and has little or no knowledge of the hazards of having a reactor on its doorstep, nor indeed of the hazards of radiation. In fact, Britain at the present time has a higher concentration of reactors than anywhere else in the world: by 1985 up to a third of Britain's electricity generating capacity will be nuclear, with a total capacity exceeding 100,000 MW.

Even if the safety margin is wider in Britain compared with the United States (and for the sake of the British one hopes it is) there can be little doubt that if we continue to commit ourselves to nuclear energy we are going to leave our successors with some very unpleasant disposal problems, even if no major radiation accidents should occur. Surely it is now time for the nuclear industry whether in the United States, Britain or wherever, to reflect again on precisely what sort of world they are going to leave us and our children?

The amount of 48·0 million tonnes of oil used in 1969–70 for industrial and commercial purposes is equivalent in heating value to about 81 million tonnes of coal, which if used for the same purposes would have produced about 0·23 million tonnes of smoke and 2·3 million tonnes of oxides of

Pollution by Radioactivity

sulphur. The total amount of 6·26 million tonnes of oxides of sulphur is 1·94 per cent of the total coal equivalent of 322·7 million tonnes; the total amount of oxides of sulphur in 1968 was 2·00 per cent of the total cost equivalent.

16 POLLUTION BY PESTICIDES

Kevin P. Shea

Scientific Director, *Environment*

In 1946, if you had told a farmer in Nebraska that the poison he was spraying on his crops might seriously affect the reproduction of a group of oceanic birds nesting on an island in the Atlantic 800 miles off the coast of North America, he might have been a little reluctant to believe you. The same reluctance might have been encountered even 10 years later. But now, nearly 25 years after the first widespread use of DDT and related insecticides, it is becoming increasingly clear that even minute amounts of certain pesticides can drastically affect some of the vital processes of living systems. These tiny amounts are far from lethal, but the changes they inflict upon important reproductive processes could be far more important than the frequent massive losses of wildlife caused by direct contact with lethal amounts of the same poisons.

The first evidence that pesticide levels now commonly found in the environment may be associated with subtle changes in the reproductive success of birds was observed by a group of English ornithologists concerned about the sudden decline in certain bird populations, notably some birds of prey. Bird populations are known to fluctuate from year to year depending upon the abundance of food, weather conditions and a variety of other factors which affect birth and death rates. However, the populations of the peregrine falcon and sparrow hawk had been declining steadily since the early fifties, and there seemed to be no obvious explanation. Reproductive success in the golden eagle was also declining.

After an investigation of various ornithological records, one peculiarity was found to be common to all three species. The number of nests containing broken eggs rose sharply midway through the century.[1] In 109 peregrine nests examined between 1904 and 1950, only three nests contained prematurely broken eggs. During the period 1951–66, 168 nests were examined and 47 contained broken eggs. The same pattern was observed in golden eagle nests in Scotland. Of 35 nests examined between 1936 and 1950, only two were found with broken eggs; while between 1951 and 1963 twelve of 48 examined contained broken eggs. The nests of the sparrow hawk showed a similar increase in egg breakage.

The decline in populations of birds of prey, a sharp increase in the incidence

164

Pollution by Pesticides

of egg breakage, and the widespread use of chlorinated hydrocarbons were all roughly coincident. At that time there was no real reason to suspect a causal relationship between these events, but the English scientists studying the problem took important steps towards solving the puzzle.

Some ornithologists, both professional and amateur, are avid collectors of eggs, and private collections and museums all over the world house large numbers of shells accumulated over several generations. This hobby, once scorned by scientists, now proved valuable, for in these collections resides a unique history which could be examined in no other way.

Dr D. A. Ratcliffe of Monks Wood Experimental Station in England began measuring the thickness of the eggshells of the three species, peregrines, sparrow hawks, and golden eagles, using eggshells collected as early as 1900. He found a striking difference in the thicknesses of those eggs laid prior to 1947 and those laid after that time. In the peregrine falcon the difference amounted to a 20 per cent decrease in some parts of England. The sparrow hawk eggs showed a decrease of 24 per cent, and the golden eagle an 8 per cent reduction.

The reports of population declines among birds of prey in England and the events associated with the declines prompted American scientists to investigate the situation in the United States. Joseph J. Hickey and Daniel W. Anderson of the University of Wisconsin published a report in 1968 which revealed a nearly identical situation to that found in England.[2] In eggshells collected prior to 1947 there was little variation in thickness, while in those collected after that time there were decreases in thickness similar to those found in English eggs. East Coast peregrine eggs were 26 per cent thinner after 1947. Osprey eggs from New Jersey were 25 per cent thinner and bald eagle eggs from an area in Florida declined in thickness 19 per cent. Hickey and Anderson carried their investigation one step further than the British scientists. In order to test the hypothesis that the recent changes in eggshell thickness were the result of exposure to chlorinated hydrocarbon compounds, they collected the eggs of herring gulls at five different locations and analysed them for pesticide residues and measured their thickness. The two biologists found that those eggs from colonies with the highest average residues also had the thinnest shells and those from areas of smallest residues, the thickest shells.

While the ornithologists were amassing observational data on waning bird populations, physiologists and biochemists began looking for the mechanism by which tiny amounts of persistent pesticides could cause such declines. As so often happens, the first suggestion linking pesticides with the observed decline in bird populations was the result of an accident.[3] In 1963 a group of scientists in the Department of Pharmacology at the State University of Iowa were studying the effect of starvation on drug metabolism in rats.

165

Normally, starvation reduces the ability of the liver to produce enzymes which are capable of changing the chemical structure of drugs (in this case barbiturates) and thereby rendering them ineffective. In one group of starved rats, the scientists found that enzyme activity was higher than in any group they had studied before. An investigation revealed that the rats used in this experiment had been exposed to chlordane (like DDT, a chlorinated hydrocarbon) one week before they were used in the test. Chlordane had been sprayed in the room used to house the experimental animals to eradicate an infestation of bed bugs.

With this lead the Iowa scientists set out to determine if the exposure to chlordane was causing the increase in drug-metabolizing enzyme activity.

Adult and weanling rats were given doses of chlordane ranging from 10 to 100 parts per million (ppm) of body weight, all less than lethal doses. The researchers found a significantly higher enzyme activity in the rats receiving the chlordane doses than in the control animals. Furthermore, unlike other chemical agents known to stimulate drug metabolizing activity, the effect of chlordane lasted more than just a few hours. Three consecutive doses of 100 ppm stimulated the production of enzymes for as long as 29 days after the final dose was administered. It was postulated that since the chlorinated hydrocarbons are soluble in fatty tissues they were at first stored in those tissues and then gradually released to the circulatory system.

Chlordane was the subject of further tests on rats conducted in 1964 by a group of scientists at Wellcome Research Laboratories in Tuckahoe, New York.[4] It was discovered in these experiments that chlordane was not only capable of inducing the production of enzymes which inhibited the effectiveness of certain drugs by changing their structure but that one of the enzymes induced in this way (a steroid hydroxylase) could alter the structure of sex hormones. When chlordane was administered to female rats at 10 mg per kg once every 2 days for 14 days, it increased the metabolism of a female sex-hormone (oestradiol-17β) by 385 per cent over the untreated controls.

The same effect was shown in birds in 1967 by Dr D. B. Peakall working at the Upstate Medical Center in Syracuse, New York.[5] In his experiment both male and female White King pigeons were used. The males were analysed for changes in testosterone, and the females were analysed for changes in progesterone. Some birds were fed DDT, others dieldrin, and a third group was given both chemicals. At the end of the one-week feeding period the birds were killed and the portion of the liver containing enzymes was extracted. To this was added tiny amounts of carbon 14-labelled progesterone and testosterone. A highly significant increase in the rate of breakdown of both the sex hormones was found in all of the tests. Testosterone metabolism was increased two-fold by DDT, three-fold by dieldrin and five-fold by a combination of the two.

166

Pollution by Pesticides

These studies have resulted in the most widely published hypothesis regarding the way DDT affects eggshell thickness. Sex hormones are present in all birds and mammals and play an especially vital role in bird reproduction. Just prior to egg-laying, calcium from the hollow parts of the bone is transferred to the ovaries and shell gland via the bloodstream. Much of the calcium is used in the formation of the eggshell. These activities are mediated by the sex hormone oestrogen in the bloodstream. Any interruption of this crucial chain of events could result in some of the symptoms observed in declining bird populations. Excess production of enzymes which break down oestrogen might decrease the level of this sex hormone in the bird's bloodstream, leading in turn to inadequate calcium mobilization and thinner eggshells.

There are other possible ways in which DDT may be affecting calcium metabolism and hence eggshell production in birds. There is some evidence that DDT mimics certain hormones and may interfere more directly in the hormone balance. Other possibilities that are being investigated, according to Lucille Stickel in an interview with *Environment*, are that DDT interferes with the metabolism of Vitamin D, with enzymes in the shell gland (especially carbonic anhydrase), or with other more general enzyme systems. Still other possibilities are probably being explored, but 'the people with the best ideas aren't talking', according to Dr Stickel.

The way in which DDT acts may still be obscure, but the fact of its effect on eggshell thickness has now been demonstrated in laboratory tests.[6] This was done at the Department of Interior's Patuxent Wildlife Research Center in Patuxent, Maryland. Birds from a colony of wild-stock mallard ducks were fed diets containing 10 and 40 ppm of DDE or DDD (DDT breakdown products) and 2, 5, 10 or 20 ppm of DDT. In their second breeding season, ducks fed DDE, the form in which DDT is usually present in the environment, cracked or broke 24 per cent of their eggs as compared to 4 per cent for the control birds. As expected, even the sound eggs produced by the treated birds had thinner eggshells, 11 to 13½ per cent thinner than the control birds. Further, eggs that appeared sound and began to develop produced only about one-third to one-half as many healthy ducklings as did the eggs of untreated birds. This indicates that egg-breakage due to thin shells is not the only detrimental effect of DDT.

Controlled study of predatory birds was a much more difficult problem. A colony of American sparrow hawks was started in 1964 at the Patuxent Laboratory, and the problem of care was not resolved until 1967. This was a considerable achievement in itself – no predatory bird had ever been reared in captivity with enough success to permit experimental studies. During 1967 and 1968 experiments were conducted in which some of the birds received 5 ppm of DDT and 1 ppm dieldrin in their diets.[7] Another group received 15 ppm DDT and 3 ppm dieldrin, and a third group received no pesticides at all. Again, eggs laid by the treated birds were thinner, averaging 8–16 per cent thinner than those of the undosed birds. Another important observation was made by these scientists. There was no significant difference between the high and low dosage in either of the birds tested. The level at which no effect would occur must therefore be even less than the small amounts fed in these studies.

Although the subtle effects of chlorinated hydrocarbons on the reproductive success of wild populations of birds have not been fully explored, research in this area continues to sort out bits of information. For example, it has been recently discovered that DDT has another and distinctly different effect on the reproductive system of both birds and mammals: its ability to induce in female rats, chickens and quail a reaction similar to that produced by estradiol, a female sex hormone.[8] Further, it was found that two different molecular forms of DDT had distinctly different female hormone-like effects. When chickens were injected with three consecutive daily doses of 50 mg of one form (*o,p'*), it increased the weight of the oviduct and the amount of glycogen present in the oviduct to the same extent as did three consecutive daily injections of 500 mg of oestradiol. On the other hand, the *p,p'* form had no effect at such low doses. Commercial DDT is usually made up of 15–20 per cent of the active (*o,p'*) form, and 80 per cent of the inactive (*p,p'*) form.

In 1950 an experiment was conducted in which White Leghorn cockerel chicks were given doses of DDT ranging from 15 mg per kg of body weight in the beginning of the experiment to 300 mg per kg near the end.[9] The experiment lasted a total of 89 days. At the end of the experiment a striking difference was noted in both the primary and secondary sexual characteristics of the roosters. The combs of the treated birds averaged 7·56 cm in length while those of the untreated control birds averaged 11·7 cm. An even greater difference was found in the size of the testes. The treated birds showed an average testicular weight five times smaller than that of the untreated birds. The DDT used in the experiment was identified only as being purified and having a melting point of 109° C. The effect, however, was exactly what would have been observed if the birds had been given an oestrogen compound. It was suggested that the explanation may lie in the fact that the DDT molecule is similar in structure to diethylstilbesterol, a non-steroid sex hormone.

In another experiment with caged birds (Bengalese finches), a correlation was found between the amount of *p,p'* DDT in the diet of the birds and the interval between mating and egg laying.[10] The higher the dose (up to 1,200 ppm) the longer was the delay. Again, the author attributes the delay to the interference of DDT in the hormonal balance which times the onset of ovulation. In this case it was postulated that DDT somehow interferes with the secretion of hormones from the pituitary gland. Two of these hormones

Pollution by Pesticides

are associated with the growth of the testes in male birds, and one is associated with ovulation in the female. If the pituitary is the site of action it could explain the inhibiting effect of DDT on the growth of the testes in cockerels and the delay in ovulation of the Bengalese finches, since it has been shown that injections of oestrogen can inhibit the secretion of hormones from the pituitary gland. The explanation, however, may not be that simple. Since the secretion of hormones from the pituitary is controlled by the brain it is quite possible that the nervous system is actually the site at which all the trouble begins. In any case, before the exact method by which DDT affects reproduction in both birds and mammals is known, a great deal more unravelling of this complicated process will have to be done.

The numerous and sometimes catastrophic episodes in which large numbers of fish, birds and lower animals have been killed are in some ways more spectacular than the recently discovered enzyme and hormonal complications caused by DDT. Even this aspect of pesticides in the environment is somewhat of an enigma because the exact method by which these chemicals kill is not fully understood. It is known only that DDT attacks the central nervous system by becoming bound to nerves and somehow preventing their proper functioning.

In many instances extensive losses of wildlife have been directly associated with insect control programmes or have occurred when large amounts of a poison were accidentally released into waterways – especially when the chemicals used have been of the more toxic type such as endrin and dieldin. More often though, such losses occur unexpectedly and are the result of a build-up of the poisons through food chains to levels high enough to cause death. Furthermore, the young are often the most affected.

Such was the case in 1955 when a complete loss of lake trout fry was experienced in the Lake George, New York, fish hatchery.[11] The young fish began to die shortly after hatching. A repeat of the die-off occurred in 1956. In 1957 the eggs from Lake George female trout were distributed to two other hatcheries to determine if the hatchery water or the procedures were causing the failure of the fish to develop, but the fish did not survive in the other hatcheries. A study was then undertaken which eventually showed that DDT used in the Lake George watershed for the control of mosquitoes, blackflies and gypsy moths was related to the loss suffered in the hatcheries.

Samples taken from individual female fish in 1960 showed extremely high levels – over 400 ppm DDT in fat and over 60 ppm in muscle tissues. Developing eggs from the same females contained levels as high as 200 ppm in the fat and 15 ppm in other tissues. By comparing residue levels from fish and eggs from eight other lakes, it was determined that mortality occurred when levels in the eggs reached 2·9 ppm or above. These levels, however, did not interfere with the hatching of the eggs, and mortality occurred only after the yolk sac had been absorbed. Newly hatched trout live for several days on

169

nourishment absorbed from a large yolk sac attached to their bodies. The yolk contains a high percentage of fatty material derived from the mother fish and it is in this material that large amounts of DDT can be stored. As the yolk is absorbed, the DDT is released into the circulatory system of the young fish and eventually causes death.

A similar situation accounted for the loss of 680,000 Lake Michigan coho salmon fry in 1967.[12] A study was conducted to compare the Lake Michigan residues in coho salmon fry to those of fry from Lake Superior and from Oregon, where the cohos originated. Levels from the Lake Michigan fry were five times higher than those from Superior and sixty times higher than those from Oregon. Mortality ranged from 15 to 73 per cent in individual rearing groups of the Michigan fry, while no mortality was experienced in the fry from the other localities.

In both of these cases the young fish which suffered the mortality were the progeny of apparently healthy parents that were taken from waters in which the level of DDT was barely detectable. In Lake Michigan DDT is present in the water at about 1 part per trillion. These are examples of the frequently-observed accumulation of DDT in food chains (see *Environment*, July–August, 1969).

Young birds are subject to the same kind of mortality from poisons accumulated by their mothers. In an experiment with caged Japanese quail, it was found that when adult females were fed high levels (200 ppm) of DDT in their diets for two weeks, 62 per cent of the chicks hatched from their eggs died within seven days of hatching.[13] At the same time the DDT had no effect on the hatchability of the eggs. The survival of pheasant chicks is affected by low levels of DDT as are bobwhite quail. As in young fish, yolk absorption plays an important role in survival. The final absorption of the yolk occurs several days after hatching at which time concentration of DDT or related compounds in the blood can rise quickly. If a food shortage occurs at the same time, as it often does in nature, the situation is even more critical since the DDT is released as the fatty tissue is consumed and remains circulating in the blood. High chick mortality due to excessive levels of DDT and similar chemicals is thought to be largely responsible for the decline in numbers of the Sandwich Island tern and the cause of the predicted extinction of the already rare Bermuda petrel.[14] Indirect effects such as shell thinning may also be involved.

It has been estimated that over 1 billion lb of DDT alone are circulating in the biosphere and it can certainly be expected that a large amount of this will eventually reach the oceans (see *Environment* July–August, 1969).[15] Most sea life carry residues of DDT, but the effects of these residues have been studied in only a few species, with no indication so far of detrimental effects. The commercially important San Francisco crab may be an exception.

Pollution by Pesticides

Laboratory experiments have shown that levels as low as 50 parts per trillion can kill newly hatched crab larvae, a level which is one thousand times lower than that found in adult crab ovaries.[16] The annual crab harvest a decade ago was about 9 million lb, but it has steadily declined until it now averages about 1 million lb. Part of the decline is probably due to overfishing, but, according to Dr Robert Poole, a state fisheries biologist investigating the problem, low survival of crab larvae due to DDT-contaminated parents has contributed heavily to the decline.

Another report has shown that concentrations of DDT as low as 100 parts per billion in sea-water can drastically reduce photosynthesis in the tiny marine plants which are responsible for more than half of all the photosynthesis which takes place on the globe.[17] Although levels in the oceans are far below 100 parts per billion, the ecological implications of this experiment are clear.

Probably the most controversial and least understood aspect of the ubiquitous occurrence of DDT and its relatives is their possible adverse effect on human health. A series of experiments conducted in the 1950s in which adult male prisoners were fed DDT in amounts far exceeding those encountered in normal diets laid to rest, until quite recently, any suspicion that DDT and other related compounds were dangerous when consumed in small amounts. Scientists are still a long way from proving that the amounts of chlorinated hydrocarbons found in the fat tissue of the average human adult are of any significance at all, but a recent report seems to make the possibility a little greater. Between January 1964 and June 1967 in one Florida county, all autopsies with a history of liver, brain or neurological disease were selected for a study which compared pesticide residues in fat, liver and brain tissues with those from cases with normal organs of the same kind. A consistent relationship was found between elevated pesticide levels in these tissues and patients with cirrhosis of the liver, cancer and hypertension. The authors emphasized however, that the correlation they found by no means proves that a causal relationship is involved. They were more impressed by the great variability in pesticide levels found between individuals and suggested that this variability could not be accounted for if it was assumed, as is generally done, that food is the major source of pesticide residues in the human population. Data obtained by interviewing next-of-kin revealed that there was a strong correlation between pesticide residue levels and home use of pesticides. Reinforcing this correlation was the fact that dieldrin and heptachlor epoxide levels did not vary between the subjects, a fact that could have been predicted since these compounds do not normally occur in preparations intended for home use.

The recently aroused suspicions are not based so much on new and incontravertible evidence that persistent pesticides are a threat to public health as they are on a new awareness that has accompanied the discovery of the enzyme-inducing capabilities and oestrogenic activity of these compounds. More disturbing and even less well understood is the possibility that some may be carcinogenic. The question is no longer how much will kill this or that animal or even how much will make it sick, but instead, what are the long-term effects on a population of animals in which very small amounts of pesticides are known to be biologically active?

There is no question that man has changed the chemical environment of the globe considerably within the last 25 years and that this change has had a measurable effect on numerous species. The uneasy feeling is becoming widespread that we are not so far removed from our fellow-species as to be immune from similar measureable effects. It is therefore concern about human health as well as about wildlife that has led to the increasing pressure to eliminate persistent poisons from our arsenal of pest controls.

Note on pesticides

Synthetic organic insecticides are generally classified into three broad groups, the chlorinated hydrocarbons, organophosphates and carbamates. Within each group there is a great variation in toxicity to different animals as well as a difference in their ability to persist in the environment.

Acute toxicity, the most direct hazard to man, is evaluated by determining the amount of a compound it takes to kill 50 per cent of an experimental population of white rats. It is usually abbreviated as the LD_{50}. This is only a comparative value, however, and tells very little about the compound. For example, TEPP is one of the most toxic chemicals registered as a pesticide, yet it can be used on a crop twenty-four hours before it is harvested with no danger of leaving a detectable residue. On the other hand, DDT is far less toxic but remains in the environment for years and accumulates to damaging levels in food chains. Other peculiarities exist among some compounds. Carbaryl, a carbamate, has a relatively low toxicity for mammals but is a deadly killer of honey-bees and related insects, far more so than its relative Zectran which in turn is more deadly to mammals.

All groups have two things in common. First, they are highly soluble in fatty tissues. Because they should kill insects on contact they must be able to penetrate the thin layer of hard fatty material that covers the body of insects. This feature accounts for the fact that the persistent materials can build up in fatty tissues of many kinds of animals.

Secondly, they kill by disrupting the transmission of nerve impulses. The method by which the organophosphates and carbamates accomplish this is quite well understood. They change the structure of a chemical generated at nerve junctions. The change allows the repetitive firing of the nerve and results in convulsions and death. The chlorinated hydrocarbons also attack the nervous system, but the precise mode of action is not fully understood.

172

Pollution by Pesticides

There are over 100 commonly used insecticides and about 1,000 different formulations. They are used as dusts, sprays, aerosols, granules, pellets and baits. They are sometimes fed to animals to control parasites. They are incorporated into many consumer products, including paints, clothes, floor waxes, wood products and room deodorizers, to name just a few. In short, it is impossible to avoid contact with a wide variety of insecticides.

The following table contains a few of the most widely used chemicals and their relative toxicities:

	LD_{50} mg per kg (white rats)	LC_{50} at $11°$ C mg per litre (fish)
CHLORINATED HYDROCARBONS		
Aldrin	40·0	0·0082
Dieldrin	46·0	0·0055
DDT	250·0	0·005
Endrin	12·0	0·0044
Heptachlor	90·0	—
Lindane	125·0	*n.e. at 0·03
Toxaphene	69·0	0·0022
Endosulfan	110·0	—
Telodrin	4·8	—
ORGANOPHOSPHATES		
Malathion	1,500·0	0·55
Parathion	8·0	0·065
Methyl parathion	15·0	**ir at 1·0
Azinphosmethyl	15–25	0·055
TEPP	1·6	—
Mevinphos	6·0	0·83
Ethion	208·0	0·42
Temik	1·0	—
Trichlorphon	450·0	*n.e. at 1·0
CARBAMATES		
Carbaryl	540·0	—
Zectran	15–36	*n.e. at 1·0

*No effect
**Irritated

LD_{50} – lethal dose for 50 per cent of experimental population
LC_{50} – lethal concentration for 50 per cent of experimental population

REFERENCES

1 RATCLIFFE, D. 1967. Decrease in eggshell weight in certain birds of prey. In *Nature 215* (5097).

2 HICKEY, JOSEPH and D. W. ANDERSON. 1968. Chlorinated hydrocarbons and eggshell changes in raptorial and fish-eating birds. In *Science, 162*.

3 HART, L. G., and R. W. SHULTICE and J. R. FOUTS. 1963. Stimulatory effects of chlordane on hepatic microsomal drug metabolism in the rat. In *Toxicology and Applied Pharmacology, 5*.

4 KUNTZMAN, R., *et al.* 1964. Similarities between oxidative drug-metabolizing enzymes and sterile hydroxylases in liver microsomes. In *Pharmacology and Experimental Therapeutics, 146*.

5 PEAKALL, D. B. 1967. Pesticide-induced enzyme breakdown of steroids in birds. In *Nature, 216* (5114).

6 HEATH, R. G., J. W. SPANN and J. R. KREITZER. 1969. Marked DDE impairment of mallard reproductions in controlled studies. In *Nature*.

7 PORTER, R. D. and S. N. WIEMEYER. 1969. DDT and dieldrine-effects on eggshells and reproduction in captive American sparrow hawks. In *Science*.

8 BITMAN, JOEL, *et al.* 1968. Estrogenic activity of *o,p'*-DDT in the mammalian uterus and the arian oviduct. In *Science, 162*.

9 BURLINGTON, H. and LINDEMAN, V. F. 1950. Effects of DDT on testes and secondary sex characters of white Leghorn chickens. In *Proceedings of the Society for Experimental Biology and Medicine, 74*.

10 JEFFRIES, D. J. 1966. The delay in ovulation produced by *p,p'*-DDT and its possible significance in the field. In *Proceedings of the Society for Experimental Biology and Medicine*.

11 BURDICK, G. E., *et al.* 1964. Accumulation of DDT in lake trout. In *Transactions of the American Fisheries Society, 93*.

12 JOHNSON, HOWARD and C. PECOR. 1969. Coho salmon morality and DDT in Lake Michigan. In *Transactions of the 34th North American Wildlife and Natural Resources Conference*.

13 JONES, F. J. S. and D. B. SUMMERS. 1968. Relations between DDT in diets of laying birds and viability of their eggs. In *Nature, 217*.

14 WOODWELL, G. M. 1967. Toxic substances and ecological cycles. In *The Scientific American, 216* (3).

15 PERLMAN, D. 1969. How DTT is killing crabs. In *San Francisco Chronicle*, May 3.

16 WURSTER, C. F. Jr. 1968. DDT reduces photosynthesis in marine phytoplankton. In *Science, 159*.

17 HAYES, W. J. 1956. The effects of known, repeated oral doses of DDT in Man. In *Journal of the American Medical Association*, October 27.

17 POLLUTION OF THE SEAS

J. David George

Marine Ecologist, *Natural History Museum*

If one considers pollution as the introduction of harmful matter into the environment as a result of human activities, then pollution has been occurring since Man entered the ecosystem of this planet. In the first few hundred thousand years of his existence his number and knowledge was such that he was unable to upset the overall balance of the ecosystem in which he had developed. Now, however, his population is so large and his technology so advanced that his impact is felt in the remotest parts of the world and even extra-terrestrially.

In his efforts to improve his own lot in the world, Man at times has forgotten that balanced systems of life, which have taken millions of years to evolve, exist all around him. By destroying organisms, either intentionally or by accidental pollution, the equilibrium of the eco-structure may be upset to such an extent that the system can never, or only with extreme difficulty, be returned to that which existed previous to his interference. Plainly this is what has happened in parts of the terrestrial environment during the last two or three centuries where Man has unwittingly converted fertile land into lifeless waste and now in some areas of the world is spending millions of pounds attempting to return it to its former state. It is only in the last few years that we have realized that our lakes, rivers and streams are not the place to put waste products of the Industrial Revolution; for we have seen with our own eyes that many of these sites have become stinking and virtually lifeless.

Restrictions placed on the deposition of waste in freshwater have, among other things, caused increasing use to be made of the oceans in which to dump unwanted by-products; but is the ocean a limitless drain in which to pour the products of our technological age? Most marine ecologists believe that the sea is not infinite in its propensity for self-purification and that irretrievable damage will be done to marine life if the escalation in addition of pollutants is allowed to continue unchecked. Already serious concern is being expressed about the fate of marine life in restricted areas such as the Black Sea, Baltic, Mediterranean and North Sea. What is the evidence on which these fears are based?

FERTILIZERS AND SEWAGE. In Britain many millions of gallons of sewage-

175

laden water flow into the sea daily from rivers and coastal habitations. This water is often already rich in dissolved minerals such as nitrates and phosphates from fertilizers applied to the land and from breakdown of domestic waste in sewage treatment works. Under normal conditions plant productivity in the sea is limited by the quantities of nitrates and phosphates naturally occurring there. Presented with unlimited supplies of these chemicals in the sea, minute plants (phytoplankton) often proliferate rapidly producing a phytoplankton bloom. In open waters this rarely presents a problem to the herbivorous animals which feed on the phytoplankton, and indeed, an increased yield of fish may result. However, in estuaries and other areas where water exchange with the open ocean is limited, overproduction of phytoplankton is often damaging. In extreme cases the phytoplankton may become so thick that the gills of fish and filter-feeding mechanisms of other animals, such as shellfish, become clogged. The waste products produced by blooms can be extremely poisonous to other marine life. For instance, blooms of certain phytoplanktonic single-celled organisms known as dinoflagellates produce a particularly virulent type of nerve toxin which can kill or incapacitate thousands of larval and adult fish, and other animals. Beds of filter-feeding shellfish (oysters, clams, mussels, cockles) can be rendered unsaleable as a result of build up of these toxins within their bodies. Indeed, many human deaths have resulted from eating shellfish polluted in this way. The increasingly regular occurrence of poisonous algal blooms is giving rise to some concern in certain parts of the world, including the Scandinavian and North European countries.

Organic matter piped or dumped into the sea produces similar signs of over production as marine bacteria break it down and minerals are released. Significant contributions to the quantity of organic material present on the sea bottom can result from a rain of dead phytoplankton produced in quantity as a result of high levels of dissolved nutrients. The decomposition of organic matter uses up oxygen and in many sheltered areas where excessive organic material is present deoxygenation occurs near the bottom, and in some cases throughout the water column. This results in death or decrease in viability of animals that are unable to move away from the area. The fauna thus tends to become impoverished with only a few of the most tolerant species remaining. An influx of non-toxic organic waste can cause serious deterioration of certain fish, shellfish and prawn feeding and nursery grounds in several ways:

1   The oxygen levels are so reduced that adults cannot stay in the area.
2   The adults are able to spawn but there is too little oxygen for hatching of the eggs and development of the larvae.
3   The organisms on which the animals feed have been eliminated or seriously reduced in numbers.

Pollution of the Seas

4   The profuse growth of bacteria in these polluted waters is injurious to the hatching of eggs and survival of larvae.
5   The turbidity of the water is increased to such a degree that it influences development and survival of pelagic eggs and larvae.

All of these influences have been proved to operate in laboratory and field experiments. The Oslofjord is one site among many where growing evidence reveals that as a result of conditions caused primarily by sewage discharge the stocks of commercial marine animals are steadily declining.

The discharge of organic matter and effluent rich in minerals into the sea has many long-term disadvatages. These effluents could seemingly more profitably be returned to the land from which they came (*Ecologist, 1* (5)).

RUBBISH. Some organic products are very resistant to breakdown by bacteria and the current use of plastics and other durable material presents a difficulty of disposal as landfill areas become scarce, which has been 'solved' in some cases by dumping in nearshore waters. Reports have been made of such debris obliterating the habitats of many organisms, leading to the impoverishment of local flora and fauna. Even the deepest trenches of the ocean now frequently yield products of our civilization. The unrestricted dumping of refuse from ocean-going vessels has led to the strandlines of even the remotest shores being cluttered with beer cans and plastic containers. The age of the non-returnable container is upon us! The production of disposable containers cannot go on *ad infinitum* as the sources of material for construction are finite. It is surely better to make a greater effort now on seeking methods of recycling our rubbish than to wait until the cupboard is bare.

PULP MILL LIQUORS. Industry, because of the demonstrable harm already done by its waste products on land and in freshwater, tends now to expel much of its liquid waste into the sea, but here also the effects on marine life are being noticed. Sulphite liquors from pulp mills have been seen to interfere with the assimilation processes of phytoplanktonic organisms which are the first essential link in the food-chain of most marine life. Although in low concentrations liquors do not kill animals outright, feeding and growth of oysters can be interrupted, larval development and behaviour of herring affected and many species of fish suffer respiratory difficulties.

HEAVY METALS. Many types of industrial waste contain heavy metals in solution. These metals are normally present in minute quantities in unpolluted sea-water where their concentration has been reasonably constant for millions of years. Marine organisms therefore have not evolved mechanisms to protect themselves from large fluctuations in metal concentration.

M

Thus most organisms are unable to prevent the concentration of metals within their body tissues passively rising to a level which, even if not lethal, may affect their body chemistry. In fact, some filter-feeding animals, especially those with calcareous shells, will actively concentrate metals to a level many thousands of times higher ($\times 200,000$) than that in the surrounding seawater.

COPPER AND ZINC. The growth of the large brown seaweeds of inshore waters is adversely affected by an excess of copper and zinc in the water, and when a quantity of copper sulphate was dumped in Dutch coastal waters the mortality of mussels in beds several miles away was alarming. Experiments on other shellfish more resistant to heavy metal poisoning have shown that sub-lethal amounts of copper and zinc lead to regressive changes in the gut diverticula and damage to the stomach wall. Predatory animals which do not normally accumulate metals may as a result of their feeding behaviour attain a sufficient quantity of these metals to kill them. For example, an inshore demersal fish feeding on the ragworm may die as a result of the worm's ability to concentrate copper in its tissues. Copper and zinc discharged from estuaries may prevent Atlantic salmon reaching their spawning grounds, for it has been discovered that they will avoid waters containing these pollutants even at very low concentrations.

MERCURY AND SILVER. The industrial uses of mercury compounds are numerous; they are used as fungicidal seed dressings, in paper-making and as catalysts in the manufacture of PVC. Numerous cases of sterility of seed-eating birds and predators, including man, have been traced to the habit of seed-dressing with mercury compounds. This practice is also a hazard to coastal marine life which is exposed to mercury as a result of freshwater run off. A recent research report that a very low concentration (1 part per billion) of fungicidal mercury is sufficient to cause a 50 per cent drop in photosynthetic activity of a phytoplanktonic test organism is particularly alarming, for, such concentrations are frequently found at the mouths of rivers draining agricultural land and near industrial outfalls. It is possible that inshore phytoplankton (and consequently those animals that feed on it) is being seriously affected.

The concentration of mercury and silver found around certain industrial outfalls is also sufficient to cause abnormal or inhibited development of eggs and larvae of certain barnacles and sea urchins. Other marine organisms, however, may accumulate metals without any readily apparent harm being done to them. Some shellfish and fish have such a high concentration of mercury within their tissues that people are advised not to eat them for fear of being poisoned. From 1953 to 1960 almost one hundred people were killed

Pollution of the Seas

after eating fish and shellfish taken from Minamata Bay in Japan. The cause of their death was a lethal amount of mercury in the bodies of the marine life derived from the mercury-laden effluent of a plastics factory.

The danger of mercury in the marine environment has now been recognized by many governments, but how many other metals may be accumulating undetected in the bodies of sea life?

From the few examples cited it can be seen that the directly poisonous action of heavy metals is not the only consideration, for there is evidence that long-term accumulation and concentration of metals by marine organisms can lead, if not always to their own death, to death of others that eat them. Clearly discharge of heavy metals into coastal waters should be actively discouraged.

PESTICIDES AND PCBS. Pesticides are deliberately applied in the terrestrial environment in order to control insect pests, weeds, fungi, *etc*. They reach the sea not only as a result of land drainage but also from the atmosphere. Indeed, it has been concluded by some American workers that the observed distribution of the chlorinated hydrocarbon pesticide DDT and its residues off the coast of California can only be explained by assuming distribution through the atmosphere. Corroboratory evidence for atmospheric distribution comes from the fact that organochlorine residues can be detected in ice and in the fatty tissues of penguins and seals from the Antarctic where pesticides to the best of our knowledge have never been applied.

Polychlorinated biphenyls (PCBs), unlike pesticides, reach the environment by accident. They are used in the manufacture of paints and varnishes, as softeners in plastics and for improving electrical insulation in cables. Many high-temperature lubrication oils now contain PCBS. PCBS reach the ocean in liquid waste from industrial and domestic sources, from decomposing rubbish dumped at sea and from the atmosphere polluted by smoke from industry, motor vehicles and rubbish dumps.

The danger of both chlorinated hydrocarbon pesticides and PBCs is that they are extremely stable and persist for long periods of time without biodegrading into a harmless form. Some organochlorines have been in use for 30 years or more so that if only minute quantities have been reaching the sea during this period they have had time to build up in the water and sediments. In addition many invertebrates have the ability to concentrate them many thousands of times and store them in their fatty tissues in much the same way as metals are concentrated and stored.

Many planktonic species of animal and plant as well as fish and benthonic invertebrates are extraordinarily sensitive to organochlorine pesticides, especially in the earlier stages of their life history, and can be killed outright by residues reaching the sea by land drainage and in effluents from manu-

179

facturing plants. The waste from a parathion manufacturing plant on the Danish North Sea Coast led to many dead and dying lobsters being cast up on local beaches. Other species higher up food-chains may be poisoned by eating animals and plants that have accumulated pesticides in their tissues. Sandwich Terns dying in tremors and convulsions in the Danish Wadden Zee were found to have been poisoned by chlorinated hydrocarbons passed on from herrings and sand eels which in turn had been feeding on planktonic and benthonic copepod invertebrates with a high level of organochlorine entering their diet due to pesticide discharge from the Rhine. By the time the pesticides had reached the Terns they had been concentrated many thousands of times. Due to the greater sensitivity to pesticides of some marine species as compared with others the balance of certain ecosystems can be seriously affected, animals at the top of the food-chain dying as a result of non-availability of a particular food source. The demise of the Californian Sardine industry has been attributed to such a situation.

As disturbing as the direct kills attributed to pesticides are the numerous sub-lethal effects that have been reported in scientific papers. These include alterations in body chemistry, disturbance of growth and gonad formation, interference with thermal acclimation mechanisms, lowering of resistance to disease and changes in the basic behaviour patterns of various species. Of necessity much of this experimental work has been carried out on commercially important shellfish and fish but this does not mean that other groups of animals are any less affected.

Organophosphorous and carbamate pesticides which are now being used increasingly for pest control are much less stable than organochlorines and consequently do not accumulate through food-chains to the same degree. There is thus less chance that animals higher up the food-chains will receive sufficiently large doses of pesticide to affect their biology.

The chemical similarity between PCBs and organochlorine pesticides suggests similar physiological effects on marine organisms. However, at present little is known of the adverse effects of PCBs, although in laboratory experiments it has been shown that these chemicals can affect the production of sex hormones in such a way that animals are rendered infertile. It may not be entirely coincidental that the fertility rate of guillemots at breeding sites on the British west coast is dropping. In September 1969 between 10,000 and 15,000 dead sea-birds, mostly guillemots, were washed up along the west coast of Britain. Although it is by no means certain what caused their deaths, fatty tissues of the birds contained relatively high amounts of PCBs.

Marine life will be increasingly placed at risk if the release of chlorinated hydrocarbon pesticides and PCBs into the environment is allowed in anything but very small quantities. No one will deny the short-term benefits that have been reaped by the use of DDT and its derivatives but we have got to

180

consider the long-term consequences of their use. Already in a confined area like the Baltic marine species contain on average eight to ten times more DDT than the same species in the North Sea. Organochlorine pesticides should only be used in an emergency and should not be applied as a prophylactic.

RADIOACTIVE WASTE. Radiation has long been recognized as a factor constituting a potential hazard to human populations, if not to marine life. Radioactive materials reach the sea (1) from the atmosphere, (2) as a result of natural leaching of rocks containing radioactive compounds, (3) from containers of radioactive waste dumped at sea, (4) from outfall pipes of coastal nuclear installations.

Due to concern over the wide dissemination of radioactive dust following nuclear explosions in the atmosphere very few tests of atomic devices now take place above ground. Hence only very small amounts of radioactive dust in excess of the background quantities now reach the sea via the atmosphere.

In certain coastal areas of the world high background radiation is present due to naturally occurring radionuclides in the soil. Unfortunately, there is as yet no published information available on the effects on marine life in these areas, although statistical surveys on human populations in one of these regions has shown a significantly higher than normal rate of occurrence of chromosome abnormalities.

Radioactive wastes of short half-life can be stored at the point of production until inactive, but the problems of storage of wastes which decay at a slow rate are enormous. Much radioactive waste is stored in heavily shielded containers on land, but other wastes are encased and dumped in selected deepwater sites in the ocean. Due to the high cost of providing adequate shielding for dumped containers, some do not completely prevent escape of radiation. It must be accepted, therefore, that damage to marine life may occur in the region of these dumps.

The continuous discharge of low-level radioactive wastes from coastal nuclear plant may also be causing sub-lethal damage to marine life in the vicinity of the discharge point. For it has been shown experimentally that low levels of radiation can cause chromosomal damage, with subsequent growth abnormalities, in both marine invertebrates and vertebrates. Effects may be even more subtle, as their is some evidence to suggest that exposure of fish to radiation can reduce their ability to tolerate changes in temperature and salinity.

Marine organisms, such as algae and shellfish, which concentrate metals cannot discriminate between radioactive and non-radioactive elements. Thus the radiation levels in certain organisms may be many thousands of times higher than that in the surrounding sea-water. For example, oysters gathered

181

some 250 miles from a nuclear source were seen to contain 200,000 times more radioactive zinc than the surrounding ocean. In theory the existing regulations relating to the discharge of radioactive waste take into account the ability of many organisms to concentrate elements in their tissues. However, the number of species examined in relation to the number occurring in coastal waters is very small.

It is certainly unwise to set any acceptable dose levels of radiation as far as marine life is concerned in view of the subtle nature of radiation damage unless they are based on long-term statistical experiments.

OIL. Every year more and more crude and refined oils are transported across the oceans and the hazard of pollution of the sea by oil increases. Oil reaches the sea in some areas of the world as a result of natural seepage but the vast majority of oil present in the oceans today has been introduced by man either by accident or deliberately. The public are very much aware of the aesthetic threat posed by occasional major marine disasters which instantly release many thousands of tons of oil into the environment. However, much of the oil entering the sea accidentally results from minor spillages while oil is being loaded or off-loaded, from leaks at marine oil-well heads and from river water and untreated sewage containing tars, fuels and lubricants. Small craft when present in sufficiently large numbers may cause significant pollution.

By far the largest quantity of oil reaching the sea at the present time is deliberately discharged by vessels flushing out their oil tanks and pumping out contaminated ballast and bilge water. Happily the major oil companies of the world now only allow oil-contaminated water to be discharged into oil separators at their shore installations. At present, International Conventions do not completely prevent discharge of oil at sea but only limit it to specified offshore areas. Thus oily residues can be found floating on the surface of the sea anywhere in the world, although, of course, they are found more frequently in the shipping lanes. If, as seems likely, at a future date the deliberate discharge of oil is completely banned anywhere at sea we can expect to see a drop in oil pollution.

Oil deposited at sea may affect marine organisms either mechanically or chemically. Crude oil consists of a complex mixture of hydrocarbons. The aromatic hydrocarbons represent its most dangerous fraction and are very poisonous to all marine life. Other fractions, although not necessarily acutely toxic, often cause long-term damage by affecting many body processes.

While oil films remain floating at sea they do not present a physical hazard to marine life other than that which exists or feeds at the air/water interface. There is a specialized surface community, known as the neuston, which may be seriously affected mechanically by the oil, and the gills of fish feeding on

Pollution of the Seas

the neuston also may become clogged by oil. Air-breathing marine vertebrates belonging to the reptiles, birds and mammals may find their air passages and lungs become obstructed with oil, preventing gaseous exchange.

All sea-birds (diving birds in particular) are very susceptible to oiling of the plumage which prevents them flying and eventually leads to their death by drowning or by starvation. The birds in their efforts to clean themselves ingest quantities of oil which cause enteritis and other damage to the digestive system. Toxins present in the ingested oil cause degenerative changes in the liver and kidneys of sea-birds, and there is evidence that they may lead to a reduction in breeding success. This knowledge combined with the fact that the species most usually affected by oil already have a low reproductive potential leads one to the conclusion that several species of sea-bird may be in danger of extinction as a result of oil pollution.

The neuston and other planktonic organisms are liable to be affected by the toxicity of soluble oil fractions disseminated from oil floating on the surface. Experimental exposure to oil of phytoplankton from the Black Sea, Mediterranean, Red Sea and Atlantic shows that death or retardation of cell division can result. The sensitivity of different species varies by several orders or magnitude, thus in estuaries or other sheltered waters where persistent oil pollution occurs the more sensitive species are probably slowly being excluded.

The eggs and larvae of many pelagic and benthic animals spend many weeks in the surface layers of the sea during their development. The egg and larval stages of the commercially important plaice and herring, for instance, display high mortality and various ontogenetic abnormalities when exposed to small quantities of various oil fractions. The larvae of hermit crabs and prawns are similarly affected. Generally speaking, however, development stages of wholly planktonic species are more sensitive to the toxins in oils than are the development stages of animals that do not spend the whole of their life-cycle in the plankton.

The severity of damage to marine life depends to some extent on the type of oil released into the environment. Refined fuel oils seem to cause considerably more immediate damage than crude oils. Thus when a spillage of diesel oil occurred in a restricted area as the result of the grounding of the *Tampico* on the western seaboard of North America only four species of attached plants and two species of benthic animals survived. Similar mass mortality of benthic organisms has been reported as a result of the spillage of refined oil from a fuel barge which struck submerged rocks off West Falmouth, USA. In contrast the Kuwait crude oil reaching the beaches of south-western England after the *Torrey Canyon* disaster appeared immediately to kill animals and plants only if it was so thick as to smother them. This does not mean, however, that animals surviving the initial onslaught of the oil survived unharmed, for it has been shown in long-term experiments that the filter-feeding mechanisms and guts of shellfish may become so clogged with oil that the animals slowly die of starvation. In addition water-soluble substances in crude oils have a narcotizing effect on the rate of ciliary beat in filter-feeding animals such as oysters and barnacles. Water-soluble fractions further damage the feeding potential of oysters by retarding the growth of one of its major plant-food sources.

In the region of certain refineries sufficient oil pollutants are present in the aquatic environment to cause tainting of shellfish, and many incidents have been reported of resistance to stress, and reproductive potential, being adversely affected by sub-lethal amounts of oil.

Once oil pollutants enter the tissues of animals they are retained for long periods of time without breaking down and thus they become a potential hazard to predators. Prolonged contact with refined oils leads to skin cancers in man and there is now evidence to suggest that some marine organisms are similarly affected.

Many fish rely on the reception of chemical clues to find their prey, sexual partners and areas in which to spawn. The presence of high boiling-point saturated and aromatic hydrocarbons in the sea, even in minute concentrations, can block their ability to receive such signals.

Although occasional spillages of oil in coastal areas may cause severe local damage to marine life, it is unlikely that this type of pollution will destroy a sufficient number of individuals of a particular species to endanger any shallow-water species (other than diving birds), as repopulation will take place from the surrounding areas within a few years. However, continuous low level pollution may cause a change in the ecology of a region bringing about a slow decline in the variety and quantity of marine life.

It is obvious that the danger to marine life from oil and its compounds is such that every available method of preventing entry of oil into the sea should be used.

OIL DISPERSANTS ('*Detergents*'). Oil spills which foul beaches and shore installations, as well as slicks at sea which are considered a potential danger to the coastline, are often treated with oil-dispersing liquids. The justification for deliberately dispersing oil through the water column instead of leaving it as a compact film on the water surface is primarily an aesthetic one, for nobody likes to see our coastline befouled by oil. One cannot fail to be upset by the pathetic sight of sea-birds coated with oil washed ashore in their hundreds. The plight of some diving-bird species is undeniably grave and justification can be found for dispersing oil when it occurs in quantity near their feeding areas.

Dispersal of oil into small droplets permits microbial action to proceed more rapidly than normal thus allowing oil to be removed from the environment more quickly than would otherwise be possible. However, in the majority of cases the use of dispersants is not justifiable since emulsification of the oil only distributes it more evenly through the environment making it virtually certain that every organism in the area will be exposed to the toxic fractions present in the oil. It has been found that many marine organisms, such as fish, which can normally avoid oil slicks, ingest and assimilate fairly large quantities of well-dispersed hydrocarbons.

Until just recently the only 'detergents' available for oil dispersal were dissolved in low boiling point aromatic hydrocarbons – the most toxic fraction of crude oils! Unfortunately, these dispersants are still very much in general use and can result in the death of many marine organisms when being used to clear oil. At the time of the *Torrey Canyon* disaster several shores were so thoroughly cleaned with detergent that it was difficult to find a live marine organism on them.

The sub-lethal long-term effects of these dispersants are less well known but it has been noticed that the growth of many phytoplanktonic and attached algal species is seriously impaired. Among inshore species of animal, larval growth of clams and oysters is slowed and adult shell growth interrupted. Dogwhelks that have recovered from near-lethal doses of detergent show growth disturbances in the shell.

Behavioural patterns of animals can be modified as a consequence of detergent pollution. Observations made at the time of the *Torrey Canyon* spill showed that dispersant-laden sea-water caused inhibition of the normal climbing response in winkles and topshells, and led to razor shells and heart urchins coming to the surface of the sand in which they are normally buried. Such effects put the animals at a competitive disadvantage and make them more susceptible to attack by predators.

Sub-lethal doses of dispersants can interfere with the life-cycle of shallow water species, preventing some animals from reproducing and the planktonic larvae of others from settling.

The obvious damage to marine life caused by these emulsifiers has led to the evolution of a new generation of dispersants in which the lethal aromatic carrier solvents have been replaced by far less toxic ones. Even so, long-term effects are still noticeable, and it is these that are the most important in the long run.

The use of oil dispersants, therefore, does nothing more than introduce another poison into the sea and makes the toxins present in crude oil more readily available to marine life. Unless used in moderation on the shore and in sheltered coastal regions where regular oil spills occur they cannot help but lead to a reduction in the variety of marine life existing there.

I have only mentioned some of the more common pollutants entering the ocean and affecting its inhabitants. There are many thousands of other substances released into the sea whose effects on the ecosystem have yet to be investigated. Nevertheless the evidence put forward is, I hope, enough to convince people that waste products from our society cannot be introduced into the marine environment without causing damage to marine life. The effects may not be immediately apparent but may be noticed only over a period of years as the natural stability of the ecosystem is upset in that area. The reduction in variety of marine life existing in the heavily polluted inshore areas of North-east England is already very marked. Even more worrying is the decline in abundance over the last 20 years of many characteristic species of phytoplankton and zooplankton in the North-east Atlantic and North Sea; for the plankton is the grass of the sea on which all other life in the oceans is ultimately dependent.

Attempts to stop further pollution leading to the slow decrease in diversity of marine life in our oceans, should take into account the adage 'waste not, want not'. It is an admission of defeat by society that we cannot recycle our own waste products. Perhaps it is only a sick society that already has the ability to recycle many of its waste products, but finds it more 'economical' to throw them away. The onus should be placed on potential polluters to prove that the products they wish to introduce into the sea are harmless to marine life in both the long-term and the short-term. In other words the wastes should be considered 'guilty until proved innocent'.

We have reached a point where we cannot simply think of the quality of the environment as some nebulous entity to be sacrificed on the altar of technological advance. For in the long-term it is only an ability to remain in balance with the rest of life on this planet that will save man from disaster.

REFERENCES

ARTHUR, D. R. 1969. *Survival: Man and his environments*. London: English University Press.

BARDACH, J. 1968. *Harvest of the Sea*. London: Allen and Unwin.

CARTHY, J. D. and D. R. ARTHUR (Ed.). 1968. The biological effects of oil-pollution on littoral communities. In *Field Studies, 2* (supplement).

FONSELIUS, S. H. 1970. Stagnant sea. In *Environment, 12* (6).

HEDGPETH, J. W. 1970. The Oceans: World sump. In *Environment, 12* (3).

HOULT, D. P. (Ed.). 1969. *Oil on the Sea*. New York: London: Plenum Press.

KINNE, O. and H. AURICH (Ed.). 1967. International Symposium: Biological and Hydrographical problems of water pollution in the North Sea and adjacent waters. In *Helgoländer wiss Meersunters, 17*.

MELLANBY, K. 1970. (2nd edition.) *Pesticides and pollution*. London: Collins.

Pollution of the Seas

RISEBROUGH, R. and V. BRODINE. 1970. More letters in the wind. In *Environment*, *12* (1).

SMITH, J. E. (Ed.). 1968. *Torrey Canyon: Pollution and Marine Life*. Cambridge: CUP.

WILBER, C. G. 1969. *The Biological Aspects of Water Pollution*. Springfield, Illinois: Thomas Books.

18 POLLUTION COSTS

Edward Goldsmith

Editor, *The Ecologist*

In what way does pollution affect the country as a whole? What is its total cost to us? This is difficult to answer as no one has really defined the term 'cost'. It normally refers to 'economic' cost, *i.e.* to cost that can be measured in terms of the units of measurement used by economists. But are these the right units of measurement? One cannot, for instance, measure social and ecological costs in these terms; at least, not until they begin to affect economic life. This, of course, they must do in the long run, and perhaps one can take them into account by referring to them as 'delayed economic costs'.

Thus, for over 150 years, industrial waste has been poured into the air, rivers and seas, without any apparent adverse effect on our economy, so much so that it is assumed by many people that the world's capacity for absorbing waste products is infinite. Unfortunately, this is not so. The environment can absorb a finite amount of different wastes; beyond that these tend to accumulate so that even if the annual amount disposed of was constant, which as we know is not the case, the total amount in the environment would be increasing more or less exponentially, depending on their persistence.

Also there must be thresholds beyond which levels for different pollutants become lethal. Before these thresholds are reached, the effects are not easily observable. This does not mean that biological damage is not being done and that ecological costs are not being incurred, but that they will only be translated into economic costs once they have led to a reduction in economic activity.

The reason why there has been this sudden interest in pollution is that many of these thresholds are now being reached and pollution is beginning to affect our economy.

There appear to be few satisfactory studies of the cost of pollution to our society. However, in the United States, Lester B. Lave and Eugene Seskin[1] of the Carnegie–Mellon University estimate that roughly 25 per cent of all respiratory disease is associated with air pollution. This means that the cost of air pollution to health in the United States was about $2 billion in 1963, the last year for which usable data is available.

Professor Thomas D. Crocker, of the University of Wisconsin, and Pro-

Pollution Costs

fessor Robert J. Anderson Junior, of the University of Purdue,[1] have estimated that an increase in air pollution of from 5 to 15 per cent, reflected in off-colour paint, ailing shrubbery, sooty surfaces and unpleasant odours, takes $300–$700 off the value of a house. On this basis air pollution in 1965 was costing America $621 million in reduced property values.

The *Beaver Committee Report* put the cost of air pollution in Britain on our health and property at £350 million. This was 16 years ago, and it was probably even then a conservative estimate (see Albone, Chapter 14).

Gerald H. Michael, Assistant Surgeon General, has calculated that the 173 million tons of contaminants ejected annually into the atmosphere in the United States costs Americans $10–$20 billion a year in medical bills and cleaning bills.

According to the National Air Pollution Control Administration, the figure is between $14 and $18 million.[2]

The harm done by sulphur dioxide alone to crops in the United States has been estimated at more than $500 million a year. The damage done by the countless poisons we pour into rivers and seas in terms of reduced fish catches must also be colossal, and can only go on increasing. Mercury alone has been considered responsible for an annual billion's-worth of damage world-wide.

Representative James Murphy of Staten Island, member of the Merchant Marine and Fisheries Committee, asserts that pollution in general costs the United States more than $30 billion a year and predicts that this figure will rise to $60 billion by 1980.

From these terrifying figures, it must be apparent that pollution control is not the luxury many people think it is. To refuse, for economic or political reasons, to install pollution control equipment is not to save money, again as many people think but simply to pay the cost of pollution in a different currency: in reduced plant yields, in larger cleaning bills, in higher medical costs, *etc.*

Also the amount of money spent on pollution control has up till now been but a minute fraction of total pollution costs. In Britain the £32 million spent on air pollution control is less than an eleventh of total cost as estimated by the Beaver Committee. In the United States the $10 billion that President Nixon proposes to spend before 1975 (assuming that it is in fact spent, which is by no means sure) is also but a fraction of what it will really cost to clean up that country's polluted environment. Let us briefly examine this.

The cost of eliminating water pollution depends primarily on the degree of cleanliness we seek to achieve.

As urbanization progresses, the amount of sewage requiring secondary treatment must increase. In the United States by 1973, according to the

189

Federal Water Pollution Control Agency, 90 per cent of the urban population will need secondary sewage systems.[2]

According to the Federal Water Pollution Control Administration this would require over $8 billion in water treatment plants (exclusive of land costs) and over $6 billion in sewers. Secondary treatment of industrial wastes will cost another $5 billion in construction. To separate storm and household sewers could cost anywhere from $10 billion to $48 billion and to control thermal pollution will cost yet another $2 billion. In addition, operating costs for all these facilities would be almost $2 billion for the municipal plants, $3·5 billion for the industrial plants and about $1 billion for the thermal processes.[2]

If America really wants clean water and decides to build tertiary treatment plants, then the construction costs would jump from $31 billion to about $90 billion. This figure is not far off Professor Barry Commoner's estimate of $100 billion to clean up US rivers.

The Federal Water Pollution Control Administration estimates that between $26 and $29 billion will have to be spent between 1969 and 1973.[2] A National Survey in July estimated that between $33 and $37 billion will have to be spent within the next 6 years.

In Britain, there are few estimates of the cost of fighting water pollution. We have 20,000 miles of rivers, of which 5,000 are polluted and 2,000 grossly polluted. According to Mr Anthony Crossland, in a speech at the Guildhall, January 1970, it would cost £30 million to clean up 4 miles of the River Tyne, but this is a particularly bad stretch. The *Jeger Report* estimates that the GLC must spend £100 million on cleaning up the Thames Estuary.

Tees-side Borough Council has calculated that £22 million are needed just to clean up the River Tees over 10–12 years. £500 million has been estimated as the sum required to bring 1,000 miles of grossly polluted British rivers just to tolerable standards.[3] Once more, the cost of control must depend on the degree of cleanliness we require, and this can only go up as we depend more and more on our rivers for drinking water.

According to the *Jeger Report*, 3,000 of our 5,000 sewage works are at the moment overloaded and produce effluent below the quality associated with secondary treatment. Mr Craig Sinclair of Sussex University estimates that £260,000,000 a year must be spent on sewage works, which is twice what is spent at the moment.[3]

Estimates of the cost of controlling air pollution are even more difficult. According to Professor Goldman, they range in the United States from $300 million to $3 billion a year simply for construction costs. In the latter case, this would mean capital expenditure of a little less than $100 billion by the year 2000. This only covers emissions from stationary sources. Air pollution from motor-cars is an even more serious problem and in many

190

Pollution Costs

US cities motor vehicles are responsible for as much as 80 per cent of it. According to Professor Goldman, controlling air pollution from cars might add up to another $2–$3 billion a year. A recent survey suggests a figure of $400 per car or a total of $40 billion.

Dr Ernest Starkman, Chairman of the Technical Advisory Committee of the California Air Resources Board, asserts that, if air pollution were to be cut down to 'levels that would keep the atmosphere clean', one would have to expend an extra $1,000 per motor-car or approximately $100 billion, if every one of the cars at present in use in the United States were appropriately equipped.

The actual cost clearly depends on what percentage of total pollution one wishes to eliminate. It is important to realize that we can never get rid of all of it. As Professor Goldman writes, 'Institution of $100 billion worth of air quality controls would not mean the elimination of all air pollution nor of the costs that arise from it,' but it would considerably reduce the cost of air pollution in terms of medical bills and cleaning bills and help defray the costs of operating expenses.

In Britain, up till now there has been practically no legislation to reduce pollution from motor-cars as it has been considered too expensive. The recent report of the Royal College of Physicians on air pollution and health, has revealed that the savings are largely illusory. Nevertheless, in order to justify the government's short-sightedness, the government's official position has been that there is no evidence that air pollution is bad for people, at least at existing levels.

Recently, there seems to have been a radical change of policy as Mr Peter Walker announced very firmly on 1 December 1970, that the government intends to introduce very strict measures to control pollution from the exhausts of motor cars.

One can also expect in the United States and eventually here measures to reduce lead pollution of the air which we know to have a very serious effect on human health. The cost of tetraethyl additives from petrol which will be responsible for much of this pollution is likely to be particularly expensive. According to the Ethyl Corporation, these additives save the United States 215 million barrels of oil each year. The cost of this extra oil consumption would amount to at least $3 billion for the public to pay each year and $6 billion to be met by the oil companies. If octane ratings are to be maintained, then further changes are required which will probably give rise to other forms of pollution and hence require further costly controls.[4]

In the United Kingdom Lord Rothschild, head of the government's new Capability Unit recently said that the exhaust from cars could be purified at a cost of an extra £50–£100 per car, while £5–£10 would be required to get rid of the lead.

According to Geoffrey Charles, Americans have already spent $10 billion on anti-pollution devices for their cars and it is estimated that they will have to spend another $15 billion.[5] Businesses must undoubtedly foot a considerable part of the bill, as the principle that businesses must pay for the disposal of their own waste is rapidly becoming accepted both by government and industry.

In the United States businesses spent an estimated $1·5 billion to control air and water pollution created by them, which is an increase of 40 per cent over the previous year. The National Industrial Conference Board estimates that investment to control air and water pollution rose from 2 per cent of manufacturer's capital outlay in 1967 to close to 4 per cent in 1968. A good number of companies questioned by *Fortune* report that they are spending 10 per cent of capital outlays, and in extreme cases the figure was 30 per cent.[6]

In Japan where public awareness of pollution is of recent origin, already 5 per cent of capital expenditure, according to a recent Ministry of International Trade and Industry report, is devoted to pollution control equipment, while in the chemical industry, the figure is closer to 12 per cent. These figures are increasing every year and must continue to do so at an ever greater rate.

The chemical industry is among those most affected by pollution control problems. It is producing an ever-wider range of chemicals which are ending up in our rivers and hence in our water supply. The Institute of Water Engineers warned that, as a result, our water supply is in a precarious position. Many of the chemicals cannot be identified, let alone filtered out. Clearly very tight controls will have to be imposed. Pollution of water supplies with detergents, insecticides and artificial fertilizers is also becoming a matter of national concern and it is but a matter of time before controls are adopted that will seriously reduce the profitability of the industries producing them. In the meantime the major chemical companies are planning large increases in their expenditire on pollution control.

In the United States Du Pont has made a cumulative investment of $125 million in air- and water-pollution control. Its yearly operating costs for this purpose run to over $25 million.[6]

In the United Kingdom ICI plans to spend £60 million over the next 10 years on equipment to control its effluents.

The paper industry is also likely to be severely affected. According to Professor Barry Commoner, $300 million a year would have to be spent in this industry just to meet current US pollution standards. This would apparently reduce the industry's profits by one third.

Macmillan Bloedel has announced that in addition to the $19 million it has already spent on pollution control, it proposes to spend another $30 million in the next 5 years. Meanwhile in the United States an ever-increasing number

192

Pollution Costs

of paper mills unable to meet pollution standards have been forced to close down.

The steel industry is also vulnerable. In the United States it is estimated to use 8 billion gallons of water per day for cooling and other purposes, and causes extremely serious pollution to waterways. It is already spending considerable sums. US Steel has invested $235 million up to date.

Bethlehem Steel plans to raise annual capital expenditure of 6 per cent per annum to 11 per cent.

Armco Steel spent $74 million from 1966 to 1969. The American Iron and Steel Institute states that reporting members are spending $325 million per year for pollution control.

In the United Kingdom British Steel is currently spending £5½ million a year on construction costs. Of this, £4 million are spent on air-pollution control and £1½ million on water-treatment plant. Operating costs are £1·2 million for the former and £750,000 for the latter. Expenditure is expected to increase by 50 per cent over the next 5 years.

The cost of controlling pollution from power stations must also increase very radically. In New York, Mayor Lindsay is faced with the serious dilemma of whether to allow Consolidated Edison to build more power stations, thereby increasing the already serious levels of air pollution in the city of New York or else face an ever-worsening chronic power shortage. The solution adopted will clearly be to build more power stations but to impose ever more drastic pollution control standards.

New York Consolidated Edison has already spent $16 million on pollution control equipment including $10 million on a precipitator to curb smoke pollution.

The Illinois Commerce Commission is forcing Commonwealth Edison to spend more than $30 million a year in the next 6 years. A 4·5 per cent price increase will provide this company with $16 million a year of this money. The rest must come out of profits. The Boston Edison Company announced recently that new air pollution regulations would cost their customers $22 million more a year. This is mainly the result of being forced to use low sulphur fuel oil. They calculate that it will add 7 per cent to the cost of domestic lighting bills, 8 per cent to the bills of commercial users and 14 per cent to industrial bills.

The cost of eliminating noise pollution is also exorbitant. For instance, to fit the entire commercial aircraft fleet in the United States so as to reduce noise to acceptable levels is estimated at $500–$750 million according to the Secretary of Transportation, James E. Beggs. A more dramatic programme to 'retrofit' the whole US airline fleet with engine silencers would cost $2 billion. If supersonic transports are banned from landing at US airfields which is a definite possibility, then the cost in terms of money wasted on research will be colossal. More than £800 million have already been spent in Britain on the Concorde, and the French must also have incurred very high costs on this absurd project.

The cost of controlling pollution of the seas may be highest of all. Practically all our waste products end up in the seas, and they cannot absorb it all indefinitely. Strict measures will undoubtedly soon have to be taken to curb oil pollution by tankers. Nuclear power stations will have to find ways of reducing levels of radioactive waste at present ejected into the seas. Pesticide levels will have to be reduced which simply means that farmers will have to use less of these poisons, though this may in the long run represent a saving both in expenditure and crop yields. There will also have to be a limit to the amount of solid waste indiscriminately tipped into the sea. At present the cost of collecting solid waste in the United States including 7 million cars, 100 billion tyres, 2 million tons of paper, 20 billion bottles and 48 billion cans adds up to about $2·8 billion. Much of this ends up in the seas. More sophisticated means of disposal are clearly required, and this must radically increase expenditure.

The total cost of controlling all different types of pollution, has I am sure never been calculated. Senator Gaylord Nelson estimates that in the United States it will be between $25 and $30 billion a year. 'No administration has understood the size of the issue. It is much more important than space programmes, weapons systems or the money we are wasting in Vietnam.'

Professor Goldman estimates that the cost of controlling air and water and solid waste pollution will be between $130 and $180 billion in construction costs, and will involve between $12 and $17 billion in annual operating costs. These amount to approximately 1–2 per cent of the annual Gross National Product (GNP) and to 4–7 per cent of the value of industrial, agricultural, mining and transportation output. This only includes the cost of secondary sewage plants. If tertiary sewage plants are installed, then construction costs go up to $200 billion.[2]

This figure does not include construction costs involved in reducing pollution from motor-cars or aeroplanes, nor any undertaken to reduce noise pollution or pollution of the seas, save by improving the quality of effluent to our rivers. Estimates for a more comprehensive programme of pollution control would thus be considerably higher.

How important is it that this money should be spent? There are two ways of looking at it. Firstly, pollution control must tend not only to reduce the short-term economic costs but also long-term or delayed economic ones, *i.e.* long-term social and ecological costs. From this point of view money spent on pollution control will have a far more beneficial effect than might be supposed. Also, pollution control can also be regarded as maintaining or restoring those conditions that will permit further demographic and economic

194

growth. As such, it is too a means of suppressing some of the more noxious symptoms of these processes which can only serve to render them more tolerable and contribute thereby to their perpetuation. In this way pollution control will favour the continued depletion of our natural resources, the disintegration of society and other calamities brought about by continued growth.

Pollution control in other words cannot by itself provide a solution to the environmental crisis. It is but a short-term expedient, a useful, indeed a necessary one so long as we realize that it is basically only a means of gaining time and can only be of long-term usefulness if this time is used for what are the only really effective measures, *i.e.* reducing demographic and economic growth. Meanwhile, let us try to predict how the cost of pollution will be affected by developments in the next few decades. Firstly, one must realize that pollutants over and above that level that can be absorbed by our environment tend to accumulate. This means that even if they are being generated at a constant rate, the total amount in the environment will increase by something approaching compound interest depending on their persistence. Unfortunately since the amount generated is roughly a function of economic activity, so a growing economy will mean a still greater rate of pollutant accumulation.

As already mentioned, it is important to realize that the effect of pollutants on biological organisms is unlikely to be linear. There are likely to be thresholds below which concentrations have only sub-lethal long-term effects, but above which serious biological damage becomes apparent. When these thresholds are reached, observable and measurable damage to crops, wildlife and humans will start soaring.

With oil transported across the seas trebling every ten years, interest in the long-term sub-lethal effects of oil pollution has increased. Dr Max Blumer in the United States and Dr J. D. George in the United Kingdom have pointed to its very serious nature. It is possible that in the next decades the accumulated effects of oil pollution will become very costly in terms of fish resources.

The levels of pesticides in marine organisms, birds and surprisingly enough in our rainwater is also on the increase – not surprisingly as pesticides in the United States are a $450 million business, and in the United Kingdom £20 million worth are sold, a sum that is increasing at 6 per cent per annum.[7] It must be but a question of time before these levels are no longer tolerated and start taking their toll in human lives.

I think that one can take it as axiomatic that governments and businesses will spend as little on pollution control as they can possibly get away with. Conservationist pressure can force their hand to a certain extent. Political and economic necessity, however, must be the ultimate determinant of the amount of money spent on pollution control.

Thus DDT was banned for 2 years in Sweden only when herrings were found to contain higher than permissible levels of this poison, which rendered them unsaleable.

In Britain the Clean Air Act was passed only after 3,000 people had died from the effects of smog in the winter of 1952.

In Northern Italy businesses are spending a lot of money on water-pollution control equipment, and advertising the fact in the popular press to show just how socially responsible they are. The fact is that they are running out of usable water and their choice is clear cut: either to spend the money or close down.

Situations of this sort are likely to occur more and more. For instance, in Japan, pollution is so bad that in certain industrial areas, further expansion is simply no longer viable. Manufacturers are getting round this by setting up manufacturing facilities in other countries, mainly in South-East Asia, though Toyota is apparently looking around for a suitable site in Europe.

We have here a totally new phenomenon, 'Industrial Nomadism'. Manufacturers pollute an area until it is incapable of supporting further industrial growth and then move off to another one.

The trouble is that growing social and ecological problems will tend to make economic imperialism ever less easy. As problems multiply, foreigners are bound to be singled out as responsible for a country's growing ills and discriminated against, as nationalism grows. In the next few decades one can undoubtedly expect more and more foreign firms to be nationalized in developing countries, and more and more protectionist legislation proposed.

Japan and other industrial countries that will soon find themselves in a similar plight will thereby be forced to spend ever greater sums on pollution control to permit economic growth and eventually simply to maintain existing output.

One of the beneficial effects of the growing shortage of raw materials must be the increased profitability of recycling waste. Take the example of sulphur dioxide. Monsanto has developed a means of recycling it and providing sulphur at £30 a ton which is just about twice the world price. A shortage will clearly make this recycling possible.

In the United States approximately 23 million tons of sulphur dioxide are discarded into the air each year; in the United Kingdom approximately 6 million tons. This could provide 5 million tons of sulphur or 15 million tons of sulphuric acid in the United States and about a quarter of this in the United Kingdom. It will soon be impossible to waste this precious material, and when that day comes, the huge cost to plants, animals, human health and buildings will be avoided simply because it will be profitable to do so.

The development of ever more efficient recycling methods will tend to have

196

Pollution Costs

a similar effect. Also, as Sanford Rose writes, 'Once society, by one means or another, begins charging rent for use of the environment's capacity to absorb wastes, engineers will have to think about pollution control as an integral part of plant design rather than as an afterthought. A lot more research funds will be allocated to pollution control, and costs may go down faster than anyone expects.'

Recycling will have to be resorted to more and more for other reasons. At the moment much of the money spent on pollution control is aimed at shifting pollution from one place to another rather than suppressing it. Thus high chimneys are built to keep smoke out of urban areas. Clean air is achieved in cities at the cost of causing hideous pollution to the Welsh valleys where the Phurnacite or smokeless fuel is made.[8]

Even the sophisticated after-burners used to cut down exhaust suffer from the same deficiency. According to *Bio-Science* they simply break up the exhaust into minute particles which stay in the air longer because of their small size. A single motor-car will emit about 100 billion such particles per second. Instead of forming condensation centres for raindrops, they form centres for tiny ice crystals, or mist droplets, that tend to remain in the air or descend very slowly. As Professor Wayne Davis comments, 'The result is that in regions far from the pollution centres, we now have developing misty covers, which can cut down the amount of sunlight reaching the earth.'

It is clear that as pollution becomes more and more a global problem, so the devices used to combat it must become correspondingly more sophisticated. Effective recycling must tend to replace less sophisticated systems and costs must increase proportionately.

The amount spent on pollution control must also increase as scientific research reveals the ever greater damage done by different pollutants to biological organisms and in particular to human health.

Things considered harmless are slowly becoming incriminated as research progresses. It is in fact gradually being revealed to scientists, who should already know, that man has developed phylogenetically as an adaptive response to much more specific environmental conditions than we think, and that any undue modification of these conditions will affect him adversely.

Take sulphur dioxide; there is as yet no legislation calling for its control. Yet we know of its adverse effects on plant growth and we learn from Dr Robert Shapiro that it has a significant mutagenic effect, and can thereby cause infant malformations and probably cancer. It seems probable, Shapiro writes that sulphur dioxide constitutes a genetic hazard to living organisms.[9]

Research on the effect of radioactivity of biological organisms is constantly leading to further reductions in permissible levels. Recently, Doctors Tamplin and Goffman of the AEC have provided evidence to show that the effects of

197

low level radiation are much more dangerous than previously thought.[10] It was pointed out that if their recommendations were to be adopted, the effect on the nuclear power industry would be disastrous.

One reaction was that it would simply put America out of business.

Clearly, as research continues to reveal more and more adverse effects of pollution, so standards of pollution controls will have to be increased as will the costs involved.

It is also essential to realize that a large amount of pollution can only be controlled by cutting down on economic activity.

How else, for instance, can heat from the combustion of fossil fuels be reduced? Clearly, only by cutting down on power consumption.

How can the damage done by agricultural chemicals be controlled? Only by closing down the factories that produce them or persuading them to produce something else, and at the same time returning to sounder methods of husbandry that do not require them.

This must mean reducing economic activity, which implies more costs to our economy.

How are these likely to be met?

The reasonable thing to do would be to cut down on less important expenditures, notably those on superfluous consumer products. We can do without electric toothbrushes and plastic buckets but not without air to breathe and water to drink.

Also the government should cut down on other expenditures that are clearly not so urgent, such as many aspects of welfare and education, defence, *etc*. It is unlikely, however, that their sense of priorities is likely to undergo so violent a transformation as to render such acts conceivable, though a typical Conservative government is likely to go quite a long way towards reducing the costs of that vast cumbersome bureaucracy set up by its opponents.

Social disintegration will require ever greater expenditure on police, prisons, de-alcoholization centres, psychiatric hospitals and every type of welfare for an ever less adaptive population. Growing unemployment will call for still more welfare and will also contribute to further social disintegration. The declining health of urban man will mean still more expenditure on our health service and the ever-increasing demand for education will further increase costs in this direction.

Governments will undoubtedly try to make business pay as much of the bill as possible. However, there is a limit to the extra costs they can absorb without increasing prices.

The government will thus have to finance much of the anti-pollution programme by inflation.

This, of course, will lead to a measure of social chaos. The public will obviously clamour for higher wages to maintain their standard of living, which will simply lead to further inflation.

As ecological principles begin to be understood and concern with the environment increases, so we can expect people to become more willing to accept some reduction in their standard of living to finance pollution control. In the United States a national survey by the Information Research Centre showed that 57 per cent of adults interviewed would accept taxation increases if it were the only way to keep town and country clean and pleasant to live in. A survey in Sweden showed a similar result.

In the long run as industrial production is ever more seriously handicapped both by pollution and by the cost of its control, living standards calculated in terms of consumption of manufactured goods must inevitably fall whether by consent or by sheer social and ecological necessity.

The only scientific attempt to predict the effect of pollution control on the US economy that I have come across confirmed these conclusions.

Economist Robert Anderson built an effective model of the US economy which was used to predict changes in 1962–4 with reasonable accuracy.[1] He altered some investment and price inputs to reflect stringent air-pollution control measures. For instance, he assumed that manufacturing industries would increase investment on air-pollution devices at an annual rate of $1·2 billion. Public utilities, he assumed, would increase their expenditure at an annual rate of $320 million and new car prices would rise by 1 per cent so as to meet new air-pollution standards. He then reran the model for the same period (1962–4). As expected, the GNP went down to $617 billion whereas without the assumed pollution controls it would have been $625 billion. Unemployment was up to 5·3 per cent instead of 4·8 per cent. Prices also rose by about 1·2 per cent.

This model, as Sanford Rose points out, did not take into account the effect of improved technology. This may be so, but all forms of technology, as we have been at pains to point out in this book, are subject to diminishing returns, and these are already beginning to manifest themselves and are likely to do so more and more in the next few decades. Anderson's model clearly points out the basic trends associated with the sort of massive pollution-control programme that must inevitably be adopted in industrial nations. Indeed, as Professor Commoner said at an AAAS meeting in the summer of 1970, 'We, the prosperous, will have to give up big automobiles, big defence projects and big man-in-space programmes to pay the required ecological and social bills.'

REFERENCES

1   ROSE, SANFORD. 1970. The economics of environmental quality. In *The Environment* (ed. Fortune Magazine). New York: Harper & Row.

2   GOLDMAN, MARSHALL I. 1970. The costs of fighting pollution. In *Current History*, August.

3   MARINE POLLUTION BULLETIN. 1970. December.

4   CHEMICAL WEEK. 1969. Vol. 105, p. 71.

5   THE TIMES. 1970. December 10th.

6   DAVENPORT, JOHN. 1970. Industry starts a big clean-up. In *The Environment* (ed. Fortune Magazine). New York: Harper & Row.

7   HEADLEY and KNEESE, A. V. 1970. Economic implications of pesticide use. In *Annals of the New York Academy of Science*.

8   MACLEAN, CHARLES. 1970. Smokeless Hokus Pokus. In *The Ecologist, I (6)*.

9   JOURNAL OF THE AMERICAN CHEMICAL SOCIETY. 1970. June 28th.

10   GOFFMAN, HOHN and ARTHUR TAPLIN. 1970. Radiation: The invisible casualties. In *Environment, 12 (3)*.

PART FIVE

Social Consequences

19 OVERCROWDING AND SOCIAL TENSION

Claire and W. M. S. Russell

Authors of *Human Behaviour* and *Man, Monkeys and Violence*

'In 1900 a visitor from another sphere might reasonably have decided that man, as one met him in Europe or America, was a kindly, merciful and generous creature. In 1940 he might have decided, with an equal show of justice, that this creature was diabolically malignant. *And yet it was the same creature under different conditions of stress.*' These words occur in *The Shape of Things to Come*, published (in 1933!) by H. G. Wells. For thousands of years, there have been two schools of thought about human aggression and its expression in violent crime, riot and war. Some people have said that human aggressiveness is human nature, an innate disposition in man. Other people, like Wells, have taken the view that human aggression is a response to intolerable frustrations, and that violence is a symptom of stresses in human societies and in their relations with their natural surroundings. The records of past history, right up to the middle of the present century, appear to favour this second view, that violence is a reaction to stress, notably the stress of shortage of food. Clear evidence for this connection can be found by studying the incidence and severity of public violence in many times and places, such as Imperial China, Japan in the seventeenth and nineteenth centuries, Tudor England, eighteenth century France and medieval Europe from Brittany to Bohemia. By 1932, evidence of this kind had convinced most civilized people that human aggression is a response to stress, and not an innate and ineradicable taint. This was the verdict of the members of the *American Psychological Association*, replying in that year to a questionnaire, by a majority of 346 to 10. But in the 1950s voices began to be heard again in favour of man's inherent aggressiveness. This change of opinion results from events in

201

modern highly industrialized societies of W. Europe and N. America. These 'affluent' societies have much higher national incomes than other nations, or than they themselves had in earlier periods. True, it has been estimated that nearly one-seventh of the British people, and more than one-quarter of the American people are living in serious poverty. Nevertheless, the affluent societies are genuinely affluent in one important sense. By comparison with Tudor England or Imperial China or *modern* India, most people in the affluent societies are free from really serious shortage of food.

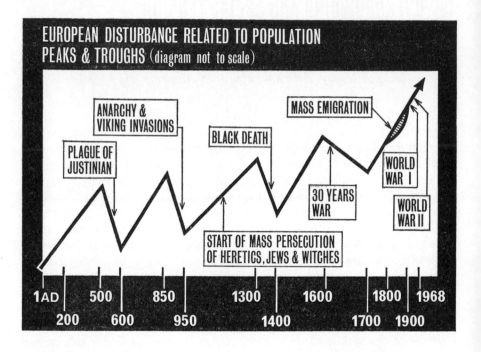

If violence is a response to stress, should not this real improvement have the effect of substantially reducing violence in these societies? What has actually happened is precisely the reverse. In England and Wales, between 1950 and 1960, the annual number of violent crimes per 100,000 people more than doubled. In the United States, between 1960 and 1967, violent crime increased nearly six times as fast as population. Does this mean that people are indeed inherently aggressive whatever their conditions?

At this point we can get new insight into the problem from studies of the simpler societies of monkeys (including apes), and especially from comparing their behaviour in the wild and in the zoo. By now we have accounts of some

202

Overcrowding and Social Tension

fifteen species in the wild, at least eight of these same species in zoos or other close forms of confinement and some species in a variety of different intermediate conditions. We find that differences between wild and zoo behaviour are common to all species studied, and amount to a total change or reversal of all aspects of social behaviour and social life. In monkeys living under completely relaxed conditions in the wild, quarrelling is always rare and violence is practically non-existent. In monkeys living under the stresses of an enclosure, quarrelling is frequent and violence appreciable, sometimes leading to serious wounds and death. This contrast applies to all the species studied: any monkey species in the zoo is more quarrelsome and violent than the same or other species in the wild. Hans Kummer made a direct comparison of hamadryas baboons living in the wild in Ethiopia with hamadryas baboons at the Zürich Zoo. He found that aggressive acts by males were 17·5 times as frequent in the zoo as in the wild, and that serious bite-wounds were commonplace in the zoo, though *never* occurring in the wild. This contrast seems to be typical for all monkey species studied.

AFFLUENT MONKEYS. The zoo monkeys are clearly getting an ample food supply, and can be regarded, so to speak, as materially 'affluent' societies. What they lack is *space*, since a band of monkeys in the wild normally roams an area of several square miles, whereas a zoo community must make do with an area of several hundred square yards. Hans Kummer found in the wild hamadryas baboons that such quarrelling as did occur was commonest in areas where cliff-ledges (and hence *space* for resting in safety from predators) were in short supply. *Crowding* is the crucial stress. Further confirmation of this comes from observations on rhesus monkeys by C. H. Southwick at the Calcutta Zoo and by Hilary and Martin Waterhouse at the Bristol Zoo. At Calcutta, halving the cage area for the same number of monkeys roughly doubled the amount of aggressive behaviour. At Bristol, halving the number of monkeys in the same enclosed area reduced the frequency of fights by 75 per cent.

The uniform peacefulness of wild monkey bands reflects the nature of their social organization. The forms of social structure and political control vary between monkey species. In the patriarchal democracy of the hamadryas baboons, leadership is dispersed among all experienced males; in cynocephalus baboons and rhesus monkeys, a small establishment of leading males controls the society; in Japanese monkeys, though male leaders generally control the movements of the band, a male can only become a leader if he is acceptable to the leading females who live at the core of the band. The one form *never* found in relaxed wild conditions is arbitrary dictatorship by a single individual. In the more oligarchic societies there is a sort of constitutional president but he does not differ sharply in rank from his aides, and owes his position entirely to the support of his male colleagues and, in Japanese monkeys, to the approval of the females. In a group of cynocephalus baboons observed in Nairobi Park, for instance, the leader could be driven away from a piece of food by a stronger baboon if both were some distance from the rest of the band. But normally, whenever an argument arose, the leader's authority was supreme, for he was always loyally supported by two colleagues, and a group of three can outrank any trouble-making individual. At Takahashi, a Japanese monkey male, individually capable of dominating any other male in the band, could never enter the leader class, for every time he approached the centre of the band, where the leaders live, he was driven out by the leading females. From these and other instances it appears that a highly aggressive male cannot expect to rise high in a band of monkeys under relaxed conditions. Since his position is owed to support by others and not brute strength, the leader does not appear much higher in rank than his supporters; on the other hand, he need not fear displacement as his physical powers decline. In chimpanzees and hamadryas baboons, elderly males are known to be respected; and in two Japanese monkey bands the top leader has been seen to retain his position to the end of his life, thanks to the active support of his leading colleagues.

BENEVOLENCE AND RANK. The basis of social rank among chimpanzees has recently been studied by Vernon Reynolds and Gillian Luscombe. The observations were made at a USAF base in New Mexico, and concerned a community of redundant chimponauts. These chimps had all been trained to work in space vehicles. As everyone knows, human astronauts have taken over their jobs. The apes were therefore gathered together in honourable retirement in a spacious enclosure of 30 acres at Holloman Base. They rapidly resynthesized a community similar in many ways to those Vernon Reynolds had observed in the wild in Uganda. In these relatively relaxed conditions, Reynolds and Luscombe made observations for six days on thirty-four individuals. Each individual was scored for the amount and kind of food he obtained. A clear-cut rank order emerged, with marked differences between high-ranking individuals, who ate plenty of their favourite fruits, and low-ranking chimps, who had to make do with monkey pellets.

Records were also made, for each individual, of all his social interactions with other individuals, that is every time he did something in relation to another individual. These interactions were classified into two groups: aggressive and friendly. Aggressive interactions included slaps, bites and a stand-up threat display which made the threatened individual take to flight. Friendly interactions included grooming, greeting, play and the like. When all the scores were compared it was found that the chimps of high rank, evidently the most self-assertive ones, were *not* the ones with the most

Overcrowding and Social Tension

aggressive behaviour, but those with most friendly contacts, the best-liked individuals. The most successful chimp of all had nine times as many friendly contacts as the average score. The chief way to win friends and influence people was apparently to perform a noisy but unaggressive display, quite different from the threat display; this cheerful hooting and banging about seemed to attract friendly attention and interest, and led to numerous friendly contacts and high rank and privileges as a result. When two or more bands of chimps meet in the wild at a fruit tree, which has just come into season, they engage in a regular beat session which may go on for 55 minutes, drumming on tree-roots and rushing about the trees. This may help to arrange ranks and priorities among chimps who do not know each other well. Clearly, under relaxed conditions, self-assertion and aggression are totally different things, expressed in posturally different displays. In a wild monkey band, aggression is not the way to social advancement.

DICTATORSHIP IN ZOOS. In the zoo, under sufficient crowding stress, dictatorship by a physically powerful individual is a commonplace observation. In rhesus colonies observed by Michael Chance at Regent's Park and by Vernon Reynolds at Whipsnade, the top male was in each case an absolute dictator, of whom all other monkeys were terrified. In a group of chimpanzees in a small enclosure at Regent's Park, observed by Caroline Medawar, we can see the extreme contrast to the civilized community at Holloman Base. In this crowded group, the boss was a strong male with a positive dislike for personal friendly contacts: he would attack and viciously wound any of his subjects who made friendly approaches even to each other. In these conditions there has been a total reversal: high rank is now attained by brutal aggression and nothing else.

Between the two extremes, there are two intermediate situations. At Whipsnade, Reynolds drew up diagrams of the aggressive and friendly inter-relations between each of the individuals in the colony. The chief male was found to be at the top of the aggressive hierarchy, liable to attack anyone below him, but also at the top of the friendly hierarchy, receiving grooming and friendly contact from many subordinates. In a community of rhesus monkeys at the Bristol Zoo, Hilary and Martin Waterhouse found two individuals at the top of the rank order in terms of food access and freedom of movement: one of these was at the top of an aggressive hierarchy, the other at the top of a friendly hierarchy. These two intermediate situations throw some light on the transition from a relaxed to a stressful society. Evidently, when a society is under sufficient stress, brute strength and ferocity take the place of friendly mutual support and responsible leadership.

It is no wonder the result is frequent quarrelling and not infrequent violence. A dictator monkey in a zoo colony, touchy about intrusion or disturbance in the confined space, is constantly liable to attack subordinates. He may suddenly rush upon a group of neighbours and scatter them – just as the police suddenly scattered a group of peaceful demonstrators in Lincoln Park, during the 'police riot' in Chicago in the summer of 1968. In a study of 118 quarrels described by Reynolds among the rhesus colony at Whipsnade, we were able to identify a number of processes which in the wild make for peace, but which under the protracted stress of crowding actually spread, amplify, prolong and intensify quarrels. A wild leader will repress a quarrel between two others by means of a mild threat; the zoo dictator will simply attack one of them as a *punishment*. In the wild, a monkey suffering momentary frustration from a superior may work off his feelings by redirecting resentment into a threat against some monkey of still lower rank, who can simply move away. In the crowded community, a monkey punished by the dictator will go off and attack somebody else by way of *redirection*, illustrating the observation of the great law reformer Sir Samuel Romilly, that 'cruel punishment will have an inevitable tendency to produce cruelty in the people'. When one monkey threatens, a neighbouring monkey will often threaten in the same direction, even if he cannot see the object of the first one's threat. In the wild, this automatic reaction ensures prompt support for the leader from his colleagues, who are always close to him, in suppressing, by threat and without violence, aggression by subordinates. In the zoo, this same reaction causes other monkeys to join in the quarrel on the side of the aggressor. By all these means, quarrels reverberate round the crowded society. Monkeys of low rank are liable to become the butts of redirection by all the others. This mass redirection can reduce an individual to the status of an outcast. This happened to a male at Whipsnade, who finally had to be removed when the others broke his arm in their unprovoked persecution of him.

STRESS-INDUCED AGGRESSION. We have now seen that rank criteria, social structure and a variety of social interactions all change completely under stress. When brute strength becomes the basis of social order, females and young, as the weakest members of the society, are the principal victims. In relaxed conditions in the wild, male leaders show the utmost chivalry towards females and young, and protect them instantly from even mild attacks by others. Under stress, the dictators of the zoo colonies are capable of savagely biting and even killing females and young. In a colony of hamadryas baboons at Regent's Park, observed in the 1920s by Sir Solly Zuckerman, 8 out of 61 males died by violence, but 30 out of 33 females and 5 out of 5 babies were killed in this way.

Monkeys, in short, have two totally different kinds of social behaviour, 'kindly and merciful' on the one hand, 'diabolically malignant' on the other.

Overcrowding and Social Tension

Some social mechanisms, as we have seen, are actually designed to promote peace under relaxed conditions and violence under stressful conditions. Other mammals present a similar picture of reversal of social behaviour under stress, notably under crowding. The fundamental change is in parental behaviour, from a protective to a competitive attitude. For, as the Dutch zoologist Adriaan Kortlandt has shown, parental behaviour is the starting-point of all other mammalian social behaviour. In its relaxed and positive and its stressful and negative forms, it is the origin of love and hate. The advantages of positive social behaviour are obvious: what could be the significance of the diabolically malignant behaviour under stress? Studies with rapidly breeding mammals, such as rats and voles, have shown that a population bred in a confined space, though supplied with unlimited food, will not exceed a certain density. As soon as the population density reaches a certain level, the reversal of behaviour begins, and the tension and violence and attacks on females and young have the effect of halting population growth and even reducing the population for some time. V. C. Wynne-Edwards has pointed out that if a population of animals only began to fight when its food supply was running short, that supply could be irretrievably depleted. By reacting to crowding, a population can be reduced in time to allow the food supply to recover.

The effects of crowding and violence are not restricted to death by wounds. There are physiological effects on the females which impair reproduction for a couple of generations, and a disturbance of the machinery of immunity which renders the animals vulnerable to infectious disease, so that epidemics complete the crash of the population. The whole system of reversal of social behaviour can thus be seen as a means of response to a crisis in which population is in danger of outrunning resources. It may, indeed, get out of hand and go too far; this may have happened to the red squirrel in Britain. Under relaxed conditions, then, mammals are incredibly peaceful and, so to speak, civilized. Under population pressure, their societies are brutally unequal, cruel, tense and violent. Where man is concerned, we can make no such easy comparison. For man has probably never, or hardly ever, enjoyed completely relaxed conditions. Technological advance is the outcome of human intelligence, but it has always hit human societies as if it were an external force, since they have never recognized the need to regulate and allow for its effects. Every such advance, changing the relation between human societies and their natural surroundings and resources, has made possible an increase in population: every time, the increase has gone on without regulation, so that sooner or later population out-stripped resources. As a result, man has been under virtually continuous population stress, and hence virtually continuous social inequality, tension and violence. Hence some people have supposed that these evils are the normal inherent lot or nature of man. But while all mammals are capable of fiendish cruelty under stress, man differs from them all in having an even more highly developed positive parental urge. This is clear from the long and increasing period of parental care in man, and from the unique social achievements of our species, with refinements of social welfare even for adults, all stemming from our parental behaviour. Even under frightful stresses, where almost all mammals would kill their young, many human beings continue to love and protect them at great sacrifice to themselves. It is not the violence in man's desperately stressful career that should astonish us, but the quality of human intelligence and human feeling in the most awful circumstances.

Nevertheless, under sufficient stress, a proportion of human beings do wound, kill, even eat their own children, and thoroughly mammalian atrocities do occur in man. We do not have human societies in totally relaxed conditions for comparison, as we do with monkeys; but we can compare human societies under greater or lesser degrees of stress, in different places and times. When we do so, we find striking differences, enough to suggest that, if we could eliminate population stresses altogether and forever, our societies could eventually be as free, friendly and peaceful as those of wild monkeys, and of course infinitely more creative. F. H. McClintock and others studied the incidence of violent crime in London in 1950, 1957 and 1960. They found violent crime at first concentrated in areas of dense, bad housing. As the British population crisis continued, other districts also became densely populated, and violent crime spread to these, though it showed no sign of appearing in suburbs where housing was still good and population relatively sparse. At Newcastle, the city planning department recently studied various social and medical symptoms in different districts. The sharpest contrast was between the most crowded and least crowded third of the city. The most crowded third produced more than five times as many offences against the person, more than four times as many larcenies, seven times as many people on probation, three times as much juvenile delinquency, more than five times as many cases of neglect of children, five times as much venereal disease and 43 per cent more prenatal deaths.

In his *Autobiography* H. G. Wells thus described his life in a slum at Westbourne Park. 'I looked, so to speak, through a hole in my life of some weeks more or less, into a sort of humanity coarser, beastlier and baser than anything I had ever known before ... I think the peculiar unpleasantness of that episode lies in the fact that we were all too close together. We were as congested ... as zoo monkeys.' The settled civilized populations of mankind have generally had high normal death rates, of 3–4 per cent annually, but even higher birth rates of 3·5–5 per cent, resulting in a natural annual increase of up to 1 per cent. If this had been the whole story, it has been calculated that by now the world population would form 'a sphere of living flesh, many

208

thousand light years in diameter, expanding with a radial velocity many times faster than the speed of light'. In real life, as opposed to the wonderland of mathematics, nothing of the kind can happen: indefinite natural increase is absurdly impossible, and either birthrates come down or deathrates go up. In fact, every time the human civilized populations seriously outran their resources, they entered a population crisis, marked by very acute social tensions, leading to extensive, unrestrained violence and stress, the collapse of the population under epidemics and the decline and fall of many a civilization. These population cycles were out of phase in different regions; thus India succumbed to a population crisis in the eighteenth century, China in the nineteenth, and hence the Europeans gained control in India a century earlier than they did in China. Europe was for long the least densely populated region of the civilized world, and most recent creative advances in technology and social organization were achieved in Europe during the precious respites between crises, when population was for a while in balance with resources. The current population crisis differs in two ways from previous ones: it is world-wide and it is marked by very low normal deathrates, making for explosive population growth.

Our century is therefore exceptionally cruel and violent, and getting more so. Civilians, including women and children, made up 5 per cent of the dead in the First World War, between 50 and 75 per cent of the dead in the Second World War and 84 per cent in Korea. According to Senator Edward Kennedy, quoted by *The Times* on 3 December 1969, more than 300,000 civilians had by then been killed in Vietnam since 1965. Even if we could tolerate the suffering and waste entailed by the population crisis response of social tension and violence, we can no longer afford it even for its old evolutionary function, since a world war with modern weapons, far from sparing our natural resources, would irretrievably damage them by its ecological effects. But we can avert all this. We can do what no animal can do. We can substitute voluntary birth control for involuntary death control, for what Paul Leyhausen has called 'the old, cruel, methods by which Nature balanced our numbers'. With our modern technological resources, and a reduced world population, we can find out how to create truly relaxed conditions for human societies. Everything we know of mammals and man suggests that, if we can do this, we can build a lasting, peaceful and creative civilization. We can choose whether our species is to be kindly, merciful and generous or diabolically malignant: for it is the same creature under different conditions of stress.

REFERENCES

BURTON, H. 1968. (2nd edition.) *Peasant Uprisings in Japan of the Tokugawa Period.* New York: Paragon Book Reprint Corp.

COHN, N. 1957. *The Pursuit of the Millenium.* London: Secker & Warburg.

GRAHAM, H. D. and T. R. GURR. 1969. *Violence in America. A Report to the National Commission on the Causes and Prevention of Violence.* New York, Toronto and London: Bantam Books.

REYNOLDS, V. and G. LUSCOMBE. 1969. Chimpanzee rank order and the functions of displays. In *Proceedings of the 2nd International Congress of Primatology, Atlanta, 1.* Basle and New York: Karger.

RUSSELL, CLAIRE and W. M. S. RUSSELL. 1968. *Violence, Monkeys and Man.* London: Macmillan.

RUSSELL, CLAIRE and W. M. S. RUSSELL. 1969: Sociological factors in fertility control. In *Journal of Biosocial Science, 1.*

VIRGO, H. B. and M. J. WATERHOUSE. 1969. The emergence of attention structure amongst rhesus macaques. In *Man, 4.*

VIZOSO, A. B. 1970. Squirrel Viruses. In *Proceedings of the Royal Society of Medicine, 63.*

WALKER, D. 1968. *Rights on Conflict. A Report to the National Commission on the Causes and Prevention of Violence.* New York, Toronto and London: Bantam Books.

210

20 PRICES, WAGES AND POPULATION

W. M. S. Russell

Lecturer in Social Biology, University of Reading

In the last decades of the sixteenth century, in the reign of Elizabeth I, some people with more money than imagination were claiming that England had never had it so good, or, in the more eloquent Elizabethan words of the Bishop of Salisbury, 'never was it better ... in abundance of victuals'. Yet at this very time England was experiencing a ferocious rise in prices. The real situation was well summed up by the Elizabethan historian John Stow: 'there was no want [lack] of anything to him that wanted [lacked] not money'. In the last decades of the twentieth century, in the reign of Elizabeth II, our situation is similar. If there is a surge of wage claims, it is not due to perversity or greed. It is simply that prices are rising even faster than they were in the days of the first Elizabeth. For most people, from the commuter to the pensioner, from the shopper buying a loaf to the young couple trying to get a house mortgage, the most immediately frightening fact of life in the later twentieth century is the persistent rise in prices, or, to put it another way, the persistent fall in the value of money.

The cost of living in Britain by 1970 was about six times as high as in 1913, and about four times as high as in 1938. In the first quarter of 1970, manufacturers' prices were reported to be rising at a rate of 7 per cent per year. Some costs, notably housing and transport, are rising especially steeply, but virtually all kinds of costs are affected. In 1970 there have been rises or threatened rises in the cost of food and drink, fuel and light, council house rents and commuter fares.

Until the Second World War, wages in most occupations were rising even faster than prices, so that people in employment were generally getting higher and higher *real wages* – that is, they could buy more and more goods and services with their pay. Thanks to this, and to the development of social services since the war, our standard of living has risen substantially since Victorian times. In 1900 it was estimated that about 28 per cent of the British people were living in dire poverty; by 1960 the probable percentage had gone down by a half, to about 14 per cent. However, since the war, wages in many occupations, especially the lower paid ones, have begun to lose the race with prices, so that real wages have begun to fall. To judge from past experience, if the rise in prices continues, wages will lag increasingly behind prices, and the standard of living for the great majority will inevitably go down. It is no wonder that prices and wages are always in the news, that one cartoonist (Cummings) has introduced the demon figure of Mr Rising-Price, and that governments are more and more obsessed with Prices and Incomes Policy.

This is by no means a new concern of civilized government. It is probably the oldest concern of all. The earliest extensive code of laws is that of the city-state of Eshnunna in ancient Iraq, promulgated at the beginning of the second millennium BC. This code begins with a list of fixed prices and wages, and some miscellaneous decrees on other matters are appended at the end almost as an afterthought.

Probably no government in history has been completely indifferent to the movement of prices and wages. But governments have varied in the degree of control they tried to exercise. At one extreme, the governments of classical Athens and Victorian England made very little attempt to control prices and wages. Both societies were enjoying exceptional trading advantages as the most advanced industrial states of their respective worlds. Most governments have tried harder to control prices and wages by legislation. But their regulations have been largely ignored, and prices and wages in such societies have generally gone their own way, rising and falling in great smooth waves.

At the other extreme, we find such highly regulated societies as the city-states and empires of the ancient Near East, or the modern Soviet Union. In such societies, the government itself is such a big spender and such a big seller that it is a major factor in the economy, and its regulations have some force. All modern governments have been increasing their expenditure, and hence moving in this direction. It is therefore important to realize that even governments of this kind can only exert a temporary control over price and wage movements. They can hold up a rise for a time, only to have it finally break through with a jerk: price changes therefore occur in sudden steps instead of smooth curves. As the historian Fritz M. Heichelheim put it, such a society has 'a comparatively static economy with sudden periods of adjusting'. During a single year of the reign of King Ammizaduga of Babylon (seventeenth century BC), the price of barley doubled. In June 1962 the government of the Soviet Union was obliged to increase the purchase prices of meat and meat products by 35 per cent, since the supply of these goods was not adequate to meet the demand. They had held the prices constant for some time, at considerable loss to the government, but finally had to accept this sudden large price rise.

Since even the most influential governments can do so little directly by regulation and decree, the only way to solve the problem of rising prices is to understand and deal with the fundamental causes. When day-to-day changes in the prices of particular products are examined, under the microscope of

212

Prices, Wages and Population

economic analysis, a bewildering variety of interacting factors appear. But we are not really concerned with these ripples, but with the great long-term movements of prices as a whole. These are best studied through the telescope of world history. When we do this, we find there are three fundamental factors involved: money, resources and population.

Prices are undoubtedly affected, in the short run, but the amount of money or credit in a society, relative to the amount of real resources and hence goods to be bought. When there is too much money about for the available goods, the value of money falls – in other words, prices rise. There are many examples in world history to show that prices rise when a large addition is made to the supply of money in a society, without a corresponding increase in goods. This happened when Alexander the Great captured the gold hoard of the Persian kings, and put it into circulation. It happened in the sixteenth century AD, when the Spaniards began to exploit the silver mines of Zacatecas, Guanajuato and Potosi in their New World empire. It happened in the nineteenth century, when new gold deposits were discovered in turn in California, Australia and South Africa. But in all these cases, prices were already rising, for other reasons. Moreover, at least in the long run, such changes must affect prices *and* wages equally, since the amount of money is increased relative to both goods and labour. If all goods cost twice as much, but all wages are also doubled, nothing has really happened. It is only when prices rise faster than wages that real wages fall, and vice versa. In the long run, money is only a symbol of the relations between population and resources. The same principle applies when the amount of money or credit is reduced. If it is made more difficult to get mortgages, house prices may show a transient fall. But in the long run people *have* to have somewhere to live, and if the pressure of population on housing continues, house prices will soon rise again. This has been common experience in Britain in the past few years. The most fundamental factors of all are supply and demand – real resources and population.

The major price rises of the past have come about in this way. Population growth outstripped the production of some *essential* resource. Until the middle of the nineteenth century, this key essential was generally cereal grain, or the flour or bread made from it. Since demand exceeded supply, the price of bread rose. This meant that the *proportion* of income spent on bread had to increase, often drastically. It has been calculated that in February 1789 the price of bread in Paris was such that a factory worker would have had to spend 97 *per cent* of his income on bread alone. The result was that wages simply had to rise, and this meant that the price of other goods rose too, by a vicious spiral. But in these conditions the rise in wages lagged steadily behind the rise in prices, and the standard of living inexorably went down, especially for the lowest-paid workers, who in any case spent the

213

largest proportion of their income on essentials. The very increase in population, which made prices rise, also kept wages from rising as much or as fast as prices. As well as too many mouths, there were too many hands. With a surplus of labour, wages remained as low as they could be without starving the labour force out of existence altogether. In these recurrent population crises, the problem was often accentuated by an increase in the frequency and destructiveness of wars. For warfare, by throwing part of a society's real resources down the drain, reduced yet further the amount of goods relative to the population, and so accentuated any rise in prices. Eventually, malnutrition and stress rendered the population vulnerable to epidemics, and there was a drastic fall in population. With reduced demand for goods, prices fell; with reduced supply of labour, real wages rose, and conditions improved steadily until the next time population outstripped resources.

This sequence can be illustrated in many times and places. In the ancient world, we can detect such trends in Babylonia in the second millennium BC, in classical Greece, in the Hellenistic kingdoms, in the Roman and Byzantine Empires. In medieval and modern times, the process can be followed with more certainty and in more detail in many places, for instance in France, Spain, Italy, Germany, Sweden. In England a careful study of prices and wages extending continuously over seven centuries has been made by E. H. Phelps Brown and Sheila V. Hopkins. From this and other evidence we can construct in outline the course of events in England since the thirteenth century. Until Victorian times, apart from minor differences in detail, the story was very similar for the whole of Western Europe.

During the thirteenth century, the population of England and Wales was growing fast. Some people think it even reached 6 millions, a level not reached again till the eighteenth century. Certainly the production of cereal grains could not keep pace. People began to cultivate poor soil, and to concentrate on crops at the expense of livestock, with a loss in manure for the crops themselves. By the end of the thirteenth century, crop failures began, especially in the poorer lands, and production began to shrink. In 1315–17 there was a catastrophic famine, and throughout the fourteenth century a succession of epidemics reduced the population, till by 1400 it was little more than 2 millions. The biggest of these epidemics was in 1348–9, the famous Black Death.

Because of the pressure of population on resources, prices increased throughout the thirteenth century, and well into the fourteenth, as productivity actually declined. Real wages fell, and people suffered increasing misery. The reduction of population in the fourteenth century changed the whole picture. Prices did not begin to fall till the 1370s. But wages rose spectacularly from the Black Death onwards, in some cases by as much as 200 per cent. In 1351 the government brought in the Statute of Labourers to freeze wage rates at

Prices, Wages and Population

their old values. It was completely ineffective. Labour is like anything else: when it is in short supply, people are bound to pay more for it.

From 1380 to 1510 the much reduced population grew very little. Prices remained very constant, wages somewhat increased, so real wages rose to a high value: they never reached this value again until 1880. The great Victorian economic historian Thorold Rogers called the fifteenth century a Golden Age for the English people. But eventually, with much improved nutrition and a rising standard of living, the population began to increase again, and soon all the gains were being thrown away.

Between 1510 and the middle of the seventeenth century, prices increased about six-fold. Wages rose too, but not nearly so much, so that during this period real wages fell to half their value at the beginning. This drastic change is called by historians the Price Revolution.

Some early economists ascribed the rise in prices entirely to the import of silver into Europe by the Spaniards during the sixteenth century. In 1803, in the second edition of his great book on population, Thomas Robert Malthus swept away this hypothesis. 'Depopulation,' he wrote, 'was loudly complained of at the end of the fifteenth and beginning of the sixteenth centuries, and a redundancy of population was acknowledged at the end of the sixteenth. And it was this change in the state of population, and not the discovery of the American mines, which occasioned so marked a fall in the corn wages of labour' (*i.e.* real wages in terms of the corn they would buy). Modern research has fully confirmed Malthus's view. Decades before significant amounts of silver began to be imported from the New World, prices began to rise, in parallel with population increase, in all parts of Spain itself and in France, England and Sweden.

In England and Wales the population considerably more than doubled between 1510 and 1650, when it exceeded 5 million. In a recent history of the British cost of living (1969), John Burnett has shown that the whole chain of events occurred in two stages. Population and prices rose, and real wages fell, throughout the reigns of Henry VIII, Edward VI and Mary (1509–58). In 1556–8 there was a very serious epidemic of 'sweating sickness' (possibly influenza), which may have reduced the population by as much as one-fifth. Prices and wages stabilized for the next couple of decades. After that, the growth of population was resumed, and the price revolution continued until the English Civil War. The drop in standard of living was catastrophic. By the end of Elizabeth's reign 'almost half the population was hovering perilously close to hunger and destitution' (Burnett). In the early seventeenth century malnutrition became widespread and the vitamin-deficiency disease of rickets made its appearance. The weakened population was subject to a series of epidemics, of which the Great Plague of London in 1665 was the worst.

215

Because of malnutrition and disease, but also because people now began to use birth control on an extensive scale, population remained almost stationary until about 1750. Accordingly, throughout this period, prices remained stable and wages rose somewhat, producing a rise in real wages and in the standard of living from the very low levels of the mid-seventeenth century. Agriculture made great advances. Without much machinery or any agricultural chemicals, it was becoming capable of supporting a considerably larger population than in medieval times. Nutrition improved, and wheaten bread (as opposed to barley or rye bread), hitherto a luxury, became a staple food at least in southern England. Along with nutrition, health improved and infant mortality began to decline. Finally the country entered another period of rapid population increase, more than doubling again by 1820, when it reached 12 millions.

This new population increase, from 1750 to 1820, had all the old consequences. Prices more than doubled, real wages fell back to their seventeenth-century level. Under the population pressure, cultivation again spread to poor land, 'though the use of land which was unsuitable for crops under normal conditions only forced up prices further' (Burnett). The population crisis in Europe had culminated in the Napoleonic Wars which, through waste of real resources, also pushed up prices. The misery of the British working classes was extreme. This was the period in which Malthus drew the attention of the world to the whole problem of population pressure, and in which Francis Place began to urge the workers to use contraceptives, in order to reduce their population and thus increase their bargaining power. In the long run, as he rightly observed, 'every suggestion which does not tend to the reduction in number of the working people is useless'.

From about 1820 to 1945, a whole set of new factors came into play. Malthus had foreseen them, and had rightly warned that they were unique and would not recur again. Population continued to increase throughout the period. The rate eventually fell considerably, but towards the end of the period the absolute number of the population was so large that even small percentage increases meant the addition of large numbers of people: the absolute increase between 1911 and 1951 was greater than between 1801 and 1841 (nearly 8 millions compared with nearly 7 millions). By 1951 the population of England and Wales was nearly 44 millions.

Despite this staggering population rise, prices actually fell on the whole until the First World War; by that time they had got back to the level of the late eighteenth century. By that time also, real wages had more than doubled since 1820, and were higher than they had ever been before, even in the fifteenth century. Both the World Wars were accompanied by unprecedented price increases, but real wages continued to rise until the Second World War. It is only since that war that they have begun again to lose ground.

Prices, Wages and Population

This new turn of events was made possible by several developments. In the nineteenth century Britain became the first industrialized nation in the modern sense, and long maintained her lead in the new industrial world. People sometimes imagine that industrialization in itself will make possible a large increase of population. This is magical thinking: you cannot eat machine tools, however many you make. British industrialization made possible a large increase in the British population because simultaneously vast new lands were opened up for crop agriculture – chiefly the prairies of North America, ploughed up with the help of the new steel ploughs. By the 1850s Britain was importing nearly a quarter of her wheat, by the 1870s more than half, paying for it by the export of manufactured goods. Raw materials other than food, and luxuries of all kinds, could now be imported from abroad. Great new lands were available for emigration, to take off any surplus of labour. By the 1860s it was becoming difficult to man the Navy. The standard of living of the British people was steadily rising, reflected in the rise of real wages.

But this bonanza could not last. Classical Athens had lost her favoured position when other peoples began to make fine pottery. Britain began to lose her favoured position as other nations industrialized. She began to have difficulty in paying for her imports – what we call a 'balance-of-payments' problem. Such problems began in the 1930s, and have multiplied since the Second World War, with the final loss of the British Empire. With the loss of the special world privileges that buffered them against price rise and real wage decline, the British people are now once again exposed to the penalties normally incurred when population outstrips resources.

As a food-importing country, Britain is now extremely vulnerable. But her food supply is still adequate. Ever since the Industrial Revolution got under way, the key essential resource in Britain, constantly outstripped by population, has been *housing*. The rapid growth of industrial towns in the early nineteenth century produced an immediate housing shortage, and the ground then lost has never been made up. All the work of the Victorian charitable trusts, clearing slums in London from 1845 to 1875, was sufficient to house only 6 months of London's population increase; the demand today is, of course, far greater. In 1970, with births still exceeding deaths by 800 per day, a new city the size of Leeds is needed every year.

Rents rose steeply all through the nineteenth century, and in the past 50 years housing costs have probably increased ten- or fifteen-fold; 'the most important single price-change in the period is, no doubt, in housing' (Burnett). Council house rents had by 1969 risen about six-fold since the 1930s. Since the Second World War housing costs have rocketed, in part because of the varied pressures of population density on land itself. The price of agricultural land in southern England doubled between 1962 and 1964. The cost of building land in London rose about seven-fold between 1951 and 1963. Between 1960 and 1970, the price of a new house, including the cost of land, more than doubled; between 1969 and 1970 the average price of a new house rose by some £300. Already in 1900 it was estimated that 11 per cent of all expenditure was on rent. By 1965, among the lowest-paid workers and the pensioners, housing, together with fuel, light and power, made up the same percentage of family expenditure (31 per cent) as food itself. It is thought that growing numbers of old people in Britain die each winter of diseases associated with 'under-heating', because they cannot afford enough fuel. For many working people, as a by-product of urban development, commuting transport has become another essential, and transport accounted for about 10 per cent of all personal expenditure by 1965.

In earlier periods, high food prices had several results. They regularly led to demonstrations and riots. At times, in eighteenth century England and France, these took relatively restrained forms: bakers and millers were forced by indignant crowds to sell at prices considered reasonable. The modern analogy could be some form of popular rent control by squatter groups. More serious riots were, of course, common, and the incidence and severity of riots have been shown to correspond closely with the occurrence of high food prices, in France in the eighteenth century, in Japan in the seventeenth to nineteenth centuries, in England in the sixteenth, eighteenth and nineteenth centuries. A modern equivalent would be the occurrence of serious housing riots, not yet seen in Britain. All this, of course, makes up the background of the more serious civil violence and war that forms part of every population crisis.

Food shortage has also regularly led to malnutrition, vulnerability to disease and hence to high mortality in epidemics. The stresses of crowded commuting, the stresses and sanitation hazards of crowded and inadequate housing, could obviously have similar effects, in a society where population pressure is already placing a severe strain on health and sanitation services. All the ingredients could be present for a reduction of the British population by a considerable rise in the death rate.

What are we to do about prices and wages? We have seen that simple decrees about price levels, and manipulations of money, are both ineffective. What about increasing the production of real resources? Certainly we need more houses at present. But there are overwhelming objections to what Edward Goldsmith has called 'the cult of productivity' in general. First, for purely mathematical reasons, no conceivable production of goods can keep pace indefinitely with even a modest natural increase of human population. Second, it is equally impossible to sustain an ever-increasing market for export products. Third, considerations of exhaustion of resources and pollution of the environment are making it more and more imperative to *reduce*

218

industrial production, far from increasing it. In Britain, we cannot build many more houses: we are running out of land.

What, then, will become of Britain by 2000? One thing is certain. Population and prices will not continue to rise for the next three decades. By the turn of the century, either the death rate will have risen – or the birth rate will have dropped. For there remains the solution of Francis Place – voluntary birth control – supported by generous government provision of education, information and facilities. Such a policy will more than pay for itself, almost from the outset. A voluntary birth-control programme, started in Mecklenburg County, North Carolina, in 1960, is estimated to have saved $250,000 in welfare payments within 3 years; the operating expenses totalled one-twentieth of the savings. In the past, substantial reduction of population, even the cessation of population growth, have resulted in rising real wages and a rising standard of living. We do not need the horrors of a Black Death to achieve this. No doubt we shall need much skill and much research to take the fullest advantage of the opportunity so provided. But the opportunity will be there.

REFERENCES

BORTON, H. 1968. (2nd edition.) *Peasant Uprising in Japan of the Tokugawa Period.* New York: Paragon Book Reprint Corp.

BURNETT, J. 1969. *A History of the Cost of Living.* Harmondsworth: Penguin.

CHECKLAND, S. G. 1964. *The Rise of Industrial Society in England, 1815–1885.* London: Longmans.

DRAKE, M. (Ed.). 1969. *Population in Industrialization.* London: Methuen.

GOLDSMITH, E. R. D. 1970. The Cult of 'Productivity', In *The Ecologist, 1.*

GRYTZELL, K. G. 1969. *County of London. Population Changes 1801–1901.* Lund (Sweden): Royal University of Lund, Department of Geography and C. W. K. Gleerup.

HAMILTON, E. J. 1960. The History of Prices before 1750. In *XIe Congress International des Sciences Historiques, Rapports.* Stockholm.

HAMMARSTROM, I. 1957. The 'Price Revolution' of the Sixteenth Century, some Swedish Evidence. In *The Scandinavian Economic History Review, 5.*

HEICHELHEIM, F. M. 1970. *An Ancient Economic History.* Leyden: A. W. Sijthoff.

JONES, A. H. M. 1953. Inflation under the Roman Empire. In *The Economic History Review, 5.*

LEVITAN, S. A. 1966. New Directions in Aid of the Poor. In BOWEN, H. R. and G. L. MANGUM (Ed.). 1966. *Automation and Economic Progress.* Englewood, Cliffs, N. J.: Prentice-Hall.

LUTZ, H. F. 1932. Price Fluctuations in Ancient Babylonia. In *Journal of Economic and Business History, 4.*

MILLER, M. 1965. *Rise of the Russian Consumer.* London: Institute of Economic Affairs.

219

MOLLER, H. (Ed.). 1964. *Population Movements in Modern European History*. London: Collier-Macmillan.

PHELPS BROWN, E. H. and S. V. HOPKINS. 1962. Seven Centuries of the Prices of Consumables, Compared with Builders' Wage-Rates. In *Essays in Economic History*, *Vol . 2*. London: Edward Arnold.

ROGERS, J. E. 1884. *Thorold Six Centuries of Work and Wages*. London: W. Swan Sonnenschein & Co.

RUDE, G. 1970. *Paris and London in the 18th Century*. London: Collins.

RUSSELL, C. and RUSSELL, W. M. S. 1968. *Violence, Monkeys and Man*. London: Macmillan.

SAGGS, H. W. F. 1965. *Everyday Life in Babylonia and Assyria*. London: Batsford.

SLICHER VAN BATH, B. H. 1963. *The Agrarian History of Western Europe A.D. 500–1850*. London: Edward Arnold.

SMITH, W. 1968. *An Historical Introduction to the Economic Geography of Great Britain*. London: Bell.

TITOW, J. Z. 1969. *English Rural Society 1200–1350*. London: Allen & Unwin.

WALLAS, G. 1925. *The Life of Francis Place*. London: Allen & Unwin.

21 SOCIAL DISINTEGRATION: CAUSES

Edward Goldsmith

Editor, *The Ecologist*

When social systems (or any other systems) join together to form a larger one, they are said to integrate. When the opposite occurs, the larger system must be regarded as disintegrating – in other words, its order is being reduced; the bonds holding it together are being weakened until eventually they can hold it no longer. At this point it breaks up into smaller systems.

This process can occur at all levels of organization. A modern state is often an unstable system held together externally by a vast bureaucracy. It may be made up of different territorially based ethnic groups, each with its own culture and traditions that will furnish it with stronger and more lasting bonds than those linking it to the other groups in the national state. It is not difficult for such a state to disintegrate into such ethnic groups. Austria in the thirties and Spain during the Republic are particularly striking examples.

It may also disintegrate into ethnic groups that are not territorially based, but that, before disintegration set in, lived symbiotically with each other as did the whites and the Negroes in the United States when the latter worked on plantations in the Southern states and more spectacularly as do the different castes in India.

When this occurs, then the natural state ceases to be a self-regulating unit of behaviour; it becomes unstable and has to be run externally by a bureaucracy and an autocrat.

In such cases, the new social units into which the original society disintegrates can become viable, self-regulating societies if conditions are right, though in the latter case it would require granting each group its separate territory.

If a society disintegrates beyond the clan or village level, it ceases to be a viable social unit. Such disintegration can qualify as pathological. The peasant societies described by Banfield are pathological. The largest unit of organization is the family and above this, no effective co-operation is possible. According to Banfield, such a society will display a number of related characteristics. For instance, 'no-one will further the interest of the group or the community except as it is to his private advantage to do so. In other words, the hope of material gain in the short run will be the only motive for concern of public affairs . . . the law will be disregarded when there is no

221

reason to fear punishment . . . an office holder will take bribes when he can . . . but whether he takes bribes or not, it will be assumed by society that he does.' Clearly such a society will not be capable of running itself, *i.e.* of constituting a self-regulating system. Rather, it will require a bureaucracy and other external controls to keep it together.

Similarly, a society in which the families themselves have disintegrated and in which the largest unit of effective organization is the individual or the incomplete, single-parent, family, is even more clearly pathological. An example is that found in certain urban slums. According to Oscar Lewis, the main social and psychological features of such a society 'include living in crowded quarters, a lack of privacy, gregariousness, a high incidence of alcoholism, frequent resort to violence in the settlement of quarrels, frequent use of physical violence in the teaching of children, wife-beating, early initiation into sex, free unions or consensual marriages, a relatively high incidence of the abandonment of mothers and children, a trend towards mother-centred families and a much greater knowledge of maternal relations, the predominance of the nuclear family, a strong predisposition to authoritarianism, and a great emphasis upon family solidarity – an ideal only rarely achieved. Other traits include a strong present and time orientation with relatively little ability to defer gratification and plan for the future, a sense of resignation and fatalism based upon the realities of their difficult life situation, a belief in male superiority which reaches its crystallization in "machismo" or the cult of masculinity, a correspondingly martyr complex among women, and finally, a high tolerance for psychological pathology of all sorts.'

He regards this related set of behavioural traits as a culture all of its own which he refers to as 'the culture of poverty'.

It is to be found not only in the slums of Mexican cities, in which Lewis carried out most of his work but also in a large number of other urban societies. 'It seems to me that the culture of poverty has some universal characteristics which transcend the regional, rural, urban and even national differences.' The 'culture of poverty' is thus a behavioural response that occurs spontaneously when environmental conditions are propitious.

The main features of such a culture is that it is very rudimentary. As Lewis says, 'Poverty of culture is one of the crucial traits of the culture of poverty.'

It is thereby incapable of ensuring self-regulatory behaviour at the level of a community or even of a family, and appears to be exclusively associated with the lowest possible level of social integration; that in which the unit of behaviour is the individual or the incomplete nuclear family.

To predict its behaviour, probably the most important thing to know of a society, is the extent to which it is integrated, *i.e.* its degree or order. Un-

222

Social Disintegration: Causes

fortunately, no terminology is available to classify societies in this way. One is thus forced to coin one's own. I suggest using the prefixes *ethno-* (a nation), *oikio-* (a family or hearth from which *eco-* as in economics and ecology is a corruption) and *ego-* (the self) together with a suffix – *telic* (from *telos*, an end or goal), which would give one the terms *ethnotelic, oikiotelic* and *egotelic* to designate these three degrees of integration.

These terms are, needless to say, crude ones, as there are clearly different degrees of ethnotely, oikiotely and egotely.

Thus extreme egotely or social entropy would be temporarily achieved by putting together on an island a mass of heterogeneous people of different race and culture and speaking different languages, *i.e.* with nothing whatsoever in common. Before long, they would start organizing themselves into couples, families and eventually small communities, so as to be able to meet environmental challenges – at the same time developing the basis of a common culture. Indeed, as Whyte has shown, the members of even the worst slums are linked together in some way; there is some sort of community life, however rudimentary. That is why slum-clearance schemes usually increase egotely rather than decrease it.

It is important to realize that social systems exist in time as well as in space. They are four-dimensional. Disintegration is not only spatial but also temporal. As pathological disintegration sets in, so one must expect to see a corresponding decrease in their temporal organization.

An individual in a stable, ordered society considers himself one stage in a long process, of which his ancestors were the previous stages and his descendants the subsequent ones. That is why there is little fear of death and little concern with the after-life in such societies. A man considers that he will simply live on in his children. This is particularly well illustrated by Hsu with regard to traditional Chinese society. As a society disintegrates, a man tends to regard himself more as isolated temporarily as well as spatially. That is why he is over-concerned with his own petty interests to the detriment of those of his community, and with the present and short-term to the exclusion of the long-term. As a result, there is nothing to hold together the larger four-dimensional social system, save a set of precarious external controls which is unlikely to prevent further disintegration both in space and in time.

CAUSES OF DISINTEGRATION. A society can be subjected to many modifications that will adversely affect its capacity for self-regulation, and hence adaptation. Apart from those that are to all practical extents unpredictable, modifications are most likely to occur during periods of rapid growth. As such they can be regarded as feedback controls preventing growth beyond the optimum point.

223

How they operate is best studied at the level of a simple tribal society which often displays a very high degree of order.

Ordered societies do not require any external controls in the shape of formal institutions. This in itself makes for greater stability. If a society is controlled by one man, his demise leads to a vacuum which often cannot be filled very easily. If, on the other hand, it is achieved by the society as a whole, there is no way of upsetting its organization save by extermination.

It also means that the society behaves in a way that favours its own interests as opposed to those of one of its parts. In other words, the controls are themselves subjected to the control of the system as a whole.

As Lowie writes, 'It should be noted that the legislative function in most primitive communities seems strangely curtailed when compared with that exercised in the more complex civilizations. All the exigencies of normal social intercourse are covered by customary law, and the business of such governmental machinery as exists is rather to exact obedience to traditional usage than to create new products.'

This essential principle is clearly established by Lucy Mair in her book, *Primitive Government*.

The function of government is assumed by the citizens as a whole. The most important influence is tradition, any deviation from which is severely frowned upon. The ancestral spirits, the council of elders and public opinion in general combine to oppose and chastise any unnecessary departure from the traditions and customary law that is handed down from generation to generation. Even where there is a king, the latter's authority is still strictly limited. Thus, among the Ashanti and other West African people, he can be de-stooled by a mere show of hands.

The same was true of the Hellenic kings of Homeric times.

The real power did not reside in them but in the 'Demouphemos' or public opinion. Later this was institutionalized into the 'Demoukratos'. The latter without the former, as we find in most modern states, is of no value save to provide a façade behind which powerful individuals and groups will vie with each other for the real control of the society.

On the other hand, once the society has totally disintegrated, its capacity for self-regulation breaks down.

As Fortes and Evans-Pritchard write, 'The evidence at our disposal suggests that cultural and economic heterogeneity is associated with a state-like political structure. Centralized authority and an administrative organization seems to be necessary to accommodate culturally diverse groups within a single political system, especially if they have different modes of livelihood.' Indeed only an elaborate bureaucracy run by a shameless autocrat can hope to control a heterogeneous mass of people deprived of a common culture and a sense of duty towards their society.

224

Social Disintegration: Causes

It is customary today to criticize certain autocratic governments such as that of the colonels in Greece.

Little do people realize that the choice in such a society is not between dictatorship and democracy but between dictatorship and chaos. Democracy in the sense of self-government only becomes possible once the people become bound together by a common culture, and once a strong public opinion develops to sanction any deviation from the established code of behaviour.

What is likely to happen during rapid growth of a society that can lead to disintegration, and hence a breakdown in the process of self-regulation?

Let us seek examples among simple self-regulating societies. In Fiji, a tyranny was possible when a chief with limited authority over his people allotted land to refugees fleeing from another locality. These formed a minority that did not belong to the body politic, and who therefore developed personal allegiance to the king, greatly enhancing his prestige and authority and hence his ability to tyrannize his subjects.

The rise of the Kazak and Mongul Khans can be attributed in the same way to the attachment to their court of Nokod or soldiers of fortune, who being outside the body politic and owing personal allegiance to the Khans, served as a core to his organization for future conquest. Similarly the Emperor Frederick II, hampered by the obedience owed to the pope by his subjects, transferred 16,000 conquered Moslems from Sicily to Apulia where they founded a colony, forming a troop directly responsible to him and immune to excommunication.

If a society embarks on a career of conquest and establishes hegemony over alien peoples, the would-be tyrant is then in a position to use any of these alien peoples against his own citizens. In addition to this, in order to maintain sway over heterogeneous peoples held together by no social bonds, a personality cult is likely to develop. The king or leader becomes the principle bond holding them together, which will make possible the most autocratic behaviour on his part. To maintain control over these people, an army will probably be required; the bigger his empire, the greater the necessity for such an army and the greater the probability that it will degenerate from being a citizen army that owes allegiance to the community as a whole, to a professional one with allegiance to its leaders only.

This is precisely what happened during the latter part of the Roman Republic and the subsequent Empire. It was this that rendered possible the civil wars between Marius and Sulla and later between Pompey and Caesar.

The most common cause of social disintegration and the emergence of an autocracy is the development of a proletariat. In a sense, this is an unsatisfactory term. It tends to be identified with the working class, which is wrong. The latter includes trained people with a definite role and place in society. The proletariat should really be used to designate the unintegrated members of a society – those parts of a social system that have come into being by multiplication as opposed to differentiation; what Homer called 'the tribeless, clanless, hearthless ones'.

Plato described the proletariat of a Hellenic city 'as he who dwells within the city without falling into any of the categories of the city, whom one can call neither trader, nor artisan, neither knight nor hoplite, but only poor or indigent'.

The Plebeians originally fell into this category. The history of the Roman Republic is to a great extent the history of the slow absorption of the Plebeians, of their transformation into citizens capable of participating in the government of the city. How little they were integrated to begin with is well illustrated by the story of their mass departure from Rome and voluntary exile to the Sacred Mountain. They left, 'since the Patricians wish to possess the city for themselves, let them do so at their leisure. For us Rome is nothing. We have neither hearth nor sacrifices nor fatherland. We are leaving but a foreign city. No hereditary religion attaches us to this site. All lands are the same to us.'

However, their voluntary exile was short-lived. This structureless mass of people was incapable of creating a city on the model of that which it had left and which was the only one it had known. Consequently the Plebeians returned to Rome and after many struggles established themselves as citizens of the Republic.

They were absorbed, but Rome never succeeded in absorbing the vast mass of slaves and foreigners who thronged to Rome towards the end of the Republic, and throughout the period of the Empire, and which undoubtedly caused the disintegration of this great civilization.

It is the main theme of Aristotle's *Politics* that tyrannies in the ancient world invariably arose as a result of the alliance between the king, or ruler, and the proletariat against the citizens. This was so in the case of Pisistratus at Athens, Theagenes at Megara and Dionysius at Syracuse.

A proletariat tends to develop once a city becomes prosperous. It can thus be regarded as a feedback mechanism preventing the development of excessive wealth rather than too high a population.

The mechanism is simple. With prosperity, food can be bought from abroad to feed more people than previously. Starvation no longer exerts a control over population. People come from the surrounding country to take advantage of the prosperity. Even if a different culture, they are welcome, as the developing economy requires cheap and abundant labour. They may come as slaves as they did to Rome, as peasants from the surrounding countryside to the developing cities of Flanders, Bohemia and Southern Germany during the late Middle Ages, or as foreign immigrants to the industrialized countries of Northern Europe at the present time.

226

Social Disintegration: Causes

Rome fell not as the result of the Barbarian invasions but as the victim of internal disintegration, due to the urbanization of the yeomanry, and the vast population of liberated slaves and their transformation into the structureless and depressed proletariat entirely dependant upon state welfare for its livelihood and entertainment: free corn and the public games. Chelhod describes the fall of Mecca in very similar terms.

Norman Cohn traces the growth of a proletariat in North European cities of the Middle Ages, and the Messianic movements that arose to reintegrate the alienated masses into a new society by providing them with a separatist culture of their own. Kornhauser shows that totalitarian movements are only possible in societies that have lost their basic structure, mass societies as he calls them.

It is one of Durkheim's principal themes that a vast centralized bureaucratic machine destroys a society's essential structure and renders it so unstable that it loses its capacity for self-government. He writes, 'The social forms that used to serve as a framework for individuals and a skeleton for the society, either no longer exist or are in course of being effaced, and no new forms are taking their place. So that nothing remains but the fluid mass of individuals. For the State itself has been reabsorbed by them. Only the administrative machine has kept its stability and goes on operating with the same automatic regularity.'

This must be so as it destroys the spirit of self-reliance, the sense of duty to the community and all the associated cultural traits that together permit social self-regulation.

Societies that, over a long period, have been governed by an autocracy or a vast bureaucracy, lose the habit of self-government and are thereby condemned to be governed by a succession of tyrannies from which they become incapable of extracting themselves.

The principle involved is the law of economy. A society like any other system will display the minimum size and also the minimum organization or order necessary to face a given environmental challenge. Autocratic government reduces the need on the part of a society to furnish any effort. So it simply loses the capacity to furnish this effort.

Welfare does exactly the same thing. Peasant society as Banfield shows can only exist because the state provides it with all sorts of services that it would normally have to provide for itself, being forced to organize itself into larger units to do so.

He writes, 'Amoral familism (or oikioletic society as I have referred to it) is not a normal state of culture. It could not exist for long if there were not an outside agency – the state – to maintain order and in other respects mitigate its effects. Except for the intervention of the state, the war of all against all would sooner or later erupt into open violence, and the local society would either perish or produce cultural forms – perhaps a religion of great authority … Because the larger society has prevented indigenous adaptation of this kind without making possible the full assimilation to itself of the local culture, the Montegrano ethos (named after the village in which he conducted his study) exists as something transitional and in this sense, unnatural.'

If welfare is pushed further to usurp functions that should be fulfilled at a family level, as well as those that should be fulfilled at a communal one, then the family unit itself will tend to disintegrate, and the society will become egotelic.

The extended family as Murdock has shown (which may be bilateral, matrilineal or patrilineal) is a feature of all simple stable societies so far studied by anthropologists.

The nuclear family made up of two parents and their children is unstable. Thus if one parent dies, the remaining one is incapable of fulfilling all the necessary functions required to bring up the children. Whereas in the extended family, countless relations are available for this purpose.

The nuclear family is usually a feature of a disintegrating society. *A fortiori*, the one parent family, and the isolate, can only survive in an environment which does not display sufficient challenges to justify the existence of the larger family group – such as the modern welfare state. Free education, a free health service and family allowances make it quite unnecessary for a father to struggle so as to be able to cater for the basic requirements of his children. The effect of behaving in a less fatherly manner will be to lead his children to behave in a less filial one.

Crèches and nursery schools are available for the mother who wishes to forgo the satisfaction and duty of bringing up her own children, while if she wishes to abandon them altogether, there are institutions to which they can be consigned. A highly developed pension scheme means that people do not have to depend on their children to provide for them in their old age.

It is a serious error to suppose that poverty is the main cause of social disintegration. One of the most apparent features of oikiotelic society in Southern Italy is the gloom and general feeling of hopelessness. The Italian peasants refer to it as 'la miseria'.

Banfield writes … 'La miseria arises as much, or more, from social as from biological deprivations. This being the case, there is no reason to expect that a moderate increase in income (if by some miracle that could be brought about) would make the atmosphere of the village less heavy with melancholy. On the contrary, unless there were accompanying changes in social structure and culture, increasing incomes would probably bring with them increasing discontent.'

The same is true of an egotelic society.

A slum is a slum, not because its inhabitants are poor nor because its housing facilities are bad, though these may be contributing factors. It cannot be turned into a sound and stable community by pumping money into it, nor by lodging its inhabitants in brand-new blocks of flats. These measures, by reducing social bonds, are in fact likely to do more harm than good.

This tends to be confirmed by the fact that the squatter communities that have appeared in many towns of South America, and who live in far worse physical conditions than the conventional slum communities, display few egotelic symptoms.

According to Mangin, the squatters establish themselves by taking over empty lots on the periphery of the big cities. If this were done in a haphazard way, they would be driven off by the police, so a sort of military operation is required whereby some thousand squatters take over the lot in one fell swoop under cover of darkness so that when the morning dawns a new shanty-town has appeared, too big to be demolished by the police without causing a serious popular outcry. The city authorities react by refusing to recognize the very existence of the new shanty-town. As a result, its inhabitants have to fend for themselves, organize their waste disposal system, police, schools, *etc.* For this purpose they form neighbourhood committees in which all participants elect their own leaders and soon develop relatively sound communities that contrast only too sharply with the conventional welfare-maintained slums. As Mangin writes, 'Although poor, they do not live the life of squalor and hopelessness characteristic of the "culture of poverty" depicted by Oscar Lewis.'

Welfare is clearly not the only factor tending to reduce the challenges that justify the survival of such essential social structures such as the small community and the family in a stable, ordered society. Modern industry is another. The family in a stable, ordered society is an economic unit. People get married because they want children but also because the co-operation of the different members of the family is required for the fulfilment of those tasks necessary for survival. With the development of modern industry there has been a radical reduction in the number of tasks that have to be fulfilled at the communal level and even more so at that of the family. The wife no longer has to bake the bread, or tend to the vegetable garden nor gather faggots for the fire. Bread, vegetables and any other food, can be bought at the supermarket, and the home will probably be central-heated.

With the proliferation of tinned and frozen foods, she no longer even has to do much cooking, an activity which until the last generation, took up most of the time, skill and ingenuity of the average housewife in countries as advanced as France and Italy. Men can open tins and thaw out meat as well as women and the economic necessity for a family unit has correspondingly decreased.

The modern dogma that men and women are psychologically, if not physi-

229

cally, fit to perform the same tasks and the development of an educational system in which women acquire the same information and are provided with the same social and economic aspirations as the men, has led to a further disintegration of the family. What bonds are there to hold together two people who both have similar jobs, earn the same amount of money and live in a household in which all the household chores are done for them by big corporations?

Sexual attraction is about all that is left, and in this respect it is interesting to note that of all the 3,000 or so societies so far examined by anthropologists, ours is the first in which sexual attraction is regarded as a reason for marriage. It is undoubtedly the most unstable of links; too much so to serve as the principal, let alone the only, bond to a union on whose duration must depend the stability and mental health of the children born of it.

The modern industrial state also favours the disintegration of the family because of the proliferation of communications media which increase the influence of random sources of information (to the detriment of the familial ones) in determining a child's moral and intellectual development. Increased mobility, principally as a result of affluence, also reduces the parents' influence.

One of the most powerful disintegrative forces, however, is the rapid changes to which our society is being subjected. It is basically 'experience' that the elders communicate to youth, and this is of little value in a changing situation. To maintain social stability, environmental changes must simply be kept within certain limits.

This brings us to another consideration. A culture develops as an adaptive response to a specific environment. If the latter undergoes a radical transformation, then the culture is no longer adaptive – and it must itself be transformed. However, for a new one to develop, the original one must first of all disintegrate. Thus religious conversions are usually of a purely 'terminological' nature, unless the culture of the society to be converted is first of all destroyed. The same is true of a human personality. As Sargant shows, a nervous breakdown is adaptive in that it ensures the breakdown of a behaviour pattern, that in changed environmental conditions may no longer be adaptive. Similarly, during historical times, many societies have disintegrated because changed economic conditions removed their very *raison d'être*. This was probably the case of the cities of South Arabia after the main trade routes shifted to the Mediterranean – also of the Mediterranean maritime cities such as Genoa, Pisa and Venice when trade shifted to the North Sea and the Atlantic.

Our culture developed to adapt our society to economic, and in particular industrial, growth, which is becoming increasingly less viable, and it may have to disintegrate before a new post-industrial society can hope to emerge.

230

Social Disintegration: Causes

It remains to determine how social, and in particular family, disintegration affects the individual, hence the society of which he is part.

REFERENCES

BANFIELD, EDWARD C. 1958. *The Moral Basis of a Backward Society*. New York: The Free Press.

BARTH, FREDERICK. 1968. Ecological relations of ethnic groups in Swat, North Pakistan. In MANNERS, ROBERT and DAVID KAPLAN, *Theory in Anthropology*. Chicago: Aldine.

CHELHOD, G. 1958. *Introduction à la Sociologie de L'Islam*. Paris: Besson.

DURKHEIM, EMILE. 1958. *Professional Ethics and Civil Morals*. London: Collier/Macmillan, Glencoe Free Press.

FORTES, M. and E. E. EVANS-PRITCHARD. 1965. *African Political Systems*. Oxford: OUP.

GLOTZ, G. 1921. *The Greek City and its Institutions*. London: Routledge & Kegan Paul.

GOLDSMITH, EDWARD. 1970. Religion in the light of a general behavioural model. In *Systematics, 8*.

HSU, FRANCIS L. K. 1942. *Under the Ancestor's Shadow*. London: Kegan Paul.

KORNHAUSER, WILLIAM. 1960. *The Politics of Mass Society*. London: Kegan Paul.

LEWIS, OSCAR. 1966. The culture of poverty. In *Scientific American, 215*.

LOWIE, ROBERT. 1921. *Primitive Society*. London: Routledge & Kegan Paul.

MAIR, LUCY. 1962. *Primitive Government*. Harmondsworth: Penguin Books.

MALINOWSKI, BRONISLAW. 1927. *Sex and Repression in Savage Society*. London: Routledge & Kegan Paul.

MANGIN, WILLIAM. 1967. Squatter settlements. In *Scientific American, 217* (4).

MURDOCK, G. P. 1960. The universality of the nuclear family. In BELL, NORMAN and EZRA VOGEL, 1960, *A Modern Introduction to the Family*. London: Routledge & Kegan Paul.

SARGANT, WILLIAM. 1957. *Battle for the Mind*. London: Heinemann.

WHYTE, WILLIAM FOOTE. 1943. *Street Corner Society*. Chicago: Chicago Press.

22 SOCIAL DISINTEGRATION: EFFECTS

Edward Goldsmith

Editor, *The Ecologist*

Most schoolteachers and social workers would agree that the children who give them the greatest trouble are those with family problems. Such children may have a father who for various reasons does not fulfil his fatherly functions – in all probability he will be simply displaying one of the many symptoms of anomie or egotely – or a mother with similar problems, or he may simply come from an incomplete, or one-parent, family. Whatever the exact situation, the child will have suffered from some form of family deprivation which is bound to affect him profoundly and colour every aspect of his behaviour throughout his life. Such children are often referred to as emotionally disturbed. However bright they may be, they will tend to find it very difficult to fit into their social environment, the reason being that the early and most important stages of socialization were badly impaired. The earlier family deprivation occurred, the more will this be the case, for as D. O. Hebb[1] shows, the effect of early experience on adult behaviour is universally correlated with age.

Sadly, it is rarely possible for socially deprived and emotionally disturbed children to be satisfactorily socialized. No amount of school education can do much for them.

Children who have grown up in isolation from their fellows are even further incapacitated. They are incapable of the normal familial and communal functions and sometimes seem indistinguishable from congenital idiots. This subject is treated in Zingg's remarkable study, *Wolf Children and Feral Man*.[2] Experiments with animals, such as those conducted by Harlow with monkeys, lead one to the same conclusion.[3]

Emotionally disturbed children are characterized by inability to accept any social constraints. They are unable to concentrate on their work and are only interested in things which are of apparent immediate advantage to them. Regardless of their intelligence level, they are thus extremely difficult to educate. They are particularly concerned with the present, and the short-term, and are predisposed to all pathological forms of behaviour such as delinquency, drug addiction, alcoholism and schizophrenia.

What is worse, when they grow up, they are unlikely to be capable of fulfilling their normal family functions; their children consequently also deprived of a normal family environment, will in turn tend to be emotionally unstable.

John Bowlby went so far as to compare a delinquent with a typhoid carrier.[4] He is as much a carrier of disease as the latter – of a disease of the personality, which will affect his family and his community for generations, until his descendants are eliminated by natural selection.

Socially deprived, emotionally disturbed youths are a feature of disintegrating societies. In the black ghettoes of New York and other large American cities, they are the rule rather than the exception. The low standard of achievement and the high rate of crime, and various forms of retreatism that characterize such societies, is mainly attributable to family deprivation.

If a child is seriously affected by being deprived of a satisfactory family environment, an adult is also adversely affected by being deprived of a satisfactory communal environment. In an ordered society a man is a differentiated part of a family or of a community which is made up of a large number of interwoven groups of different kinds. In a typical tribal society he belongs to a paternal and a maternal kinship group. He may also be a member of an age group, of an economic association, of a secret society, of a military group, *etc.* It is his position as a member of each of these groups which provides him with his status or identity as a differentiated member of his social system.

In a disintegrating society, he loses his identity. He is lost in an anonymous mass of humanity. It is this lack of identity which is normally referred to as alienation or anomie. It is that terrible feeling of loneliness when surrounded by a vast number of people that is so much worse than loneliness in a desert.

In an ordered society, a cultural pattern provides an individual with a complete goal structure and an environment within which these goals can be satisfied.

In a stable society the principal goal appears to be the acquisition of prestige, to be looked up to by one's family and community. In each society this is achieved in a different way. In a hunting society it requires skill in the hunt, while in a society earning its livelihood from agriculture, it must be skill in husbandry.

But this is not sufficient. Such skill is nearly always regarded as associated with what the Polynesians call 'mana', a special sort of power which can be acquired by performing the rituals and observing the ethical code which together make up society's culture.[5a,b] At the same time an individual's personal stock of this power can be reduced by breaking any of the society's many taboos. In our industrial society, prestige is achieved in a variety of ways, including the right education, entering a socially acceptable profession and perhaps most important of all, making money.

The proletariat, as well as members of different ethnic groups, may for various reasons, find these avenues of success barred to them. In such conditions they have no alternative but to develop a substitute set of goals. Cloward and Ohlin[6] interpret the development of a criminal sub-culture in the slums of a big city in these terms. It provides people with a new set of goals which they can achieve. Once crime becomes big business, and requires the same sort of qualities that permit success in the mainstream culture, then a further substitute outlet is required.

It is in these terms that Cloward and Ohlin interpret the 'violent gang' sub-culture which also has its own ethic and goal structure, so different from the mainstream culture. However, those who have not succeeded in shedding the latter's values find themselves incapable of participating in it. They are forced to indulge in one or other form of retreatism – to isolate themselves psychologically from an environment which not only fails to provide them with an essential goal structure but also denies the setting for it.

Merton[7] describes a retreatist in the following way: '. . . Defeatism, quietism and resignation are manifested in escape mechanisms which ultimately lead him to "escape" from the requirements of the society. It is thus an expedient which arises from the continued failure to near the goal by legitimate measures and from an inability to use the illegitimate route because of internalized prohibitions, this process occurring while the supreme value of the success-goal has not yet been renounced. The conflict is resolved by abandoning both precipitating elements, the goals and the means. The escape is complete, the conflict is eliminated and the individual is asso-cialized.'

In a disintegrating society one would tend to find sub-cultures developing along all these different lines in varying degrees, *i.e.* there will be an increase in delinquency, violence and all the various forms of retreatism, such as drugs, drink, strange religious cults, *etc*, and mental disease. Such a society will be characterized by a general feeling of aimlessness, a frantic, almost pathetic search for originality, over-preoccupation with anything capable of providing short-term entertainment, and beneath it all a feeling of hopelessness of the futility of all effort.

Margaret Mead[8] writes, 'Juveniles who affect aberrant dress and modified transvestism . . . are a group who see life as a blind alley. They are in an economic situation which offers them no hope of a kind to satisfy social identity.' A student from Mason City, Iowa, could not put it more clearly when he writes in *Time Magazine*, 'I am a student at the University of Northern Iowa, and from the present state of the college I can see a direct relationship, almost a reflection of the entire world situation. On the campus one can find a small percentage of social drop-outs, another small percentage of dedicated students, while the vast majority are lost in a maze of non-purposeful lives.'

234

Social Disintegration: Effects

CRIME. Crime is very rare in a really stable and ordered society. Social constraints prevent all deviations from the cultural norm. Often these appear to the outsider to be of a very mild nature. Ridicule, for instance, is often quite sufficient to prevent anti-social behaviour. As Linton[9] writes, 'The Eskimos say that if a man is a thief no-one will do anything about it, but the people will laugh when his name is mentioned. This does not sound like a severe penalty, but it suffices to make theft almost unknown.'

In societies like that of the Comoro Islands, where feasts play a big part in people's lives, those given by people who have committed anti-social acts will be boycotted. This is a terrible insult and a most powerful deterrent. If it does not suffice, then there is the ultimate punishment: exclusion from the tribe or village.

Such a fate is considered worse than death. The victim is thereby deprived of his essential social environment and goal structure. He is lost in a hostile world to which he is not adapted culturally. He is condemned to the life of an isolate.

It must follow that in a stable society there is no need for a police force, nor for lawyers, tribunals, prisons, burglar-alarms, *etc*, that vast and elaborate superstructure required to control crime in a disintegrating society. It is interesting that in a modern industrial state, those areas where life most closely approximates that of a primitive society are precisely those where crime is the lowest, while it is where social structures have most conspicuously broken down – in big cities – that it is most frequent.

In the United States, according to Mr John Mitchell, Attorney-General, crime in cities of more than 250,000 inhabitants is two and a half times that of the suburbs, which in turn is twice that of rural areas. Crime, needless to say, is on the increase. In the United States it has doubled in the last 10 years. In 1969 there were 2,471 crimes per 100,000 inhabitants. There were 655,000 violent crimes and 4,334,000 crimes against property, 14,590 murders, 36,470 rapes and 306,420 aggravated assaults.

This reports an increase of 12 per cent over the previous year. In the United Kingdom, crime is increasing at a similar rate. In 1970, according to a *Newsight* investigation, there were $1\frac{1}{2}$ million indictable crimes, 300,000 in London alone, an increase of about 10 per cent over 1969.

Crimes of violence and burglary and battery in particular are increasing at the fastest rate, at more than 15 per cent per annum. These are at present 66 crimes of violence per 100,000 people in the United Kingdom as opposed to 324 per 100,000 in the United States. At the present doubling rate of five years it will take approximately 12 years to achieve the US rate of 324 per 100,000, which is so bad that life in cities has become intolerable and economic activity seriously menaced.

Professor Michael Banton of the Department of Sociology, Bristol University, told the British Association for the Advancement of Science that 'increased disorder is part of the price we pay for the adaptation of our social arrangements to an economic system which brings us such great material benefits'.

Crime is part of the price of affluence, or more precisely, of the egotely that affluence creates.

Perhaps the most damning indictment of our industrial society is the behaviour of people when the elaborate mechanisms of the law are for some technical reason put temporarily out of action.

In Montreal, during a 24-hour police strike, shops were pillaged, women raped and houses burgled.

In London a power strike, theft increased to such an extent in shops and department stores that many had to close until the light came on again.

Nothing better illustrates what can happen when the self-regulating mechanisms which normally ensure the orderly behaviour of the members of a stable society break down and are replaced by a precarious set of external controls.

ILLEGITIMACY. As the family unit breaks down, it is not surprising to find that illegitimacy, another symptom of social disintegration, increases. Nor is it surprising to find that it is closely linked with other systems of social disintegration. According to W. R. Lyster, an Australian statistician, 'Crime and illegitimacy rates are simultaneous in their incidence. The illegitimacy rate in England and Wales per hundred of all births has increased since 1955 from 4·7 to 7·8; crime has increased from about 45 per ten thousand to 120 per ten thousand; thus, both have more than doubled.'

Illegitimacy is costing the government £52 million per year. In industrial slums and other societies that have reached the more advanced stages of disintegration it is not unusual to find that up to 70 per cent of children are illegitimate.

W. A. W. Freeman, President of the Children's Officers Association, has recently reported a startling increase in the number of women who are simply abandoning their children, something which would not occur in a stable and ordered society.

DISCIPLINE. As a society disintegrates, there is a general reduction in discipline.

It is surprising just how disciplined people are in simple, ordered societies. The Hellenes, who prided themselves on their liberty, were in fact subjected to laws that we would consider the most shameful infringements of personal liberty.

Many Greek cities made it illegal for men to remain bachelors after a certain age. At Locrai, at Miletus and at Marseilles, women were forbidden

236

Social Disintegration: Effects

to drink wine. In Sparta there were strict laws on women's hairstyles, and in Athens, the law forbade women to take with them on a journey more than three dresses. In Rhodes the law prescribed shaving. In Sparta moustaches were forbidden. In Byzantium, the mere possession of a razor incurred a fine.[10]

The laws concerning involvement in public issues were strict. Neutrality, or indifference, to the politics of the city was punished by the loss of civil rights.

As society disintegrates, every rule and convention is questioned and discipline increasingly relaxed. We eventually find a situation in which everyone can do precisely what he pleases, and any attempt to enforce any discipline in the interests of the society is opposed.

ALCOHOLISM. The correlation of alcoholism, another form of retreatism, with anomie or egotely occurring as a result of the breakdown of social order, is well established.

This thesis is well presented by Field[11] who shows that it is universally proportionate to the cohesiveness of the family, clan and tribal groupings. It is significant that in the disintegrating society in which we live, alcoholism is increasing, and this despite alternative forms of retreatism, such as drugs, being more readily available.

William Madsen[12] examines the cause of the alcoholism among the semi-acculturated Mexican Americans along the Mexican–Texan border. The 'Gringo', or semi-acculturated Mexican, finds himself alienated from his normal family and communal social structures, without having succeeded in becoming integrated in Anglo-American society. He is thus a marginal man. 'Alone among two cultural worlds, the Agringado frequently finds alcohol the only mechanism available for anxiety relief.'

Madsen concludes, 'Although the specific etiology of alcohol is unknown, the cultural setting involving value concepts resulting in loss of identity with community seem to be conducive to alcoholism particularly when the individual has been exposed to the tradition that alcohol may function as an escape mechanism or as a prop to some core value.'

Clearly all drinking is not associated with egotely. Among other things, it is known to have a definite integrative effect on society. It provides a cathartic outlet for the tension and anxiety that exist in any society.

For each specific cultural pattern there must exist an optimum degree of alcohol consumption. It is likely that increases over and above this level will be in direct proportion to the development of disorder within the society itself. The number of offences of drunkenness proved in England and Wales for the year 1967 is greater than the number of offences proved in previous years. The increase as expected occurred in the large cities, the City of

London having 476·43 offences for each 10,000 of its population. The Home Office with characteristic ignorance of basic sociological matters writes, 'No reason for the increase can be adduced. There was no significant change in the liquor licensing laws.'

According to the National Council on Alcoholism, alcoholism is costing the country about £250 million a year, mainly by absenteeism from work. About seven workers out of every thousand have drinking problems, and there are about 400,000 alcoholics in the country, a figure which is increasing annually.

DRUG ADDICTION. Drug addiction is another form of retreatism which tends to increase with social disorder. Clearly a model capable of describing the rate of drug addiction would take into account other variables as well. In India, for example, because of religious aversion to alcohol in certain castes, drugs of various sorts play a big role among available cathartic outlets. They also play an important part in the rituals of many primitive peoples. Nevertheless, drug addiction as a form of retreatism undoubtedly increases with social disorder. Cloward and Ohlin[13] show that drug addiction as a form of retreatism is resorted to by deviants for whom both the legitimate and illegitimate avenues to social advancement are closed.

It is well known that drug addiction is increasing at an exponential rate in most of the industrial societies of the Western world today. At the 1969 meeting of the UN Commission on Narcotic Drugs[14] it was stated that the abuse of narcotics is assuming 'alarming proportions'. In Britain, according to the British representative, it is estimated that up to 125,000 people may be showing some dependence on barbiturates and up to 100,000 on amphetamines. The latter are the staple diet of the discotheques. The National Health service is responsible for issuing some 400 million tablets a year and millions more are obtained on private prescription or simply stolen.

In the United Kingdom the number of known heroin addicts increased 60 per cent between 1968 and 1969 to 2,782, 1,775 of which were fifteen- to twenty-three-year-olds.

According to the Home Office Inspector for Drugs, cases could be expected to multiply by five between 1969 and 1972. If these predictions were projected to the year 2000, there would be 546,750,000 cases – and practically everyone in England would be a drug addict!

According to *The Times*, heroin deaths in New York City have multiplied two-fold in 3 years.

In March 1970 there were an estimated 25,000 youngsters on heroin. Dr Donald H. Houria, President of the New York State Council on Drug Addiction, predicted 'within a couple of years, every high school and every college in the country will be inundated with heroin'.

Social Disintegration: Effects

In Washington, according to Dr Robert Dupont the head of the Police Department's Narcotics Treatment Agency, there are estimated to be 15,000 addicts of whom half are juveniles. A survey conducted by him revealed that in Washington 45 per cent of gaol inmates are heroin addicts.

The connection between drug addiction and more apparent psychotic states, which we know to be connected with anomie, was revealed in a study conducted by Dr Hekiemann and Gershon among random samples of 112 of the 560 drug abusers admitted to Belle Vue Psychiatric Hospital from January to July 1967. Dr Hekiemann said the most important reason for taking drugs was to escape from a strange underlying depression. Half of the drug abusers were found to have had definite pre-drug signs of schizophrenia and had been seen by psychiatrists before they had turned to drugs.

MENTAL HEALTH. Social disintegration is a major cause of mental disease. When an individual deprived of his essential social and physical environment is incapable of building a substitute one, or fails to isolate himself from the one he can no longer tolerate, by means of drugs or alcohol, his behaviour pattern, no longer adaptive to an environment for which it was not designed, tends to break down. One remaining position of defence is to build up his own personal world of fantasy which contains just those environmental constituents of which he has been deprived, and which he most requires.

There is considerable evidence to show that members of a society undergoing acculturation, whose culture is breaking down under the influence of an alien one are particularly prone to mental disease.

This point is made by Wittkower and Fried.[15] 'Change which affects basic cultural values, ideals or attitudes, traditionally the core of inter-personal relations, adversely affect mental health.' They also say, 'Evidence is accumulating to substantiate the hypothesis that mental health problems grow in direct relation to the disturbing of traditional bonds which hold families and communities together. It is suggested that individuals socialized under such well-knit family conditions may suffer when they are estranged from traditional systems of security arrangements, previously rooted in the family.'

Anthony Wallace[16] points to the same tendency: 'Anthropologists frequently have made note of the fact that primitive groups, who have been forced into situations of culture conflict and of partial, unorganized acculturation, seem prone to a higher frequency of the milder neurotic and personality trait disorders. Chronic anxiety and tension, psychosomatic complaints, alcoholism, narcotic addiction, delinquency and crime, witch fear, regressive or stunted personality development: such disorders apparently proliferate under the conditions produced by culture conflict and partial acculturation.'

Demarath,[17] in a careful survey of the evidence, concludes that 'wherever

239

schizophrenia has been reported, the society in question has been in the process of acculturation'.

Wittkower and Fried,[18] from research carried out in 1966 in Peru, found evidence that migrants from a tightly knit family background are especially vulnerable in an urban setting, and isolated from the security of their relatives. Involved in such movements are all the stresses and difficulties inherent to the tremendous readjustment immigrants must make to a novel and often hostile social cultural environment.' Similar practice is reported from Formosa, 'where mainland migrant patients show a parallel tendency to develop psychosomatic symptoms, as an unconscious defence against anxiety and tension.'

Dr D. C. Madison came to a similar conclusion as a result of a study of Polish migrants in New York State. He writes, 'There is a substantially higher percentage of Polish migrants in mental hospitals than would be expected from the incidence rate for the country as a whole.'

Malzberg and Lee in the study of hospital admission for the period 1939–41 in New York State, concluded that 'the rates of first admission to hospital for mental disease are markedly higher for migrants.

'Far more prone to mental disease than the migrant who lives among his own people and retains his own culture is a member of a minority group who is in the process of abandoning his culture in favour of a new one and who is thus undergoing acculturation.'

Malzberg and Lee found that 'the rates of first admission for total psychoses were much higher for recent than for earlier migrants'.

Victor D. Sauna,[19] in a study of personality adjustment among different generations of American Jews and non-Jews shows that Jews leading the ghetto life are very conservative and orthodox and have a low rate of mental ill-health. The Jew who is marginal, *i.e.* between two cultures, is submitted to far greater tension.

It appears that whereas the second generation of Jews, the marginal ones between two cultures, had a high rate of mental illness, third-generation Jews are far less marginal, having succeeded to a certain extent in adapting themselves to the world of the non-Jews, and thus again come out of it with a better mental-disease level.

Wilson and Lantz,[20] in a study of state hospital admissions, showed that the Southern Negroes pay a heavy toll in mental illness for their partial emancipation. When they were living entirely among themselves, or even as slaves, mental health was much better. 'It appears that negroes, when refusing to abide by the white man's dictum of where one belongs in society, occasionally lose the security of the earlier position.'

Gillin,[21] who has conducted research on this subject in Central America also observes: 'So long as the Indian stays within the framework of his culture,

240

Social Disintegration: Effects

he is less prone to be beset by anxieties and frustrations, which the Ladino culture almost inevitably creates.'

As national boundaries break down, small communities are swallowed up by vast urban conglomerations, mobility is increased and people move about the place in search of better pay, so cultural patterns break down.

In the United Kingdom, mental disease is increasing at a phenomenal rate. According to Ministry of Health statistics 169,160 people were admitted to hospitals in England and Wales in 1967 suffering from mental illness, two and a half times as many as in 1951.

There were 600,000 mentally disordered people in England and Wales in 1967, 186,901 of them occupying hospital beds or 46·6 per cent of all hospital beds. Thirty-two million working days every year are lost because of mental illness, representing a cost to the nation of £100 million, and local authorities spent £20,250,000 in mental health, more than six times what was spent in 1957.

SUICIDE. Durkheim[22] regarded suicide as the ultimate manifestation of anomie. He found that the suicide rate was particularly low in poor rural communities where social structures were intact, and high in disintegrating affluent societies, especially among the working classes and even more so among immigrants, in this case Italians, to the cities of Lorraine.

He goes so far as to say that 'suicide varies in inverse proportion to the degree of integration of the social groups to which the individual belongs'.

Dr Ralph S. Paffenberger, Junior, headed a recent study whose object was to determine the traits in youth that predisposed them to suicide. The survey was carried out among 50,000 college graduates whose histories after leaving college were carefully traced.

The trait found to be the most significant was the loss of the student's father in pre-college days, *i.e.* to the disintegration of the family unit in early youth.

In Britain the suicide rate has fallen over the last 6 years by about 200 a year. Nevertheless, according to the Samaritans, a lay organization that helps depressed and potentially suicidal people, the number of potential suicides has more than doubled in the last 2 years.

In 1967 their seven London area branches dealt with 5,999 new cases. In 1969 the same branches dealt with a further 11,641 cases. The Reverend Basil Higginson an official of this organization, estimated that in 1970 there would be about 60,000 new cases.

CONCLUSION. There is every reason to believe that the social ills at present afflicting our society – increasing crime, delinquency, vandalism, alcoholism as well as drug addiction – are closely related and are the symptoms of the

241

breakdown of our cultural pattern which in turn is an aspect of the disintegration of our society. These tendencies can only be accentuated by further demographic and economic growth. It is chimeric to suppose that any of these tendencies can be checked by the application of external controls or by treating them in isolation, *i.e.* apart from the social disease of which they are but the symptoms.

It is the cause itself, unchecked economic and demographic growth, that must be treated. Until such time as the most radical measures are undertaken for this purpose, these tendencies will be further accentuated – until their cost becomes so high that further growth ceases to be viable.

REFERENCES

1   HEBB, D. O. 1961. *The Organisation of Behaviour*. New York: John Wiley.
2   ZINGG, ROBERT M. and J. A. L. SINGH. 1942. *Wolf Children and Feral Man*. New York: Harper.
3   HARLOW, HARRY. 1962. Social deprivation in monkeys. In *Scientific American*, November.
4   BOWBEY, JOHN. 1965. *Child Care and the Growth of Love*. Harmondsworth: Penguin Books.
5a   JANHEINZ, JAHN. 1958. *Muntu*. London: Faber & Faber.
5b   KAGAME, ALEXIS. 1966. La Philosophie Bantu-Rwandaise de L'Etre. In *Academie Royale des Sciences D'Outre Mer*.
6   CLOWARD, RICHARD E. and LLOYD E. OHLIN. 1966. *Delinquency and Opportunity*. New York: Collier/Macmillan.
7   MERTON, ROBERT K. 1967. *Social Theory and Social Structure*. New York: The Free Press.
8   MEAD, MARGARET. 1959. Mental health in world perspective. In OPLER, MARVIN. 1959. *Culture and Mental Health*. New York: Macmillan.
9   LINTON, RALPH. 1965. *The Study of Man*. London: Peter Owen.
10   LECKY, WILLIAM EDWARD HARTPOLE. 1890. *A History of European Morals*. London: Longmans.
11   FIELD. 1961. *Social Psychological Correlation of Drunkenness in Primitive Tribes*. Harvard University: Unpublished thesis.
12   MADSEN, WILLIAM. 1964. The Alcoholic Agringado: Alcohol Symposium. In *American Anthropologist*, April.
13   CLOWARD, RICHARD E. and LLOYD E. OHLIN. 1966. (Above).
14   JOURNAL OF THE AMERICAN MEDICAL ASSOCIATION. 1968. July.
15   WITTKOWER, ERIC D. and JACOB FRIED. 1959. Some problems of transcultural psychiatry. In OPLER, MARVIN. 1959. *Culture and Mental Health*. New York: Macmillan.
16   WALLACE, ANTHONY. 1967. *Culture and Personality*. New York: Random House.
17   DEMARATH. 1942. Schizophrenia among Primitives. In *American Journal of Psychiatry, 98*.
18   WITTKOWER, ERIC D. and JACOB FRIED. 1959. (Above.)

Social Disintegration: Effects

19   SAUNA, VICTOR. 1959. Differences to personality adjustment among different generations of American Jews and Non-Jews. In OPLER, MARVIN. 1959. *Culture and Mental Health*. New York: Collier/Macmillan.

20   WILSON and LANTZ. 1957. The effect of cultural change on the Negro race in Virginia. In *American Journal of Psychiatry, 114*.

21   GILLIN, JOHN. 1951. The Culture of security in San Carlos, New Orleans. In *Middle American Research Institution, Publication No. 16*.

22   DURKHEIM, EMILE. 1952. *Suicide; a Study in Sociology*. London: Routledge and Kegan Paul.

CONCLUSION: WHAT OF THE FUTURE?

Edward Goldsmith

We are now in a position to make a few tentative suggestions as to what the future holds in store for the inhabitants of these isles.

First of all, a serious world food shortage appears inevitable. The demand for food is increasing at 3·9 per cent per annum. Production up till now has only increased by 2·6 per cent, while in 1969 for the first time there was actually no increase at all. The FAO plan for feeding the world is based on the extensive use of high-yield wheats and the intensification of agriculture throughout the third world. For many reasons (see Allaby, Chapter 4) it is extremely unlikely to prove successful, save perhaps in the very short-term.

With regard to food from the seas the situation is similar. We are currently taking 70 million tons of fish from the seas, four times more than we were 25 years ago, and expect to increase this to 140 millions by the turn of the century. This will clearly never be achieved. In fact, in 1969, for the first time, world catches actually fell.

It is certain that, well before the end of the century, there will be a very severe food crisis with widespread famine in the poorer and more densely populated areas of the world.

It would be extremely naïve to suppose that we in Britain will not be affected by these developments.

At the moment we import half our food. By the end of the century, as a result of foreseen population growth alone (see Allen, Chapter 2) demand for food will have increased by possibly 20 per cent. If economic growth occurs according to plan, it will have more than doubled. In any case, we shall have to import more food than we do now. But who is going to sell it to us? Is it likely that countries threatened with starvation will be willing to export essential foodstuffs in exchange for manufactured goods of dubious utility? If they were to sell them at all, surely it would be only against essential basic raw materials which by then will also be in short supply. Also it is by no means certain that we shall remain capable of producing the manufactured goods whose sale has so far permitted us to purchase the food and other resources that are so desperately required for the proper functioning of our industrial society.

Whatever happens we will have to rely more and more on our own agri-

244

What of the Future?

culture We shall have to try to feed ourselves. But will this be possible? Agricultural yields have increased by 50 per cent in the last 20 years. Our experts tell us that they can be increased still further by further intensifying agriculture. However, both on theoretical and empirical grounds this thesis cannot be accepted.

Firstly, we are likely to run out of many of the essential inputs such as arable land (see Waller, Chapter 9 and Powell, Chapter 5), water (see Steele, Chapter 13), minerals (see Cloud, Chapter 11) and power (see Bunyard, Chapter 12). In addition we must expect diminishing and eventually negative returns on the technological inputs required for intensive food production, pesticides (see *Environment* Staff Report, Chapter 6), fertilizers (see Powell, Chapter 5), antibiotics for intensive stockbreeding (see Harrison, Chapter 8) as well as on the various devices such as sonar and radar equipment made use of in modern fishing. Once more we are forced to face facts. We cannot increase indefinitely the amount of food from a fixed area, and we are rapidly reaching the point where every possible expedient will have been tried.

It is difficult for those living in present-day affluent Britain to accept that they are soon to be faced with a serious food shortage, yet this is the only conclusion that is consistent with the available information.

This food shortage is likely to have a seriously demoralizing effect. It will tend to reduce resistance to disease, capacity to work and faith in the values of our industrial society.

As food becomes scarce and expensive, more and more marginal land will be turned over to agriculture. This means that any nature reserves and national parks with agricultural potential will be brought under the plough. Conservation in the face of continued demographic and economic growth is a pretty hopeless task. On the other hand, the more marginal the land, the more the technological inputs such as irrigation and fertilizers that are required. Since these will be in shorter supply there must eventually be a trend in the opposite direction, and wildernesses may begin to appear once more.

Meanwhile industry will undoubtedly fully exploit the wide open market for synthetic foods of every type. But these cannot be made out of nothing and many of the materials required for this purpose will be becoming scarce or unobtainable: petroleum products, for instance. Also, if our food is to be manufactured in factories instead of grown on the land, our requirements of ever scarcer resources, such as water and fuel, will correspondingly increase, and such methods of food production will cause pollution which our environment will be ever less capable of absorbing. There is likely to be an eventual reaction against synthetic foods, when the side effects on human health of the countless chemical additives become more apparent.

In the long run, once it is generally accepted that technology cannot indefinitely increase the short-term food supply, there is likely to be a gradual return to traditional methods of husbandry, which means smaller farms, less reliance on the agro-chemical industry and replacement of machines by men – all very beneficial tendencies which, as Waller points out (Chapter 9), would probably not only maximize food production in the long run but lead to the re-establishment of a stable and healthy community.

But to enjoy these benefits we must first of all survive the initial chaos and reduce our population in one way or another to that level that can be fed without resorting to the gimmickry of modern agricultural methods.

A further condition for the survival of our industrial society is the availability of the requisite raw materials. This, as we approach the turn of the century, is extremely unlikely.

Cloud (Chapter 11) shows that the world's mineral resources are nearing exhaustion. By the end of the century there will be practically no tungsten, copper, lead, zinc, tin, gold, silver or platinum. Other minerals essential to industry will also be in short supply.

Shortages are likely to occur and prices are likely to increase dramatically long before stocks are actually exhausted, as producing nations will be increasingly reluctant to sell precious non-renewable resources which can be used for their own development. Producing nations will tend to import technological know-how and manufacture their own goods.

Scientists and technologists will attempt to develop all sorts of substitutes for these apparently indispensable resources. Many will be found, but it is unlikely that they will satisfy all our requirements. Whatever these materials are made of is likely to run out some day. Plastics, for instance, are normally made from petroleum products which will become progressively scarcer.

In the meantime, everything will be done to recycle existing stocks. Recycling is likely to be the basis of a major industry but it cannot hope to satisfy our ever-growing requirements. There is always a loss during a recycling process from, if nothing else, friction and oxidation. In the case of metals, the loss is likely to remain high in spite of the very efficient techniques that are bound to be developed.

It is not difficult to predict the short-term effects of a shortage in minerals. Our economy will be radically affected, businesses will have to close down and there will be increasing unemployment.

Once more the long-term effects are likely to be beneficial. There will be a tendency towards engineering craftsmanship and away from the throwaway economy. Also it will become economic to recycle countless waste products at present causing serious pollution.

Both Cloud and Bunyard point to the fact that the world's supply of fossil fuels is nearing exhaustion. There is only enough natural gas for another 25 years or so, and oil reserves are only likely to last another 70 years.

246

What of the Future?

Long before stocks run out, oil is likely to be both scarce and expensive. The producing nations will become more conscious of their hold over the West. Indeed, by withholding oil supplies as they threatened to do in Teheran, they can bring about the total collapse of our industrial society.

Nuclear power is unlikely to provide an alternative source, as there is no solution in sight for the safe disposal of radioactive waste. The world's only remaining important and viable source of power is coal, of which there appears to be enough for a few hundred years. There should be a considerable revival of the coal industry, though to persuade people to work in coalmines once the original mining communities have broken up might present a challenging problem.

The fuel shortage which appears inevitable will also favour a return to small labour-intensive units both in agriculture and industry. It will also favour political and economic decentralization. However, it will take a long time before these beneficial effects are felt. In the short-term, the fuel shortage will seriously depress industry and cause widespread unemployment.

A third condition for the survival of our industrial society is our continued ability to transform raw materials into finished products. This is likely to be seriously compromised by many factors, including the increasing cost of pollution and its control.

As our environment's capacity to absorb pollutants of different sorts is slowly being reached the economic cost of each increment of pollution rises. The seriousness of the problem of air pollution and its harm to our health is pointed out by Albone (Chapter 14). The extent of marine pollution and its possible long-term effects on marine life are described by George (Chapter 7), and the very serious damage to animal life caused by pesticides essential to intensive agriculture are pointed out by Shea (Chapter 16). Further demographic and economic growth can but aggravate these problems.

It is becoming evident that their costs in terms of increased medical care, extermination of wildlife, stunted plant growth, cleaning bills, *etc*, are very much higher than is generally accepted.

Industry will have to bear an ever-increasing proportion of these costs which will mean higher prices and reduced economic activity. The government will also have to spend exorbitant sums on pollution control. Relatively clean air and clean water in the United States might cost as much as $200 billion, which vastly exceeds what the present or any future government is likely to spend. Mr Nixon has proposed an expenditure of $10 billion for this purpose before 1975, and even this sum is unlikely to be granted him by Congress.

As a result pollution is likely to get worse until such times as a shortage of raw materials makes recycling economic, and finally, as economic activity begins to fall off.

The public is also likely to become ever more pollution-conscious and conservation pressure must build up more and more, especially as in the next 30 years we can expect a number of serious ecological disasters. It is possible, for instance, that the Baltic Sea, the Mediterranean and the Black Sea will, before the end of the century, have become biological deserts devoid of any fish life. In addition, much of the fish life in the Atlantic and the Pacific may well be so contaminated as to have become inedible. Outbreaks of new diseases caused by specific pollutants, such as Minamata disease in Japan, are likely to occur, perhaps causing death and disablement on a large scale.

Such catastrophes must slowly affect public opinion. They must lead to increased pressure on the government to deal with pollution problems and increase the disenchantment with the industrial way of life, especially among the young.

The deteriorating health of urban man is also going to be costly. The degenerative diseases associated with a faulty diet and exposure to pollutants in our food, water and air will also remain on the increase (see Waller, Chapter 9).

The conditions for the reappearance of large-scale epidemics are rapidly becoming more and more favourable. Population density is increasing. The resistance of urban-dwellers to disease is being progressively reduced as the levels of the different pollutants build up in their bodies. Mobility is increasing, thereby effectively spreading disease to areas where the population has not developed natural controls; and germs are rapidly becoming resistant to antibiotics. The development of the appropriate vaccine may prevent a serious epidemic from spreading throughout the world but if it were to originate in a country with a high population-density such as England, it might wipe out a considerable proportion of the population before eventually being brought under control.

Whether or not there are epidemics to add to our afflictions, a serious recrudescence of infectious diseases can be expected. Contrary to popular belief, these have not been conquered. The so-called miracle drugs have only granted us temporary respite. Gonorrhoea, for instance, which a few years ago was considered totally under control is now, after the common cold, the second most widespread disease in the United Kingdom.

In general, there is bound to be increasing disenchantment with modern medicine whose short-term benefits will be found to compensate less and less for their biological and social side-effects.

Our continued ability to transform raw materials into finished products is dependent on the maintenance of social order. This essential condition is increasingly unlikely to be satisfied.

The conditions that lead to social disintegration all appear to be intimately linked with demographic and economic growth: as Mishan (Chapter 1) and

What of the Future?

Allen (Chapter 2) show, both lead to greater reduction in the quality of life. Both lead to urbanization and overcrowding, which, as the Russells show (Chapter 19), have the most serious social consequences, in particular increasing crime and aggression. These tendencies, if unchecked, lead to further social disintegration which in turn must increase the need for all types of state intervention – bureaucratic control, police action, state welfare – all of which inevitably give rise to further disintegration.

The ills from which industrial societies are at present suffering – delinquency, crime, drug addiction, alcoholism, mental disease, suicide, *etc* – are the closely inter-related symptoms of social disintegration. As our population continues to grow, so these tendencies will further assert themselves.

As ever less consumer products become available to an ever-increasing population (see Russell, Chapter 20), there will be ever rising inflation, which will cause further social tension and disintegration.

Growing unemployment will also have serious social consequences.

It is common knowledge that few things are more demoralizing than prolonged unemployment. Apart from the material deprivation involved, a man is deprived of his status which in an industrial society is largely determined by the work he does. He also loses his goal structure and his self-esteem. Galloping inflation will make matters still worse.

A further problem is the presence in this country of a large and expanding immigrant population which, as in the United States, will tend to concentrate in the city centres. The West Indians are likely to adapt badly to industrial life, their society displaying most of the symptoms of 'anomie' or 'egotely', and will tend to become particularly dependant on welfare. They are also likely to develop an ever-increasing resentment of the mainstream of society, which is likely to manifest itself, as with the Negroes in the United States, by violence and rioting. When the unemployment level is really high, tension is likely to build up against these groups who are the obvious scapegoats for society's ills. Racial strife is certain to develop.

We have taken the ability and inclination of our trading partners to purchase our finished products, as one of the basic conditions permitting the survival of our industrial society. Our trading partners are mainly industrial nations, like ourselves, and are likely to suffer from the same problems. This means that they will have to spend much more on imported raw materials and food than at present. Pollution-control will also take up an ever greater proportion of their national budgets, as will control of the various manifestations of social disorder. As a result, they must have correspondingly less money to spend on non-essential manufactured goods. The industries on which they depend for their livelihood will also tend to be menaced by competitors from countries that, not being so advanced along the road to industrialization, may not be suffering quite so badly from its side-effects.

The obvious reaction would be to introduce protectionist measures such as import duties, quotas, *etc*.

Mounting inflation is also likely to lead Britain's trading partners to adopt protectionist measures to safeguard their currency. The protectionist spirit is already beginning to gain ground in the United States, and businesses are already obtaining subsidies, price supports and credit guarantees. At the moment of writing the US government is trying to persuade the Japanese to apply voluntary limitations to the export of textiles to the United States. A Maritime Bill has been passed which is overtly protectionist and which, among other things, trebles the number of merchant ships eligible for government subsidies. The Mills Bill which was designed to protect 120 manufactured products from foreign competition actually passed the House of Representatives to be narrowly defeated in the Senate. One can expect considerably more legislation of this type in the next decades.

The British government will do everything possible to combat the inevitable unemployment. Among other things it will attempt to encourage economic growth regardless of its environmental consequences. At the moment of writing, President Nixon is doing just this. In spite of the essential correlation between economic growth and environmental disruption that his Council for Environmental Quality cannot have failed to point out to him, he has poured $2·2 billion into the sagging economy. The reason for this is obvious. He simply cannot afford a slump with widespread unemployment. Its cost in terms of votes and social unrest would be prohibitive. In his position, a British government would do exactly the same thing.

On the other hand, conservationist pressure is building up and will continue to do so. It is bound to act as an ever greater brake to economic growth, each increment of which causes more noticeable environmental deterioration. To increase the water supply of our industrial conurbations, we will have to flood valleys of ever greater value to naturalists or put up barrages across increasingly beautiful estuaries. To build the countless new towns and motorways that we will require in the next 30 years will mean destroying ever finer scenery and depriving the country of ever more valuable agricultural land. The difficulty encountered by the government in siting the third airport is but an example of the sort of problems that will be encountered more and more as demographic and economic expansion threaten what remains of the British countryside.

On the other hand, it is likely that a powerful anti-conservationist movement – and ecology backlash, as it is already known in America – will spring up, mainly among the industrial working classes and particularly the unemployed. They will tend to regard conservation as a conspiracy to deprive them of the benefits of our industrial society already reaped by the middle classes who form the bulk of the conservationist movement.

250

What of the Future?

Eventually there may well be a new political alignment with no-growth conservationists on the one hand and a growth orientated alliance between big business interests and the trade unions on the other.

The latter is likely to be the more influential, at least to begin with, and it is more than likely that it will be able to apply sufficient pressure on the government to keep the latter firmly committed to economic growth in spite of mounting difficulties.

Whatever happens, there is likely to be an increasingly marked polarization between the political parties. This will clearly render parliamentary government correspondingly more difficult and will create a tendency towards authoritarianism in order to maintain some semblance of social order, however superficial. Unless the British government transforms itself into a ruthless dictatorship, one is forced to predict the eventual breakdown of political control.

In the ensuing chaos one can foresee various attempts at social reintegration in the form of religio-political messianic movements, many of which influenced by ecological teachings, will preach a return to nature. Like all messianic movements, these are likely to be violent and must further contribute to the general disorder, further reducing, in this way, the viability of what remains of our economy. The social system most likely to emerge is best described as feudal. People will gather round whichever strong men can provide the basic necessities of life, and offer protection against marauding bands from the dying cities.

To what extent can all this be avoided? Industrial society can clearly not survive for long. Nevertheless it should be possible to ensure a gradual transition to a different type of society whose survival does not depend on the maintenance of such specific and highly vulnerable conditions.

How can such a society be established? *The first and most urgent task is to control our population.* Not only must any further growth be avoided, but its present level must be reduced probably at least by half.

It is only in this way that this country can hope to feed itself in the long-term. All possible means, however irreconcilable they might be with our present set of values, should be made use of to ensure that this goal be eventually achieved.

Next we must reduce the impact of each man on the environment by cutting down, in particular, on his energy consumption. An energy tax would clearly be a useful expedient but the most effective method must be to decentralize our society, politically, administratively and economically. This would lead to that other prerequisite of stability – the development of small self-regulating communities.

The totally absurd notion that bigger things are better, must be abandoned

251

and with it the false ideal of 'maximizing' productivity – the pretext normally given for making things larger and more centralized.

Indeed it should be a precept of government, as it is of the organization of nature, that everywhere there should be the maximum decentralization. Nothing should be done at village level which could be done by the family, nothing at county level which could be done by the village, and so on all the way up.

A nation consisting of 56 million people can constitute a society only if it is highly organized into families, small communities, provinces, *etc.* Their members must be responsible for running their own affairs. They must be self-regulating for only in this way can they be stable.

Among those activities which must be radically decentralized is welfare. At the moment the State, by usurping those responsibilities that should be fulfilled at the communal and family levels, is contributing to their disintegration by rendering them largely redundant.

Economic activity should also be decentralized. Small traders, artisans and businessmen are on the whole stable citizens who tend to take pride in the quality of their work and in the services that they render the community. This should more than compensate for their lack of short-term 'productivity'.

Agriculture must also be decentralized. Contrary to what is generally thought, its output is probably increased by reducing the size of units rather than by increasing them.

The flight to the towns must also end. The destruction of rural life and the elimination of the small farmer, who should normally constitute the backbone of a stable society, is a social disaster whose cost to the community cannot be over-emphasized.

The most serious challenge at present is the provision of alternative employment for the countless millions of people who depend on technology for their living.

Decentralization would contribute towards this by furthering the development of divergent cultural patterns, and of new activities to replace those that are no longer possible.

The construction of beautiful buildings, the manufacture of fine furniture, the development of local arts and crafts, the revival of local festivities and religious ceremonies; all these things will provide a worthwhile substitute for the haphazard accumulation of manufactured goods to which our society is at present geared. In this economic activity could be 'ritualized' as is 'aggression' among stable societies (both human and non-human). Ritualized aggression provides a satisfactory outlet for a society's aggressive requirements without its leading to the annihilation of its enemies. Similarly, ritualized economic activity could be regarded as providing an outlet for man's essential requirements for creative work in such a way as to minimize the resultant damage to the environment.

Decentralization would also result in a reduction of mobility. If people are employed where they live, less transport will be required. By reducing our dependence on technology, decentralization would fulfil yet another essential function: that of reducing our vulnerability. The complex and self-regulating systems of nature would be allowed slowly to replace the relatively simple and externally regulated systems of our technosphere, a substitution essential to the establishment of ecological stability.

Clearly the transition to such a society would not be easy. The principal problem would be how to provide satisfactory employment for so many people. New occupations that do not require the use of power, would probably take some time to develop. The dole does not solve the serious psychological problems of unemployment. It is at best a palliative. The only alternative is to accept that a vast amount of work is required to clean up the mess resulting from 150 years of uncontrolled economic growth.

A sort of national service for conservation on the lines of the Conservation Corps could be instituted, and the more decentralized its organization, the more effective it is likely to be, as people would surely be keener to help clean up their local environment than that of people living at the other end of the country.

Moreover, it must be accepted that people should be employed whether or not their employment is justified on 'economic grounds'. This is already the case in the Soviet Union. 'Economically unproductive' work of this sort would undoubtedly lead to a situation in which there would be more money around than goods to buy, again as is the case in the Soviet Union. The dissatisfaction this might give rise to would be partly offset by the development of the new occupations already referred to, as economic activity becomes ever more 'ritualized'. Meanwhile there will certainly be inflation – but on nothing like the scale that would accompany the total breakdown of our society, which is possibly the only alternative.

A more serious objection is that the transition of a stable society would probably have to be carefully orchestrated as a single programme. If any part of it is left out, because it is regarded as objectionable by some sector of society in terms of current ethical norms, then the whole programme may well be a failure.

It follows that this social transformation can only be ensured by a government having a mandate to plan and implement such a programme as painlessly as possible, *i.e.* over the maximum period consistent with avoiding the catastrophes with which our society is at present menaced.

Is it likely that the British government will undertake a programme of this sort? The answer is unfortunately 'no'. It would require first of all a degree of long-term planning of which we are undoubtedly incapable. It would also require subjecting a host of short-term requirements on the part of practically the whole population to wider and longer-term considerations. This would be very difficult as our society is geared to specifically short-term ends. A businessman simply must declare profits at the end of the year if he is to survive, and to make these profits he is often forced to adopt methods detrimental to the society he lives in and also to his own long-term prospects.

A doctor must above all else relieve pain or lose his patients. To do this he currently administers drugs and uses diagnostic techniques such as X-rays and radio-isotopes that must inevitably increase disease in the long-term.

The farmer, in order to survive, as we have been at pains to point out in this book, must make use of highly unsound agricultural methods that must eventually lead to a reduction in output.

The scientist must above all succeed in achieving whatever short-term goal he has been set by the business enterprise or the government department he works for. He is likely to have neither the means nor the inclination to judge for himself what are the long-term effects of the work he is doing on the society or the ecosystem of which he is part.

A politician must win votes if he is to remain in office and to do this he must satisfy the countless short-term requirements of a predominantly ignorant and egoistic electorate, even when these are in direct conflict with the long-term interests of the society he has been called upon to direct. Neither the businessman, the doctor, the farmer, the scientist, the politician, nor anyone else in a position of authority, appears capable of questioning the basic assumptions underlying our industrial culture.

The tendency will thus be to blame all ills on technicalities that can be dealt with without having to modify these assumptions – leaving the real causes untouched – as in the case of the tribal rainmaker or the Jivaro Indian warrior mentioned in the introduction to this book.

Overcrowding, we shall persuade ourselves, is the result of poor urban planning; delinquency of insufficient state care and drug addiction of faulty education.

Pollution, we shall insist, is the avoidable result of the niggardliness of industrialists, lung cancer of insufficient money spent on cancer research and the world food shortage we shall attribute to the backwardness of agricultural techniques, and so on with all the other ills that must afflict us.

In this way vast sums of money will be wasted on more urban planning, more state care, more education, more cancer research, more pollution control and more poisonous agro-chemicals in a vain attempt to suppress the symptoms of the disease which we are incapable of treating as we are culturally unadapted to the life style that must constitute its only remedy.

254

What of the Future ?

To treat the symptoms, however, is to render the disease correspondingly more tolerable and to contribute thereby to its perpetuation.

Thus growth is not likely to cease as the result of a conscious decision on the part of anyone in authority but simply because the specific conditions in which it can occur will slowly cease to obtain.

As that moment draws near so we are entering a radically new phase in our history: the post-industrial age.

INDEX

256

Index

257

Index

destruction of cultural constraints *48*
conservation of the environment *48*
self-regulation *49*
multi-ethnic societies *51*
resources *52*
disposal of waste *52*
pollution *52–3*
complexity *53*
systematic adaptation *53*
asystemic regulation *54*
conclusion *55*
Nature Conservancy *32, 76*
Nebraska *164*
Negentropy *45*
Netherlands, The *33, 147*
Nevada *159*
New Caledonia *122*
New Earth Village *65*
New Scientist 32, 131
New York State *157*
New Zealand *39*
Newcastle Planning Committee *38*
Newsom, Dr L. D. *82*
Nicaragua *84*
Nickel *122*
Nigeria *67*
Nitrogen *72–3*
Nixon, Richard *16, 189, 247*
Nuffield Institute of Comparative Medicine *111*
Numata, Dr Makoto *65*

Oats *70*
Ohlin, Lloyd E. *234, 238*
Optimum Population of Britain, The 34, 38
Organ transplants *51*
Organophosphates *80–3, 86*
Oslofjord, Norway *177*
Overcrowding and social tension *201–9*
affluent monkeys *203–4*
benevolence and rank *204–5*
dictatorship in zoos *205–6*
stress-induced aggression *206–9*

Paffenberger, Dr Ralph S. Jun. *241*
Panama *80*
Parathion, Methyl *81*
Parker, Dr Albert *129, 134*
Parkes, Sir Alan *34*
Patuxent Wildlife Research Center, Maryland *167*
Peak National Park *38*
Peakall, Dr D. B. *166*
Pendleton, Dr Robert *159*
Peregrine falcons *164*

Perils of the Peaceful Atom, The 162
Peru *83, 85*
Pesticides *61–2, 70, 73, 79–92, 115–16, 148, 164, 169, 172, 179–81*
Petroleum *122–3*
Phelps Brown, E. H. *214*
Philippines, The *60*
Phosphorus *72*
Pigou *24*
Pigs *73, 78, 103*
Place, Francis *219*
Plains Indians *52*
Platinum *123*
Plowshare Program *155, 160–1*
Polanyi, Karl *18*
Polychlorinated biphenyls (PCBS) *179–81*
Pollution, air, *11, 15, 28, 54, 143–52*
soil *11, 15*
noise *11, 28, 54*
oil *12*
water *11, 15, 28, 104, 139–40, 175–86*
radioactive *154–63*
grit and dust *154*
wildlife *164–73*
marine life *175–86*
fertilizers and sewage *175–7*
rubbish *177*
pulp mill liquors *177*
heavy metals *177–8*
copper and zinc *178*
mercury and silver *178–9*
pesticides and PCBS *179–81*
radioactive waste *181–2*
oil *182–4*
oil dispersants ('detergents') *184–6*
Poole, Dr Robert *171*
Population Commission (UN) *64*
Population explosion *57–8*
Potassium *72*
Potatoes *70*
Poultry *70, 73, 78, 94, 103–4*
Powell, L. B. *39*
President's Science Advisory Committee (US) *148*
Primitive Government 224
Protestant Ethic and the Spirit of Capitalism, The 19
Putnam Palmer *132, 134*

Quezon Province (Philippines) *60*

Radcliffe Hospital, Oxford *108–9*
Radioactive dust *12*
Ratcliffe, Dr D. A. *165*
Report of the British Government's Working Party on Sewage Disposal 141
Report of the Department of Health and Social Security, 1970 (Britain) *37*
Resources and Man 129
Reynolds, Vernon *204–6*
Rice, 'Miracle' (IR8) *60, 62, 63*
Rickets *110*
Rifle, Colorado *160*
Ritchie-Calder, Lord *66*
Roman Empire *225–6*
Roman Republic *225–6*
Romilly, Sir Samuel *206*
Rose, Sanford *197*
Rothschild, Lord *191*
Royal College of Physicians (UK) *149, 191*
Royal Society of Health (UK) *108*
Rulison Project, The 160
Russell, W. M. S. and Claire *3*

Sahara, The *60*
St Louis *146, 150*
Salmon, Atlantic *178*
San Francisco crab, The *170–1*
Sandwich Island Terns *170*
Sargent, William *230*
Sawna, Victor D. *240*
Schleswig-Holstein *95–6*
Science 128
Scurvy *110*
Searby, P. J. *128, 131*
Seifert, Prof. Alwin *95*
Seskin, Eugene *188*
Sewage strike, The *55*
Shape of Things to Come, The 201
Shapiro, Dr Robert *197*
Sheep *70, 74, 78*
Sheffield, George *77*
Sierra Leone *67*
Silver *123*
Simms, M. *41*
Sinclair, Craig *190*
Sinclair, Dr Hugh *103, 110–11*
Singapore *32*
Smog *145–6, 196*
Social disintegration, causes of *223–31*

259

Brand Warriors

Brand Warriors

CORPORATE LEADERS SHARE THEIR
WINNING STRATEGIES

Edited by Fiona Gilmore

■ HarperCollinsBusiness

HarperCollinsBusiness
An imprint of HarperCollins*Publishers*
77–85 Fulham Palace Road,
Hammersmith, London w6 8jb

Published by HarperCollins*Publishers* 1997
2 3 4 5 6 7 8 9
Copyright © Springpoint 1997

The Authors assert the moral right to
be identified as the authors of this work

A catalogue record for this book
is available from the British Library

isbn o oo 255867 X

Set in Janson and Ellington by
Rowland Phototypesetting Ltd, Bury St Edmunds, Suffolk

Printed and bound in Great Britain by
Caledonian International Book Manufacturing Ltd, Glasgow

Contents

Acknowledgements

Putting this book together has been quite an adventure. Every step of the journey has been very demanding and yet immensely rewarding; a book of this nature is demanding in its structural ambitions and logistical complexity. What has been most rewarding for me is the team interaction and enthusiasm.

My colleague Katrina Symons deserves special mention. She joined the project at an early stage, bringing the team together, unwavering in her support and tenacity.

I would like to give special thanks to Sarah Butterworth, my assistant, who has demonstrated remarkable gifts of diplomacy and patience, and to other colleagues from Springpoint, in particular Gary Broadbent, Patricia Perchal and my business partner, Mark Pearce.

My deep thanks also to Lucinda McNeile of HarperCollins, who has provided excellent editorial guidance, and to Bob Garratt, who has added insight and new ideas, right up to the last moment.

I gratefully acknowledge my debt to the contributors: Bob Ayling, Jos Brenkel, Alain Evrard, John Hawkes, David Heslop, Shigeharu Hiraiwa, Nick Hodges, Robert Holloway, Tim Kelly, Archie Norman, Alan Palmer, Robert E. Riley, Fred Smith, Sir Clive Thompson, C. C. Tung and Allan Wong.

My grateful thanks go to Meg Carter, Laura Mazur and Alan Mitchell, for their assistance over many months.

I would also like to thank the following: Kim Balling, Valérie Banino, Pat Barry, Rick Bendall, Eddie Benoilum, Jim Carroll, Simon Chalkley, Eric Delamare, Lynn Downey, Kate Ecker, Anne Forrest, Sylvie Gagnot, Cindy Gallop, Martin George, Clarence Grebey, Charles Grimaldi, Michael Harvey, Michèle Heyworth, Jackie Holmes, Richard Hytner, Joyce Jui, David Kisilevski, Jill Kluge, Annie C. H. Loi, Greg Rossiter, Justine Samuel, Gregory Sendi, Stanley C. Shen, Geoff and Rachel Skingsley, Emma Smith, Robert Triefus, Charles Tugendhat, Stephen Webb, Dominic Whittles, Elin Wong and Jim Wood-Smith.

Lastly, I would like to thank my husband, Richard, for taking over some family responsibilities during the eighteen months I was working on this book, and for his support.

Fiona Gilmore
July 1997

Contributors' Biographies

Robert Ayling

Bob Ayling was appointed chief executive of British Airways in January 1996. He joined the airline in 1985 from the Department of Trade, and headed the legal side of the British Airways privatization in 1987 and its acquisition of British Caledonian in 1988. He has also held the positions of group managing director, director of marketing & operations, director of human resources and company secretary.

Bob originally qualified as a solicitor and has been involved in air transport and international commerce throughout his career.

Jos Brenkel

Jos Brenkel is director of the Personal Systems Group at Hewlett-Packard's European Marketing Centre and is responsible for ensuring the company's success in the European market for personal information products, such as portable notebook computers and PC products. He joined Hewlett-Packard in South Africa in 1986, moving to Grenoble the following year where he held various management positions within the marketing centre.

Alain Evrard

Alain Evrard has been L'Oréal's zone director Africa, Asia Pacific since 1990, and his work covers Africa, the Middle East, East and South-East Asia, the Pacific and French foreign territories. He joined L'Oréal in 1981 from Solvay & Cie of Belgium, where he held management positions in Austria and Italy.

Alain graduated in Economics and Finance from the University of Brussels. He has been Conseiller du Commerce Extérieur de la France since 1988.

John Hawkes

John Hawkes is senior vice president of McDonald's UK. He joined the company in 1982 as marketing executive, was promoted to marketing manager and from there moved to McDonald's Development Company as marketing director, with responsibility for Scandinavia and other Western European countries. He was appointed to his current position in April 1994.

David Heslop

David Heslop is chairman and managing director of Mazda Cars (UK) Ltd. He joined Mazda in 1984, and worked his way through sales and dealer operations before being appointed managing director in 1991. He began his career as personal assistant to the chairman of Trebor.

David is a graduate of the London Business School, and is a member of the Institute of Directors.

Shigeharu Hiraiwa

Shigeharu Hiraiwa is director and president of Mazda Motor (Europe). After graduating in Industrial Engineering from the Tokyo Institute of Technology, he joined Mazda Motor Corporation (then Toyo Kogyo) in 1965. Since then he has worked in a variety of roles and is now responsible for overseas marketing and sales and European R&D.

Nick Hodges

Nick Hodges was appointed group chief executive of London International Group plc in 1993. He joined LIG in 1982 as sales director of the UK operation, LRC Products, rapidly moving through the ranks to managing director of LRC Products and Regent Hospital Products with worldwide responsibilities. In 1991 he became divisional managing director, Europe/Middle East/Africa, joining the main board in 1992.

Nick previously worked for Kimberley-Clark, Golden Wonder and Johnson & Johnson. He is a graduate of London University.

Robert Holloway

Robert Holloway joined Levi Strauss & Co. in 1982 and has held a wide range of marketing and merchandising positions in Europe. He was a key member of the team behind the Levi's® brand's European marketing successes over recent years. In January 1996, he relocated to the company's San Francisco global headquarters to become vice president of the new Global Marketing team.

Tim Kelly

Tim Kelly joined Guinness plc in 1995, and is based in Dublin as marketing director for the Guinness Ireland Group. He is responsible for marketing the Guinness brand, and franchise brands such as Budweiser and Carlsberg.

Tim began his career at Unilever in 1982 and worked for Van den Berghs for four years on a variety of brands. He left in 1986 to join Coca-Cola & Schweppes Beverages as brand manager on Coca-Cola, and later held the position of marketing director from 1994.

Tim is on the Board of Cantrell and Cochrane (a joint venture between Allied Domecq and Guinness) and is on the editorial board of the *Journal of Brand Management*. He was educated at the Oratory School and Warwick University.

Archie Norman

Archie Norman joined Asda in 1991 as group chief executive, from King-fisher plc. He became chairman of Asda in 1997. He was educated at Cambridge University and Harvard Business School, and his early career took him to Citibank and McKinsey and Co. where he was a principal.

Archie is a non-executive director of Railtrack plc, a Fellow of the Marketing Society and Member of the Council of the Industrial Society. He was voted Yorkshire Businessman of the Year in 1995 and UK Retailer of the Year in 1996. Archie is vice chairman of the Conservative Party and Member of Parliament for Tunbridge Wells.

Alan Palmer

Alan Palmer was appointed marketing director of Cadbury in 1993, and has been involved in drawing up a programme to focus investment and development behind the Cadbury brand.

Alan began his career as a graduate trainee with Cadbury Schweppes in 1974, from where he broadened his experience at Cadbury Typhoo, before beginning a six-year period at Cadbury Ltd. He later moved to Schweppes as marketing director, and has also been marketing director of Trebor Bassett.

Robert E. Riley

Robert E. Riley is managing director of Mandarin Oriental Hotel Group. He holds a Bachelor's degree from Randolph-Macon College, a law degree from University of Virginia and has extensive experience in the real estate and hotel businesses.

Robert E. Riley began his career in 1974 as an attorney practising corporate and tax law in New York. He first became involved in the hotel business when he worked for the Ford Foundation which supported various urban redevelopment projects in the USA. In 1979, he changed his career and joined a Texas-based commercial real estate and hotel developer. He continued to work in the fields of real estate and hotel investment, development and management and joined Mandarin Oriental Hotel Group in 1988.

In 1994, Robert E. Riley became chairman of the Asia Pacific Hotels Environment Initiative in liaison with the Prince of Wales Business Leaders Forum.

Frederick W. Smith

Fred Smith is chairman, president and CEO of Federal Express Corporation, the world's largest express transportation company.

Fred graduated from Yale in 1966 and served as an officer in the US Marine Corps until 1970. He founded Federal Express in 1971.

Fred serves as director on the boards of various transport, industry and civic organizations.

Sir Clive Thompson

Sir Clive Thompson is chief executive of Rentokil Initial plc which he has led for the past fifteen years, transforming it into an international service group operating in every country of Western Europe, North America and Asia Pacific.

Sir Clive graduated in Chemistry from Birmingham University and began his career in marketing with Shell. He subsequently moved to Boots, becoming the company's general manager in East Africa before returning to the UK in 1971 to join the Jeyes Group.

He is a vice president and a Fellow of the Chartered Institute of Marketing, a Fellow of the Institute of Directors, and a Companion of the British Institute of Management. He is deputy president of the CBI and will become president in July 1998. He is a member of the CBI President's

Committee, the CBI Finance and General Purposes Committee and of the CBI National Council.

Sir Clive is currently a non-executive director of BAT Industries plc, Sainsbury plc, and vice chairman of Farepak plc. He is also a member of the British Overseas Trade Board.

He was knighted in the 1996 Queen's Birthday Honours.

C. C. Tung

C. C. Tung is chairman, president and CEO of Orient Overseas (International) Limited (OOIL), a position he has held since October 1996. His involvement in the company spans twenty-five years and from 1986 to 1996 he was vice president.

He studied at the University of Liverpool, where he received his Bachelor of Science degree, and later acquired a Master's degree in Mechanical Engineering at the Massachusetts Institute of Technology.

C. C. Tung currently holds the following positions: 2nd vice chairman of the Hong Kong General Chamber of Commerce; chairman of the Merchant Navy Training Board of the Vocational Training Council; chairman of the Port Welfare Committee of Hong Kong; a member of the Port Development Board, a member of the Hong Kong/Japan Business Co-operation Committee and a member of the Hong Kong/United States Economic Co-operation Committee.

Mr Tung is also a non-executive director of Sing Tao Holdings Limited; chairman of the Hong Kong-America Center; a member of the Council of the Hong Kong Polytechnic University; a member of the School of Foreign Service, Georgetown University's Board of Visitors and a member of the University of Pittsburgh's Board of Trustees.

Allan Wong

Allan Wong is chairman of VTech Holdings Ltd. Educated at the University of Hong Kong and in the United States at the University of Wisconsin, he obtained degrees in electrical and computer engineering before joining NCR Manufacturing as a design engineer in 1974.

In 1976 he founded VTech to pursue the design and manufacture of microprocessor-based products. VTech has since grown to become the largest and most successful electronics company in Hong Kong and China, with worldwide sales exceeding $700 million, with 18,000 employees in thirteen countries.

In 1991 Allan was awarded Industrialist of the Year by the Federation of Hong Kong Industries. He serves on various business and technology committees and is also a director of the Bank of East Asia.

Introduction: Brand Championship

FIONA GILMORE

Business is war; the objective is competitor destruction through superior industrial economics. *Brand* warfare is different: the brand warrior identifies the key conquest as the customer, not the rival. Beating the rival follows inexorably from winning over the customer's heart and mind, so the process of nurturing a brand is a crucial aspect of the warrior's attack.

Branding is ultimately about securing the future of a company, its products and services, by building loyalties using emotional as well as rational values. Such values matter because they are exchanged for cash in the marketplace and affect the perception of a company's products and services as well as its ability and its freedom to manage its future.

The companies which are rated by marketeers as the rising stars for the future are those with very clearly positioned, confident corporate brands. These companies deliver through their core competencies and, more importantly, have a coherent core value and emotional brand proposition for the consumer.

A brand is inclusive. It is the tangible and intangible benefits provided by a product or service: the entire customer experience. It includes all the assets critical to delivering and communicating that experience: the name, the design, the advertising, product or service, the distribution channel, the reputation.

Brands need to be cared for in much the same way as parents care about their children: brand custodians need to know and understand the quirks, the specialness and the faults of their brands.

Increasingly, however, business leaders do not have the same parental relationship with the brands in their care. For reasons which are understandable, the typical brand owner cannot give the required time to managing brand equities as he or she used to. So, just when consumers are more open than ever before to buying into well constructed, motivating brand positionings, many brand owners have reduced the amount of time they spend thinking about their brands.

The economic case for branding

Sometimes the marketing hype overshadows the economic advantages of branding, but, as *Brand Warriors* shows, branding survives because it enhances the present value of future cashflows. This simple economic value comes from both the price premium justified by effective branding, maintaining and growing markets, and from building brand loyalty, to deter new entrants and substitutes, thereby making future earnings more secure.

In purely financial terms, the importance of brands is clearly shown by the price that companies have been prepared to pay for them. Nestlé, for example, paid £2.5 billion (more than five times the book value) to win control of the Rowntree group in 1988. Similar acquisitions can be seen in Figure 1.

Branding is *the* differentiation strategy. The cost of differentiation must naturally be less than the perceived value, but com-

Figure 1: Examples of goodwill payments

Acquirer	*Target*	*Goodwill (% of price paid)*
Nestlé	Rowntree	83
GrandMet	Pillsbury	88
Cadbury Schweppes	Dr Pepper	67
United Biscuits	Verkade	66

Source: Greig Middleton & Co. Ltd

panies must be alert to the temptation to erode differentiation by cost cutting, or other short-term tactics.

Good business leaders set about the nurturing and caring inherent in good brand management because they know it pays off. Investment bankers and other financial professionals become uneasy because even though the cost of differentiation can be quantified, its benefits cannot: shutting an inefficient factory is easier to justify than building cost into a product or a significant investment in marketing.

The economic arguments concerning brands might be characterized as the 'cost fixation' versus the 'art' schools of management: to the cost fixated, branding adds cost of uncertain value, so it is driven out and joins the other downsizing initiatives. This to me is the classic short-term view. Renting a brand share encourages brand promiscuity, where a customer shows little loyalty.

Most, if not all, consumers like choice. Observers of the British supermarkets' struggle for share attribute part of Tesco's dramatic overturn of Sainsbury's historical leadership to Tesco's commitment to brand choice. In many other product categories, consumers like the intrinsic or extrinsic reward of branding. Who buys training shoes without explicit branding? The secret, surely, of good marketing is understanding customers' underlying motivations, the deep psychological needs and moods. For this reason, it is dangerous to assume that 'mystique' per se is still credible or relevant. Even today, there are brand custodians who, when asked to sum up their brand's positioning, confide knowingly, 'Well, it's mystique, isn't it'. Today's customer cannot be bought so easily. *Brand Warriors* shows that mystique has to be replaced by a true psychological contract between customer and company.

Charismatic branding must go hand-in-hand with delivery of the functional product values. The equation is not based on an addition but on multiplication:

Brand values × product delivery = customer satisfaction.

If either brand values or product delivery equals zero, you will not deliver customer satisfaction.

The two schools of management ('cost fixation' and 'art') illustrate the perennial dilemma of the director's task. The multiplier effect can give significant leverage. How do you strike an appropriate balance between the two sides? Careful benchmarking of where your brand *really* is, rather than where you have convinced yourself it should be, is central to this process. Successful brands operating in aggressively competitive markets have acquired these disciplines out of necessity. Brands which have flourished in monopolistic environments have greater difficulty in coming to terms with self-criticism. While companies will never achieve perfection in both product delivery and soft values, *Brand Warriors* confronts this dilemma.

The economic arguments are more difficult for the 'cost-fixated' manager. Branding needs the sustenance of investment, but everyone knows that at least half of it is wasted. It is easy to see that successful brands command a price premium and that their branding creates a volume demand, which can provide scale economies in procurement, manufacturing, distribution, R&D and even marketing. Plus, critically, once these are achieved, they are *real* barriers to entry.

Cost-fixated managers, even if they are not comfortable with the art of branding, ought at least to know about the risks of high sunk costs in market entry caused by better-scaled branded competitors. The final nail in the coffin of the cost-fixated view is the inexorable temptation to reduce price. The quickest way of eroding profits is by reducing prices; and it is very hard to raise them again. Low cost and differentiation are not alternative strategies. Most of the greatest branded businesses have always pursued both with vigour; exploiting all possible economies of scale to deliver lowest cost and differentiating via product, service and branding. This combination is the key to superior returns, higher profit margins and less likelihood of disruption by new entrants.

Short-term pressures on performance have destroyed the Procter & Gamble paradigm of 'brand manager as managing director of the brand'. Today's brand manager is often the custodian of tactics to maximize short-term profitability, not the custodian of brand positioning and brand values. In these circumstances, the custodian of brand positioning and brand values clearly needs to be the CEO with the support of the team. Only he or she can balance the short-term/long-term trade-off. *Brand Warriors* illustrates the importance of not being distracted from managing the brand.

The custodian's role should not be underestimated. Brands need a lot of love. Fred Smith, founder and chairman of FedEx, has a clear view about his role: 'maintaining [the FedEx] reputation and its brand image is a top priority for me, since it is one of the most valuable things the company has.'

Allan Wong, chairman of VTech, has admitted that many companies in the Far East are only now starting to appreciate the importance of developing a brand: 'being too focused on cost and not nurturing and investing in the brand has been typical of many companies in this region. Perhaps people here are very good merchants but are not necessarily also good at building brands.'

Brand warriors need courage to take difficult decisions. In 1997, British Airways chose to cut costs, rationalizing its workforce, and also decided to build on traditional values and invest new values in its brand through a costly redesign programme.

For maximum effectiveness, everyone must work together towards the same goals and with a realistic degree of harmony. The old adage of partners sharing the same bed and dreaming different dreams is an issue for every business. As Archie Norman of Asda once put it: 'a company like this tends to be like a large orchestra: it's no good having the lead violins ahead of the rest.'

Realizing the dream: local or international

The senior management team may not always agree about their international aspirations and strategy. Nick Hodges, responsible for the Durex brand, refers to the pitfalls of local baron warfare. Clarity of vision and acceptance of that vision are crucial. Otherwise, life becomes ambiguous and tiresome for everyone involved, resulting in a weakening of brand positioning and management drive. When British Airways decided to become a global brand, a massive change in structure, attitude, behaviour and communication was required. As *Brand Warriors* shows, a lot of energy and management time must go into similar exercises.

The single-minded, global strategy has been embraced by American brands such as Levi's and Coca-Cola, and Japanese brands such as Sony and Canon. Few other Asian home-grown brands have become universal household names, but this is all changing, as the Asian entrepreneurs realize the benefits of developing the brand.

In Europe, there is a growing number of companies recognizing the value of an international vision. Two of the biggest fast moving consumer goods (FMCG) companies, Unilever and L'Oréal, have been moving towards greater focus on core competencies and commitment to global branding. There are certain attractions to developing brands in new regions: remarkable market growth and significant consumer respect for international as opposed to indigenous brands. Achieving economies of scale through harmonization, such as product format, advertising and design, can obviously bring huge rewards. These emerging regions, however, bring new challenges and some of these are described in the chapters about L'Oréal and McDonald's.

Brand Warriors illustrates dilemmas and challenges both local and international. For example, Durex (LIG) is looking to adopt one brand-name worldwide and Guinness is capitalizing on the universal appeal of the 'Irish soul'. The imperialistic approach is rejected in favour of a listening attitude. Nick Hodges of LIG suggests: 'You always see the corny expression, "think globally, act locally", well, even big brands must take local action . . . We can't decide to roll out a brand globally and just do it. Local attitudes, approaches and sensitivities must all be taken into account.'

McDonald's makes certain that its menus reflect the cultural framework; so the Maharaja Mac™ is the Indian version of the Big Mac™. The brand's emotional values remain unchanged, but the 'rest is about tailoring it for local markets'. As Robert Holloway of Levi Strauss suggests: 'The emotional chords any global brand needs to strike will have many similarities worldwide. It is how you hit them successfully in executional terms that ensures the brand's continuing success.'

Effective implementation and relevance can only be achieved using strong local teams which understand the particular cultural, historical and economic nuances that are likely to influence brand appeal. The conversation should never be one-way. L'Oréal's management team is open to ideas and insights from anyone, anywhere: 'We soon realized it would be very difficult to develop an effective long-term strategy ... without our own organization, our own "family" to give us feedback from the ground.'

Sensitivity manifests itself in executional terms. The Mandarin Oriental Hotel Group's fan symbolizing the Eastern quality standards of personal service is central to its service proposition, but given increased relevance as well as charm by being interpreted differently for each market. As Robert Riley says: 'This kind of originality gives life to our identity – it's not a rigid, static thing.'

Deeply committed to being a global brand, British Airways symbolizes its intention through its new visual identity introduced in June 1997. British Airways has chosen to dispense with the Union Jack motif and heraldic crest, replacing them with a logo, suggesting wings and speed, but curved to create a warmer feel, adorning the tailfins with ethnic and abstract works of art. The British Airways plane feels less like a flying bus and more like a feathery friend, showing off its bright plumage.

This is a fascinating change as it represents a swing in mood within society as a whole. The 1997 identity suggests a more open, less arrogant and jingoistic spirit for the brand. Those who choose the British Airways badge, in the future, will by association be showing an interest in a multi-cultural world and a curiosity to discover diverse, creative forces. The pre-1997 identity now looks not only dated but is a perfect historic icon of the mood of the 1980s, where a more didactic corporate tone of voice was admired. The new identity has lost any possible imperialistic overtones and suggests 'we come in peace'.

British Airways is, at the very least, demonstrating both ortho-

doxy and unorthodoxy (the paradox of Britishness) in its new
identity; namely, respect for relevant heritage and equity combined
with courage and vision to break new ground. An identity can be
both fixed and flexible. It is fixed in the sense that there are familiar
icons suggesting the inherent consistency in the brand and its offer.
It is flexible in the way it has been dramatized through the variations
of art form, reflecting the creature characteristics of the brand. In
this way, it has life and spirit; it is a true living brand.

Many see there are strengths in combining globalization and
localization. Jos Brenkel of Hewlett-Packard states: 'Centralization
means cost saving. Localization means being closer to your
customer.'

Figure 2: Brand architecture options

Monolithic (single dominant corporate brand)	Fixed Endorsed (strong, strait-jacket endorsement)	Flexible Endorsed (flexible in terms of high level, low level variations, depending on relationship to heartland)	Discreet (corporate brand is not used overtly with consumers)
Levi's			
Canon	Kellogg's	Cadbury's	
Sony	L'Oréal		Procter & Gamble
FedEx	Guinness		(e.g. Ariel,
OOCL◄- - -┤	Mazda		Pantene, Pampers)
Rentokil Initial			
Mandarin Oriental	Durex ◄ - - -┤		
British Airways ◄ - - -			
VTech ◄- - -			
McDonald's			
Hewlett-Packard	There are many endorsed strategy options ranging from high		
Asda	level to low level, strait-jacket through to flexible		

© SPRINGPOINT 1997

Developing the brand architecture

I use the term 'brand architecture' to define the strategic relationship between corporate brands and product brands and I have identified four types of brand architecture. (1) The 'monolithic'
approach, with a single dominant corporate brand, such as Levi's,
is highly focused and cost effective. (2) The 'fixed endorsed'
approach, with a strong strait-jacket endorsement, such as Kellogg's, allows clear product line differentiation but ensures the
'master brand' remains all-powerful. (3) The 'flexible endorsed'
approach, such as Cadbury's, allows sub-brands to become heroes,
with the Cadbury's signature acting as endorsement. (4) The 'discreet' approach, deployed by Procter & Gamble with brands such
as Ariel, Pantene and Pampers, ensures that the corporate brand is
not used overtly with consumers (see Figure 2).

Clearly there are pros and cons to each approach. The 'discreet'
approach is costly – each brand needs clear differentiation and
support – but the 'monolithic' approach can be limiting. Then
again, 'monolithic' and 'fixed endorsed' approaches are the most
economic methods of support, as it is difficult to afford a range of
product brands without a corporate umbrella endorsement.

In 1989 I ran a worldwide assessment of corporate architectures
and predicted that more and more companies would focus on their
corporate brands, as competition and economic pressures increased.
Brand Warriors illustrates how this refocusing is taking place. British
Airways, for example, has recognized the primary role of the corporate brand, and is now reasserting its commitment to the brand's
status, appeal and reputation. It has rejected its 1980 'pillar branding' strategy which, although it was created to *support* the corporate
brand, ultimately placed too much emphasis on product brands and
thereby diluted the core brand.

When Nestlé took over Rowntree, it wasted no time in introducing a corporate brand endorsement to all the original Rowntree
product brands, which had historically been most coy about their
corporate brand. Owing to the range of products in Nestlé's portfolio, it is unlikely to choose an even stronger corporate branding

approach which could become too rigid and too limiting. A range of endorsement strategies is available and has to be tailored according to the proximity between the core brand values and products.

Successful brand champions assess the complex value matrices of each individual brand, and endeavour to communicate the varying offers without alienating particular customer groups. There will be those who buy BA First for business travel, but BA World Traveller, or another brand, for holidays. Other consumers will buy Marks & Spencer's underwear but insist on Jaeger or Armani for business clothes. This is a more complex jungle than the choice between Nescafé and own-brand coffee. A great challenge for more dominant corporate branding is to manage these apparent value gaps successfully without eroding one side or deterring the other.

Brand dilution has often been the result of greedy expansion, diversification and meaningless extensions. Today, there is greater awareness of the benefits of concentration. As Alan Palmer of Cadbury reflects: 'it is probably no accident that those branded entities that have survived and prospered under a single company's ownership owe their success to deep-rooted management competencies and considered investment over time in the core values of their products.'

The other dimension is the discipline of concentration on core competencies. Rentokil Initial's growth was based on this belief: 'over time, we have carefully developed and extended the brand according to our core competence', the core competence in this case being a range of service activities.

Levi's has survived the pitfalls. According to Robert Holloway: 'Perhaps the most common mistake when you become successful is to try to stamp your brand on everything . . . It often takes a calamity to focus a company's collective mind. When you're doing very well the temptation is to keep adding bits here and there. Ultimately you risk losing your core consumer.'

And as Nick Hodges of Durex says: 'Diversification had led to management losing sight of the core business – the Durex brand and Biogel surgical gloves – and the heritage of the company.'

One of the benefits of the monolithic approach is, as Sir Clive Thompson of Rentokil Initial says: the 'leverage from one activity to another. The down-side is potential dilution of the impact of the brand, because it acts as an umbrella rather than being sharp and focused on the single activity.'

Another confident, highly respected corporate brand is Virgin, an exception to this principle of core competency focus. This is a brand based on a highly seductive proposition, 'I'm one of you', that is, not one of them, one of those corporates. A 'people's champion' brand is very pertinent to the mood of the late 1990s, and building a brand on a psychological plane, rather than on functional product offer, allows for much more elasticity. Virgin can credibly cruise from music to airline, from vodka to financial services.

So many companies are excited by what Virgin has achieved that they too will be developing their corporate brand architecture in a similar vein. This more fluid, organic development of a corporate brand is certainly inspirational, particularly for young marketeers. Virgin's protagonist, Richard Branson, is a folk hero in parts of the world and in this respect a traditional corporate monolith cannot so easily engage young wannabes. Retailers who own conventional distribution channels have also demonstrated brand elasticity; major multiples, such as Asda, can offer a wide range of products and services and are beginning to challenge the conventional high-street banks.

The world is big enough to accommodate contrasting types of corporate brand and endless brand elasticity is not necessarily appropriate. Perhaps, more importantly, it is a question of deciding what you want to be, and doing it in full knowledge of the implications. L'Oréal builds its own brand on emotional, aspirational values as well as product superiority, and, like Cadbury, has a powerful signature.

Some products have the same values and emotional offer as their parent brand, but they carry additional and specific benefits for smaller, niche audiences. These offspring are sometimes called sub-brands. They should be clearly positioned (as, for example, Durex Fetherlite) and their differentiation should be consonant with the corporate brand values. Mutual reinforcement, the multiplier effect, can be a central benefit in a brand architecture strategy. A symbiotic relationship can often be particularly beneficial to the parent corporate brand, as in the case of Mazda MX5.

Sometimes, the sub-brand begins to contradict rather than reinforce the parent's core values, resulting in loss of brand coherence. In certain markets, such as toiletries, product brands have proliferated to the extent that the consumer is more likely to be bewildered than bewitched. *Brand Warriors* shows that the ultimate decision-makers have to determine how those relationships should be developed, but they need to do so in collaboration with the ultimate brand champion: the consumer.

The benefits of mutual reinforcement, such as credibility, impact, cost efficiencies and product brand freedoms (frameworks within which to operate), have been central to the debate for many of the brands discussed in this book. Building business alone is not enough. 'The moment you produce something that disturbs ... the soul of the brand – you're in trouble,' says Robert Holloway of Levi Strauss & Co.

Cadbury too has achieved a sophisticated and successful model where the positioning of a new product is considered carefully in relation to the core values, and all aspects of communication, including visual identity, reflect that relationship faithfully. The coherent and yet inherently flexible Cadbury architecture provides an increasingly attractive strategy for FMCG brands, which need the strength of a single brand proposition and product offers individually designed with precision. European FMCG brand companies such as Unilever and L'Oréal have been particularly inventive in this respect in recent years.

Keeping the brand relevant

It takes skill to understand the needs and moods of your customers, to connect them with the brand proposition and then to *deliver* it. First Direct is a perfect example of making the right connection with users who were frustrated with the traditional methods of banks and were open to new distribution channels.

Many admit to past failures because they did not understand customer needs and moods. For example, Mazda admits: 'For too long we have been product- rather than market- and marketing-led.' The mature brands have often learned this lesson the hard way: the challenge for Levi's 'is to remain relevant to a target audience that regenerates itself every four or five years; and . . . to avoid the distractions of success . . . History is one element of the brand-building equation. The other part is adapting our history to a life-style that is relevant and interesting to today's consumers. A classic mistake brand managers make is to become too obsessed with their own culture, talking to consumers in ways that are too remote from actual experience – preaching history.'

Guinness is another mature but outward-looking brand whose management is directly and constantly involved in consumer research. Stimulated by creative methods of research and serious benchmarking, the Guinness managers teach their people to listen hard.

Not so long ago, a worldwide brand leader still claimed 'the *mysterious* beauty fluids help'. Consumers in both developing and advanced economies will no longer be patronized. Today, customers seek greater knowledge about products and services. The 'smart home' (real or virtual) gives more power to the consumer, so the product or service performance benefits are more crucial than ever. Activism on the part of the tourist, the patient, the mobile phone user, the utilities' user and the investor is increasingly evident. In this environment, the people own the brand.

While trying to maintain relevance to the consumer, the company must also tread with care. The opening of McDonald's in Russia is a case in point: 'We keep reminding ourselves of what makes us successful. We cannot just rush into new countries if it means we cannot achieve the level of quality and consistency our customers expect. It is much better to do the right thing and guarantee quality than to go for speed. And it works: the Moscow McDonald's is now the busiest in the world.' In Levi's case, in

Europe, 'by hitting the right note, sales for the Levi's brand went up 800 per cent'.

With any brand, the offer has to be coherent in every aspect for a brand's appeal can be fragile. A few years ago Asda lost its appeal, and since then the company has worked hard to regain it. A feeling of Asdaness or Guinnessness can be engendered through delicately balanced messages, themes and variations.

The level of sophistication employed to ensure brand relevance varies among the companies featured here. At Levi's, for example, a European research pilot covered 500 of the core youth target group in each of seven key territories. It has now been rolled out as 'a measure of total brand image strength, breadth, depth and salience across Europe'.

Anticipating future needs is both a skill and an art. Insights from research, combined with imaginative leaps can create exciting opportunities. Fundamental needs never change, but the way in which these needs can be reinterpreted and given new meaning is one of the most rewarding activities of a brand engineer.

Creativity and its value

Imaginative leaps are not the preserve of consultants bearing the title 'creative'. Everyone involved in the development of a brand should be encouraged to make leaps in thinking. Ultimately, a brand dies if it is allowed to stand still, and therefore the culture of an organization has to be dynamic in order for it to progress. Shigeharu Hiraiwa of Mazda believes in continuous progress: 'brands are not static things, they have to evolve.'

The brand custodian must never neglect his or her duty to encourage the team. An organic, creative process begins with the tone of the leadership. Brand warriors encourage their colleagues to think freely. Lateral thinking is a rare gift and should be valued much more than it is.

Technology industries welcome change: it is in their bloodstream. Hewlett-Packard's Jos Brenkel comments: 'We have to hire people who like change, but who understand that change must never affect product quality, or compromise our core values.'

Anticipating needs has been of prime concern to Fred Smith of FedEx: 'for a growing number of major corporations, our air fleet has become their 500-miles-an-hour warehouse: we take over their entire logistics functions ... And now, FedEx is ready to provide the distribution infrastructure the Internet commerce needs. What the clipper ship and railroads did for nineteenth- and twentieth-century trade, we are ready to do for the twenty-first century ... That skill – the ability to meet the needs customers don't know they have – is what continues to drive our business forward.'

Brand supremacy cannot be assumed. Competition is a positive trigger. Bob Ayling has no doubt that British Airways has to give customer service new meaning: 'the quality of customer service we give and the reputation we have for customer service must get better and better. What some people might think are dangers to our business could be stimulants to its growth.'

An unconventional corporate identity can attract new prospects who may have hitherto rejected a brand for being too staid. That's fine, as long as the core loyalists are not alienated. A niche sponsorship programme aimed at opinion-formers can appear indulgent, but may in fact be part of a focused, long-term campaign.

Take Mazda's approach to sponsorship. The idea of sponsoring is an old one, but the idea of reflecting the spirit of your brand in a new concerto commissioned by your company is exciting. The striving for harmony is fundamental to Mazda and therefore to this new Michael Nyman concerto. Thematically linked communications, where the core values of the brand are echoed consistently, require imagination. Otherwise, the result can be ponderous and dull.

More and more companies are exploring scenarios for the future, matching advances in technology and design trends with projected needs. The 'leapfrogging' approach is particularly favoured in the Asian region, where companies learn from others' mistakes, thereby avoiding pitfalls. VTech recognized that its competitors suffered from the absence of an in-house technology capability. VTech has the know-how to produce a constant flow of unique offers.

Making proper time to *think* is tough in a world obsessed with instant results. Brand champions make the time. They also know there will be disappointment as well as success. Guinness' Tim Kelly accepts: 'you won't succeed unless you make an effort, and in making an effort, sometimes you will fail.' Fred Smith, with over twenty-five years' experience, professes: 'our goal is perfection, but we live in an imperfect world.'

Mobilizing creativity through fluid structures

The value of the people who can make creative leaps is increasingly recognized. Seeing things differently will be a greater valued skill, particularly in markets where standard performance differentials are eroded.

The most effective brand developers are structured to allow these creative leaps to see the light of day with, for example, global marketing teams who stand distinct from the day-to-day local or regional management, as in the case of Unilever and Levi's.

Levi's Global Marketing group was created in 1996 to 'act as visionaries, outside national and regional constraints and to build and manage global developments such as the Internet, media, sponsorship, Original Levi's Stores and brand equity management tools.' It allows Levi's to 'transfer best practices from local markets to global markets, bringing a new perspective to the individual and local businesses that previously didn't exist.'

Hewlett-Packard's 'entrepreneurial flexibility is fostered by decentralized business units which have a fair degree of autonomy'; its consistency, in terms of consumer perceptions across a wide range of products, 'has arisen from both culture and behaviour'. As Jos Brenkel states: 'We have had over fifty years to build up values based on our people, customer support and service, the products, innovation and active citizenship.' He admits, though, that 'trying to cement together this very diverse company with its 112,000 employees can still be a challenge.' For the global brands such as Hewlett-Packard, the intranet has transformed work processes and enabled a faster, more comprehensive exchange of ideas.

McDonald's franchised structure allows it to work 'based on long-term commitment' so it has built an infrastructure to facilitate that. As John Hawkes says: 'In order to achieve consistency, we need partners who can not only understand us, but also live by our standards.' McDonald's identify its franchising system as one of the organization's greatest strengths: 'franchisees . . . bring a wealth of individual flair into the business . . . and the franchisees have typically signed up for twenty years and because it is their livelihood, they bring a great deal of dedication and energy to a restaurant's development.'

For many featured in *Brand Warriors*, the direction, tone and style with which things are done are established at the top. That means that not just the intellectual tone – the strategy framework – but the way that people work, and what they do, can now be assessed by the use of competencies.

L'Oréal's structure, with its segmented approach to brands, as well as giving it a prominent position in the three main channels, allows each signature to function as its own business. It fosters the notion of internal competition which, the company believes, is vital to keep it fit.

Many companies are adopting a more mobile, less hierarchical shape. Flat structures have replaced pyramidal structures and the benefits derived from this include more accountability, greater speed and efficiency and, crucially, real focus. Holistic strategy with local implementation is the most attractive approach. A recurring theme from each contributor is the importance of this creativity. It's apparent in the way each tells his story. The L'Oréalian idea of 'poet and peasant' is the very heartbeat of the company's culture. Imaginative people who are both ambitious and generous are selected early on and then they are valued, respected and motivated to stay.

Respecting your roots

Giving a brand some meaning, something engaging and appealing to consumers is crucially important. Keep things simple, but not simplistic, otherwise you patronize your audience.

Perhaps the most important question for the contributors to address is, 'What meaning do you attribute to your brand?'

We often gain insights into the culture of a country by exploring the essence of a brand. We can sometimes understand a brand better by knowing the culture of the country of the brand's origin.

McDonald's and Levi's are symbols of the casual, unpretentious American lifestyle. L'Oréal's personality exudes French charm, flair and finesse. British Airways reflects some of the British virtues of stability, subtlety and yet unorthodoxy. OOCL mirrors typical Hong Kong characteristics: boldness, pride, free spirit. Guinness reflects much of the attraction of Irish soul; in fact, Guinness seems to be doing a grand job for the Irish tourist industry. The Mazda philosophy is a product reflecting Japan: renowned for its high quality, high standards and modern technology.

In other instances, the roots of a brand have less to do with the culture of one specific country and are more concerned with the founder's moral and philosophical motivations. This is true in the case of Cadbury and FedEx.

When Archie Norman proclaims 'to thine ownself be true', as Asda returns to its Yorkshire roots for inspiration, perhaps there is a message here for all brands. Take care not to throw away your cultural roots, jettisoning your equities. A business, in its bid to act globally, can become enfeebled by its acceptance of lowest common denominator values. While certain aspects of a traditional culture convey parochialism, these characteristics may be some of the brand's most distinguishing and motivating assets. A defensive move towards putative commonality can herald the beginning of decline.

Living the brand

OOCL and VTech are corporate brands that have recognized the importance of sharing the brand vision. Chinese companies have historically been typified by the brilliance of their merchants. Now, they are building expertise in long-term branding and this will encourage people to articulate their brand values in a more deliberate way.

Perceptions of the ideal corporate brand vary widely from country to country but, in many countries, social status brands still hold sway. Recent research conducted by Springpoint shows that, in advanced economies, the ideal corporate brand is friendly, enjoys life and has imagination. It is interested in profit, but considerate to staff and suppliers. It is not dogmatic and hears others' opinions. Many Europeans say, 'they promised us the caring 90s, it's turned into the scaring 90s'. That is why brands which mouth platitudes such as 'We are a caring, trustworthy brand' may no longer be credible. The didactic, authoritarian approach to building trust values can alienate people.

Security is a deeper, warmer, more human notion. A 'caring brand' can gain meaning through its ability to understand the psyche of its customers. The British Airways Business 'larder' for the middle-of-the-night snack is a good example. Levi's 'Personal Pair' jeans, tailor-made to your size, is another.

Getting it wrong *within* a company can also alienate people. Motherhood and apple pie propositions which are not followed through are a waste of space or, at best, a sop to a divisive board. Levi's teach people to 'walk the talk'. Hewlett-Packard believes: ' "Just be." In other words, don't advertise your values, just live them.'

A mismatch between the external and internal protection of a 'caring' brand is upsetting to employees and suppliers. When you get it right from within, as is now the case with Asda, your brand attains a deeper resonance. 'Getting it right from within' is echoed by every service champion. For example, OOCL, Mandarin Oriental, FedEx and McDonald's recognize that *the brand is delivered by the people*. This message is not only pertinent to service brands, but is more relevant than ever today for FMCG brand champions than it was when times were easier.

Branding in the future

Some argue that brands will wither away, particularly in the super-market arena. Certainly, the trends in economies such as Western Europe suggest that more discerning consumers, prompted by increasing fragmentation of distribution channels, greater know-ledge and, in some respects, greater insecurity, show increasing willingness to buy own label. Retail Own Brand can, of course, be a brand. The retailer is a trusted supplier and the major multiple retailer can offer any product or service relevant to his customer, where he has an edge. Fuel, OTC products, insurance and financial services – there appear to be no restrictions.

Retail Own Brand has eroded traditional brands' shares across many parts of Europe. Carrefour, the French chain of supermarkets, has been selling own label computers since 1995. Décathlon, the French sports goods retailer, sells own label sports goods across France and Spain. Its own range includes sports shoes, clothing, bikes and trekking kit. In 1997 this retailer had become the sixth biggest sports manufacturer in Europe, and the second in France. Corte Ingles is one of the main distributors for credit cards in Spain. Sectors which historically were exclusively branded are now open to this retail competition (see Figure 3).

The reality is that own label has lost any social stigma it once had (see Figure 4). Interest and experience can provide people with the confidence to buy own label and avoid well-known brands.

Once upon a time, there was a simple world where a stable line of manufacturing brands dominated a market. Retail Own Brand has now gone so far that the old order of Brands and Commodities has disappeared for ever in certain parts of the world. The conven-tional model has gone and, as in chaos theory,* a bifurcation has

---

* *Chaos* by James Gleick (London: Heinemann, 1988; Minerva, 1996).

Figure 3: Acceptance of own label brands – not just FMCG products. Those who could imagine buying the following own label products when offered for sale by their local supermarket

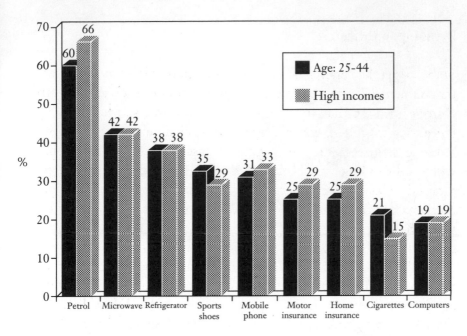

Source: The Henley Centre, *Frontiers: Planning for Consumer Change in Europe 1996/7*

occurred: there are now FMCG brands and retail brands. Within this turbulent environment, there appear to be new 'spikes' of order, breaking into four, then eight lines, as distribution channels fragment. For example, Eismann provides home delivery of frozen foods and First Direct promotes telephone banking.

Within this apparent chaos, however, a new regularity will emerge. In the future, with the convenience of shopping on the Web, product choices are likely to be more concerned with quality/ value trade-off. Interactive media can be regarded as both a threat and an opportunity for companies. Technology is a key driver, changing the way markets are and will work. Ultimately FedEx, UPS and DHL may become the channel; and the mechanics will be the Web, mail, phone. There are risks to conducting transactions

Figure 4: Percentage of high earners who agree, 'I would be prepared to pay more for a supermarket "own label" champagne if I thought it was better.'

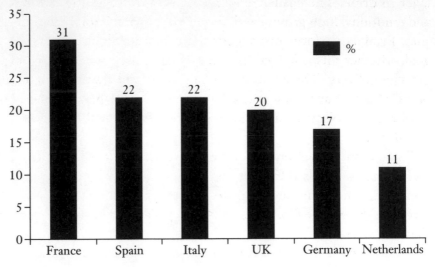

Source: The Henley Centre, *Frontiers: Planning for Consumer Change in Europe 1996/97*

simply on the Web, however. If you reduce all your exposure to a consumer down to a transactional, rational level, do you undermine your own ability to create the myth which is the heartbeat of a brand?

Levi's raises this question and many companies today are grappling with this issue. However hard we try to be rational about product choice, we are not purely logical in our responses. As we have discussed earlier, brand appeal and reputation are created not only through the product experience but as a result of both controlled and uncontrolled communication (such as the hostile publicity that Unilever's Persil Power received in the mid-1990s in the UK).

Intangible values may evoke a range of emotional benefits, ranging from self-enhancement, romance, fun, through to deeper, spiritual yearnings. Even City analysts are liable to form opinions about corporate brands in this way. For many years the City has tried to perpetuate a myth of a rational relationship between institutional investment and performance. In reality, many individuals buy and sell shares with the same fickleness as they choose which premium lager to drink. The challenge is therefore to own *both* the rational and emotional high ground and, in this way, own the total relationship. Product performance superiority continues to be a desirable goal, whether this is judged in terms of customer service or actual product delivery. The emotional high ground will always influence brand choice, but in new ways. For example, the ethical stance of a company, projected through its corporate brand, will engender a moral contact.

Perception will always be crucial. As Robert Holloway says: 'What makes Levi's different, and allows them to be priced at a premium, is how they are branded and *perceived*. As a result, Levi's earn Levi Strauss & Co. twice the profit that other manufacturers' jeans earn them.'

To cope with the diverse challenges of fragmented distribution and more sophisticated competition, the warrior must demonstrate his ability to resist the temptation to compromise on the big ideas. He or she will need to reduce layers of bureaucracy even further and empower innovation or breakthrough groups to create the revolution in corporate brand positioning, architecture, concept, creation and product development. These groups will be so structured, as to be able to form and re-form according to the nature of the project. A headache to manage well, such teams are immensely effective.

Recruitment and management development policies will adapt as corporations build new kinds of teams, where creative talent is allowed to shine through and make an impact.

Brand positionings will be more distinctive and more engaging. Trademarks will be respected as only part of a brand identity and a brand identity will be seen as an important part, but only one part, of a brand experience.

Brands are about people and ideas. *Brand Warriors* explores the ways in which people and ideas come together to make a profit. United in a common mission, the brand is fuelled by an inner fire. The warmth and glow of this fire radiates and creates the *charismatic* brand. The brand warrior can light and tend the fire, controlling its flames. Unmotivated people let the fire rage out of control or allow it to die. Motivated people deliver a fire that glows and radiates warmth. In *Brand Warriors*, all the brands selected have in common an inner fire.

Marketing in the third millennium will be tougher than ever before. Brand warriors, as individuals, will be thinking in unconventional ways about new kinds of distribution channels, media strategies, distinctive brand positionings, architectures, moral dilemmas, quality of life aspirations and a new vocabulary for brand development. The challenge for every business leader, outside commodity sectors, will be his or her ability, every day, to be a true brand warrior.

1 | Asda: The Accelerated Repositioning of a Brand

ARCHIE NORMAN, *chairman*

To thine own self be true

If there is one lesson to be drawn from the Asda experience it's this: the secret of successful branding is 'to thine own self be true'. In retailing especially, your shoppers define your brand, and knowing what your brand stands for and how it appeals to its core customers is key. The successful revival of the Asda brand was the result of a determined return to powerful core brand values that had once made it popular, but had been lost, forgotten or deliberately rejected.

From its origins in the 1970s, Asda was a pioneer. It had a unique positioning as the place you could go to get everything you needed at the lowest prices. It was the UK's first superstore, selling a wide range of groceries and non-food items such as clothing, washing machines and toys. It pioneered the idea of permanent low pricing before it became a fashionable concept. And, long before others began to see the vital importance of the shopping experience, it consciously tried to craft a better way to shop – one that would appeal to the whole family.

By the late 1980s, the business had comprehensively lost its way. Its roots had been abandoned in an attempt to copy the strategies of rivals J. Sainsbury and Tesco which were more upmarket and up-margin. At the same time, the group had invested heavily by diversifying into other businesses such as furniture and carpets.

Asda had started chasing after the customers it thought it would like
to have and, in its search for higher margins and a more upmarket
customer base, it had begun to suppress the very brand identity
that had made it so popular. In doing so, Asda became caught
up in a vicious circle, losing customers, pushing up margins to
compensate for that loss, thereby accelerating the customer exodus,
responding by pushing up prices even further, and so on.

By the time a new management team took over in 1991, sales
per square foot were two-thirds that of the market leader, a £1
billion debt mountain was piling up and the group's share price
had entered a tail-spin. The organization was in the grip of a triple
crisis: a crisis of confidence, an identity crisis and a financial crisis.
If it was to survive, all three had to be tackled. Fast.

By 1996, Asda's debt mountain had been eliminated, the company's profitability was restored and rising and, in fierce competitive
conditions, its sales growth was outstripping its rivals. The brand
had staged a dramatic and comprehensive recovery.

Move fast and focus on your strengths

To turn Asda around, everyone had to understand that things had
to change if the organization was both to survive and to thrive, and
that the change would be major, radical and painful.

Clear overall directions were set out – directions which came
from the roots of the business. Asda's stores are in areas of Britain
with lower-than-average demographics and tend to be older and
larger than those of the competition. So it was clear that Asda had
to trade in a way that exploited its floor space while tapping into
the powerful brand heritage.

To create scope for the radical change needed, two new projects
were set up within the first hour I was in the business. One was
called Renewal; its task was to create an idea of what the Asda store
should look like in the mid-1990s, what it was aspiring to achieve.
The other project subsequently became known as Dales; it was all
about creating Britain's best wide-range discount formula.

This overall direction was quickly confirmed by research, which showed Asda's customers still remembered the old things about it: an honest, no-nonsense 'Yorkshire' brand synonymous with value. Everything subsequently centred on reinterpreting those brand values for the 1990s, and focused on four key elements:

- Asda is a family shop. A greater percentage of people who shop at Asda have children and shop with children. They also stay in the store for longer. So Asda must stock a range wide enough to satisfy customers' basic needs; it must be a place where they can solve problems such as what to give the kids for tea on Friday night; and it should have a cafeteria so that customers can sit down and relax for a moment too. As such, the Asda store should be closer to the community than its rivals.

- Asda has 'Yorkshire heritage'. That means it is honest in what it does. It is authentic. It has integrity. It is ordinary and every day, without pretensions.

- Asda is committed to value. Instead of adopting yo-yo pricing policies and promotional gimmicks so that customers are never sure how much things will really cost, it opts for steady, permanently low prices. This delivers recognizable value to the customers, and it reduces the manipulation, thereby positioning the brand as the housewife's champion. Any promotions must be authentic. In other words, if Asda buys for less, the customer buys for less. If it gets a good deal on pineapples, or finds a way of engineering better value into the system, it is passed on to the customer.

- It must be an enjoyable shopping experience. Partly, this is connected with Asda's family focus, but it is also about the experience in store: Asda is a place people enjoy going to because it contains a lot of interesting things, things customers didn't expect to find, things which solve problems they have been worrying about. It's all about creating a sense that this store is for its customers and that staff are there to serve. And that means integrating service throughout Asda stores, actively helping and stimulating the shopper.

Live the legend

Once these brand values had been clarified, Asda set about living the legend. First and foremost that meant cutting costs. If Asda were to offer value for money, which means lower prices on goods overall than its major competitors, then there would have to be lower costs. That meant starting from the centre. For the first year, there was a complete wage and salary freeze. Overheads were quickly reduced by a third, by trawling through each department and store to find ways to cut costs.

At the same time, Asda had to find ways to express all the core brand values, using a process called 'sauna-ing'. It involved an intense review of every aspect of the business and the store: from cost structure to store layout, design and format, and the way customers were served. For example, before the new team began, the first thing a customer encountered on entering a store was clothing. But food values are fundamentally important to Asda, and so food is now right up front. And, to communicate a no-nonsense, market trader feel, it is now displayed differently. Whereas in some rival stores everything is arranged so perfectly that the shopper feels afraid to pick up a piece of fruit, Asda piles it up, giving the impression of relative abundance; the place looks lived in.

At every twist and turn, Asda looked for ways to express its brand values. One way which emphasized the value-for-money proposition was to put prices on blackboards as though the local produce man had chalked up the price of tomatoes that morning. Wider aisles were installed for easy traffic flow for the whole family. Samplings and tastings were introduced to involve and entice customers and to create a sense of personality, warmth and theatre. And the store layout was planned as though it were a good book. As they come out of the store, people should be able to tell you what the highlights were, what the chapter headings were, and why it had an exciting ending. What you don't have is a really exciting first chapter, a boring bit in the middle and a punch-line at the end. It has to be paced – at the end of each aisle there must be something exciting.

Only after the sauna-ing process was well under way and Asda was truly delivering what mattered, was mass media advertising appropriate. The whole idea of 'Asda price' (which had been abandoned) was revived, re-creating Asda's once famous tap on the pocket, 'pocket the difference' imagery.

The challenge in retailing is that your customers experience your product directly. They actually walk through the store for an hour every week. That has much more impact than any amount of media coverage or advertising. They see everything, buy everything, and talk about it. What they experience in the store is the brand. So stores have to be both internally and externally coherent. The way the brand is projected and advertised externally reflects the way it lives and works internally.

The new advertising campaign fulfilled three key objectives. First, it announced to the world that 'We're back', that Asda had returned to its roots and its heritage. Second, it was a clear statement of intent. Some change, some improvement, was already visible. Asda was effectively promising that there would be lots more to come. And third, we were signalling all this to our own staff.

From the beginning Asda had worked on the assumption that whatever it said externally would be said internally too, and this was an extension of the theme. It was not always easy to unite a workforce consisting of tens of thousands of staff, many of them part-time. But as soon as they saw the TV commercial, colleagues understood the mission statement. They knew what they had to do, and for many it was back to the Asda they grew up with.

Finally, it was consistent *brand* advertising. Unlike a lot of retail advertising, which is about this 'summer saver' or that 'half-price meat offer', in every commercial we focused on our commitment to value for money.

Align the culture and the brand

To create, live and communicate an Asda culture, it was crucial to change the way people operated and felt about things.

One of the most important initiatives was the teams set up to look at the future of Asda stores. They were 'risk-free zones', working outside the main body of the organization, resourced with some of the best people, regardless of cost. This was important in two ways.

First, people in a crisis-ridden company lose their ability to help themselves. That's because innovation generates a high proportion of failure to success, but if you are in a position where you don't dare fail, then you don't dare take risks. For this reason, the project teams were specifically briefed to collect all the ideas that people had, to push the boat out, to create a sense that everybody was wanted and had a chance to play a part. This was critical to mobilize staff for the long haul back to viability.

Second, people from outside were hired to help with the creative process and search for good ideas. Being able to do this without feeling defensive is a good test of a company's culture. Many people become tremendously defensive at the notion that an outsider can think of anything they have not thought of. So the successful repositioning of Asda results partially from its ability to gather and apply ideas from organizations like Wal-Mart in America, or from people like Julian Richer, who concentrates on customer service and staff motivation. The key, however, lies in knowing how to translate these ideas and turn them to advantage in an Asda sort of way; retailing especially is a very cultural, people-based business and just because an idea is good, it doesn't mean it's right for Asda.

Another crucial step was the formation of a close leadership team to see through the programme and to live the vision. The leadership tone was essential to what had to be achieved. The direction, tone and style with which things are done are established from the top. That means not just the intellectual tone – the strategy framework – but the way management works and what it does.

If you set the right leadership tone, the right direction and the right mini-examples – ones that deliver solutions with a high degree of understanding, detail and quality (so that you can focus on the issues that are central to what you are trying to achieve) – then the organization starts to take care of itself.

One such mini-example was the way the stores were visited. Thus, instead of the chief executive arriving in an imperial caval-cade, informal wandering around taking notes became, and has remained, the norm. Initially, store managers were amazed that the chief executive was writing down what they said. It gave them a tremendous sense of importance. It positioned the chief executive as being there to listen, and it positioned the manager as someone who had something to say for the company.

Another effective cultural change was to give store managers their head, focusing them on sales rather than costs. That is what Asda is about: driving sales. If you drive the sales, customer service naturally follows. And selling is something everyone should be involved in – a universal responsibility.

As a result, store managers became confident that they were central to the success of the company. They then started doing things locally that they wouldn't have done otherwise, the vast majority of which were highly productive for the company.

Also central to the Asda proposition is straight talking. It would have been a mistake with a company like Asda, which had been drifting downwards for so long, to try and pretend that things were better than they were. Trying to motivate and lead employees using the feel-good factor in such a situation would not have been cred-ible: they knew too well what things were really like. What was needed was a sense of grip. So, right from the start, everyone was told it was going to be tough and we might not make it. With the management at last openly facing up to reality, the main reaction was one of relief.

Likewise, from day one, the strategy was explained to share-holders. They were told it would take three years before Asda would have a sustainable basis for profit growth and that the new team was not focused on short-term growth. Indeed, if reducing the next

year's profit happened to be the right thing to do, that's what would
be done.

Continue the revolution

Once the main direction has been established and results have
started coming through, in retailing especially it's essential to maintain momentum. You have to move on, avoid complacency, be
relentless. And, to move with pace in a high employment business
– Asda employs 75,000 people – you have to have a strong culture.
It's this that helps you manage behaviour. It creates a way of doing
things, a set of principles that people recognize and work with.

We have deliberately tried to create an Asda culture,
encompassing three words: Selling, Personality and Involvement.
Our attitude to service, for example, starts from a different base
from our competitors. We believe in service with personality. Good
service comes from the heart. It has to be experienced, not advertised. And it doesn't come from a training manual. It should not
be necessary to say 'Make sure you have good eye contact and
smile'. It's much better to recruit people who smile in the first place
and to put them in a position where they feel they are respected and
where they think this is a smiling sort of place, that this is a bit of
fun.

The next task is to get them motivated about the business – to
believe that the business is trying to do a good thing in the marketplace and trying to help its customers. Everybody can subscribe to
that; it gives them an incentive to sell. Then you start to deliver
service. It will happen in a way that combines selling and personality.

The same goes for involvement. We seek to involve customers
in stores with tasting and samplings. And we seek to involve staff.
We are an open sort of company. If you walk around our headquarters in Leeds you will find people who don't actually work for
us foraging around, hopefully making a contribution. We feel at
ease with that. We also have the biggest employee share-ownership

plan in Britain. Since it was launched in July 1995, 36,000 colleagues have taken up share options.

And we have pulled down every partition wall in the building. There are no offices, no meeting rooms that don't have windows. Why? Because we try and operate a single status business in which people are not judged by the size of their office. We want open communication. It's lively, vocal, noisy and sometimes it seems a bit chaotic, but it's got personality.

We are also maintaining the momentum in communicating the Asda brand values. Having revived 'Asda price' and the famous 'pocket tap' in our advertising, we moved on to create a Yorkshire farmer to express some of the things which are central to the Asda proposition: calling a spade a spade; good honest value; a little bit of old-fashioned craft skills; bringing back to supermarkets some of the things that used to belong in the High Street, such as fresh food; plus a sense of trust and being on the customer's side.

This sense of 'being on your side' is very important – and it's another area where we have expanded the Asda brand. Being a champion of the consumer was always part of Asda's stance but we have deliberately added a crusading element, campaigning on issues such as perfume prices, the Net Book Agreement and retail price maintenance in medicines. To some extent, we enjoy being a northern, anti-establishment company. More importantly, by becoming 'Britain's value crusader' we are bringing our customers and colleagues together, allowing them to feel good about what they are doing.

Some people say that there is a PR, gimmicky element to our crusading. Certainly, there is a PR element to it. It does create enormous opportunities for expression in store. But then, all good marketing relies on strong communication. Asda is not the biggest and cannot afford the marketing budgets of some of its competitors, but we can find campaigns that matter. This is not a stunt. We do not enter these campaigns for cheap publicity. We do and will go to court to see things changed.

We have also changed our policy on own label. In the beginning we cut back on many own label lines. They were lower quality, me-toos and failed to offer genuine added value. Now we are developing a theme of 'only at Asda', starting with an excellent fresh food offer, with the George clothing brand, and with an improved own label offer. Own label is a crucial method of delivering customer value. If own label is as good as leading brands (as ours is now), and if we sell it at a discount of 10 to 15 per cent, the more the customers buy own label, the better value they get. Therefore, own label penetration is essential to delivering value in the basket overall. Also, we believe we are a food company first and foremost, and therefore developing a unique product is part of what we should do. Early on Asda had to catch up, but now we believe we can do some pioneering.

We are also exploiting assets like our larger stores to enhance that sense of personality. Take a little thing like doughnuts. After three hours, a doughnut loses its freshness. But with an operation where the doughnuts are fried in-store and sold within the first three hours, you will have a product that nobody can match. It may not be the cheapest way of producing a doughnut but it's not expensive either if you sell the volume. And, of course, the margins are tremendous.

Asda's competitors which have smaller outlets don't have the facilities to do this. Nor do the discounters. Asda, as a result, has more personality. Bakers baking the bread, people making up the salads, butchers cutting the meat – this is how you start creating a sense of humanity, personality, theatre and excitement. These are the things that shoppers hanker after.

Themes like these are coming together under our new strategy of Breakout. Breakout is about continuing the revolution, creating not just a good business, but something that is special and which is capable of sustaining profitability and growth even where the market is competitive and mature and even when we have to accept we will never be the biggest grocery multiple.

Being the biggest is not an option for Asda. Instead, we have prioritized something we do have control over. We want to be the biggest operator of large-scale, wide-range superstores at the best value. We want to have the best value, fresh-food operation in

Britain and to re-create the craft skills which can deliver, in-store, prepared and finished fresh foods that nobody else can match.

Accelerated repositioning is possible – but it still has to be real

Many people believe that Asda's performance has improved basically because of price. We have improved on price. We are better value for money. But our performance improvement stems from the whole renewal programme: refocusing the Asda brand. The small moves, central to repositioning and integrated right across the business – the display, merchandising, presentation, ranging – make things happen and make the difference, not a single idea.

You certainly can accelerate things. At Asda, there was no time for exhaustive strategy reviews. We simply had to create a tremendously accelerated run at change and get the organization moving very, very fast. Nevertheless, a company like this tends to be like a large orchestra: it's no good having the lead violins ahead of the rest. It just won't work. In the end, you cannot be a different type of store or retailer unless you have a different type of business behind it. In retailing, the store is the business. You can't reposition the brand without repositioning the business.

2 | British Airways: Brand Leadership Results from Being True to Our Long-term Vision

ROBERT AYLING, *chief executive*

When British Airways started using the slogan 'The World's Favourite Airline' in 1983, it was perceived to be extraordinarily arrogant and self-regarding. It was. That was the whole point. It was not something that British companies did. At the time it was probably quite unjustified in the sense that British Airways was by no means everyone's first choice. Today all that has changed. People no longer say that British Airways has no right to call itself the world's favourite airline, but how terrific it is to have a company that is one of the world leaders in its industry based in the UK.

One of the most critical elements in that success has been the concentration on our customers: you have to give customers not only what they expect but more than they expect. And that is a very difficult thing to achieve. Understanding what customers want better than the competition does has to be at the heart of everything we do.

The crucial role of branding

The balance between functional and emotional delivery has taken years to fine-tune, and branding plays a crucial role in this. We have created certain expectations of the British Airways brand: it stands for a professional Western style of service of the highest calibre where passengers are treated politely, professionally, in a friendly way and where they are cared for.

The British Airways brand experience is of course not just about the tangible aspects of the airline – seats or food, for example – although we are constantly improving what we offer. It is also about softer values – the emotional side of the brand. Creating and sustaining these softer values is critical in creating and sustaining the success of the company.

Good design and innovation are central to the brand proposition. For example, the new seats in First give a significant product advantage for British Airways, and have won numerous design awards. They also build the brand equity for a key customer group. Research among our most loyal passengers clearly indicated how we could reduce yet more of the stresses of travelling: they wanted privacy, space and flexibility, and we've been able to deliver in a way that's never been done before.

The need to relaunch

The first time we transformed ourselves, culminating in privatization in 1987, we changed the airline from being a company criticized for its bad service into one of the most profitably privatized companies and the world's leading international airline.

Since then we have enjoyed fourteen good years of profit to become the 'world's favourite' airline. It became clear, however, that more of the same just wasn't good enough. We had overhauled a good many parts of what we offer our customers, but the company itself clearly needed to be relaunched.

Our research confirmed that we needed to change again if we wanted to continue to be the industry leader into the twenty-first century. So, over two years, we planned a new corporate identity which would create a global personality for British Airways.

The new identity is a visual promise to our customers and staff of the many improvements that will come from the company's repositioning for its customers – 60 per cent of whom come from outside Britain. We are blending the best of traditional British values with the best of today's Britain – diverse, creative, friendly, youthful and cosmopolitan in outlook.

Our new identity represents an outward sign of significant change within the organization. It is part of a larger programme, launched in 1996, to prepare the airline for the next millennium.

It is linked to a £6 billion investment programme which covers new aircraft and new buildings. Hundreds of millions of pounds are being ploughed back into improved services and products for leisure and business travellers. A programme of new training initiatives will ensure even better customer service. As part of our programme for the new millennium, we are improving our efficiency by ensuring that all of our activities match external cost levels, and by working our assets harder.

The aim is to ensure it is fully equipped with the right people, with the right skills, in the right places to meet the challenges of the new millennium. Driving the overall programme is a new corporate mission – to be the undisputed leader in world travel. British Airways is aiming to set new industry standards in customer service and innovation, to deliver the best financial performance and to evolve from being an airline to a world travel business, with the flexibility to stretch the brand into new business areas.

The new livery, the efficiency programme and the change in staff skills are all designed to show employees and customers that the airline is changing, as we need to do. To become the world leader in world travel, we have to do again what we did in the last decade – put clear blue sky between us and our rivals. We have to reach out to people around the world and deliver a service that meets their needs. Our customers want to deal with people who speak their language, and eat food that suits their palate. In short, they want to feel as if they are travelling home from home.

British and global

The airline's British heritage is reflected in our corporate colours of red, white and blue, but the heart of the new identity is the creation of more than fifty 'world images' which will appear on the entire fleet. They will also be seen in the designs on ground vehicles, stationery, signage, timetables, baggage tags and ticket wallets – everything that bears the British Airways name.

Through these world images, British Airways is turning its fleet into a flying gallery – one of the world's largest art commissions. The new identity is aimed at presenting British Airways as an airline of the world, born and based in Britain with a community of people passionately committed to serving the communities of the world. To show this, what we have done is to find art that represents different communities, which we then take to other communities on our tailfins. We are sending an important message to our existing and new customers everywhere: British Airways wants to be your favourite airline and is responsive to your needs.

We are moving the brand's formal British style of the 1980s to a more international one. Instead of being perceived as 'professional but reserved', British Airways is becoming less formal and more flexible, catering more to our customers' individual needs.

Our change ensures we are now British *Airways* instead of *British* Airways. We are proud of the name of the company, and we never considered changing it. Keeping British in the name is a strength because, although the British are perceived in some countries as being a bit reserved, they are also seen as caring, ready to help and responsible. These are all very good characteristics to have if you are running a business in which people trust you with their lives, because uppermost in people's minds is their safety.

Customer needs in the new millennium

Global demographic trends were a factor in the change in brand focus. In addition, we are aiming to enhance our customers' experience by delivering an individualized service.

Ultimately, each of our customers expects to be treated as an individual. Each one has a different reason for travelling, a different reason for choosing British Airways, and different expectations of us.

Recently, in order to understand better the needs of our cus-

tomers as individuals, we have been listening to them and exploring
their social values. We have found that they are the kind of people
who like to explore all new options. They take nothing for granted,
and do not necessarily accept the status quo – so our challenge is
heightened. In our favour is the fact that many of our passengers
have 'heavily invested' in British Airways. They tell us that, as well
as investing commercially (choosing to give us both time and
money) they are committed to British Airways at an emotional
level.

Breaking down the 'them and us' between British Airways and
its customers is important. Many of our passengers are as involved
with the company as are the staff themselves. They wish to be
recognized for that and treated as 'insiders'. In fact, they tell us
they want British Airways to succeed and feel let down when things
do go wrong.

Not sub-brands but segmentation

The brand is British Airways. In the 1980s, it all became too complex – sub-brands with distinct personalities. What we learned was
that our customers ultimately purchase British Airways.

The British Airways brand has been developed in close collaboration with our customers. The research findings conclusively
showed that they wanted a global airline, by which they meant big,
safe and reliable. However, they also wanted an airline that cared
for each customer, addressing individual needs wherever they came
from. In all our communications we therefore aim to combine scale
with humanity, to appeal to the heart not just the head.

The aim became, and remains, to be the airline that customers
choose first in all the markets we serve. Ultimately, all who travel
with British Airways should feel so much at home with us that they
choose us in preference to their national carrier.

We have to segment the market to some extent, however. That
is why we offer a number of services like Club World, Club Europe,
and World and Euro Traveller. But to call them sub-brands can

be misleading. What we have is the one main brand, British Airways, which offers a number of different services. Travellers know what they will get depending on which service they have selected. For example, travellers in First and Club Class know they will get off first, their baggage will be in the hall first, and that they have the use of a lounge.

Concorde is a different case. While it is part of British Airways, it is seen as a brand in its own right. The British Airways name is on the outside of the aircraft, but otherwise all the branding inside the aircraft is Concorde. The Concorde brand stands above all for speed, for getting from London to New York in three hours, twenty minutes. It represents a very exclusive means of travel, and in some ways it is also an exclusive club.

It also stands for a particular form of engineering excellence. It might be twenty-five years old but it has never been bettered. It is still the most remarkable sight in the skies. When it flies over everyone looks up, and not just because of the noise. In fact, the British Airways and the Concorde brands are complementary. Concorde helps the British Airways brand by giving it cachet.

The implications for the brand of strategic alliances

Apart from the competitive issues, one of the most difficult branding issues British Airways is facing is what happens to the brand as strategic alliances are formed with other airlines. The laws in Europe forbidding foreign airlines from having a majority stake in domestic airlines have recently been liberalized. We took advantage of this by taking stakes first in TAT and then in Air Liberté in France and in Deutsche BA in Germany. In these we have control over their operations, but the way the global aviation market is moving means that we will have to form alliances with players as big as ourselves to stay alive.

When British Airways formed a relationship with Qantas in Australia, in which we have a 25 per cent stake, all sorts of possible corporate branding ideas were considered. It soon became obvious, however, that none of the ideas – such as, for instance, Global Airlines – would work. Both James Strong, chief executive of Qantas, and I were clearly of the view that his airline should remain Qantas and ours should stay British Airways.

Changing the name of an airline might be fraught with danger, but there are times when it can be done. When British Airways took over British Caledonian it was rebranded overnight. We were in one market and both operating out of the same airport, so it made sense. Changing 'British Caledonian' to 'British Airways' worked because we told the British Caledonian employees about our values as a company and helped to make them keen to project them. Many of the British Caledonian staff still work for us.

Qantas and British Airways are both resonant, motivating brands with loyal customers; they are discrete propositions which risked being diluted if combined. However, over time, there will be aspects of what we do with alliance partners – the seats on the aircraft, the style of our catering, the sort of cups and glassware we buy – where it would be crazy not to seek economies of scale. None of this will affect the brand in a significant way. If people believe that travelling on Club World on British Airways has similarities with Business Class on Qantas or other partners, that is fine. But the personalities will remain different. When we sell British Airways and Qantas services together, customers are offered the airline of their choice.

In terms of brand protection, the key issue on alliances is that there must be an alliance of equals when it comes to the quality of service. We have taken the view that passengers prefer one carrier or the other so market share might be lost if the two were merged. However, the service levels clearly need to be in line with customer expectations. If a customer is transferred to the partner airline, the comfort and quality of the alternative provider must be the same, throughout the journey.

Franchising has also proved an effective way of developing our business. Franchising at British Airways dates back to 1993 and is central to our growth strategy. We tend to franchise where we don't have the right size of aircraft, or expertise in a particular market, or legal rights to fly. For example, we cannot fly from

Johannesburg to Durban for these reasons, so Comair flies it as a franchise.

For many of the routes operated, the best way for British Airways to earn money on them is from the licence fees. For example, British Regional Airlines flies football fans from Shannon to Manchester under our name. Our franchising agreement allows other airlines to use British Airways' intellectual property – logo, style, trademark and service standards – provided they deliver product consistently to our specifications. As with Hertz, which has franchised 70 per cent of its operations, the customer would be hard pushed to tell the difference.

Staff levels have increased from 55,000 to 60,000 as the business has grown and, of these, 1,000 extra members of staff have been employed to service the franchisees. We already have ten franchised airlines carrying about 6 million passengers a year, and we have ambitious plans to continue to develop in this way.

The staff as embodiment of the brand

A vital part of the brand's personality is its closest interface with our customers: the staff. Good customer service is essential. It is central to our competitive edge as it increases our customer retention and our overall efficiency.

Our approach can work only if we have a clear vision, deliver the basics reliably and consistently, and employ staff who have a passion for delivering excellence in customer service. Their personality and attitude will project the image of the brand.

A culture has to be created which is strong enough to transmit the brand values without having to repeat them every day to every person. You have to persuade everyone who works for the company that customer satisfaction is the only criterion that matters.

Keeping a finger on the pulse of the brand

The chief executive has to act as the guardian of the brand. Keeping a finger on the pulse of the brand means that when I fly, which is at least once a week, the key thing is to look around. I notice the way our staff treat our passengers. We don't want people to be gushing but polite, friendly, helpful, always thinking of something they can do to make passengers' lives easier.

I notice things like the quality of announcements. If they are being made on a flight from Frankfurt, can the staff speak German or do they put on a tape? How do the captain and co-pilot cope with things like delays – are they informative without being overly informative? Do they keep the passengers in touch? I look at the quality of the service, not just the meal service. I look at the interior of the aircraft, whether there are any broken seats, whether the carpet is stained, and I do this almost without thinking about it because it is all part of the brand. If there are things that are not quite right, everyone needs to know. Feedback is a very powerful tool for upholding the brand values.

It is like visiting someone's house. When someone comes to your house you want a certain impression to be created. It would be different from the impression created by anyone else. Your house is organized and presented in a particular way, and it is the same with the aircraft.

My job is to be responsible above all for the reputation of the company. The day British Airways starts losing its reputation is the day it starts losing money. So, looking after the company's reputation is my job since the branding of the company and of our products and services is really about our commercial reputation. It has to be taken very seriously.

For example, in summer 1996 Egon Ronay said some really quite unflattering things about our shuttle breakfasts. There was a lot of press coverage at that time about the American Airline alliance and the share price, which was all very important, but the one thing that really caught my attention was this criticism about our breakfasts. That is what our customers are going to be interested in. If people really don't like the breakfast on the shuttle, then we have to find out about it. After all, it is the brand's reputation that is at stake.

Global consistency

It is also crucial to protect the brand by being consistent on a global scale. That means having strict controls over advertising, the use of the name, and representation of the company's products in the marketplace. There has to be a high level of discipline but the marketing managers in different countries must be able to say what they need for their particular markets.

We now translate the offer to meet local needs with appropriate food and local cabin crew. Regular tracking, worldwide, ensures we stay alert to our customers' evolving needs. Our research has stressed the need for multi-cultural and multi-functional teams. Although this approach involves more work and debate, it is important to involve people early and encourage their input.

With this in mind, we have developed our marketing team over the last six years to build our knowledge, understanding and sensitivity with regard to different markets.

We also needed to work more closely as a team with our creative partners. In the early 1990s we reviewed how we were communicating worldwide and were concerned at how patchy things were, particularly in view of the plethora of ways in which we have contact with our customers. Whether via computer screen, letter box, or sales shop, the brand needed to be managed consistently across these channels to ensure clarity for our customers.

One area that is harder to control is publicity. We think long and hard about the impact any form of publicity has on the company and the way we deal with it. We have to ensure that we communicate in a tone of voice that is consistent with our brand. British Airways will do so in one way, while another company would do it differently.

Growing the brand

British Airways is fortunate because we are in an industry which is growing. More people each year want to travel by air. Provided that we can maintain our share of the market, then we will continue to grow. Over the next few years the objective is to make British Airways more international, in the sense that people from other countries identify with the brand as much as people in the UK do. Beyond that, the quality of customer service that we give and the reputation we have for customer service must get better and better.

Our mission to be the undisputed leader in world travel means that we must move forward. We have been relaunching the various sub-brands every three or four years. In future we will have to do it more frequently, to match evolving consumer needs and to respond to aggressive activity by the competition, which is always trying to catch up.

In addition, there are many international marketing opportunities for the brand. 'Brand stretch' is a central theme of our mission to be the undisputed leader, and it comes from our desire to offer more to our customers. Extending our brand into other travel-related products fits our business well, and is of great interest to our customers.

There is a limit to how much we can stretch the brand, however. The brand is so closely associated with travel and air travel in particular that it would be impossible to market something like a British Airways motor car.

There are a number of things that could change the nature of the industry over time, such as electronic communication. On the whole, more communication leads to more travel, because as more people contact each other by non-physical means, they want more contact with each other by physical means. What some people might think are dangers to our business could be stimulants to its growth.

One of the big branding challenges British Airways has faced over the last few years is that as a 'mature' brand it has to keep the brand fresh in the face of 'new' brands. The many new entrants not only make us increasingly aware of the competitiveness of the marketplace, but also make the company think more about what it stands for. New entrants coming into markets which have been dominated by large, previously state-owned businesses, challenge the establishment and status quo, and we are forced to react.

It would be a mistake to compete on others' terms. We will never win with that. It can sometimes be rather frustrating because we feel that some of British Airways' qualities are going unnoticed. But that is part of the game. And if you cannot take that, go and do something else.

3 | L'Oréal: Achieving Success in Emerging Asian Markets

ALAIN EVRARD, *zone director Africa–Asia–Pacific*

How to win when you're starting from scratch

At the beginning of the 1990s, L'Oréal brands were strong in most regions of the world, including Europe and North and South America. But in the emerging Asian markets, the company's presence was limited to two subsidiaries in Hong Kong and Indonesia, as well as agents in other countries, for example, Thailand and Malaysia.

We decided we had to establish a major presence with our brands there because the markets were changing shape. The markets of developing countries tend to follow a certain pattern. At the outset, there is always a thin layer of people who want and can afford luxury goods, and buy higher-priced cosmetics such as Lancôme. Below that lies a very wide and unsophisticated mass market. But, as income per head starts moving over $2,000, the middle class begins to grow and have aspirations that are reflected in purchasing brands which offer quality and the right image. Many of the countries in South-East Asia, with the exceptions of Vietnam, Burma and Laos, have reached that point. For example, between 1989 and 1993 the markets for health and beauty products grew by 94 per cent in Indonesia, 93 per cent in Malaysia, 60 per cent in Taiwan and 90 per cent in Thailand.

The women in these countries increasingly want more sophisticated mass-market cosmetics. They have moved beyond using basic toiletries, shampoo and soap brands and, like women all over the world, want products to help them take better care of themselves. We realized that they increasingly fit the profile for the brands within the L'Oréal Paris signature, which are for women who are a little more affluent than average, are sensitive to style and fashion, believe in technology for beauty products, and have a modern attitude to self-service shopping.

Although we were already selling a small amount of haircare products in the area, we were basically starting from scratch. Is this a handicap? We don't think so. Our chairman, Lindsay Owen Jones, said recently that he strongly feels that it is never too late to capture a market if you have a better performing brand. It just has to be new, different and better.

The three critical factors in the success of L'Oréal brand development

We build our brands and base their success on three critical factors. First is performance, which comes from constant innovation through a deep commitment to research and development. For example, in 1995 the group spent 3 per cent of sales on research in cosmetology and dermatology, and registered over 270 patents. Second, communication of performance is essential, whether through advertising, point-of-sale material and sampling, or partnerships with groups such as retailers, hairdressers and journalists.

Finally, the third key element of success is the internationalization of our brands. Until the late 1960s, L'Oréal, which was founded in 1907 when Eugène Schueller invented the first synthetic hair dye, was mainly a French corporation. Then came considerable expansion in Europe and, following that, North and South America. In 1980 L'Oréal sales of cosmetics in the US market were about $100 million. By 1995 that had grown to $2 billion. Now almost 80 per cent of sales are outside France.

How the branding structure works

The name L'Oréal is both the corporation and a brand signature. The corporation, L'Oréal, had a turnover in 1996 of $11 billion. It is made up of a pharmaceutical division and four operating cosmetic divisions: consumer, perfumes and beauty, salon, and active cosmetics. These four divisions account for up to 80 per cent of the turnover.

Within each of the cosmetic divisions are several 'signatures' which are applied to a basket of brands and which appear prominently on the packaging. Each signature has its specific image and advertising. For example, in the consumer division, which is the largest and which contributes half of all cosmetic sales, the main signature is L'Oréal Paris. The brands include products in hair colouring (Excellence and Récital), skincare (Plénitude), haircare (Elsève) and make-up (Perfection). These are leading-edge products for people who care more about the way they look and will pay more. The positioning of L'Oréal Paris is French, technology, a bit elitist, and top of the mass market in terms of pricing. The slogan, 'L'Oréal, because I'm worth it', summarizes this specific positioning.

The second signature in the consumer division is Laboratoires Garnier, which contains portfolio brands like Synergie and Neutralia. These are more popular and accessible products based on the use of natural, mostly plant-based ingredients that are both gentle and safe, but without compromising performance. The next grouping is Gemey Paris and more recently, through acquisition, Maybelline New York and Jade, a well-known German brand. These are entry level brands with a feeling of the 'girl next door'. There is also a range of mainly French brands under the 'Lascad' signature.

The perfume and beauty division, contributing almost 30 per cent of cosmetics sales, has in its portfolio international luxury brands like Lancôme, which covers skincare, make-up and fragrances, Biotherm for skincare and make-up, plus prestige fragrance brands such as Guy Laroche, Ralph Lauren, Helena Rubenstein and Paloma Picasso. Over 90 per cent of this division's sales are outside France.

The third division has brands aimed at professionals in salons, such as L'Oréal Professionel, Kérastase and Redken, and accounts for 13 per cent of sales of cosmetics.

The fourth division is involved with what we call the active cosmetics division, and has a portfolio of mainly European signatures such as Vichy, Phas and LaRoche-Posay which are usually sold through pharmacies. They contribute about 6 per cent to the cosmetics revenues.

Securing a prominent position through segmentation

This segmented approach to the brands gives the company a prominent position in the three main channels for distribution of cosmetics products: professionals in salons, mass market at different levels, and selective distribution channels such as department stores and perfumeries. It also means that innovation can filter down from the top end through to the mass-market brands, once ways to do so at lower costs are found.

Also, because the corporate name, L'Oréal, is not used on all the products, except within the L'Oréal Paris signature brands, we can sell not only the French way of life with signatures like L'Oréal Paris and Lancôme, but other cultures as well: the American way of life with Ralph Lauren at one end of the scale, and Maybelline New York at the other, Italian values with Armani and so forth.

This flexible approach means that there is no limit to marketing our brands consistently around the world: it is about the spirit, the image, the values of the way of life.

Each signature can function as its own business. This fosters the notion of internal competition, which we believe is vital to keep the company fit. It means as well that the advertising works harder and more effectively; since the consumer sees ads with a strong emphasis on the signature as well as the brand, the share of voice increases. And, because we have a certain vision of, for instance, the L'Oréal Paris woman, who will be the same in New York, Paris or Kuala Lumpur, it solves the key problem of what models we use for international advertising. It does not matter whether she is American, French or Chinese. She has to have something more than the average woman.

The only time this segmented strategy can present a few obstacles is in terms of corporate image, when we enter countries where we are relatively new. When it comes to hiring people in South-East Asia, for instance, we have to make them understand that they are joining not only a company manufacturing skincare which they may use, or for which they may have seen advertising, but one which is the number one cosmetics company in the world.

Anything we do can go global: the determinism of success

When a molecule is performing (and by molecule we mean a product molecular invention), we patent it and there is no good reason why we can't take it to the whole of the world.

To manage these brands we have to strike a delicate balance between harmonizing them internationally, and at the same time encouraging the entrepreneurial spirit in the individual countries. We do not force countries to take products, but we believe that the products we create can go global, and more often than not they do. It is what a former chairman called the 'determinism of success': when you have true performance in one market there is no reason you cannot do the same worldwide.

However, although we project the same brand-names and images in all markets, we do adapt products for different hair and skin needs in different countries, with the appropriate languages on the packaging. For example, hair colouring suitable for Asia can differ from that which will be successful in Denmark, although the active molecules are often the same. Similarly, with skincare products, we will sell more oil-free products in South-East Asia than in Scandinavia.

We use the local language on the packaging and adapt the international advertising, unless there are exceptional reasons for not doing so, such as legal constraints. For example, in Malaysia and Indonesia, it is forbidden to air TV ads with non-Malay/Indonesian models so we use well-known local models while the advertising execution remains the same.

Championing the brands: keeping the moral contract

Research carried out within Singapore highlights the central role of the brand for consumers in this region. Overall, the research showed that 97 per cent of the customers purchased a specific item because of the brand-name. The comparable figure for France is 60 per cent.

This underlines the fact that in emerging markets, where consumers are offered a wide range of local brands as well as counterfeits, international brands are widely trusted. We have to deliver. The level of performance is critical if we want to have a world brand and keep our credibility. We have to keep the moral contract between the brand and the consumers. We cannot compromise on performance. We have to be brand fanatics, championing both the advantages but also the obligations of the brand.

We also have to keep in mind that the brand challenge varies in different markets. India is a good example of how we have to think very carefully about our line of attack. The company has been in India for about five years, although it has been a fully-owned subsidiary for less than three years. The challenge in India is that one tends to think of it as a new market. But it is an incredibly old one, with deep-rooted traditions and consumption patterns that go back for generations. Because the economy has been so closed, India has been perceived as a virgin market where companies could sail in and sell their products, but that is simply not the case.

The Indians have had well-established indigenous products, from companies like Hindustan Lever, present on the local market for many years, although you would not recognize them in terms of their counterparts in London or Paris. Well-established consumption habits have been accompanied by a lack of competition, so there has been little incentive to be disloyal and try new brands, a fact which newcomers have to understand and deal with.

Haircare illustrates this. Everybody in the West knows what hair conditioner is used for. The question is which brand to buy. But in India women have been using hair oil for 2,000 years. It is a bigger market than shampoo. Why should they buy your conditioner, particularly when it is more expensive?

So our approach has been broadly the same as in other developing markets, in that we say to women, here is a modern, more efficient way of keeping and enhancing your beauty with products from Parisian laboratories. For instance, Indian women take good care of their faces, doing some sort of purifying at least once a month, so we developed a face mask within the Synergie line to fulfil that demand, which has been very successful. The Synergie line now has eight products, all faithful to the Synergie concept but tailored to the Indian market.

One interesting factor for L'Oréal in the Indian market is that France and French culture are relatively unknown because the background has been British. So part of the L'Oréal evangelism is to tell customers that there is another way of looking at beauty from a country well-known for its cosmetics. It adds to the pioneering feel of what we are doing.

The Asian challenge

The least international factor is distribution. No two countries have the same distribution pattern. In Asia, there are dynamic pharmacies (like Boots in the UK), there are supermarkets, and some department stores. So there are high traffic outlets suitable for L'Oréal Paris. One of our biggest challenges is to make sure that there is space for all the explanatory material that accompanies our products. You have to help people find their way through the ranges.

When we first launched hair colour in Thailand, we saw that half of cosmetics products were available through modern distribution channels, with the rest sold through a complicated maze of small shops. Also, the established competition like Procter & Gamble and Unilever had a very strong presence in that area. We took the decision to work through the big retailers because, even though we might lose sales, dealing with the small shops would have required a large infrastructure and might also have damaged the L'Oréal Paris image. This strategy proved to be the right thing to do: in skincare now, 75 per cent of sales are made through modern distribution channels. Over the next five to ten years that figure will rise.

Asia now accounts for about 6 per cent of cosmetics sales, a figure which has doubled in five years. The challenge is to increase that, to go step by step, aiming to be first in one market in one country, then the next, and so on. We consider ourselves challengers in Asia as a company, but if we are better we will achieve leadership. If a company just wants a financial battle it might be successful in the short term, but long term it will be beaten. We have to keep on growing by fighting our main competitors on their own fields.

A 'hair colour crusade' in Thailand: the strategy in action

How the brand strategy works can be seen from one of the first major forays we made into the Far East, in Thailand. We knew that historically the L'Oréal Paris success in Europe, South America and especially in the USA had begun with hair colouring, where we consider that we have the best technology, experience and expertise. However, the problem in Asia was that this market was small. Nevertheless, we believed we had to start there and so began what we called a 'hair colour crusade'.

We soon realized that it would be very difficult to develop an effective, long-term strategy to take advantage of this booming part of the world without our own organization, our own 'family', to give us feedback from the ground. So we appointed our first general manager in Thailand in 1992. We tried to hire people who could adapt to our business philosophy, and who could be, as we like to say at L'Oréal, both 'poet and peasant'. We also held a big press conference for the press, trade and VIPs. Our vision was that, whatever product line we started, it very quickly had to become number one. We needed victories. And a victory is market leadership.

The product we chose was an existing hair colourant called Imédia, well established in Europe but one for which we had developed a new formula for Asia. Instead of pushing basic products like shampoos and gels, we wanted to put all our resources behind a product that fitted in with the image of being technically advanced and reliable. You do not need ten to twenty products to get your name known. You invade the market with one brand and push all your energy behind it. So we were evangelists. We were determined that we would be successful and create the name L'Oréal Paris in Thailand and establish a modern hair colour market, so we could follow up hair colour with skincare and then make-up.

Because there was no existing international advertising, we developed new commercials for South-East Asia. We used a top European model with dark hair and found that the ad tested well. These ads were also the first time we strongly emphasized the L'Oréal Paris signature by putting it prominently at both the beginning and the end of the advertising. The ad was shot in Malaysia, developed in Japan, and had post-production done in Paris and Thailand for the Thai text. To show that good ideas are used internationally, this ad became the basis for others used around the world.

Like all our campaigns, it focused strongly on communicating performance. Our ads can be quite didactic, underlining the rational benefits and explaining how the product works. The key point for us was to get people to try the product and see its quality.

The result is that in Thailand, now the most important hair colouring market in South-East Asia, L'Oréal has been number one since 1995 and is the international preferred brand. This is despite the fact that the competition has been active there for ten to fifteen years. We are also launching a new, improved version called L'Oréal Imédia Excellence. We have based our television commercials on the international advertising for this new product using the actress Nastassja Kinski, except we have substituted a well-known Thai personality who is an actress, TV star and model. That ad has also tested well in Singapore and in other Asian markets.

We are also number one in hair colouring in Indonesia and the Philippines. We are only in third place in Singapore, however, because their hair colour is still sold from locked cupboards. We are having discussions to try and change that. Overall, the Asian market is now expanding very quickly: for instance, in South Korea, almost three-quarters of the women who use hair colouring have only done so in the last three years.

Innovative force from 'new' L'Oréal markets

We have had similar success in these markets with our L'Oréal skincare brand Plénitude, which is sold on the concept that it delays the effects of ageing. The range, consisting of about a dozen products, is sold in a 'boutique' display which is a powerful visual marketing tool, providing a lot of clear information about the various products. When we first launched Plénitude in Indonesia in 1991, TV ads were banned so we had to use print and sampling. When TV became possible, we had to re-do the international ad using Asian women because of legal requirements. And in the early days we had a few difficulties getting the pricing right. But the big jump came last year with the successful launch of Plénitude Excell A-3.

We launched the Plénitude range in Thailand in 1995 to build on our success with hair colour. If we had launched it too early we probably would have failed. We now lead the skincare market in Australia, New Zealand, Indonesia and Singapore, we are third in Thailand and Taiwan where we launched only in 1995. We are now working even more to respond to the very specific needs of Asian women, which are linked to particularly difficult environmental factors such as heat, humidity, pollution and sunlight. Four major projects are in hand, two of which are aimed at Asian women in the area of cleansing and care. What this means is that South-East Asia will increasingly become a source of innovation for worldwide development.

The essential make-up mix

Together with hair products and skincare, our third high-performing business area is make-up. We started with a test market in Malaysia, which was interesting and strategically difficult because we had to choose a single range for consumers with varying demands according to complexion, which can range from very pale to very dark.

First we had to identify the main product types which would meet market demand for the lipsticks, foundations and eye make-up, and then choose what we considered the strongest lines. We found that Malaysian women typically want products which are non-oily, anti-ultraviolet and offer protection against pollution, and are lightly perfumed or even perfume-free. Colour preference is for matte tones, although they also like red and orange shades. As with all markets, the wide range of items is constantly monitored.

We are now in first place in Malaysia and second in Singapore. Interestingly, our recently-acquired signature Maybelline New York is in first place in Singapore and second in Malaysia. As with skincare, partnership with retailers is crucial in order to have the most effective display. For example, we offer an exclusive display unit for the make-up range which was originally created for the US market and which is accessible, modular and designed to meet the needs of self-service.

Living the L'Oréal philosophy: the poet warrior

The important thing when starting up in a country is to put a good team together, send them to Paris so they can see the big company they are part of, and train them in the specific L'Oréal way of doing things. The culture is a key element. To start with, no matter what the nationality, the manager who starts the business has to live the culture from within, it cannot just be taught. We need someone who can explain every day why we do this or that, or why, for example, we decide at the last minute to change something that has been prepared for weeks.

Recruitment in any country is not only based on getting the best students from the universities. We are also interested in personalities and talents, in imaginative people who are both ambitious and generous and who can develop projects for markets which are becoming both more diverse and international. The human resources framework is very international, which allows for a permanent exchange of culture and abilities. It is a strategic decision to recruit and train managers locally to understand local issues and habits. Most of the managers in Asia are native Asians.

We also encourage people to stay with the company by putting great emphasis on experience and by helping to nurture both professional and personal growth for the long term.

Being committed to the long term means we have to help people to improve constantly but also accepting that sometimes they fail. We do not have it written in the form of a constitution but the right of error is officially accepted. What we are really passionate about is creating warriors for our brands. When we enter new countries, particularly in Asia, we feel we have a tremendous story to tell and excellent products to which people respond, which makes us ever more enthusiastic.

Because L'Oréal does not go into markets with huge budgets and cut-and-dried marketing plans that have been developed thousands of miles away, there is a sense of personal commitment to and involvement with the brands. There is a substantial element of local contribution to making sure the mix is right. Even more importantly, wherever the company is, we have to make sure we treat our employees with the same enthusiasm and respect with which we treat our brands.

4 | Levi Strauss: Focus on the Legend ... and Record-breaking Global Sales

ROBERT HOLLOWAY, *vice president, global marketing*

Levi Strauss & Co. is the largest and most successful brand-name apparel business in the world. The company sells its distinctive clothing under the Levi's®, Dockers® and Slates® brands in more than sixty countries around the world.

In March 1996, *Forbes* magazine wrote: 'Levi jeans are not so much a product as an icon. Along with Coca-Cola, Gillette, McDonald's, rock music and TV sitcoms, they are a coveted symbol of the casual, unpretentious American lifestyle.'

Dating back to 1856, when Levi Strauss opened his first store, selling supplies to California gold rush miners, the Levi's brand has had a powerful heritage. The genesis and evolution of the original, authentic American blue jeans are central to the brand's global status as an American icon.

The Levi's brand has more than endured; it has flourished. In the early 1980s, however, both the brand and our company were on the ropes. The reason? In part it was because we had ceased to focus on our core youth market – the consumers who had made Levi Strauss & Co. and the Levi's brand what they had both become. Our job then was the same job we have today: we had to refocus and restructure to ensure that Levi Strauss & Co. would remain the largest and most successful brand-name apparel business in the world (with sales now exceeding US $7.1 billion).

In many respects, the challenges of the 1980s still exist today and the solutions we developed at that time are still our guiding principles. The ongoing challenge for Levi Strauss & Co. is twofold:

first, to remain relevant to a target audience that regenerates itself every four or five years; and second, to avoid the distractions of success.

The living brand: making the heritage relevant and motivating

Our strategy for success is deceptively simple. Worldwide, the target consumer for the Levi's brand are the fifteen- to nineteen-year-old young men who buy approximately 30 per cent of all jeans sold. The history of our business has borne out that if that core target is motivated by our brands, the other demographic categories, responsible for purchasing the remaining 70 per cent, will follow.

In essence, the Levi's brand has defined and continues to define what 'blue jeans' are, and our products are able to occupy that defining point because they are the original American blue jeans. It is an important point of distinction: only one manufacturer, one brand, can say it is the original, the 'genuine article'.

From its position of prominence in the marketplace, the Levi's brand stands for many things in the minds of target consumers: rebellion, youthfulness, quality, originality, excitement, fun – all the great things about being young. To put it another way, when we're successful with young consumers, the Levi's brand will live with young people through that crucial period when they 'find themselves'. And, more than that, the brand becomes an enduring point of identification for young consumers with that period in their lives. They choose the brand as a sort of uniform or symbol of youth; and, in Western cultures, as a symbol of independence and freedom – even defiance.

Consequently, for the success of the Levi's brand, it is essential that we understand what is cutting-edge in youth culture and remain aware of social, cultural and consumer trends. But, for products like ours, with a nearly 150-year history, it's equally important that we never forget our roots, that we don't begin to stand for fads and fashions that come and go. Paradoxically, as 'the original' we are expected and even required to be an extraordinary blend of forward-looking and traditional in the way we bring the Levi's brand to market.

Another important paradox about the Levi's brand is its individuality: it's a product built on a mass consumer audience of millions that allows you, the wearer, to be more yourself. The axioms 'know thyself' and 'to thine own self be true' are the cornerstones of the brand.

Related to that impulse towards genuine self-expression is a growing desire among consumers worldwide – a desire that the Levi's brand has effectively tapped into – for clothes and objects that have a genuineness and naturalness about them. It's a heritage that owes nothing to the marketer and everything to evolution and function.

The Levi's brand, and especially Levi's 501® jeans, have been successful for decades in large part because they feed those consumer desires for genuineness and self-expression. With minor variations, such as the addition of belt-loops and the Redtab™ device, Levi's 501s today are the product that has been worn by miners, cowboys and California farm-workers since the late 1800s. Its qualities have been memorably described by fashion designer Margaret Howell: '[They] are the original Levi jeans. The design is so right it never need alter, a timeless classic of clothes. Adaptable, like any well-designed object, you can wear them with almost anything. They are good-looking, well-made, functional and unobtrusive. What is more, they improve with age and increase in value with every wash.'

The features that make Levi's jeans different from other brands are almost quaint in their simplicity. The five trademarks that make Levi's 501 jeans unique date back to the mid-1800s and include the LS&CO. embossed buttons; the two horse patch above the right back pocket; the 'arcuate' design stitching on the back pockets (the oldest American trademark in constant use); the '501' lot number; and the Redtab device (introduced in 1936 to help salesmen count and identify Levi's jeans at rodeos).

As simple as they may seem, however, those five trademarks

tell consumers they are wearing original Levi's brand jeans. They represent more than a quality product; they represent the history, heritage and associations of our company. As a result, Levi Strauss & Co. protects the value of those simple features through a rigorous ongoing trademark protection effort. We also recognize the important role of our company historians in preserving the strength of our brands. The LS&CO. company archives make the history live again for the teams of employees who develop our advertising, Internet sites, retail stores and products.

History is only one element of the brand-building equation. The other part is adapting our history to a lifestyle that is relevant and interesting to today's consumers. A classic mistake brand managers frequently make is to become too obsessed with their own culture, talking to consumers in ways that are too remote from actual experience – preaching history. Consumers don't like it. But it's an easy mistake to make, particularly with a history as fascinating as ours. The bottom line is this: as marketers, we need to be sure we're talking to consumers, not just to ourselves.

For example, the historical symbolism of our 'two horse' label design trademark – a design that appears on the patch sewn on to every pair of Levi's 501 jeans – is widely known. It depicts a strength between two horses and a pair of 501 jeans. In fact, the jeans are always tougher than the horses trying to tear them apart, a fact confirmed in 1943 by a customer who tried the test with mules, one of whom expired from the effort.

It's a great story, of course, but will it sell jeans today? Will it build the associations that make for a strong brand with today's consumers? A better illustration of the product's strength was found to be far more excitingly expressed for our European core target market in an advertisement known as 'Truck' that appeared throughout Europe. Set in the 1950s, a young man in a battered truck comes upon a couple whose car has broken down on a dusty stretch of prairie road. He takes off his Levi's jeans. The sweet girl shrugs at her besuited, geeky boyfriend and climbs in alongside the Levi's guy, leaving the boyfriend to be towed behind on the strength of his rival's Levi's 501 jeans. The jeans as tow-rope are doing fine while, unfortunately for the geek, the bumper of his car dislodges, leaving him behind. No words. Great soundtrack. End frame. The ad's punch-line: 'Separates the men from the boys.'

Nurturing the brand: striking the right chords

The emotional chords any global brand needs to strike will have many similarities worldwide. It is how you hit them successfully in executional terms that ensures the brand's continuing success. But while the umbrella messages behind the brand positioning are universal, local interpretations of those themes drive the worldwide acceptance of the product. For example, in 1984, although all agencies were working to the same brief – to refocus the Levi's brand as the original, the authentic American blue jeans – the highly successful campaigns that resulted were very different around the world. It is how a company executes a strategy that both develops brand identity and recognizes regional or cultural differences that ensures any brand's continuing success.

Recognizing those differences, in the North American market, Levi's brand ad campaigns have been more product-led than in Europe where activity has been brand and fashion-oriented. In most Asia-Pacific markets, where the Levi's brand is a relative newcomer, advertising has borrowed from both the North American and European affiliates. In new and/or smaller markets our goal is to follow successful models from other regions until resources permit local creative strategies and campaigns.

In the USA in the mid-1980s, our 'US blues' ad campaign revolutionized apparel advertising and refocused and re-energized the Levi's brand. Abandoning the 1970s mod image and traditional cowboy themes, the campaign's 'slice of life' approach captured the individualistic essence of the brand. Paid fashion models and animated characters were replaced with real people filmed in urban settings. The ads captured the soul of Levi's 501 jeans. As far as American audiences were concerned, the Levi's brand had come home.

The 501 blues campaign highlights the difference between the US and European markets in terms of how the brand positioning has been developed over time. At the core, the themes are identical: authentic, original, youthful, rebellious, individual, and so on. The ways in which these themes are portrayed, however, are quite diverse. In Europe, Levi's 501 jeans are compulsory equipment for young consumers who care about the way they look. In Europe, the core of the jeans market, fifteen- to nineteen-year-old males, have been persuaded (for the moment) that 501 jeans are the right look and the only acceptable label.

In Europe, we developed a fascination, almost a reverence, for a mythical America of the past – the America that produced Dean and Presley, the '57 Chevrolet, *The Misfits* and a host of other heroes and cult objects. The ''50s look', suitably processed for the '80s and '90s, remains current, a look for which Levi's 501 jeans could legitimately claim to be an essential feature. The 1950s and later the '60s was a time when the Levi's brand meant jeans and jeans meant youth. It was a period of perhaps fifteen years that forever changed our industry and seeded the contemporary 'jeans world' of youth, sex, rebellion and heroism. Our European ad campaigns have re-evoked these associations and have given Levi's 501s jeans ownership of them.

It's a complex formula for developing a sophisticated global brand around what is essentially a simple product. There were, and are, two carefully integrated but essentially simple messages to European consumers: the rational ('We're the American original') and the emotional ('Wow! don't they look sexy'). By hitting the right note, sales for the Levi's brand went up 800 per cent.

The distraction of success: losing the focus

The challenge faced by companies with successful brands is to decide where to take the brand after it has become established in the minds of consumers. Perhaps the most common mistake when you become successful is to try to stamp your brand on everything.

Levi Strauss & Co. learned about that mistake the hard way. In the early 1970s, the company made the mistake of expanding beyond the core product lines it had manufactured for more than 100 years and began making and marketing a broad range of products under the Levi's brand. This expansion diluted the Levi's brand and its appeal to consumers.

At the time, my reaction as a brand manager echoed what our core target consumers were feeling: I had not joined Levi Strauss & Co. to market baby clothes or polyester leisure suits.

It often takes a calamity to focus a company's collective mind. When you're doing very well the temptation is to keep adding bits here and there. Ultimately you risk losing your core consumer. By the early 1980s, when LS&CO. was haemorrhaging money, it wasn't all due to competitive or distribution issues. We had lost focus and looked to blame all the problems on external forces.

It was at that moment of crisis that the top 100 managers of the company met to review the options. The decision was unanimous – the task of refocusing on our core strengths was essential. Courageously, a 'back to basics' decision was taken and our company's diversification strategy was reversed. Each region was reorganized as a single manufacturing and marketing entity and the company's management set about the task of putting Levi Strauss & Co. back into the *jeans* market in a single-minded way.

As well as focusing on denim and the Levis's brand, the decision was also taken to focus on image not volume. The high-image flagship product of the Levi's brand – 501 jeans – would lead the company's return to profitability. The refocusing was executed extremely well. As well as ruthlessly divesting LS&CO. of all non-core businesses, all our marketing programmes put the focus squarely back on jeans.

The process wasn't quick and it wasn't easy. By the early 1990s, however, the jeans market in the USA and around the world had been rejuvenated and, by 1996, denim was a high-interest fashion fabric again. More importantly, and dramatically of course, sales of Levi's 501 jeans increased massively and became a much larger proportion of Levi Strauss & Co.'s total denim sales.

LS&CO. brand architecture: flexible yet focused

As a result of our mid-'80s refocusing, we agreed who our core target consumer was – and will remain; what the Levi's brand stands for and what our core products are.

We've resolutely stood by those decisions. Our more recent initiatives have all been built around that central premise about who our consumers are, what they want and why. As a result, if we want to get into entirely new areas, we launch new brands – as we did with the Dockers brand in 1986 and the Slates brand in the USA in 1996. Why couldn't Dockers pants be carried under the Levi's brand? It's because they are intended for a different consumer. The core product is not jeans and the brand stands for something different. Similarly, our newest brand, Slates dress pants for men, are aimed at yet another target consumer audience. Each brand has its own core market, its own approach to building an identity and set of associations with its unique consumer base.

The acid wall approach to innovation: build the brand or burn

Within the parameters we have set for ourselves, LS&CO. is continually developing and innovating products for its Levi's, Dockers and Slates brands. We bring new products to market, develop new distribution strategies and marketing programmes, refine the internal processes we use to bring our brands to consumers. But whatever the area of our business or the nature of the innovation, all new ideas are judged according to two basic criteria: do they build the brand and do they build the business?

The launch of our Levi's 'Personal Pair'™ programme is a good example of innovation. The Personal Pair programme is a breakthrough technological development in the apparel industry – the first widespread mass customization program – where a consumer's measurements are taken and entered into a computer. This information is sent directly to one of our factories and personally fitted jeans are produced and delivered on a pair-by-pair basis within two weeks.

Since its introduction in 1995, the Personal Pair programme has greatly helped push the Levi's brand to develop a genuine one-on-one relationship with our target consumers. There's nothing else like it in the market today; like the Levi's brand, it's a genuine original. It is also a truly heartland Levi Strauss & Co. concept for the modern age.

The programme also is important for another reason: size, style and colour preference details of each consumer can be stored and accessed, giving the company a wealth of valuable information about each Personal Pair programme consumer. Since these individuals tend to be some of our most motivated and loyal Levi's brand consumers, our ability to know who they are and what they want most provides us with a powerful way to ensure their continued engagement with the Levi's brand today and in the future.

One general rule with the Levi's brand is that all innovations must be 'Levi's-like'. What that means is that innovations are pursued or rejected based on their compatibility with the core values and attributes of the brand. As an example, at one of our European affiliates, this involves something they call the 'acid wall test', a technique developed by Levi Strauss Europe marketing manager Lothar Schafer. The 'acid wall' is literally a wall of their facility on which are written all the values, attributes and core associations of the Levi's brand. In considering any new products or marketing programmes, the affiliate's marketing team convenes at that wall and, one by one, considers whether the innovations are consistent with the values of the brand. Had the acid wall test and its regional equivalents been there in the 1970s, I doubt polyester suits would have got very far!

You could perhaps say that in developing brand innovations we are too cautious and may miss some opportunities. We feel that caution is not only the result of our own recent history – where the brand was sometimes treated recklessly – but also the experience of other brands that come and go because their companies don't know how to nurture them properly. So, we may miss some opportunities or are slow to respond to others, but we would argue it's a good price to pay for the focus and integrity we have with our brands and our consumers.

During the history of LS & CO., we have learned that building the equity of the brand is paramount and, with an already strong brand, equity is linked to a complex list of associations in the minds of consumers. The moment you produce something that disturbs that set of associations – the soul of the brand – you're in trouble. One can only wonder about the future of the brands that forget that simple fact.

The framework for success: structural changes

The task of keeping the Levi's brand number one for a constantly evolving group of consumers is a challenging one. One of the reasons we continue to be successful is that, while we deliver a consistent brand globally, brand managers have the freedom to execute locally. When we talk to consumers about the brand we get very consistent feedback. However, if you look at the specific projects or executions or marketing programmes, you will see they are quite different. The reason for this is that while we deliver a global brand message we deliver it to people who are very different in markets which are very different.

Our goal is to ensure we deliver to consumers what the Levi's brand stands for – indeed, what it *must* stand for to remain successful. Our activities in both the United States and Europe have continued to succeed because entire regional teams have had the courage of their convictions. We know from experience that to try to achieve such powerful results out of our San Francisco world headquarters would be naïve and almost certainly doomed to failure. How can I or our global marketing team know all the trends, or the cultural, geographical and political issues? The challenges facing someone on the ground in India, for example, are totally different from those in a developed market such as Sweden.

Consequently, our approach at Levi Strauss & Co. is to retain the highest quality local management and give them a framework within which to develop the brand in their areas. This may result in quite dramatically different executions (Europeans and Americans are, for example, perplexed by the fifteen-second commercials we run in Japan), but as long as consumers are internalizing similar basic messages about the brand, the marketing programmes are working well, as diverse as they may be.

Occasionally, something 'clicks' with consumers worldwide but, as Nigel Bogle of Bartle Bogle Hegarty has said: 'Global campaigns are born not made.' You don't start out to conceive a global campaign. They just develop as you go along.

Gradually LS & CO. has moved from a local to a regional to a global company while maintaining the respective strengths we have learned during each phase of our existence. Back in the 1970s and early 1980s we were building the brand locality by locality and each brand manager could basically do what he or she wanted without fear of impact on other markets. They were isolated. TV channels didn't span borders. The Internet didn't exist. Ten years ago, on the other hand, it became clear that consumers were hearing messages about our brand on a region by region basis. We adjusted our brand strategy to the new rules of the game. Now, with the Internet and global media, the future of our brand really is being written on a genuinely global basis. We're still learning how to make this latest leap.

One thing is clear, however. Managing a brand globally is far more complex. In large part this has been, and will continue to be, because of technological developments. Our global websites (www.levi.com and www.dockers.com), for example, provide a host of opportunities that would have been unimaginable ten years ago. They also have implications for how the brand is managed in each market. Now, more than ever, the left hand really *does* need to know what the right hand is doing.

To help bring that about, in 1996 LS & CO. established a new global marketing group and charged the group with a tough assignment: be visionaries. What we mean by that in practice is that the global marketing group operates outside national and regional constraints to support our efforts to build and manage the brand by using the latest tools and techniques; global developments such as the Internet, the media, new sponsorship strategies, our Original Levi's Stores and revolutionary new brand equity measurement tools. The group also works to communicate and transfer best practices from local markets to global markets, bringing a new perspective to the individual and local businesses that previously didn't exist. Via benchmarking of marketing counterparts at other firms, Levi Strauss & Co. also benefits from other companies' experiences on a global basis.

We're still in the global marketing group's early days but the new organization feels like a step in the right direction for the future of our brands. The global marketing group's role is, fundamentally, to incubate new products and ideas, to look after them when fragile, in their infancy. LS&CO. believes this kind of nurturing is extremely important for the future of our brands. Sometimes off-the-wall leaps of faith are vital. Experimentation and failure are important and should be rewarded.

The majority of innovations, however, are done locally or regionally. That's because there is no way for a team in San Francisco to know what's hot in Bangalore, Rio or Jakarta at the moment. In fact, there are completely different product ranges in the four regions (Europe, Latin America, Asia Pacific, North America). The Levi's brand silverTab™ line, for example, is not available in Europe, and not surprisingly there's a quite different product mix between, say, arctic Norway and steamy Singapore. There are, of course, some global products too, chiefly our flagship Levi's 501 jeans.

As 'visionary' as the global marketing group may be, it nevertheless exists to support the local experts. It is vital for the success of any of our brands that our regional and local marketing teams remain strong.

Sites for culture not just clothes: keeping a tight grip on consumers

It bears repeating that the equity for the Levi's brand is driven by a youth mind-set. For LS&CO., it's a useful coincidence that the most obsessed users of the World Wide Web happen to be young. Our Levi's brand Internet site (www.levi.com) was first established in the autumn of 1995. Since that time, our evolving presence on the WWW is being driven by a strategy of using that mind-set as a springboard and to have a broad enough voice that it can be meaningful in all kinds of cultures. The site has been designed to be a cutting-edge resource that embraces and contributes to global youth culture.

More than that, today we're beginning to recognize the Web's potential as an entirely new means of communication. As a result, we're persuaded that it won't be possible simply to take a conventional marketing approach to the WWW by simply adapting efforts from traditional media. Rather, we're establishing an entirely new approach to marketing on the Internet – an approach that creates from scratch a new, logical, credible and entertaining extension of who we are for the new medium. We believe today that the Internet provides us with an entirely new global medium through which we can leverage our position as a leading-edge marketer and brand builder.

For instance, via the Internet we can deliver messages that are much more fully developed, deeper messages than are possible, say, with conventional print or television advertising. In addition, the Web allows all sorts of two-way interactions between the brand and its audience of target consumers. As a result, time spent on-line can be a richer, more multi-layered and more self-directed media experience than has ever before been possible.

We believe that www.levi.com is particularly important because the WWW is a world where the brand with the strongest existing relationships with consumers has the most to gain. We believe the Levi's brand occupies that advantageous position and we believe the Internet is a new way to solidify our relationships with our consumers by making an interaction with the brand available to them literally twenty-four hours a day. It's a powerful tool and we intend to use it.

But the Internet is not our only strategy for creating new links to our target consumers. We also control brand presentation through various forms of retail theatre at our Original Levi's Stores around the world.

Original Levi's Stores were first established in the mid-1980s either because no jeans stores existed in a country (as was the case in Poland) or because of concerns we had about the ways our brand was being presented in a particular market. We wanted to provide consumers with a genuine, compelling, Levi's brand experience. As other successful brands have done, we have used our Original Levi's Stores as a powerful presentation of the Levi's brand expressing the core values of the brand, its history and evolution. The Original Levi's Stores are also an invaluable test-bed for new ideas, such as powerful point-of-sale strategies related to our advertising campaigns.

Initially, of course, our traditional retailers were anxious about their business when Original Levi's Stores opened up nearby. Consistently, however, the opening of Original Levi's Stores has enhanced the business of other Levi's brand retailers as well as performing well for us. We're not so much competing with existing retailers as enhancing the overall strength of the market and the presentation of the brand.

Performance has been closely monitored so case histories have been available to reassure existing retailers in new locations. There are now about 1,000 Original Levi's Stores worldwide. They offer the optimal brand experience, selection and service. In some locations they are the only source of Levi's products. Our most dramatic launch was in Moscow where we completely sold out of stock the day the store opened.

Building for the future: opportunities and challenges

With the Levi's brand established as the definitive blue jean world-wide, LS&CO. is in the enviable position of being able to lead the market from the front, pioneering and then owning new looks, styles and fits in denim and initiating programmes in other fabrics. In a notoriously fickle and unsure global market, this proactive position has incalculable value when compared with the essentially reactive position of other brands.

There are, of course, always threats and challenges to that position. For the Levi's brand, the competition from designer denim at the top end of the market looks as if it is here to stay. Unlike the 1970s and '80s when designer jeans-makers were fly-by-night companies that disappeared as quickly as they appeared, today's designer competitors seem far sounder financially and are also promoting themselves well.

We also closely monitor our competition at the lower end of the marketplace. Particularly in the USA, retailers are consolidating and finding own denim labels highly profitable.

Whatever the future holds, we believe LS&CO. is structured and has evolved to be fit and ready for new opportunities. As a company, the quality of our people and their ideas is what gives us our competitive advantage. We also have strong beliefs as an organization about the way we should be working in a global marketplace. We were the first company, for example, to establish comprehensive global sourcing and operating guidelines to benefit the individuals who make our products, and to improve the quality of life in the communities in which they live.

And last but not least, we're a company that tends to take a long view of our success; we measure it in years and decades, not in financial quarters.

Do these things strengthen our brands? We think they make us a stronger company with a powerful, cohesive common vision of responsible commercial success. And that can't help but make us a more effective organization with better ideas about the growth and evolution of our brands. The strength of our brands has always been about the strength of our company's vision. The two can't be disengaged from each other.

For that reason, the Levi's brand has been and is likely to remain central to the lives of consumers around the world. From the overalls worn by California gold rush miners in the 1870s, to 1950s James Dean Hollywood denims, to the jeans that the baby-boomers rebelled in at Woodstock, to the 501 jeans they now look cool in, the Levi's brand has evolved to fit the times while remaining faithful to the bedrock values of our company's history.

As designer Bill Blass has recently noted, we have a flagship product that is the quintessential American fashion: 'Nothing any fashion designer has ever done has come close to having the influence of blue jeans. That Levi Strauss invention – one of the sexiest items a man or woman can wear – is the most significant contribution America has made to fashion.'

So, while the future of the Levi's brand is yet to be written, we can be justifiably confident that the enduring strength of the brand in the minds of consumers worldwide is the one asset above all others that will ensure the brand's continued success and our company's vitality. We will achieve the full measure of that potential success if we remember that we succeed because of our relationships with the consumers. Out ultimate goal – a goal we can never forget – is to keep our brands relevant to them.

5 | Orient Overseas Container Line: Growth Reflecting the Rise of the Asia Pacific Economies

C. C. TUNG, *chairman*

Of all the things that we could say about our company – its role in world trade, customer service, speed, efficiency, reliability – the one thing we have picked out to highlight in our corporate logo is: 'We take it personally'. That is at the heart of our brand.

An outsider looking at a company like ours may be sceptical when we say our brand and our commercial success rest on our 'people' value. Superficially, of course, they are right. All you see when you look at a container transportation company like ours is huge ocean-going ships (some of which are big enough to carry enough containers to stretch across the English Channel), stuffed full of products from cars to frozen fish, which are loaded and unloaded at vast freight terminals.

All of these cold, hard things are fundamental to our business. But we are convinced that it is our employees' dedication that makes the difference. That is the message of our corporate identity.

'The World is Square'

To understand how we came to this conclusion, you have to understand a little more about our industry and our company. Our mission is 'to be the most successful global container transportation company ... providing the vital link to world trade'. That mission reflects the fundamental importance of the container to the global economy.

Without the container the global village would still be a concept, not a reality, because manufacturing would still be a local process. Car companies, for instance, would still have to insist that their components suppliers were located within 150 miles of their factory, as they once did.

Today, consumers enjoy cars, electronic goods, foods and garments from all around the globe because the container makes it possible to provide them at surprisingly low costs. Most people are astonished to discover that the cost of transporting a US$6,000 motorcycle from the Far East to America amounts to just $85, or that the cost of sending a bottle of whisky from Europe to the Far East adds just 10 cents to the price of a $35 bottle. That's why we say 'The World is Square' – because global trade as we know it would not exist without the square container.

If containerization has changed the world, the world of competition has changed our industry and our company. OOCL was the first Asian company to embrace containerization, and in doing so it helped to drive the development of the Asian economy. Without us, Asian companies such as Toyota and Sony would have found it harder to conquer world export markets. Back in those days, if you built a ship you could fill it with cargo. Nowadays, with every new ship launched you get more space than cargo. We are a mature industry. Load utilization rates have become critical. And we have to compete.

Some of our competitors have responded by creating lots of space on their vessels and offering it to customers at very low prices. We, on the other hand, are focusing on time-sensitive, specialized and quality-dependent products – products like refrigerated goods, garments and vehicle components that have to arrive at the right place, in the right condition and at the right time.

Achieving that requires great expertise. If a food product is to be edible at the end of its journey it must be kept within a tight range of temperatures and atmospheres, from the minute it leaves the farm or factory to the minute it is picked off a supermarket shelf. For most of that time it is in our hands and it is our responsibility. When a ship completes a thirty-five-day round trip to North

America and back it has only got a two-hour window – no matter what the weather conditions have been – to arrive at the port to meet waiting trains and trucks.

Over the last decade this last point – 'the right time' – has become particularly important because of the 'Just in Time' (JIT) movement. JIT created a complete change in customer requirements and expectations, and we had to change our business to meet them. We have had to move from a wholesale mentality to a retail mentality.

For example, companies like Boots and W H Smith are relaying scanned information from what goes through their tills back to their warehouses, and they are looking to us to help them maintain minimum stock at all times. That means we have to deliver less, more frequently. And that, in turn, means that instead of filling a ship with orders from a few customers, at any one time the ship may contain goods from between 500 and 1,000 different customers who ship small amounts frequently.

We have also had to extend our service to the store door. Before, an American importer may have ordered fifty containers of lounge chairs and put them into one warehouse and then re-despatched them, re-handling every one. That no longer happens. The importer now says: 'My store in such a city will order the following items from my supplier in Hong Kong. Please pack one container containing the following fifty orders.' Then, to avoid any warehousing, re-handling and unnecessary domestic trucking, items are shipped directly to that particular store. For that reason, we now look after containers on land as much we do on sea; the ocean link has become almost incidental. The intermodal links that connect A to B have become critical because they are the only way we can do a lot of 'store door' business.

To offer this kind of service we have to be good; nowadays, our customers are experiencing our brand virtues all the way from order to final delivery.

Becoming an information-intensive business

All these developments, however, mean that, for us, 'being good' has changed. Increasingly our industry is dominated not by the movement of physical goods but by information. With global alliances and fixed transportation structures now in place, every competitor has similar hardware, so it's the ability to manage the information that controls the movements of goods that is becoming critical. Our challenge is to find integrated and added value solutions for our customers. That means, increasingly, competitive edge lies on the software side.

It's like airlines. They all have the same aircraft, use the same airports, and meet the same safety regulations. So they compete on the softer side in customer service. The only difference is that our business is far more complex. We have far more destinations we can deliver to: we not only put you on and off the aeroplane, we remove the seat from the plane, put it on a car or truck, and deliver it to your home. What's more, we may be collecting many different items from many different sources to place into one single consolidated container. And, at every point along the way, information pops up and somebody down the road needs it.

So our business is really very complex. Ships, terminals, agents and truckers are linked with vast communication networks via satellite, computer and fax; clients now have access to up-to-the-minute information about their shipment; seamless intermodalism provides them with door-to-door service; and tracking and routing systems have become so exact that a two-week journey can be timed for arrival within fifteen minutes.

That is why we have been investing nearly $50 million in a state-of-the-art object-oriented computer system which will be the most advanced booking system in our industry. Effectively what it does is decentralize our computing, allowing marketing and operations staff to offer customers extremely rapid decisions and information while keeping an eye on their margins and their cost-effectiveness at the same time.

Nowadays, that's what the customer needs. Information. So we want each and every one of our staff to have that information at their fingertips so they can give it to our customers when they need it.

Making it personal

Even the best IT system is only a platform. It's people who actually deliver the service. Using the technologies of standardized containers and fast, accurate information, we believe it is only committed employees who can give customers a great experience of OOCL by tailor-making services to satisfy their individual business needs. What we need is a whole set of really experienced people who are able and willing to work together to deliver this service and information. In other words, the personal aspect is increasingly in demand. And to build a really strong company we need a strong set of corporate values.

Over the last five years, we have begun many initiatives designed to achieve this. We started a quality assurance process in 1990, and now that commitment to quality is embedded in our corporate identity. We say the five petals of our plum blossom logo represent the five components of our quality assurance process: customer satisfaction, management commitment, employee participation, quality partnership and continuous improvement. Our vessels carry the plum blossom on the funnel and bow symbolizing the strength of our company, and over the years it has been integrated within every facet of our organization. This commitment to quality is complete, so that, for instance, we will not use a trucker in the UK unless he is ISO certified.

This quality process was very painful at the beginning but it was also very useful. For example, initially when something did go wrong, we would say 'Right, we are committed to delivering it on time', so we would end up paying airfreight to the ship rather than miss the boat. We learned very fast that we couldn't afford to keep on doing this, so we had to fix our own organization, restructuring it so that such problems no longer happened.

Like IT, quality assurance is more of a platform than a guarantee of service. We want our slogan, 'We take it personally', eventually to become the norm in everything OOCL does worldwide. We want it to become a distinctive and unique attitude that differentiates OOCL from all other carriers. To help achieve this we have invested heavily in communications (we were the first shipping line to open up direct communications with our employees via the Internet) and we have organized special sessions to encourage all employees to think about the way they carry out their role. In particular, we are promoting a set of desired behaviours.

One of these is 'share information and encourage discussion'. For example, the first time we formulated a mission statement in 1987 we had some wise men put it together. The second time, in 1995, we asked our staff for their ideas, and a large proportion did have something to say.

We are also encouraging all our staff to develop our six core competencies, which are: customer focus, results orientation, teamwork, the drive to achieve, communication and innovation.

It is very important to stress, however, that we are not introducing a new culture. Our core values don't represent a programme that is here one year and gone the next. We are just reiterating and consolidating some of the work habits of our staff. At the same time, we cannot overestimate the importance of core values, in particular the people value. Our employees make the difference by 'taking it personally'.

How OOCL's identity emerged

If we feel clear about these things now, it wasn't always so. In the mid-1980s we had a severe financial crisis and it took two years of very hard work with 150 creditors successfully to restructure the company. During that time we went through a tremendous learning process, identifying what went wrong before and what we really needed to do from now on in order to set the company on the right course.

One of the reasons for our downfall was that we were not focused. We had been very diverse, operating in a whole host of businesses including oil drilling, hotels and travel agencies, and we did not know what we really wanted to be as a company. So we identified what we wanted to be – the best container business – and decided to focus on that. After two years of restructuring we realized that this wasn't enough. To survive you need to specialize. Then you can differentiate. And while we had succeeded as a wholesaler in container transportation, we really needed to aim for the retailers. That is how we differentiate. We will never be the biggest, nor do we want to be. But we do want to be the most profitable, and the one that people associate with quality.

We have had to change ourselves to keep up, but we have retained core brand values. In the old days, OOCL's senior managers were typically 'Asian' and middle-aged: reserved, shy and conservative. Now we have become more eager to learn, we have developed a truly international outlook, we have become more resourceful – wanting to make things happen – and we are keen to develop relationships with customers rather than strike one-time deals.

Our corporate identity has also developed in parallel – we have learned that it is a mistake not to believe in the importance of corporate branding. Before the Second World War we had the plum blossom as a sort of house flag on the chimney tops of our ships. But the logo was the script that was written on the side of the ship – first the Orient Overseas Line, then the Orient Overseas Container Line – and the two things were really treated separately.

Indeed, at that time we didn't really pay much attention to the logo other than to take the view that people needed to recognize the plum blossom and Orient Overseas. At that stage containerization was easy. Demand outstripped supply, and we were doing wholesale business where it was not important to build up a brand. Then we realized that Orient Overseas Container Line was a bit of a mouthful and we moved forward a little bit. Like FedEx we shortened our name, and started calling ourselves OOCL.

However, we still had many hybrids of the logo shape, and we didn't have a specialist dedicated to developing the brand-name. It was only after 1985 that we started standardizing the identity. At that time we felt it was really necessary to search within the organization to find out what we really stood for.

Now we have a clear identity. The plum blossom logo is for our parent company Orient Overseas International. The OOCL logo with the plum blossom in the second O is the Orient Overseas Container Line, which brings in about 95 per cent of our revenue. That is the identity we tend to promote – and on occasion it has required intervention at the most senior level to underline its importance. On one occasion, for example, an operational director decided to respray a ship a particular colour, using a certain kind of anti-rust paint. From a narrow cost point of view his decision was absolutely correct: it would need only three coats of paint. But it was totally inappropriate for the visual branding, undermining its positive, optimistic spirit. The captain of the ship objected and eventually it was C. H. Tung himself who decided that the brand image was more important, even if it did require five coats and cost more money.

There are other important aspects of the plum blossom. First, it has 'soft' values; we deliberately put a plum blossom on a massive ship of 50,000 tonnes of steel. Second, it says something about our character, our resilience. In the late 1980s we could have easily packed it in, and the brand would no longer exist. But in China the plum is a flower that blooms in the harshest conditions – in the winter, in the snow. Also there is a Chinese saying that 'You can break the saw but you cannot break the willow branch'. We like to think we have the same personality characteristic. Compared to cast iron we are resilient.

Developing the business

One benefit of having a clear focus is that we have a very good idea of where we need to invest. Over the last five years or so, hardly a month has gone by without some important development: ordering a new ship, opening a new sales office, or signing a deal with a third party trucking or railroad firm to secure intermodal links. We now have thirty liner services: half of them intercontinental and half intra-Asian. We have 144 sales outlets, including offices in Hong Kong, China, Macau, Japan, South Korea, Singapore, Indonesia, the Philippines, Thailand, USA, Canada, UK, Belgium, Germany, the Netherlands, France, and Australia. Many of them are relatively new – less than five years old.

With this infrastructure in place, and with our core values firmly established and as a driving force behind everything we do, we are in a good position to continue our strategy of selective growth. There are huge opportunities in China, a very complex market which we understand well. There are opportunities in targeting major customers we currently do not serve. We recently signed a contract with Volkswagen which has regular, high-volume shipments to Shanghai.

To achieve such gains we have reorganized our marketing and sales to be much more market-driven and customer focused. We now aim to offer most customers a single point of contact, and are determinedly developing our role as providers of solutions and not just lower-cost freight. In fact, increasingly we are training our sales people to function more as logistics consultants than standard service providers. We want them to meet the real needs of customers – not only their current needs but also their latent and future ones.

All of this is necessary if we are to avoid competing on price alone. In fact, transportation cost is a relatively small part of our major customers' total logistics expenditure, so we are increasingly trying to help them in other ways, such as reducing interest costs through minimum stocking, improving cash flow through speedy and error-free documentation, reducing customers' duty due to direct calling of suitable ports and multi-area consolidation/distribution. This is where our investment in quality, information technology, people and core values really shows through as direct customer benefits.

We have also realized that there is huge, untapped potential in smaller and medium-sized companies. We have long-term relationships with many global companies which are now household names: companies such as Ford and Michelin in cars; Sony and Philips in electronics; Acer, Gateway 2000, Hewlett-Packard and Dell in computing; Burton, Wal-Mart and Adidas in retail; United Distillers, Heineken, Bass and Guinness in wines and spirits; and Du Pont, Exxon and ICI in chemicals. Customers like these will always be of prime importance to OOCL: just 1.5 per cent of our total customer base accounts for approximately one-third of our turnover.

However, many thousands of smaller companies do not get the same sort of attention from us, and they tend to stay with us for a much shorter period of time. In fact, we recently undertook a study among our 21,000 smaller customers and discovered that, on average, they stay with us for only one year – a common figure for our industry. Improving customer retention among these smaller and medium-sized businesses could be one of our biggest opportunities for profit improvement.

By paying the smaller customers more attention, we have discovered three things. First, they are often surprised and delighted to be given this attention. Second, it is not uncommon for what we thought to be small accounts to turn out to be medium-sized opportunities after all. And third, many small customers grow rapidly – their long-term value can be extraordinarily high.

Pioneering the art of co-operation

Our customers' demands for integrated solutions, ever greater speed, quality and reliability have also prompted us to rethink our approach to business. Recently we formed a Global Alliance with four other major shipping companies; American President Lines, Malaysian International Shipping Corporation, Mitsui OSK Lines and Nedlloyd Lines. This is the first time that leading carriers from all the world's manufacturing powerhouse regions of the United States, Europe, Japan and South-East Asia have been brought together in one liner grouping.

The Global Alliance will enable us to offer new levels of customer service, and build on brand strengths. Those customers seeking more frequent deliveries of smaller orders may ask for a sailing three times a week rather than just once a week. To offer that we may need to have nine ships plying the route. It is much easier and cost efficient to do this if partners coordinate sailings and share ship space and terminals. For example, the Global Alliance now offers six weekly sailings between the West Coast of America and North and South Asia. We are also able to improve cost efficiencies by negotiating jointly with shipbuilders and forming joint consortia for the ordering of new ships. Having four big names in the industry behind such deals allows us to negotiate better terms.

One thing we are not doing is merging our marketing and sales function. And we are certainly not going to sacrifice our identity. While we cooperate on the operational side and seek to out-compete other alliance groupings in terms of service and cost structure, within the alliance we also compete as hard as ever for customers.

Promoting the brand

Now that we are clear about what we as a company stand for and we have built our brand internally first, we are in a strong position to communicate it more aggressively externally. The way we do this is by associating with events which give us a chance to explain better what we have to offer. For example, the Cirque de Soleil – a famous Montreal circus – came to us to ship their containers around the world because nobody else had the network. We had one batch of containers coming from Montreal and another from Strasbourg, and they were looped together, some coming through the Suez, some going trans-Pacific and others coming via Japan. But they had to arrive in Hong Kong on a precise day. Everything landed on time, and the big top was set up. We promoted that as an 'Amazing Journey with OOCL'.

Another example is our three-year sponsorship of the Asia Pacific Championship yacht race. The yachts are fully containerizable. They come from Sydney, the USA and from the UK – from everywhere. Everyone coordinates well, and there are no hitches. Of course, we are not like a big tobacco company throwing down $5–10 million to sponsor Formula One motor racing. But what we can offer is space on a ship, which is just an incidental cost to us. And by doing so we are able to show other people that we can perform amazing feats in transportation.

Say + look + do = reputation

This is the important thing. We have a saying which is 'Walk the talk'. As far as we are concerned, the brand-name is a combination of what we say, how we look and what we do. And what we do is the most important. If you look at the seal of GE, or FedEx or even ICI, they truly believe in their philosophy, they appreciate it, and they get their employees to practise it. Similarly, we could say what we like and have the prettiest logo but if we cannot deliver, forget it. To that extent, every employee is the guardian of the brand, particularly the last person you meet. That's why we believe the most important part of the organization is not our hardware, our ships or our containers, but ourselves: we cannot separate our culture and our brand at any time or in any place.

6 | McDonald's UK: Balancing the Global Local Demands of the Brand

JOHN HAWKES, *senior vice president*

In 1954 McDonald's™ founder Ray Kroc bought franchise rights to the embryonic chain from two McDonald brothers who operated a hamburger stand in California. By 1961, having acquired the full rights to the name, he had already licensed more than 200 McDonald's restaurants in the USA.

Now McDonald's, with sales of over $30 billion, operates over 21,000 restaurants in more than 101 countries, with a new restaurant opening every three hours somewhere in the world. Over the next few years the plan is to open 2,500 to 3,200 new restaurants, not only in existing markets but in new parts of the world.

Getting the McDonald's brand to travel to so many countries so successfully in such a relatively short time can be attributed to a number of factors. First, McDonald's is passionately committed to the brand's core functional attributes, which are about serving quality food, courteously, by friendly people in clean surroundings and at exceptional value for money. Second, we keep raising the bar on our own performance, reinventing ourselves to improve our restaurant operations and our purchasing, franchising, training and marketing skills. Getting it better is as much part of our culture as remaining focused on our core business.

There is another aspect to the way we operate that has helped us succeed in so many different countries. The brand is global and those core attributes are fundamental, but each market has autonomy in the way it delivers the vision. There is self-regulation. We hold the firm view that what is right for the brand and how we build it and maximize the commercial return in each market is best left to that market to decide, particularly as local conditions can vary so radically.

The evolution of the brand

When we first began international operations it was essential to emphasize those core functional attributes, because they were key to establishing McDonald's position in the marketplace. Our evolution in the UK illustrates how that process has worked, as well as showing how the brand strategy has to develop as markets mature. In 1974, when we opened our first restaurant in London, the idea of service, of eating 100 per cent pure beef hamburgers offered at excellent value for money, in clean surroundings, simply did not exist. The positioning of McDonald's as a restaurant which welcomed families, had high-chairs and did not mind if children made a noise, was new and different. Also, competition was very limited for the first five to six years.

By the early 1980s consumer research showed us that the perceived point of difference was narrowing, with the competition beginning to wise up and model their operational systems on us. Also, quick service restaurants (QSRs) were being seen as more of a pressured, utilitarian experience, not one that you could sit back and enjoy. So the brand went into evolutionary mode, to reassert its competitive edge and address some of the negative perceptions of the industry by focusing on our relationship with customers.

Then, from the late 1980s, as competition from companies like Burger King grew, the brand strategy began to move again, aiming at a positioning based on the unique role McDonald's plays in everyday British lives. After all, if you look at the total volume of hamburger restaurant meals consumed, McDonald's accounts for about three-quarters of them. Alternatively, in the USA, where the competition is more aggressive, heightened by price-cutting, market share is much lower.

The greatest potential weapon in our armoury in terms of building the brand for the future is to continue to reinforce that emotional connection. It is not through price discounting or short-term tactical promotional activity that we increase our brand equity. It is by building the long-term reputation of the brand through exceptional customer satisfaction and value.

That philosophy applies to other markets, where the challenge is to make McDonald's a multi-dimensional brand. As the company has grown, the brand has become bigger than the accumulation of the restaurants. Factors such as international travel and media globalization mean that more people know about our brand, or think they do. They are certainly visually aware of it, and even in countries where there are no McDonald's restaurants people still have an understanding of us. So now those functional and emotional aspects of the relationship are a lot closer together, even when we open a restaurant in a new market.

What we always have to keep in mind, however, is that although the world has moved on, particularly in terms of what people eat and how they use restaurants in general, the essence of our brand positioning, the family, and the importance of quality, service, cleanliness and value still hold.

Taking the brand to new markets

When a business is growing at such speed it is always difficult to identify defining moments in the brand's global progress. With hindsight, setting up in Russia in 1990 was probably one of these defining moments, because of the marketplace itself. McDonald's was already established in international markets around the world, but being one of the first Western brands moving into Russia in 1990, when so much change was taking place, made the brand seem truly global.

It took fourteen years from the original discussion until we finally opened the doors in Moscow. Before we were able to go ahead, we had to invest resources and integrate vertically through the local food industry, to make sure we had the quality of supplies we needed. We keep reminding ourselves what makes us successful.

We cannot just rush into new countries if it means we cannot achieve the level of quality and consistency our customers expect. It is much better to do the right thing and guarantee quality rather than to go for speed. And it works: the Moscow McDonald's is now one of the busiest in the world.

There is no pre-determined time scale for opening in new markets. It also took several years to develop in the UK. We needed to make sure prospective employees and suppliers had an understanding and acceptance of McDonald's culture, of what we were and what we required. The relationships with our suppliers are based on long-term commitment, so we have to build an infrastructure to support that. In order to achieve consistency, we need partners who not only understand us, but also live by our standards.

The strength of franchising

One of our greatest strengths has always been our approach to franchising. In some markets, up to 80 per cent of the restaurants are owned and operated by independent entrepreneurs. Almost by definition, if you are franchising to local people the delivery and interpretation of what might be seen as the culture of a US brand is automatically translated by local people, both in terms of what is delivered and the way it is delivered. The percentage of franchised restaurants may be lower in the UK, but our franchisees still bring a wealth of individual flair into the business. They come from a variety of different experiences and backgrounds, and they may well have been brought up in the local area of their restaurant, so they'll know it well. Franchisees typically sign up for twenty years, and because it is their livelihood they bring a great deal of dedication and energy to a restaurant's development.

Success in a new market comes largely from listening to the indigenous partners, franchisees, customers and suppliers. India is a good example. Along with our partners and suppliers, we have invested considerable resources in establishing operations, including the construction of restaurants, infrastructure, and developing employees and local suppliers. Our aim is to purchase products required for the restaurants locally; over several years, we have been working with Indian companies to develop products specifically for the restaurants, by sharing expertise, technology and equipment of the highest standard.

Our menus reflect the local cultural framework: McDonald's India offers products developed especially for the Indian market, especially vegetarian customers. It will serve only mutton, chicken, fish and vegetable products, not beef, pork or their by-products. Big Mac™ thus becomes Maharaja Mac™, which consists of two all-mutton patties, special sauce, lettuce, cheese, pickles and onions on a sesame seed bun. Israel has some kosher McDonald's restaurants, while Saudi Arabia has a restaurant which closes five times a day for Muslim prayer.

The fundamental essence of the menu is important to us. It needs to be limited, not only so it can be served efficiently, but also to keep the quality levels high. Most people around the world like our hamburgers, the French fries and Coca-Cola. Making small changes to account for local tastes is important. For instance, we make a pomme frite sauce for Belgium and Holland, and a special mayonnaise-based sauce that is unique to Iceland.

A part of the community

So the brand is global but it exists at the local level too. Whether you are in Moscow or Manchester, it is the experience you have when you go into a McDonald's restaurant that shapes what you think about the brand. And although our heritage is American, because we are locally managed we are not necessarily seen as an overtly American company outside the United States. We are part of the community because the employees and the customers they are serving are local. People tend to talk about their 'local' McDonald's.

The brand defines the culture

We conduct research to determine who our customers are, what they want and how they feel about us. They could probably be best described as a family, where the parents are anywhere up to thirty-five years, with children aged between three and seven.

We have always positioned ourselves as a family restaurant, but of course our appeal is very broad. Family members are individuals too, with teenagers and over thirty-fives being very important, and they can be marketed to in a different way. The restaurant, however, has to embrace all these different people and be relevant to their needs.

Once your core positioning is clearly established you can segment more easily without compromising it.

There is a very strong internal understanding of what the brand is and what is important to it, so there is a hands-on protection of core values. Every contact we have with a customer, even seemingly minor ones, can have an enormous impact on the brand. Every touch counts. It can be very easy to upset the balance of the elements that make up the total McDonald's experience.

We have a structured Operations hierarchy with people visiting the restaurants making continual checks and balances. This is not about furtively going in and observing from a distance, but about working with restaurant managers and franchisees to ensure everything is running as well as it can. However, we do use Mystery Shoppers to make sure levels of service and quality are kept up from the customers' point of view.

The 'have a nice day' syndrome is a misapprehension. We offer a personal, friendly service, and aim to have some kind of individual rapport with each of our costumers. Although consistency of service is, of course, important, we encourage our employees to add a little bit of their own personality – it's about engaging with the customer. The essence of what we do is consistent, but the rest is about tailoring it for local markets.

The promise we make through the brand is being delivered right now, to millions of people, and the emphasis on learning and improvement therefore is strong. Training is continuous through-out the company and in the restaurants this includes day-to-day coaching and technology-assisted learning programmes. Aspiring restaurant managers attend a two-week Advanced Operations and Management class at our Management Training Centre. Each year, instructors at Training Centres in the USA, Germany, the United Kingdom, Japan and Australia teach more than 5,000 students, including franchisees and corporate management, in twenty-two languages. And even people who join the company in a departmental function will usually undergo the basic training programme. As a trainee in most companies you would expect to begin work in a suit, behind a desk. Our graduate trainees start in crew uniform, in a restaurant, so they understand every aspect of the business.

Formal training about the business and operational procedures is underpinned by the cultural rub-off which keeps people very focused on the brand. We also never lose sight of our roots and once a year we hold what we call 'Founder's Day', usually in October on a Friday, when all office employees, including those in the corporate and regional offices, and many of the partners in our supplier companies, leave their desks, put on a crew uniform and work in a restaurant for the day. Remembering what business we are in is an important part of our culture.

The emphasis on developing people from within supports this. Employees may move around from one function to another to gain experience in all areas of the business. So someone who started in the restaurants may be seconded to another department as part of his or her career development programme. We also have people who move to different countries to support the development of new markets.

Global consistency, local autonomy

Within the corporate brand are trademarked products which could be thought of as sub-brands, like the Big Mac™, Happy Meal™ and Egg McMuffin™. These have to be consistent with the fundamental brand values of McDonald's.

There is sometimes a perception that, with our American heritage, we have a massive headquarters in the USA managing the business around the world. This is not the case. The management team in each country, whether there is an equity investment or local ownership, is relatively autonomous. That does not mean that employees go off and do their own thing. There is continuous communication between countries and regions, not so much for approval but for learning and sharing of best practice and to ensure consistency. We do have regional centres – for example, we have regional offices for Northern and Southern Europe – staffed by people who support, assist and facilitate the sharing of efficiencies, and make sure the wheel is not being reinvented each time we open in a new market. What is central is an understanding of the global brand.

We can, however, create new products for individual countries. There is no rule that an idea has to be able to travel to other markets, but by virtue of the networking and sharing of ideas, a lot of processes we have developed do travel well. For example, in the UK we took the lead in developing a modular building process which improved construction efficiencies enormously and it is now used in many other countries. Another way to network ideas is through our supplier-partners, who often export their products to McDonald's in other markets. Countries will test new products, new ideas, new promotional mechanics, and if they work in one market they can be adapted to work in others.

The 'not-invented-here' syndrome is a natural human characteristic. To minimize it, we credit those who innovate and then provide the encouragement and infrastructure to share. We do not worry about people taking ideas from other countries – on the contrary we do what we can to facilitate it. Rather than reinventing the wheel we seek to improve it. It is always important to remember how critical the local culture is, and that certain ideas simply will not travel. However, ultimately, there is more that is the same than is different.

We also have a senior vice president, responsible for an international team of marketing people who give guidance and help share ideas. The world is shrinking and with the advent of satellite communications and the Internet there is an increasing need to communicate more information, more quickly, about issues that arise in each country and how they may affect others. This is a vital part of managing the brand.

The power of the corporate identity

Our corporate identity, the Golden Arches, is very powerful and instantly recognized around the world. Because it is applied to so many different communication materials like stationery, packaging, signage, uniforms, literature and advertising, and by so many different people, it is important that it is used consistently.

Another misconception is that all of our restaurants are the same. This is not the case. To reinforce the brand identity, a single design for packaging is being developed, which will also save costs in production and distribution. However, our restaurant designers have broad scope in terms of the decor and furniture they use. Go into any McDonald's restaurant and the signage, the counter and the way the people serve customers will be consistent. But if you look at the architecture, the colour scheme, the fabrics and furnishings, the design, the artwork on the walls, you will find they can be very different and are often themed to the locality.

Communicating brand values at the global and local level

Apart from local marketing activity, television advertising often comes first when we enter a market, because it is the strongest communication medium. Then, as we grow and develop we will add to the media mix, whether it be radio, outdoor or press, in order to reach different audiences with different messages. Deciding the media is the last thing to do. The first task is to agree the objective and strategy, the issue we are trying to address. And then find the best way of communicating it.

Our advertising is usually produced locally. In the UK, for example, we produce our own advertising, although we have occasionally used international commercials where it was appropriate. Creating global advertising is not necessarily more cost-efficient, in terms of economies of scale, if the ads themselves are not as effective as those produced in the local market.

There are many different ways of communicating the same thing. In the USA a communication might be quite emotional, whereas in the UK the same sentiment will be communicated through humour. That is not to say, though, that a humorous commercial produced in the UK would not also strike a chord in another country.

In the UK we have occasionally adapted American ads – we may re-shoot them, or use the pictures with a different voice-over. There are no rules really, other than to be totally consistent with the brand values.

Sponsorship is another powerful vehicle for communication, whether at the global level, like the 1996 Olympic Games, the regional level, with the 1996 European football championship, 'Euro96', or at the local level. In the UK, we are the official restaurant of football's Premier League. A large proportion of the budget is directed at initiatives to encourage the involvement of families and young people. This sort of activity creates an excellent opportunity for our restaurants to become involved with the local community. It is also a way of keeping the brand alive and vital. So the management of the brand is very much in the detail. It has to work right the way down to the restaurants and bring the magic to life in the local community.

Strategic marketing alliances are another way to strengthen the brand. In 1996 we announced a ten-year alliance with the Walt Disney Corporation. McDonald's is Disney's promotional partner in the restaurant industry, giving us exclusive category marketing rights, linking our restaurants to Disney theatrical releases, theme parks and home video releases.

One of our most valuable assets, particularly in terms of our charitable and community activities, is Ronald McDonald™. He might visit a restaurant to do a magic show, and then go to a hospital and entertain the children's ward. He can also be a great teacher, for example on subjects like road safety, because children do listen to him. And he helps raise money for children's charities, including Ronald McDonald Houses™, which are homes-away-from-home for families of seriously ill children receiving treatment at nearby hospitals. At the end of 1996 there were 180 Houses in fifteen countries, accommodating 2,500 families every night.

Restaurant managers and franchisees often become involved with local charities and civic activities. The company has always had a strong corporate social responsibility stance, born out of founder Ray Kroc's desire to 'put something back' into the community. This has been adopted into the corporate culture, and community involvement and charitable fund-raising have become key features of local activity worldwide.

The brand as a living process

The challenges we face are different, market by market. The USA, for example, is dealing with issues which other countries can learn from. There are more and more opportunities for people to eat out, so it is a constant challenge for us to maintain market share. Our competition comes not just from other chains, so one of the ways we can grow is by making ourselves more convenient and taking the brand to where people congregate by using, for example, mobile restaurants. This approach is part of the objective to make the McDonald's brand and proposition available in more places. Unusual locations now include airports, hospitals, university campuses and military bases, among others. McDonald's food can also be found on aeroplanes, trains and ships.

There is a great deal of room for growth. Based on the populations of the countries where we currently operate, on a given day McDonald's still serves only 1 per cent of the population. In China, for example, there are only around sixty restaurants to serve 1.2 billion people!

It is fair to say that the business we are in is simple. But managing the brand is not a simple process. It might be relatively straightforward to sell one Big Mac to one customer. The skill lies in doing it well 20 million times a day, day in day out, around the world.

7 | Guinness Ireland: Broadening the Brand Franchise without Destroying the Mystique

TIM KELLY, *marketing director*

Ireland is, of course, Guinness' original and spiritual home market. As the brand's most mature market, it offers particular challenges that other less developed territories are yet to face. More Guinness is drunk per head in Ireland than anywhere else: one in every two pints sold is Guinness. And, despite having a population of only a twelfth of Great Britain's (5 million compared with 58.6 million), the Irish market's expenditure on the brand is nearly the same as Great Britain's. However, even in Ireland, Guinness faces competition from rival brands and is now fighting to secure future sales by increasing its appeal to a younger generation of drinkers.

In its home market, Guinness recently introduced a fresh approach. The company has tiered its brands, dividing different products into groups. 'National power brands' are Guinness and Budweiser and Carlsberg (which it brews locally under licence). These command high investment to support all aspects of the brand. Then there are 'strategic brands' (with potential to become power players) such as Kilkenny and Hudson Blue, and then there are the 'regional brands' such as Harp and Smithwicks, and they have strengths in particular areas such as Harp in Northern Ireland. The company's emphasis is to grow international business outside its most developed markets as well as expand its consumer base back home. It will have to achieve both if it is to achieve its goal: to move up from sixth position to become one of the top three beer brands in the world.

Two centuries in the making . . .

It may no longer be only an Irish business but, to many, Guinness is the quintessential Irish brand. It is a mixture of many elements: the product, the experience of drinking the product, and its history. Guinness' founder, Arthur Guinness, took over the brewery in Dublin's St James' Gate in 1759. At that time, Porter, a drink popular with the porters at Covent Garden and Billingsgate, was being exported by London brewers to Dublin and Guinness was brewing ale. Tackling the English brewers at their own game, Arthur Guinness turned his hand to 'porter' in the early 1790s. The decision led to the business becoming the largest porter and stout brewery of all time.

Today, the headquarters of Guinness plc is at Portman Square in London, where the company is listed on the London Stock Exchange. The announcement in May 1997 of the proposed merger with Grand Metropolitan, to be called GMG Brands, will create one of the largest food and drink companies in the world. At the time of writing, the merger still requires approval. Since its merger with United Distillers in 1986, Guinness has had two divisions: United Distillers, the spirits business with brands like Johnnie Walker and Gordon's Gin, and Guinness Brewing Worldwide (GBW) which handles all the beer business with brands like Guinness, Kilkenny, Harp, Red Stripe and Cruzcampo. GBW divides the world into six regions. There is Asia Pacific based in Singapore. Another is based in the United States and includes South America, Canada and the Caribbean. Ireland & Europe is based in Dublin. Then there is Great Britain, based at the Park Royal Brewery, London. The company has substantial business in Africa, and the final region is Spain, where the company bought Spain's largest brewer, Grupo Cruzcampo, in 1991. Each is headed by a regional managing director, and each is a profit centre as well as a geographic unit. Each regional managing director reports to the global managing director of GBW who, along with the managing director of United Distillers, sits on the board of Guinness plc.

Regional managing directors are autonomous but, like every global business, there is a very clear set of operating practices and targets. At GBW level, there are central staff covering the key functions such as technical, finance, personnel, marketing and public affairs. All are coordinated centrally and administered locally. So, there are the same reporting procedures and deadlines in every country. This is also important because we have people who are moving worldwide, so recruitment, employment terms and conditions and other organizational issues meet global standards. With marketing, however, GBW's role is quite different: by comparison it is quite decentralized. At Coca-Cola, central management is very strong, whereas, at Guinness, local markets have a lot of freedom and autonomy. Of course, with production there has to be a degree of uniformity, and purchasing is organized on a worldwide basis. Locally, however, there are differences in product, packaging, advertising and advertising agencies, although the core essence of Guinness is basically the same.

This structure used to be very different. Until four years ago, there were three regions: Ireland, Great Britain and International. The change was driven by the growing importance of international markets and their strong growth. Take the USA, for example, which although relatively new for Guinness is growing so rapidly it now needs its own local focus. Today, more and more decision-making is happening locally. The first US-specific TV advertising was recently shown; it was made in the USA and only for that market. Previously, the USA took everything from Dublin and London. Now it's a question of local expertise and achieving critical mass.

United Distillers has a similar structure with regional directors around the world, in local markets managing local business. But the nature of the spirits business is very different. More commonality exists. Take Johnnie Walker: it's made in one place, the graphics are the same worldwide and the advertising is the same worldwide. If a local marketing director wanted to 'break the rules', it would be discussed by head office in Hammersmith. The difference in approach comes down to the difference in product. Beer tends to be made locally; whisky is made in one place. Spirits are more of a luxury item; beer is an everyday purchase. Where spirits are purchased also differs significantly: for example, at duty-free outlets. And the quantities of each that are sold are very different. United Distillers' business is structured around local sales, marketing and distribution operations rather than manufacturing sites. As its business is bigger – UD is roughly twice the size of GBW – a different organizational model seems appropriate.

Beer is a relatively new business by comparison. The GBW structure offers a number of commercial benefits. Speed is one. Local understanding is another – we need those actually working in their market to understand that market better than anyone else. As a result, we tend to be able to recruit better people in the local market; we can offer them full freedom for that market.

'The wine of the country'

Defining the essence of the Guinness brand is something a lot of people have spent an awful lot of time doing, and we still have not found all the answers. There are some brands which you can discuss and everyone nods and knows what you are talking about. One of the difficulties of Guinness – and it is partly one of our own making – is that we have wrapped it up in a sort of language of complexity. This is complicated by the uniqueness of the product and the imagery and values which consumers attach to the brand. Marketing people have tended to cloak Guinness in jargon and unusual words. Guinness is a mainstream draught black beer for eighteen to thirty-five-year-olds. In Ireland it is an 'everyday drink'. Therefore it is the defining beer for the Irish market. In other markets it isn't. In Great Britain, for example, Guinness' share of the total beer market is in single figures and increasing, but it performs a different role, and its positioning is quite different. Here the positioning is every-day, everywhere, ubiquitous.

Now, there are a number of different elements to the brand which we map as a 'bullseye'. The core brand proposition at the centre sets Guinness as 'communion, power and exploration'.

Around this we have brand heritage, distinctiveness, complexity, naturalness, ubiquity, innovation and wit. Some of these are very similar across the brand worldwide. Others vary in significance according to the local market and consumers' perception. For example, the slogan 'Guinness is Good For You', which we used here in our advertising in the 1940s and 1950s, is still remembered in some markets. In Africa, for example, consumers have over the years attributed power to Guinness: an aphrodisiac, or a male reward. And of course we do have a heritage associated with the naturalness and benefit of the product. In Ireland, if you give blood you're given the option of a glass of Guinness, or a cup of tea, or coffee afterwards.

Then there are the physical properties of the pint: we call it 'the surge' – the way Guinness pours and settles and the ritual involved in that. This used to be peculiar and exclusive to Guinness. Now there are other brands coming in, like Kilkenny, which do it too. Even so, Guinness is still closely associated with that surge: the waiting, the anticipation. Also, Guinness is seen as natural – made from healthier ingredients to an original recipe. That's why some of the features on the packaging can be traced back to 1759 with the Arthur Guinness signature, and so on. It is seen as the original. Then there's the product, it's black – few products are only black, we 'own' the colour. We divide the emotional values of the brand into 'how it makes me feel' and 'what it says about me'. For example, individualistic, at ease with oneself, content, socially-bonded. Again, these vary market by market.

We don't push 'Irishness' in all markets around the world – in some, people may not have even heard of Ireland. However, in most there is at least a basic awareness of Irish culture: notably, Irish writers like James Joyce who memorably described Guinness as 'the wine of the country'. The greater challenge is the product itself, because it is at the root of the complexity which has traditionally surrounded the brand. It takes some getting used to if you've never tried it before. The colour is unusual compared to lager, and it has a more bitter taste.

People have explained the product and the marketing of it in terms of being complex, rewarding, deep, mysterious and so on. I believe too many people have been caught up with subtleties that may not exist. It is, after all, just a drink, a very different drink, but a drink none the less. It is usually drunk in pubs in draught format when people want to have a good time. People's needs in those situations are pretty straightforward and simple – they want to enjoy themselves. They don't want an intellectual game to be played to give them a reason to drink. There is a real risk in positioning a brand as too difficult or inaccessible. We need a more pragmatic approach.

Unravelling the mystery

Guinness has undergone two major shifts in branding and positioning in recent years. The first was in the 1970s. The second is taking place now and we call the strategy the 'Big Pint'.

In the 1970s, it would be fair to say Guinness was perceived as a cloth-cap brand. It was drunk by older people lower down the social scale, for example rural farmers, older men. Fifty-three per cent of beer drinkers were aged thirty-five or over; 63 per cent of Guinness drinkers fell into this bracket. At that time, the Irish beer market was divided into three neat categories: stout, ale and lager.

In the stout market – which at that time was in sharp decline – we had Guinness, in ales we had Smithwicks and in lager (a small but rapidly growing sector in the 1970s) Harp. Some things we did then had to change. There was a jaundiced trade view of Guinness as a company which was overall seen as caring less about its customers than its rivals. We were a typical company that had grown up successfully. As a company we had to reinvent ourselves to recognize new competition and a more demanding customer.

Guinness was failing to target the growing middle-class consumer group. And its consumer profile – predominantly male – did not reflect the growing importance of women in the market. So, in the 1980s, we developed a strategy to invest in revitalizing stout; this entailed new investment in the product, in production, the brand and its promotion. We reduced the serving temperature of the product and its quality was improved. There was a change in livery – colours were updated and packaging made more attractive, especially to women. Much of the marketing activity was designed to recruit younger people and move Guinness into outlets where it was not previously available. There was a marked difference between the old advertising focusing on the traditional male drinking market and the new.

The results were soon clear. By the 1980s, we had achieved a more upmarket consumer profile, more women drinkers and a growing share of new recruits to beer. There was real volume growth and Guinness recovered its share of all draught beer sales. At one point, stout had dropped to about 46 per cent of the total (Irish) beer market. After this initiative, it was brought back up to over 50 per cent. Successful companies can keep up to date and ahead of trends. Understanding the market and acting early is key and what Guinness managed to do was force change in the absence of a crisis.

In 1970, the majority of Guinness' total worldwide sales would have been sold in Ireland – between 70 and 80 per cent. This repositioning started in Ireland. It just wouldn't have been necessary or worthwhile elsewhere, because the sales volumes would have been so small. Since then, we have constantly worked to build on this. You can't stand still, even with an established brand. We are constantly working to improve our efficiencies, our processes, our marketing, our selling – everything. And we shall continue to do so.

Following the United Distillers–Guinness merger in 1986, there was a realization that if Guinness plc had a great global spirits business, we should fully develop our global beer business as well. Beer was already being exported, but what was required was a significant increase in resources to realize its potential. Activities were stepped up and, over the years since, as markets reach critical mass, local infrastructures have been established and local strategies set in place.

The 'Big Pint'

Today, however, we still face challenges. Research among Irish people shows tremendous loyalty towards the Guinness brand. But we must attract new, younger, drinkers if we are to grow Guinness in the longer term, and that is the essence of the challenge: to recruit new drinkers and retain current ones. Last year we switched from a local agency which had previously handled the business for many years, to London-based agency Howell Henry Chaldecott Lury & Partners. Together, we have developed the 'Big Pint' strategy. We never use those actual words, but the idea is all about size, substance, taste, texture, and worth – said in a way that is immediate, relevant and surprising but also with humour. Size matters. It's not mysterious, deep or complex. The 'Big Pint' and all the communication around it is based on the fact that Guinness is the world's biggest-selling pint. There's more to Guinness than other pints – more taste, more texture, more reward.

The thinking behind the 'Big Pint' is that Guinness is actually the biggest pint in the world. We can justify this because, as Guinness is nearly always sold in draught format, it is more often drunk as a pint than any other packaging format, which makes it the biggest-selling pint brand in the world. On its own, this says little. But explain it or show it in a way that's witty and says something about the product and brand – bigger taste, bigger density or texture – and it adds something to the brand. The next stage will be to explain the product in a new and engaging manner.

We have a reputation which requires us to keep our advertising up to date. We are always slightly nervous about a change in style; it is a delicate balance.

Because we want to secure the long-term health of the Guinness brand, we must constantly watch the market. This is why we are lowering the age profile of the brand. In hot drinks and soft drinks, as you buy into a brand and get older you don't tend to change your buying habits. But in Ireland, if you are a younger person you are likely to drink lager and be less brand-loyal. In the past, you might have moved into drinking stout as you get older, but that's not so much the case today. Young people are growing up in a world with many brand options, and they are more likely to stick to the brands they consume now as they age. We want to win over the younger drinkers. At the same time, we want to hold on to our older drinkers. They don't want themselves to be seen as drinking an older person's drink. We must make them feel good about drinking Guinness. We don't want to be so young we frighten them off.

Young people want a global brand image like Coke, Nike or Levi's. They want something for them. We used to talk about Guinness in the company as velvety, creamy, smooth, dark – the product language. These words mean little to an eighteen-year-old, who might even find them off-putting.

You could argue that it's 'old-fashioned' to have to wait for something – and Guinness is all about waiting: the 'Guinness Moment' as the pint is drawn and settles. They might say that in a Pepsi Max world the young want it now. But they'd be wrong. One of the great unique qualities of Guinness is the Guinness experience. The experience is the product. It is unique. Communicating this to younger drinkers is what we must now address. So the point of the 'Big Pint' is to use words and language that mean something to them. There are posters around using words like 'taste-tackler' – things that are amusing, or that instantly evoke an image, slightly funny, slightly tongue-in-cheek, but describing the product in a relevant way.

It's using our past but expressing it in a way that is relevant for today. We don't deny our heritage, nor do we want to. We are proud of it. We want to express it with relevance. When I first started here someone said to me 'Are you going to be a recruitment or a reassurance marketing director?' What he meant was, 'Are you going to hold on to existing customers or start recruiting new ones?' I don't believe it's an 'either/or' decision. If we recruited younger drinkers and upset older ones we'd struggle, and if we retained older drinkers and didn't win the young it would be the same. Our marketing effort is split across different age groups and targeted accordingly. We do hurling and opera sponsorship as well as music festivals. We walk a tightrope everyday between trying to attract someone in a language, a tone and with a message that's relevant to them without upsetting someone else.

Divide and conquer

One of the traps that anyone can fall into is following competitors. While new brands, like Murphys or Caffreys, have created a sense of freshness about them, we don't want to follow them. Part of the reason for our current change in strategy is to enable ourselves once more to take the lead and let them worry about how to respond.

We have also adopted a new approach to addressing our market. Now, we have 'need-states' – a world divided into different consumer needs. In the 1970s there was something drinkers light-heartedly referred to as the Holy Trinity: you started drinking Harp, you graduated to Smithwicks and then you went on to Guinness. Now the world is far more complicated than that.

Also, as market dynamics change – lager has grown at the expense of stout and ale, for example – we said rather than look at the market by sector, we would look at the total drinks market, the long alcoholic drinks market. And that's where 'need-states' come in. We've moved our market definition from Guinness being considered part of the stout market, to looking at Guinness as a proportion of the total drinks market with all the Guinness brands.

'Need-states' segment the market by consumer need. At one end, there's the need to enjoy yourself. At the other, the need to reward yourself after a busy day. There is easy sociability, everyday drinking, and there is the Friday night out, and so on. What we've got is different businesses in each need-state; each one can be quantified by volume share. We therefore can identify where we have too much of one and not enough of another, and then approach how to redress this if there is too much in a static box, too little in a growing one. We must stretch and pull our portfolio.

One of the differences in Ireland is that, unlike in other markets, we have a full range of brands aimed at different needs. We launched our first non-beer product last year: Hudson Blue, an ice cider. We have a market definition which is 'long alcoholic drinks'. This means more than just beer, and it enables us to look at the whole picture and introduce brands or packs to meet all needs. So we can cover the pitch rather than supply just one market.

To tackle the portion of the market which we don't have, we could launch Guinness either as different versions or in new packaging formats. But just how far could you stretch it? At the moment, it's only a black, draught product. Our cider is not, for example, branded as from the Guinness company, but some brand extensions have been launched. Guinness Draught Bitter is on sale in the UK and so is Guinness Extra Stout (a stronger, bottled version of traditional Guinness). But can it go only that far, or could Guinness be stretched to encompass something else? Brand stretching has seen more casualties than successes, so before we embark on any change we would have to be very confident.

Could we ever apply the same qualities Guinness has to other products? If we were to use all things consistent with the Guinness brand and do it in the right way, maybe. However, you won't succeed unless you make an effort, and in making an effort, sometimes you will fail. You have got to try several things several times to move, and all companies I am sure would like to be more innovative.

We have learned many lessons from NPD. We are far more conscious now of consumer needs, and we are becoming more innovative. Today, we do a large amount of research, and relationships with our consumers are worked on very, very hard. Many US companies are saying 'stick to core competencies – single products, single brands'. We believe there is more growth in the Guinness brand than anywhere. There are no plans to change the product.

Spreading the word

Our priority now is to grow volume in different markets. One way we are doing this internationally is with the help of the Irish pubs. The Guinness Irish Pub concept helps publicans and entrepreneurs around the world establish 'authentic' Irish pubs. Guinness is well placed to offer professional advice on how to re-create genuine Irish pub culture. There are four key elements: pub design and ambience; friendly, efficient staff; the unique appeal of Irish food; drink and Irish music – sometimes it's live, always it's there. It is a very good way of seeding interest and growing demand. When looking at a brand-new market, we must consider a number of options. Do we export? Or do we set up a plant? A few Irish pubs serving Guinness in the right way with the right music, Irish food and Irish style is a wonderful way of developing the market. It is also the perfect environment for consumers to sample a perfect pint of Guinness.

The whole Irish phenomenon has arisen over the past decade or so. Irish culture now has international appeal. The Irish pub plays a central role in this. Irish pub culture is unique. The Irish drink in pubs more than anywhere in the world. I don't know of any other European Union summit where John Major took time out to visit a local bar. But when they were in Dublin, John Major and Kenneth Clarke slipped off to the pub for a quiet pint of Guinness. What better way to present a new concept – Guinness – than in the context of the Irish pub? Imagine it arriving, by can, in a Chinese shop. Or a local bar in Peru simply starts serving it without any understanding. Remember, you need to try it a few times before you become a regular consumer.

We don't have direct investment in any of our pubs and it's not a franchising arrangement. We *do* put a lot of emphasis on quality. We have people employed worldwide who are pub retail experts, and they help to build up the relationships and build pub business. We help ensure best practice, exchange information and put the people with the money in touch with the suppliers. You can buy a bespoke kit for an Irish pub made here in a variety of designs.

Many leave here in a lorry, are unpacked, assembled and built at the other end. We are the facilitators.

The Irish pub concept is not necessarily a first step towards a global strategy for the Guinness brand. Walk into some and they are playing local, not traditional Irish music. Walk into others and you can find local musicians playing Irish music who could be mistaken for an Irish band. The point is the format allows local consumers to interpret and participate in the values it embodies.

There is, however, an emerging need to have greater uniformity for the Guinness brand around the world. In time, I think we will find more common elements – it will happen naturally. With the overall objective to grow the Guinness brand worldwide, we must develop both the home core market and new developing markets with high potential. You have got to allow freedom if these developing markets are to fulfil their potential. Even so, there is a set strategy for developing new markets: there is no need to reinvent the wheel every time.

Walking the tightrope

The Guinness brand and Guinness the company are so closely entwined in Ireland that we have to be acutely conscious of public reaction to what we do. Ireland remains a big source of volume and profit. Guinness plc has profits of about £970 million a year; United Distillers accounts for around 60 per cent of this, GBW around 40 per cent. In the Irish market we are challenged by new brands all the time. Like all businesses, there is globalization. What would once have been a local brewery in Cork is now owned by Heineken, which owns Murphy; Beamish is owned by Scottish Courage; Bass has a site in Belfast. Growing competition has meant we spend more time monitoring our product, both against our own standards and against the competition in terms of quality, taste and colour. There is an obsession, almost a missionary zeal, within the company about quality – achieving a uniform product at a particular standard – and every employee is encouraged to play a role in this. It's not just ensuring it leaves the brewery in perfect condition but that it should also be perfect when the consumer drinks it in the pub.

There is an obsessive quality in Ireland about beer. It's important here. You still hear all these stories about Guinness on the west coast not tasting as good as Guinness on the east coast because it has travelled further. And people do move from pub to pub because they say, 'I prefer it over there', or 'This is a bad day from this one'. Whether it really does taste better in Ireland than anywhere else, however, it's hard to say. Many have tried to prove it, with inconclusive results. I think it's perhaps that you enjoy yourself more when you are drinking it here.

This universal interest in Guinness is a critical factor. Our major challenge is keeping up to date, as it has been every decade since 1759. You have to work very hard at this, and not be a follower of fashion. Because markets and lead times are so short, things happen and change more quickly. We believe if you understand today, tomorrow will follow. We don't worry about five or ten years down the line, in that respect. But we do need to ensure we connect with our consumers and really understand what they are doing today and why, and why not. It is a fundamental belief. Understanding the consumer is not just an issue for the marketing department, it is an issue across the entire company.

Brand positioning, essence and relevance go beyond marketing. There is involvement and interest throughout the company. Employees ring me up and say, 'I saw that', 'I liked it', 'I didn't like it' in a way I've never experienced in previous roles. There is a special concern for quality among everyone who encounters the brand.

Custody of the brand has to sit somewhere – and that's in the marketing department. Ultimately, however, the true custodian is the consumer. In Ireland, the brand is as significant as Coke in the US or Carlsberg in Denmark – it's the national brand as well as Ireland's favourite drink. The level of attention our consumers pay to every detail is remarkable. Sometimes it makes us cautious, but we are very, very close to our market and our consumers as a company, not just as a department.

Recently, we did some work looking at companies which optimize consumer marketing. Those who do are those who are closest to the consumer. These companies include Tesco, Nike, Levi Strauss, Pepsi, Mars. Tesco, for example, has consumer panels which meet every week to say what they want and what they don't want. That sort of approach is deeply impressive. We've improved as a result. The managing director frequently consults consumer groups. In fact, he and others are now offering insights, comments and understanding of marketing in a way they would never have done previously. Marketing within Guinness has often clouded itself in secrecy and jargon, and this is an effort to break it down.

Last year we ran some ads which some of our employees didn't like. They felt frustrated because they felt they couldn't tell us. But everyone has a voice and a right to be heard. Obviously, you can't be so democratic, or afraid, that you are solely ruled by that. But people should feel confident they can tell you, that you will listen and, where applicable, that you will take it on board. If I were to draw one lesson from all of this it would be: know your consumers. And ensure you listen.

| **Rentokil Initial: Building a Strong Corporate Brand for Growth and Diversity**

SIR CLIVE THOMPSON, *chief executive*

When I arrived at Rentokil as chief executive in 1982, one of the first major decisions I had to make was on our branding strategy. We considered the two main schools of thought on branding. The first was that pioneered by companies such as Procter & Gamble: you have an individual brand representing a product category, and product categories that are sufficiently large to be able to justify advertising and promotional support at such a level that it makes a noise in the marketplace; where you have a number of well-known brands from a deliberately recessive parent company.

The second is that other group of companies which believe there are enormous benefits in having a relatively limited number of product/service categories covered by a single brand-name. Even if each individual activity is relatively small, you get the cumulative benefits of the brand and leverage from one activity to another. The downside is potential dilution of the impact of the brand, because it acts as an umbrella rather than being sharp and focused on the single activity.

In 1982 at Rentokil the approach to branding was inconsistent. While Rentokil was the name of the company, there were, in addition, a whole variety of individual brands, and the name 'Rentokil' was not commonly used throughout. This was probably the result of individual operating brands being perceived as stronger, and because managers of subsidiaries liked being independent and to develop their own brands. The second trend was a shortening of Rentokil, with the rather unfortunate word 'Rento' being associated with all sorts of different activities like Rento-Clean and Rento-Secure.

My view on joining Rentokil was that the activities we were likely to develop in industrial and commercial services were relatively small niche markets – ones where major advertising appropriation would not be affordable.

Another issue we had to debate was whether we could take a brand which had an excellent reputation for pest control, and stretch it to areas where, at first sight, customers might not feel comfortable.

We chose to go with a single brand-name and banned any subdivision of the brand. We felt that although we would be selling all our activities through separate sales and service operations, we could get a spin-off from satisfied customers for other areas of the business. We also felt we could develop the brand internationally.

My view is that to some extent you can take almost any brand, almost any name and, if the commitment is deep enough and the application is over a sufficiently long period of time, you will get to where you want to be.

Origins of the brand

Rentokil has come a long way from its roots. Back in 1920, a Professor Lefroy developed a chemical called 'endocil' for use in killing deathwatch beetles in Westminster Hall. He wanted to create a name for the generic chemical which he could register, and played around with letters until he came up with 'Rentokil'.

At around the same time a company called British Ratin emerged, which produced a rat poison called 'Ratin'. Just after the Second World War it acquired Rentokil. I like to think of the board of the newly combined company sitting down and having deep discussions about which of these two fine names they would use for the company. I suspect they made the right decision by a short head.

By the early 1980s, Rentokil was a relatively low-profile pest control and wood preservative specialist. Over the last fifteen years, through a combination of organic growth and acquisition, Rentokil Initial (as it was renamed in 1996) has become a blue-chip multinational with 140,000 employees in forty countries, and sales of £3 billion. When it was floated on the London Stock Exchange in 1969 it was capitalized at £12.5 million. That figure today is approximately £6.5 billion.

We operate in a range of services under the brand headings of Hygiene and Cleaning Services; Distribution and Plant Services; Personnel Services; Pest Control; Property Services and Security. We see ourselves very much as an industrial and commercial service company, with our markets driven by outsourcing of blue-collar activities on the one hand, and on the other by the demand by employers for an improved and/or sustained environment for their employees.

A virtuous circle

Our objective has been to create a virtuous circle. We provide a quality of service in industrial and commercial activities under the same brand-name, so that a customer satisfied with one Rentokil Initial service is potentially a satisfied customer for another. We give one operation the customer list from another, so that a Rentokil Initial sales person for pest control, for example, has a list of Rentokil Initial customers for tropical plants.

Although it was considered somewhat odd at the time, one of the reasons we moved into tropical plants was in fact to help put the brand in front of decision-makers. Our service people maintaining the plants go in through the front door and are visible to the customer. This contrasts with pest control where no one really notices unless we fail.

Over time, we have carefully developed and extended the brand by focusing on our core competence. We see this as our ability to carry out high quality services on other people's premises through well-recruited, well-trained and motivated staff. We focus on industrial commercial services as distinct from domestic and residential services. However, and this might seem like a contradiction, having decided we want to enter an activity, we don't always consider as a prime requirement whether the brand-name is perfectly applicable. We would like it to be, and if we work hard, we can often persuade ourselves that it is.

Having said that, even we have to admit that there are some areas where the name 'Rentokil' clearly would not be applicable, such as funeral services or homes for the elderly. Still, that in itself would not have stopped us going into those areas had we chosen to. It would just have been more difficult. For example, we bid for several major catering businesses, Sutcliffe and Gardner Merchant specifically, a few years ago. Although our name would certainly not at first sight have been appropriate here, this consideration was secondary to it being the right activity in terms of our core competence.

I have often said that the name 'Rentokil' is not the most favourable – Initial has many advantages over it. The word 'Initial' is a positive one – an individual's signature of approval – and it means first. Rentokil conjures up immediate negatives, but we work to transcend that by emphasizing what the brand represents. The brand stands for honesty, reliability, consistency, integrity and technical leadership.

Brand expansion

One of the main reasons we acquired the much larger BET services group in April 1996, for £2.2 billion, was to incorporate the Initial brand within our activities. Initial was a strong textile services company acquired by BET in the early 1980s, and was allowed to develop as the subsidiary's management considered appropriate. The Initial brand offered strong prospects for international growth along the lines on which we developed Rentokil. Initial would stand alongside Rentokil as a brand, and ultimately as an international brand.

The company is called 'Rentokil Initial' to make it quite clear to the observer that these two great brands, Rentokil and Initial, come from the house of Rentokil Initial. The house of Rentokil

Initial will have the same personality but it will be slightly amended according to the service activity involved, because we have also split our activities between the two brands.

Ideally, we would like to have the one brand, but the spread of activities is so great now, that to try and extend a single brand over too many businesses does risk diluting the impact and weakening the power of the original brand. And as I said before, the name 'Rentokil' isn't one that lends itself well to some activities. For example, we have bought a number of security companies and in some of the American states we would have a problem registering the name 'Rentokil' for security services, for obvious reasons. In cases like these, we will be able to use 'Initial' instead.

Having acquired over 200 companies in the last ten years or so, many of which have had strong local, national or even regional brands, we have had extensive experience of changing brand-names to Rentokil. The arguments that are put forward by the employees of those companies usually concentrate on the problems they feel they will have in the marketplace if they eliminate the original brand-name. But, in practice, most of the problems are in the minds of the employees. It is more a concern about losing independence – a perception of being submerged beneath a larger company, of being a division of a company rather than a company in its own right.

We have had to face the same challenges in picking up the Initial brand, which is a relatively small part of BET, and saying that certain companies will now be called Initial and others will be called Rentokil. In the case of Rentokil employees, their reaction was to wonder why they had to adopt the name 'Initial' when Rentokil had won the battle. So we put out the message that this was a new company that nobody had been part of for more than a few months. We were all equal and no one had an inside track. Rentokil employees might have thought this was unfair, but former BET employees thought it entirely fair.

Central control, local implementation

Corporate strategy is set and controlled by the centre, although the head office is lean and has few of the usual staff functions like marketing and personnel. We decide which activities we wish to be involved in, where, and what are the development priorities. There is no doubt that the corporate, marketing and thereby brand strategy has to be one and the same, and be centred round a focus on customers.

We operate through an extensive network of about 1,200 branches. A typical branch consists of between forty and seventy people and is run as a profit centre. The fact that each branch might have only several hundred customers encourages attention to detail in terms of quality and customer relationships, but also of cost control.

Above branch level, area managers cover four to five branches, and they in turn report to the general managers of their divisions, such as healthcare or pest control. Those general managers are answerable to the national managing directors, who report to the regional managing directors, who answer to headquarters. We have the same structure and the same organization covering each activity, wherever we are in the world.

We have fairly tight central control over presentation. In terms of an individual activity like pest control, security, tropical plants or textile services, we have marketing people who are close to the general managers of each division in each country. So the tactical promotion or advertising support of any individual service activity is done within the country and within that division, although those tactics have to conform to the presentational demands and integrity of the brand. There is therefore central strategic control, but within this narrow framework there is room for broad tactical enterprise.

Because of the nature of our markets and because we have a sharp concentration on cost control, we tend to use promotional techniques such as direct marketing which are entirely appropriate and moreover can be justified financially in the short term. There is no central advertising budget because if headquarters was seen to be splashing money around, people elsewhere in the organization would ask why. Also, unlike consumer products companies, we are not working through a distributive channel where you are not directly in contact with the end consumer, and where it can be hard to correct misapprehensions of the brand. Most of our contact is through direct mail or face-to-face so we can talk to our customers direct.

In any industry there are two requirements to achieve action: a decision and its implementation. In the oil industry, for example, the quality of a decision, such as where you put a refinery or a judgement as to what the price of crude oil will be in five years' time, has an enormous impact on the organization. The quality of the implementation has only to be reasonable to be acceptable.

In a business like ours, on the other hand, decisions are relatively simple. If you get them wrong, the results are grey rather than black and white. Implementation, however, is crucial. It determines success. What is important in our business are the people, the speed and the determination with which you carry out that implementation. That is why Rentokil Initial is such a disciplined and systematic organization. One of our greatest strengths is the quality of our implementation.

We have to keep a careful eye on the many ideas suggested by our employees. If someone comes up with a bright idea – and it is the people at the customer interface who have bright ideas, not people like me sitting in ivory towers – we evaluate whether it is potentially applicable around the world. We won't go any further if it isn't. We prefer to be technical leaders, operate to 85 per cent of the market opportunity and manage it properly.

However, sometimes our very culture can make this hard to control. People who work for Rentokil Initial are straightforward and action-oriented and they like recognition. Also, because we move people around, we are a closely-linked international company. For example, someone in Australia has a great idea about tropical plant maintenance and is allowed to test it, then he tells others around the world about it, who pick up the idea before it has been centrally agreed that it should be implemented on a broader scale.

The problem is that you don't know how long it can take to establish if something is a good idea or not, and it varies for different activities and different countries.

Getting the brand to travel

As we developed the brand internationally through the 1980s, we did not impose brand regulations as thoroughly as we should have done. What began to happen was similar to what happens to many companies as they develop internationally. There was an interpretation of how the brand should be projected in the individual countries, and it was very much in terms of the fashion or culture or sheer belief of the individuals who were running the businesses at that time. So, by the mid-1980s, we had to decide which way to go. One way was to understand and adapt our services and branding to the local culture, fashions, creeds and so on. The other was to be quite dogmatic and agree on the benefits of international branding in terms of consistent presentation of the brand throughout the world, even though that might not be ideal in terms of the local market.

We chose the second route of international branding and we devised strict rules about how to present the brand. Before we acquired Initial our colours were red and white. So all our customers saw Rentokil people getting out of vans which looked the same everywhere in the world: white with the name 'Rentokil' in red, and the Royal Warrant, which is a strong part of our corporate identity. We decided that all our services would be presented both in terms of marketing and technical aspects in the same way, irrespective of the country in which we operated.

We do not allow any modifications. As a result, we accept that we may only appeal to 85 to 90 per cent of the market. But we see the benefits of consistency worldwide, including the ability to transfer people from country to country.

There are benefits also for a number of our customers, many of whom are international, such as general managers of hotels and hospitality outlets who, if they have used Rentokil in one country can expect Rentokil to operate in the same way in another country. Also, it means we know that if we have a problem in one country, we can probably resolve it quite swiftly because we have handled it elsewhere. We have found that these are great advantages, therefore we are not prepared to amend the presentation of the brand or the technical presentation of the product. We see ourselves very much as a McDonald's or Coca-Cola. We hope there will be a large proportion of the market which will welcome this approach.

Geographically we describe ourselves not as 'global' but as 'international'. Global to me means operating in every country in the world. We specifically set out to operate in the major developed economies of the world, which are represented by the three economic groupings of North America, Europe and Asia Pacific, because the demands for our services only really exist in developed or fast developing economies. Although many of our services are hygiene-related and standards of hygiene are often very poor in developing countries, they still come way down their list of priorities.

Cultural unity

There are two things which business schools usually associate with a company's success: strategy and culture. We believe that our culture is more mid-Atlantic than British, and certainly not American. It is somewhere in between. We applaud and recognize success and do not tolerate failure. We recognize and reward the individual. We have been able to superimpose our culture upon European, North American and South-East Asian countries, where local cultures can be very different.

We have of course faced certain challenges. Some of our major problems culturally have been in continental Europe, where there are probably more cultures than in any other part of the world and where, perhaps for historic reasons, people adhere strongly to their culture. In North America, on the other hand, there is an enormous need for success. Our experience is that North Americans are more than happy to accept the challenging targets and budgets we set but, if they fail to achieve them, they simply ignore the targets and declare to themselves, their friends and their colleagues that they are a success and that the targets were irrelevant. Whereas in Asia, the issue of pride is so important that people are very wary of accepting targets which are in any way challenging for fear of failure. For them, being seen to achieve success is very important and they are not prepared to change the rules.

To say we have handled all these issues without difficulty would be wrong. It varies according to the prevailing circumstances in a certain business at a certain time. But I think, by and large, we have been successful at bringing people together by transferring people from country to country, particularly at middle management levels. It would be surprising if you were able to tell the difference between Rentokil people from different countries, apart from the way they look physically. There is definitely a Rentokil, and now a Rentokil Initial, way.

Rentokil Initial is quite a military organization in many ways. In other companies, discussion of decisions can play a big role, and if people don't agree with something they often don't wholeheartedly buy into it. At Rentokil Initial, if the organization has decided to do something, people will do it to the best of their abilities. If they can't buy into that culture they don't stay, or simply don't join us in the first place.

We frequently say there are two ways of joining Rentokil Initial. One is to join as a graduate in your early twenties, and be trained around the world in different activities. The other is to be acquired. The latter brings cultural challenges, of course. But our success results from employees knowing the Rentokil Initial way.

A branded future

We will continue to think long and hard about what we are good at and concentrate on a relatively few number of activities. We don't in any way see ourselves as being a conglomerate, because we can transfer our know-how in terms of management and culture from activity to activity in the same way, with the only difference being technical aspects. The customer base is essentially the same, and the styles and management controls are the same, so we are a single company in practice, providing a variety of products or services.

We are probably unusual in that most service companies have not really concentrated on branding, or attempting to leverage more than one service under an umbrella brand. Similarly there are no companies comparable to Rentokil Initial: operating in a number of service markets and in many geographical areas. Comparison of performance is difficult. We therefore benchmark ourselves against ourselves, branch by branch, country by country, activity by activity. The competition varies enormously, from large companies in some activities, to very small ones in others. Pick up any Yellow Pages and you will see from ten to hundreds of competing companies in different areas. But the reason there are few credible competitors is probably because the industrial commercial service industry is relatively new.

That will change, however. I believe that the service industry will consolidate and grow, so there will be a number of major international players in the next fifteen to twenty years, very much in the way manufacturers of consumer products grew from the 1920s through to the 1950s.

Concentrating on branding has definitely been of major benefit to us for two reasons. First there is that virtuous circle of delivering high-quality service and then building a reputation, and using that reputation to move into other areas. Second, there is the leverage of the brand which acts as reassurance to customers that those other services will be delivered with the same quality as the original service they received.

We see our future as becoming progressively more international while concentrating on growth in the three key geographical regions we have identified. Our goal over the next few years is for the brand to have the same recognition, the same strength and the same image wherever we operate.

9 | Hewlett-Packard: Keeping the Brand Vision Alive

JOS BRENKEL, *director of Personal Systems Group,*
European Marketing Centre, Hewlett-Packard

In 1937 two twenty-six-year-old engineers called David Packard and William Hewlett started working together in a one-car garage in Palo Alto, California. At first they made just about any sort of electrical equipment to survive, producing products such as bowling alley sensors and a shock machine for weight reduction. Their first big sale was of eight audio oscillators, which were electronic test instruments, to Walt Disney Studios to use in developing the movie *Fantasia*. In 1939, the Hewlett-Packard company was born.

As the company grew, so did the views of the founders about what the company was for. It was not just about making money, although that was essential to survive and grow. What the company was in essence, they felt, was a group of people who were assembled to do something collectively which they could not do individually. In that way they could make a unique contribution to society. By 1957, they had formalized these ideas into a set of corporate objectives, organizational values and effective strategies and practices called the 'HP Way', which is about profit and growth, but equally about customers, employees, good management and citizenship.

Brand values

The 'HP Way' is still the cornerstone of the way we operate today, although we are now a $38.4 billion global company which designs, manufactures and services electronic products and systems for measurement, computing and communication. The corporate culture has been defined by the corporate objectives and values, and reflects the company's basic character and personality. That in turn has defined what the brand stands for: reliability and quality, being somewhat conservative, no matter where it is in the world or what business it is in. The values we have established are the bedrock of the organization, our bible if you like. They encompass trusting and respecting individuals; focusing on a high level of achievement and contribution; conducting business with uncompromising integrity; achieving common objectives through teamwork; encouraging flexibility and innovation.

That brand image is strong not because of rigid rules imposed from the top. It has more to do with the fact that the brand, with its roots in test and measurement, has always been associated with reliability and quality, whether from instrumentation, to the first hand-held calculator through to medical equipment, computers and printers. Unlike Sony, for example, as an organization we have not gone out of our way to create one brand, because we are a very decentralized company. But the perception of what we stand for, across what is a wide range of products, is very consistent and has arisen from both culture and behaviour. We have had over fifty years to build up values based on our people, customer support and service, the products, innovation and active citizenship.

If Hewlett-Packard were a person, our research shows that he or she, as in some of the categories like printers, would be a reliable friend, someone you know you can ask to do something, and it will be done really well. And if he makes a mistake, he will do everything he can to fix that. He is someone who will probably be quite conservative when it comes to dress, middle to upper class, neither very rich nor very poor; also, someone who is innovative in his or her thinking but not exceptionally creative. In contrast, our research has shown that an Apple person would wear very modern dress, be very creative, with lots of ideas, but would not necessarily bring all those ideas into being. An Apple person probably talks before he thinks.

Keeping the global/local balance

We are a global company that tries to maintain a good mix between what needs to be centralized and what needs to be localized. Centralization means cost saving. Localization means being closer to your customer. Our entrepreneurial flexibility is fostered by the decentralized business units which have a fair degree of autonomy. The marketing structure is relatively fluid, with marketing being done by product divisions, by marketing centres such as the European Marketing Centre in Grenoble, and by channel marketing people. However, because wholesalers often take more than one product, there is an increasing stress on taking an integrated approach that cuts across product lines. So the regional marketing centres act as a bridge between specific product markets and their resellers and the Hewlett-Packard product divisions, as well as devising pan-regional activities.

There is also a corporate marketing communications network at headquarters and in the regions, which puts together guidelines and training to make sure we have the same look and feel in marketing. However, added complexity comes from the fact that we work through so many distribution channels. For example, if a business unit does an advertisement for a product, and the channel partner does one for it as well, there can be a problem because the unit is advertising to create awareness and preference and build the brand, while the channel partner is aiming for traffic and sales. As a result, there is a danger that Hewlett-Packard will be perceived as two different companies. We have to make sure that the money invested in the campaign by both parties goes in the right direction, which means carrying the corporate guidelines into the channel. We have an advantage here in that we are used to working across divisions, so we need to treat the resellers like another division of the company.

Where we do have stringent rules is regarding the logo, which is made up of a lozenge with the letters 'hp' inside, and the words 'Hewlett-Packard' alongside the lozenge. This system has been in operation since 1989, when our then worldwide marketing director, Richard Alberding, decided that some fairly fundamental changes had to be made because of the inconsistencies around the world, with parts of the company using different colours and different typefaces. He hired a design agency which came up with a much more systematic approach to the logo, creating a grid-like model which could cover all situations where the logo might be used, from packaging and literature to business cards, as well as modifying the logo itself for only the eighth time in its history. The modular design means there is some flexibility on how to apply it.

These new mandatory rules admittedly came as a bit of a shock to what is such an entrepreneurial culture, but, with training, people began to see the advantages of a system with templates allowing speed and cost saving, and where there was still room for creativity. With hindsight, this can be seen as the start of our becoming more conscious of our trademark as a brand.

Where we have not been centrally driven is in terms of corporate branding. For instance, we have never done corporate advertising and probably never will. There are a number of reasons for that. The philosophy of our co-founder Dave Packard was 'just be'. In other words, don't advertise your values, just live them.

Also, we have the example of IBM, which told people year in and year out that it made big mainframe computers. But that set its feet in concrete and made it difficult for IBM to encompass new offerings, which is dangerous in such a fast-moving market like high technology.

What we have increasingly realized, however, is the crucial role that branding and brand management should play in an industry noted more for being technology- than marketing-driven. A few years ago, therefore, we set up a worldwide brand equity taskforce, made up of representatives from across the businesses, which has been investigating just what the brand stands for, and how far it can stretch. This has been spurred on by our move into developing products for the home, where, although we are well-established in printers, we have had to begin to understand how easily the perception of the brand can move to other products like home PCs or digital cameras, or whether it might need some adjustments.

Staying nimble

We feel that one of our greatest advantages over the past fifty years has been our ability to move into new areas. For example, we were first known for instrumentation. That was followed over the years by a range of new products, such as mini-computers, calculators and touch-screen personal computers. Then we developed our business in workstations, then printers. We have become one of the world's biggest medical equipment suppliers. We are now one of the leading brands in home PCs, and plan to extend the consumer side with a raft of new consumer devices such as those for digital imaging. Tomorrow it will be something else. So if we positioned ourselves strongly within an individual product category, it could hinder us when we want to move into some of the new product areas that technology will create in the future. And we will be going into all sorts of new places. Innovation is crucial: each year we spend about 7 per cent of our net revenue on R & D, and more than half the company's audit in 1996 was for products introduced during the previous two years.

We like to stay flexible. We were considered late in entering the PC market, both for professional and personal users. In fact, we entered the market for consumer PCs in only 1995 with a multimedia range called Pavilion. We are now in the top five personal PC companies, while we are in the top three in terms of the large corporate PC arena. We feel we have the resources and patience to get things right even if we enter a market like PCs later than the competition.

We decided to enter the home PC market for a number of reasons. Home PCs are one of the fastest-growing segments, and one where we felt we could exploit our reputation for reliability and quality and the good-will people feel towards the brand because of their experience with our printers. Also, because the home is where new technologies like multi-media go first these days, we realized we needed to be active in domestic technologies so we can be ready to feed those technologies into the business sector. In addition, it would give us economies of scale across all our activities.

Redefining the brand

There are big challenges to face in the home PC market. First, you have to create a brand personality that consumers can associate with. The Hewlett-Packard brand-name is strong in professional and business markets, where the emphasis is on product features and technology. When you move into the home, however, you have to begin to build up brand awareness in the consumer's mind. The big problem is that in terms of branding, the home PC market overall is still relatively immature. What image do people have of Compaq or Packard-Bell, for example? There have been exceptions: Apple was good at exploiting its image of youth and creativity. And Intel has been very successful at branding itself in the consumer's mind with its 'Intel inside' campaign. But most high-technology companies are not that good at branding. Many people still view PCs the way they think about their refrigerators – as relatively undifferentiated appliances.

However, as the market moves more to sophisticated multimedia PCs, and then to communication-oriented PCs, the scene will be more and more controlled by large retailers carrying, at the most, four or five brands from highly competent suppliers, with strong brand images and close relationships with Intel and Microsoft, and who are able to manufacture and support 'mass customized' products on a global basis.

So the brand equity taskforce has had to examine all the issues surrounding our brand and where it needs to go. One of its first steps was to document the core values that make up our brand equity. A branding consultancy was hired a year or so back to look at all the volumes of research that had been carried out by our marketing people. That meant trawling through over ninety different research projects to see what was consistent in terms of the brand values that went with the Hewlett-Packard logo and whether, if you were starting afresh, you would choose those brand values for positioning the brand in the home.

Hewlett-Packard as mentor

It was found that the core values were basically good ones. People said to leave the logo alone, that its assurance of trust, quality and reliability should be constant, no matter how flashy we might make the product design or packaging. So we have decided that we should build on the positioning of being seen as people who can sort you out better than anyone else – as a mentor.

Of course, you have to be careful that you don't move a whole corporation based on a few focus groups. But the findings help to show us that as we move more into the home, if we want to crack new markets we have to adapt without moving 180 degrees away from what we do now. We want to build on that aura of professional expertise in a more positive sense, and one that stays perfectly in tune with our business-to-business stance. So it is more tweaking than outright changing, shifting from the perception that we are an understated leader to one of being a more pro-active leader.

Adding sparkle to the brand image

We do need to give the brand image a lift for domestic markets. Brand mapping has shown us that we need to consider adding some new values that will allow us to become more established with consumers. So we have been considering what sort of adaptations we have to make to Hewlett-Packard's core values.

One approach is to adapt our marketing techniques and learn from consumer goods companies, including hiring people with consumer marketing experience.

Partnering is another route: the printer business has entered into a number of joint promotions with companies such as Disney to run their interactive software on a new home colour printer. That creates a powerful combination of brand values, since such partnerships bring a sense of adventure, of liveliness and fun in terms of good, clean, family fun. In time, as we build up volumes for the

PCs, partnerships with consumer goods companies could be the way to strengthen brand awareness and enable Hewlett-Packard to become more established in the home. We have to change our way of thinking and learn to associate our brand with children and families, and not with business customers. Design is also important. We probably need to move from being seen as functional and practical to being seen as appealing and practical.

Advertising is another way to add a sense of colour to our positioning. We have run two executions for the Pavilion in the United States which have also travelled to the UK, and which illustrate what we are trying to do. One centres on sibling rivalry. A teenage boy steals his sister's diary, and then she catches him playing shadow guitar in his bedroom, wearing some very strange boxer shorts. She takes a Polaroid picture of him, runs downstairs, and enters it into the Pavilion through the photo scanner. When she demands her diary back, and he refuses to give it, she sends the photo to a girl he likes. Then his father comes in and sees the photo on the screen and wonders what is going on. The advertising is about humour and family, but it also shows the product features.

In another execution, an unfit, overweight man is running a marathon and is last in at nine hours, twenty-three minutes and fifty-six seconds. Someone takes a picture of him, which he takes home, scans into the Pavilion, and changes the nine hours to two hours. This is also about humour, showing that the HP Pavilion allows you to be creative and do what you want to do.

Sponsorship will help broaden awareness among a much bigger mass audience. In the UK, for example, we sponsor Tottenham Hotspur football club. We are also involved in Formula One motor racing. In one of the largest sponsorship deals we have ever done, we have become the official IT hardware and maintenance supplier to the organizing committee of the 1998 World Cup in France. We will be providing more than seventy-five products lines, including PCs and servers, storage devices, notebook and palmtop computers, laser and inkjet printers, scanners and some medical and chemical-measurement equipment. Virtually every piece of computer hardware will have the Hewlett-Packard brand on it. It is estimated that up to 37 billion viewers around the world will watch the tournament.

Creating power brands

A brand is something that has values beyond what the product does and it is customers who bestow the brand attributes, who buy it and recommend it. It takes time to create real brands. What we have in Hewlett-Packard are probably only two power or sub-brands, the LaserJet and DeskJet range of printers. But even here the Hewlett-Packard name adds value: store testing has shown that if the mother brand-name were removed from the range, we could lose up to half our sales.

What we do have are strong product names, like Vectra in professional PCs and the 'Jets'. As well as DeskJet and LaserJet, there are DesignJet large-format plotters and printers, ScanJet scanners, OfficeJet printer–fax–copiers, and CopyJet colour printer–copiers. These are not yet brands, although their ranges have a family name and feel. There are some inconsistencies, which is not surprising given our history of decentralized organization. The scale is huge: in fact we have 24,000 product names and numbers!

We have examined whether there are any issues arising from being seen either as HP or Hewlett-Packard. We found that half of the respondents in a survey know us as HP and half as Hewlett-Packard, but, surprisingly, there is no conflict. People seem to feel comfortable with either. So we currently have no intention of settling on just HP or Hewlett-Packard.

The HP Way

The pace of change in this industry means that we have to restructure constantly to deal with market challenges. We are always looking at our customer base, our channels, at products coming through and asking ourselves how can we get closer to our customers. We always have to be on our toes so that when we decide to move, we move quickly. That is the personality of the company. We constantly challenge ourselves to see if we can do something better even if there is nothing wrong. And that means we have to hire people who like change, but who understand that change must never affect product quality, or compromise our core values. So Hewlett-Packard hires a certain sort of person, one who can fit in with our culture. There is definitely a recognizable HP person. No matter where you go, in whichever country, HP people are the same both in appearances and in the way they react. Even the offices look the same, both inside and out. We once hired a manager for Italy who could not speak Italian because he did not need to. What could almost be called an ideology creates a corporate glue, because to succeed in Hewlett-Packard you have to buy into the values set out in the HP Way. Our co-founder Bill Hewlett defined that as 'the policies and actions that flow from the belief that men and women want to do a good job, a creative job, and that if they are provided the proper environment they will do so'.

Nevertheless, trying to cement together this very diverse company, with its 112,000 employees, can still be a challenge. One way is through our extensive Intranet system, which is beginning to act as a central nervous system. We also promote a consistent look to our Website, which has over 40,000 pages. However, the process of achieving consistency is not always straightforward. Before we could get the Website design rules finalized, Germany had to get its site up and running in time for an important fair. We let them create their site with the promise that they would conform to the guidelines as soon as they were out. But in the meantime, Taiwan and Australia had copied Germany's approach. So we have to stay on our corporate toes, although there is a lot of self-policing too. This is important as it is very easy to dilute the brand identity if it becomes fragmented.

Each individual business unit benchmarks itself against others in its field. In the personal products group we frequently benchmark ourselves against Compaq, whereas the printer division will benchmark itself against companies like Canon. It is interesting that there is no one company to benchmark ourselves against as a whole. If we did have a common competitor, that would be one of the biggest risks we could face. But we do not.

The impact of the Internet

The information explosion is going to change the way every person lives and works. Consider how quickly the Internet has made an impact. Companies now put their Website address on their ads, whether they are for washing powder or cars, so how you brand yourself through the Net will become critically important.

Our goal is to be at the forefront of this by becoming known as the leading systems integrator. Lewis Platt, the chairman of Hewlett-Packard, has said that increasingly customers are saying to him that they need help managing the chaos of so many diverse products and systems. This has resulted from the fragmentation of the high-technology industry over the years into horizontal layer of specialist companies, compared to previous times which were characterized by big, vertically-integrated giants like IBM. This proliferation of products and systems can make gluing IT systems together a corporate nightmare.

Hewlett-Packard is one of the few companies with a rich enough ecology of technologies and products to be able to help companies tie it all together. But gaining recognition means we have to work on our image as a highly branded integrator, the prime contractor who can tie the systems together, whether it is systems in large corporations or providing a small business with an instant office. The core computing strategy will be a practical approach in helping companies reach beyond their corporate environments, to create IT solutions that encompass business partners, suppliers, remote workers and customers. This will also serve as an internal unifying force, since all divisions will be looking in the same direction. So even if we do not do corporate advertising, because the different parts of the company will be focusing on this 'bundling' objective, we will be speaking with one voice.

Hewlett-Packard wants to be a brand that is going to be very well known in every sense. Currently, if you asked a child what Sony means to them, you would probably be given some sort of image. That is not the case yet with Hewlett-Packard. Over time we want that to change. But that does not mean radically changing the personality. What we want is for that personality to be known by more people in more environments.

10 | Cadbury Ltd: Harnessing the Strengths of the Corporate Brand

ALAN PALMER, *marketing director*

In the UK, Cadbury enjoys a 30 per cent share of all chocolate sales and a 50 per cent share of moulded chocolate bars, and the Cadbury brand is believed to be worth an estimated £1.3 billion in the UK, compared with Coca-Cola (UK only) at £1.2 billion and Walkers at £500 million. The company's chocolate products span a range of sub-categories headed by its so-called 'CDM Mega Brand' moulded chocolate bars: Cadbury Dairy Milk, Fruit & Nut and Whole Nut. Other categories include chocolate assortments, such as Milk Tray; 'countlines', such as Wispa, Time Out and Crunchie; and bagged chocolates, such as Buttons. Cadbury has also developed sub-brands for particular occasions, such as Cadbury Creme Egg – a product available only between New Year and Easter each year.

Cadbury has become the largest single product brand in Britain. However, its horizons have broadened in recent years. Although it is determined to retain its UK market dominance and continue to develop the market through product innovation, it also aims to develop its international business significantly. Cadbury is already one of the top world chocolate businesses, alongside Ferrero, Hershey, Mars, Nestlé and Philip Morris.

A flair for indulgence born from a Quaker heritage

Cadbury is a consumer brand which is directly shaped and coloured by the history of its parent company. The essence of the brand can be defined as 'Cadbury-ness', and it has been built over more than a hundred years. Father John Cadbury and, later, the brothers George and Richard, set up business in Birmingham in 1824, originally dealing in tea and coffee. The family were Quakers who, like many of their contemporaries, established their own commercial enterprises because of restrictions they faced in terms of education, and career. The brothers developed an interest in cocoa, initially as a beverage although they subsequently developed the manufacturing of chocolate confectionery in 1847. The social ideals of the Cadbury family created an environment and a corporate integrity that has provided the platform for a highly successful business and consumer brand. These values are difficult to distil individually, but collectively they represent care for employees, consumers and the family. Such social concerns have consistently shaped how our staff, our business partners and our consumers view us.

Cadbury had to compete in the nineteenth century with several hundred other confectionery companies – including Rowntree and Fry – and its early success was attributable to many management qualities and insights more familiar to today's business environment. Sales and marketing (although not described as such then) were in place at an early stage, as ledgers illustrate. In 1905, for example, the 'Introducers Department' spent £41,694 and 10 shillings, of which £20,000 went on advertising and signwriting; and, from the remainder, £15 and 4 shillings on customer urns! Many of today's Cadbury brands can trace their history back to 1905 when Cadbury Dairy Milk was first launched.

It is worth noting that much of the early development of the business and its product range was done under the umbrella of the Cadbury brand, with products identified by descriptive names such as Dairy Milk chocolate, Milk Tray assorted, Drinking Chocolate prefaced by the Cadbury logo, which first appeared in block letter form, and subsequently the Cadbury script, from 1928. Other Cadbury brand icons, such as the colour purple and the glass and a half of milk device date from a similar era. The combination of these icons evokes a very powerful consumer association with Cadbury's chocolate.

Over subsequent years, a focus on building strong, consumer-relevant values evolved. Coupons were introduced in 1906, gifts in the 1930s, even a Children's Club which was specifically designed to restore customer loyalty after the end of the Second World War. Once rationing ended, the chocolate market grew rapidly and sales of Cadbury, the market leader, exploded.

There can be no question that the arrival of commercial television, and its ability to capture the attention of a mass audience, became an important milestone in the development of the confectionery market, and more specifically the chocolate brands. With a history of brand communication from posters, the colour and black-and-white press, and the cinema, suddenly it became possible to add new dimensions to the sub-brands, to the extent that they developed even stronger identities than that of the Cadbury brand. Famous advertising campaigns for Dairy Milk ('award yourself a CDM'), Fruit & Nut (Fruit & Nutcase), Flake ('Only the crumbliest . . .') and Milk Tray (Man in Black) started to define how people viewed the brands from both an emotional and a rational perspective.

The medium defined the message. However, it also offered opportunities to any of the bigger brands in the market to break through and create a strong identity. Cadbury, which enjoyed a clear market leadership in the 1960s and early 1970s, found its position increasingly threatened as some new entrants, such as Rowntree's Yorkie, achieved spectacular success through the strength of their powerful advertising and product positioning. The nuclear family, in the 1960s and 1970s, sat in front of the television revelling in its novelty, and absorbing the information that was beamed at them. How much things change!

Commercial TV also enabled the company to segment its market, leading to the development of a larger number of new products which established brand ubiquity in the minds of consumers. The company's reputation for the quality of its products, and the product benefits communicated within its advertising and related marketing activities, have made a significant contribution to the Cadbury brand. Today, as the only surviving company to put its name as an umbrella across its entire portfolio, Cadbury has a unique competitive and discriminating advantage. From the consumer's perspective, Cadbury = chocolate = Cadbury, is a truism which we sought to strengthen by creating a feeling of 'Cadburyness' in much of the imagery and activity built into the brand programmes.

The 'master brand' approach

Our clear market positioning has come about through a combined process of evolution and managed change. Two factors in particular have shaped our thinking in recent years. One has been the issue of corporate versus consumer branding; the other has been diversification. Throughout the 1960s, Cadbury diversified into a number of food sectors – cocoa beverages, chocolate biscuits and others – all marketed by Cadbury Foods.

The merger of Cadbury Brothers with Schweppes in 1969 to create Cadbury Schweppes Plc brought a significant increase in the food brand range; to accommodate them a stand-alone division, Cadbury Typhoo, was created. Inevitably, the development of that business generated new brands, such as Marvel, Smash, Soya Choice and others, that were marketed under the house brand of Cadbury. Research at the time endorsed this strategy, as consumers fed back the view that Cadbury provided quality reassurance. At that time it appeared to give the business the appropriate critical mass necessary to deal with the fast consolidating retail grocery market.

During the 1980s, particularly the early to mid-'80s, the development of corporate brands became a particularly fashionable theme for a variety of reasons. Among food companies particularly, a series of contested takeovers, and the emerging trend of seeking to capture some of the value of the brand equity on the balance sheet, were sufficient justification. For others, media inflation was beginning to undermine the traditional support that had sustained brand portfolios, and thus it had appeared to be a legitimate economy of scale to try to motivate the consumer at the umbrella brand level. But for many it proved to be a leap too far. The logic of binding a corporate message on to consumer brand communication – often seeking to contemporize the corporate brand more than the individual portfolio brands – does seem, with the benefit of hindsight, to be a little thin.

By the start of the 1980s, there were growing concerns that the dilution of investment in the Cadbury brand, and the growth of some competitor chocolate franchises, needed to be addressed. A detailed overhaul was undertaken of all the aspects of the brand portfolio, the quality of the product range and, of course, the communication strategy. It was clear that the gold standards for the company's leading brand Dairy Milk needed to be re-established, and all the elements of packaging, pricing and product quality were interrogated. The advertising agency Foote Cone and Belding (FCB) developed a television campaign that ran from 1980 to 1982 called 'This is Cadbury', which set out to reinforce many of the core chocolate values embodied in the brand. The agency used techniques developed by Oxford Scientific Films to create stunning close-up imagery of 'chunks' and 'pouring milk'. It provided a new platform for the business, enabling the challenges – particularly from Rowntree's Yorkie – to be sloughed off. It gave a renewed sense of direction.

In 1986, the foods business Cadbury Typhoo Ltd was sold off to its management team and relaunched as Premier Brands. It is now part of Hillsdown Holdings. This proved to be the critical opportunity to remove the Cadbury name from a variety of previously Cadbury branded products that were not chocolate (such as Smash and Marvel). At a stroke the business refocused the Cadbury name back behind its core: chocolate confectionery, cocoa-based beverages and chocolate biscuits. Since that time, an active programme of franchising the Cadbury brand rather than organic development has taken the brand across a unique range of chocolate-based products in diverse categories from chilled desserts, through to frozen cakes and ice creams, instant beverages and even a liqueur.

The Cadbury brand is both the product brand and the corporate brand. At issue was to what extent we should communicate it as one or the other. Like any organization, we identified both corporate and consumer values. Corporate values were rational: quality and reputation. By the mid-1980s, we were running communications activities about the success of Cadbury Schweppes as an organization in addition to the brands themselves. In a fiercely competitive marketplace, you cannot afford to be complacent. We realized we had to refocus all our activities to ensure that we communicated in a consumer-relevant way. We refocused on the emotional values associated with the Cadbury name – associations with the family, children, fun and warmth. We evolved the 'working concept' of 'Cadburyness' and sought to increase the prominence of the Cadbury name, and its umbrella role for a diverse confectionery portfolio. The challenge was how to maintain a bridge between the desired corporate brand values and the essential warmth and vitality that is fundamental to successful growth.

It is interesting to contrast some of the successes and shortcomings of the initiatives in support of 'Cadburyness'. The biggest single frustration in the whole matter was the seeming inability to generate advertising of stature and effectiveness for the Cadbury Dairy Milk brand at the heart of this whole business. It had long been felt that the relationship between the brand 'Cadbury' and the brand 'Dairy Milk' was that they were one and the same. As a consequence, copy strategy and development always fell over the burden of trying to carry the aspirations and values of the broad-scale consumer brand Cadbury, at the same time as giving the diverse pack options with the Dairy Milk brand a sense of identity and role. Almost two decades of effort, with a number of agencies, and the brains and motivation of the business had generated advertising campaigns that registered only as acceptable on the advertising record.

A new model for the Cadbury brand and its relationship with the component brands in the portfolio was assembled, and it set out to establish a clear distinction between the Cadbury master brand, and the sub-brands that made up the portfolio.

The relationship between Cadbury, the master brand, and the Dairy Milk brand is clearly a dynamic one, where the values pass back and forth as if they were the blood supply between the heart and brain of a body. However, the relationship between Dairy Milk and the other sub-brands is more delicate. Hitherto it is a matter of record that the 'brands' alongside Dairy Milk, such as Fruit & Nut and Wholenut, were distinctive brands, but inspection today suggests that they are products of commercial television advertising, and are thus beneficiaries of strong advertising properties, as their buyer/consumer base overlaps heavily with Dairy Milk. It was therefore legitimate to create a Cadbury's Dairy Milk (CDM) megabrand, comprising the core Dairy Milk brand with its pure milk chocolate delivery, and added to that, Fruit & Nut and Wholenut (offering the taste and eating enjoyment of Dairy Milk but with added ingredients). It was a statement of the obvious maybe, but it explained many of the other dynamics of these sub-brands in very logical terms. The critical mass of the CDM megabrand placed it firmly at the front of the triumvirate of brands that define the chocolate confectionery market. These are CDM megabrand, Kit-Kat, and Mars Bar.

Today, Cadbury is the largest food brand in the British Isles linked by a single product, in this case chocolate. Consumers spend over £1.3 billion a year on brands bearing the Cadbury name. Cadbury Dairy Milk is the biggest brand in the chocolate market, both by volume and value; UK sales alone now exceed £230 million a year. The 'master brand' strategy has played a crucial role in achieving all of this, by re-establishing the Cadbury name centre-stage. This has not just been a cosmetic application of the Cadbury trademark on to any product containing chocolate. All recipes, including those for franchised products, are developed under the direction of Cadbury technical managers and seek to retain the essential (and unique) taste characteristics of Cadbury's Chocolate. This entire exercise is an example of how important it is for a business periodically to go back to its roots and to make sure the core elements responsible for its success are not being frittered away. Today, our sector leadership is the largest it has been in twenty years.

Fine-targeting a mass market

Confectionery enjoys between 98 and 99 per cent market penetration in the UK today. Total UK confectionery sales total around £4.9 billion. Chocolate accounts for around 70 per cent of this. Our audience is clearly mass market, but it is not a static one. Both chocolate and sugar sweets sales are steadily increasing by around 5 and 4 per cent a year. And the dynamics of the market are continually changing and evolving over time. One trend evident over the past decade, for example, has been that more confectionery is being bought by housewives as a larder item. Today, impulse purchases account for between 50 and 60 per cent of all confectionery sales. Another development has been the growth in purchases made for a particular occasion – Christmas and Easter, for example. We now have quite a specific map of the consumer market which sets out clusters of purchasing decisions. This ranges from snacking to hunger satisfaction, 'gifting' – be it a formal gift or an informal, small 'thank you' – to personal indulgence. Inevitably, some of these compete with other product sectors. In 'gifting', we compete with records, wine and flowers; in snacking we compete with soft drinks and crisps.

Today's chocolate market is therefore both sophisticated in brand make-up and complex in terms of consumer motivation. Purchase and consumption of chocolate is a balance of rational and emotional responses to the product. All confectionery brands carry an enormous mantle of emotional values. There are no models, but universal truths: such as the fact that people love chocolate and can anticipate the gratification they'll experience eating it. To a degree, science has tried to analyse the reasons for this and a number of theories have been put forward. But at the end of the day, it's about liking the taste and ease of access to the product.

The pattern of consumption is similar between boys and girls, but women have an exceptionally strong influence, purchasing nearly two-thirds of all confectionery, both for their own consumption and on behalf of the family. There is, however, a degree of life-stage influence on consumption in developed markets. The over-forties, for example, are influenced by different motivators than sixteen-to twenty-four-year-olds. Older consumers relate more to the traditions and the heritage of the brand and adopt a more thoughtful, planned approach to purchase. Younger consumers are more likely to impulse buy and purchase a broader repertoire of products.

Our marketing activities focus heavily on this latter age group. Our major challenge is to ensure that today's teens remain loyal to Cadbury into their forties, and beyond. That's why we have to support the Cadbury brand. It is easy to be seduced into the notion that commitment to a single product, like Fuse, carries equal weight to Cadbury. It does not.

Manufacturing marketing solutions

Strategically, our business has faced a number of important challenges and opportunities. First, the icons that Cadbury has established – chocolate and purple, the Cadbury logo and the glass and a half – were potent motivators but only if their individual strengths could be harnessed together. Second, functionally and psychologically, the role that chocolate plays for consumers is incredibly complex. Liberating these desires through advertising and brand development is difficult.

These challenges are set against a complex media environment with ever-increasing clutter – as more and more messages compete for consumers' attention – and media inflation. Once centre-stage in the early days of TV advertising, food and confectionery brands now find themselves overwhelmed with an increasing volume of marketing spend from financial services, retail and utilities. The differential between the UK's biggest TV spending brand, British Telecom which spends more than £90 million a year on TV advertising, and the biggest spending single confectionery brand, whose annual TV budget is a mere £4.5 million, says it all.

Cadbury took the view that there had to be a new approach. To increase the prominence of the Cadbury name, and its umbrella role for the diverse confectionery portfolio, the Cadbury endorsement was strengthened within the portfolio, using 'presence marketing' and sponsorship along with a unified endorsement strategy on packaging to provide visibility and saliency for the Cadbury trademark to complement the more targeted and specific communication that paid-for advertising could provide.

In the packaging arena, the Cadbury swatch was developed to bond the range of Countline brands more closely to the core moulded block range with a purple swatch and the Cadbury script. All the brand advertising was adapted to carry a 'tear strip' in purple, with the Cadbury logo in the end-frame corner.

A 'presence marketing' programme was devised to establish the Cadbury brand in a range of high-profile locations: volume leisure sites such as Alton Towers and the Natural History Museum, travel terminals such as airports and the Channel Tunnel, and shopping malls. The combination of an attractive location and a retailing unit provided a self-financing vehicle to draw consumers closer to the Cadbury brand. A charitable/cause-related association with Save the Children Fund set out to underpin some of the core values of social concern. When linked to sponsorship of the Cadbury Pantomime Season, which reached over 2.5 million people each year, and the Cadbury Strollerthon, involving over 20,000 charity walkers every year, this package of activities started to add texture and a more tangible bond to the brand. Meanwhile, the development of Cadbury World, the visitor attraction on the Bournville factory site, represented a hugely important piece to the jigsaw. With over half a million visitors each year, it provides an enduring bond between the visitor and Cadbury that is fundamentally stronger and more enduring than any advertising or promotional impact could be.

We also developed a more creative approach to using traditional UK media. An ideal opportunity arose with the chance to sponsor Britain's most popular soap opera, *Coronation Street* on ITV. The series celebrated its thirty-five years at the top of the British TV ratings. The association seemed logical – the coming together of two of the nation's favourites. With our £10 million sponsorship of *Coronation Street* – British TV's largest broadcast sponsorship to date – we have developed a range of marketing and promotional activities to support our association with the nation's best-loved soap.

Research confirms the effectiveness of this strategy. Seventy-one per cent of the population are aware of the association; viewers perceive it to be 'enjoyable' and 'appropriate' for Cadbury, and image enhancements for our brand have included improved perceptions of 'quality' and 'better taste' (source: Millward Brown/RSGB/Laser 1996). It has never been more important for food brands to cultivate a position of saliency, trust and relevance to their consumers.

Brand extensions

Ten years ago, I would have said the UK confectionery market was showing signs of saturation, and that the full portfolio was established. Yet, in the last decade we've seen the launch of many new brands. The market is unique in that it is still dominated by a very large number of brands that have been around for more than sixty years. The reason for this is the confectionery industry's skill in making their brands appear consistently relevant to today. Since the 1970s, one or two manufacturers have been able to develop new brands so effectively that today they are among the top twenty or thirty of all brands. As our understanding of the consumer map has expanded, we have filled in the gaps identified with new products which complement the existing portfolio. We have catered for snacking, for example, with the decline of formal meals. New product development is not only an engine for our own growth, it is an engine for industry growth.

Cadbury has launched many new brands over the past decade, driven by both technology and the developed understanding of consumer needs. Time Out was the result of unique technology which enabled flake to be put on to wafer. Whispa Gold was the result of a development which allowed aerated chocolate and caramel. Fuse, although not produced by a unique process, was a brand-new combination of ingredients. This resulted in Cadbury achieving a programme of NPD that was materially more successful than any of its competitors.

The road to new product development is littered, however, with projects that have failed. Few can remember such Cadbury brands from the 1970s: Aztec, Welcome, Rumba, Amazing Raisin. They failed not because they didn't taste nice, but because they weren't distinctive enough. It was, perhaps, a reflection that our understanding of the sector was limited. People like confectionery and are prepared to try new products. The issue is whether the new product is sufficiently distinctive to be quickly taken into a consumer's regular eating repertoire.

Typically, we have a major new product launch every two years, with a number of smaller limited edition lines rolled out annually. Also, we reintroduce old favourites periodically – for example, Freddo the Chocolate Frog. It usually takes between two and five years of a product being on the market for us to make a decision about whether or not it has worked. We are in this for the long term, and make our decisions accordingly. It would be wrong to assume that the detail of such a programme or a 'grand scheme' was all pre-planned from the outset. It was only once a pattern had been established that the business was able quickly to adopt mechanisms to fast-track success, aided by a growing level of credibility among customers. To a degree, successful new products force the launch of their own successors, as the annual sales peaks are lapped in the next year.

Around the world

Perhaps not surprisingly, the major markets that Cadbury first developed were related to British colonial influence in the 1920s and 1930s, and to patterns not far removed from the UK position. Only since the 1980s have the leading British confectionery companies really moved towards having international status. One turning point was when Nestlé bought Rowntree. Cadbury also undertook a programme of acquisition and green-field development. Today, Cadbury is an international business with managed operations in twenty-four countries and products distributed in more than 160. Our largest market is the UK. As a world player we are one of the top confectionery companies. Our aim is to ensure we remain in and move up the premier league in this fast-moving world business.

Developing markets are a significant growth area. Local manufacturing recently began in Russia, China and Poland; we continue to invest in new factories in other countries, including India and Argentina. We have a series of power-bases for our chocolate business around the world, but the UK remains our most important market with Ireland, Canada and Australia also strong. In Britain, average consumption of chocolate per head of the population is 8kg a year, not as much as Switzerland (10kg), but still high. Other developed markets range from Ireland, Austria and Benelux (8kg) to Australia (6kg), USA (5kg) and Japan (2kg). Clearly, there is a challenge, introducing a new confectionery brand to a developing market. For a start, consumer motivation can vary markedly. A typical pattern in developed countries, for example, is the growing emphasis on 'gifting' and indulging. In developing markets, the role of confectionery is different. In India, for example, there is no gift sector as such. For economic and climactic reasons the brands of confectionery sold tend to be more biscuit-based or sugar sweets.

We still believe it is possible for consumers in these developing markets to buy into the values of 'Cadburyness'. It is our intention that they bond closely with the Cadbury brand and what it stands for, so we are now converging the style and tone of our advertising and marketing communications, worldwide.

The 'Cadbury Master Brand' positioning was developed with a group of senior marketing directors representing our major companies around the world in the spring of 1995 and the 'master brand' commercial will now be adapted for other established and newer developing markets.

Inspiring indulgence

Much has been written about the declining influence of food, beverage and household brands in a more value-conscious, consumer-educated environment. Almost in the same breath, you hear talk of an emerging 'new order' of retailers, goods and services that supply food and drink packaged for the needs of today's society. These new trade-marked entities have, in many cases, yet to build the more permanent superstructures that we associate with established brands, differentiation, consumer loyalty, and imagery. They change hands with remarkable frequency, and are often submerged into the corporate hierarchy or identity of their new owners. Meanwhile, own label is a growing challenge in many sectors – although less so in confectionery where own label sales are only 6 per cent. While own label's strongest categories are in block chocolate and seasonal offerings from the grocery multiples, this is unlikely to undermine our market.

Corporate surveys undertaken by Taylor Nelson on our behalf in 1990 and 1995, have proved insightful. When consumers were asked to name spontaneously the most favoured food and drink manufacturers and retailers in the country, the number one and two positions were occupied by Heinz and Cadbury. Perhaps more surprisingly, the demographic group of fourteen- to seventeen-year-olds also endorsed the same two organizations at the top of their list, although the positions were reversed, with Cadbury at number one.

It is probably no accident that those branded entities that have survived and prospered under a single company's ownership owe their success to deep-rooted management competencies and considered investment over time in the core values of their products. We believe Cadbury is a classic example of this: its identity and pre-eminent position in the UK chocolate market have become a springboard for the development of a worldwide brand.

It has never been more important for food brand manufacturers to enjoy a position of saliency, trust and relevance to today's consumers. More parochial and within each competitive set, the tasks of sustaining category leadership and clear water ahead of our competitors require both strategic clarity and executional excellence.

11 | VTech: From Vision to Culture

ALLAN WONG, *chairman and CEO*

VTech was created with the idea of using the latest technology available to produce high-quality, innovative brand-name products that were better than anything else on the market. It would be accurate to say that everything we have done and continue to do to the present day serves this philosophy. This vision is the creative and driving force behind the company. Even when we were a modestly successful but still small manufacturer of single-chip microprocessor video games, we were driven to offer something better with every successive generation of products. The impetus is partly due to the nature of our business. Ideas and technology do not remain uncopied for long, so you must continue to produce innovative products to stay in the market and be competitive. The other force behind the company's drive is less concrete but perhaps more important, because it deals with spirit, motivation and aspiration. My colleague and I founded VTech with a passion for electronics and the determination to excel. The VTech's company personality was therefore forged in an entrepreneurial spirit and with a belief in technology. Through the years, the products have changed a lot, but the underlying vision has not.

When the company was established in 1976, the name VTech was shorthand for 'video technology'. Looking back, however, the name VTech was prescient, for it can also stand for 'vision and technology'. We make an effort to give consumers products no one else has, or which they are unable to make as well as we can. This is the reason why we have kept ourselves at the leading edge of technological advances for our core businesses. VTech is really about 'vision and technology'.

Innovation and creativity mean we place a lot of emphasis on R & D, generating an average of sixty new products a year using proprietary technology. VTech invests an average of 4 per cent of the group's annual turnover in research and development facilities. Our innovation extends not only to technology and new product ideas and features, but also to how a product can be manufactured at a lower cost and with higher reliability. All this combined has contributed to our progress and allowed us to stay one step ahead of our competition.

Borrowing the best across core businesses

One component of VTech's rapid growth has been the considerable cross-fertilization across our core businesses: electronic learning games, telecommunications and computer systems. Some companies may have expertise in one technology or maybe two, but few possess all three of the technologies for these sectors. This gives us a real advantage.

For instance, numerous VTech electronic learning toys incorporate technology that has arisen from our computer division, thus making them very sophisticated. Typically, toy companies do not have such unhampered and immediate direct access to computer technology, so they employ outside consultants or form joint ventures with computer manufacturers. The problem with this arrangement is that it cannot guarantee good results. VTech is able to draw on technological advances and expertise very easily without going outside.

The same application of cross-fertilization exists between the telecommunications division and our other divisions. A very successful product of this process is the VTech Tropez 900DX cordless phone. Integration capabilities made it possible for us to produce this unit cost effectively, passing the cost savings on to the market. Our customers receive all the benefits and power of a 900MHz cordless phone at a very attractive and competitive price.

Leveraging brand recognition

End-users of our products are blissfully unaware of the efficiency, cost-effectiveness and advanced-technology-at-our-fingertips advantages brought about by VTech's strong cross-fertilization, but they do experience its benefits in terms of performance and price. Moreover, if our end-users have children, they probably already know that our products deliver what they promise. A whole generation of children and parents now know VTech. Our first product was one of the first toys on the market to incorporate microchip technology, producing an interactive game for children. Consumers loved it. Since then parents have been looking to us for entertaining and educational toys and they buy them for their quality, originality, dependability and safety.

This recognition is of great benefit for our other core businesses when it comes to the trade. We can go to see buyers about our telecommunication products and if they don't know who VTech is, our marketing people can talk about VTech's educational toys. Chances are, however, if the buyers have young children they are already well disposed towards VTech. This crossover is also true of end-customers. After all, we sell 14 million pieces of electronic educational toys every year, and the parents who buy them are from the baby-boom generation and comprise the largest demographic segment of our customer profile. These same people are those most apt to buy our cordless phones.

Sharpening the brand focus

This is not to say we are sitting pretty. The success of VTech's electronic toys, and the solid reputation this has helped us build, are things we think serve us well in positioning the company as a whole. Our reputation rests on totally safe, high-quality products, particularly those designed for children. If you look at the dominant names in the industry of our core businesses, VTech can be seen as a relative newcomer and so we need to continue to build our brand and what it stands for. Some of the most entrenched brands in the toy industry have been around for generations. Electronic toys entered the market only in the last twenty-five years or so, and comprise only 2 per cent of the entire toy market. There is a tremendous potential for growth here, and an exciting window of opportunity for VTech. We currently have a dominant market share in the USA and Europe in electronic toys: over 60 per cent. This puts our brand in a very visible and favourable light in this high-growth market.

Courting customers with brand strengths

This is one of the reasons why we are paying more attention to branding, and focusing on brand identity as a competitive advantage. When we first set up VTech, the market was small and we could beat everyone else with our innovations. However, as the market has become bigger there are also more competitors. It becomes harder to stand out and be seen as appreciably better than everybody else. As the gap between us and other companies narrows and the market grows larger, we will rely increasingly on brand recognition to differentiate VTech from 'me too' competitors.

Our game plan is to build brand recognition, bolstered by our reputation for trustworthiness and reliability, not only with end-users but also with the buyers in the middle of the process. We want to strengthen all of our relationships and have people associate the VTech brand with first-class quality and performance. We want our buyers and business partners to regard VTech as their most reliable supplier. And we would like our end-users to perceive VTech as honest, reliable and innovative, with top-notch customer service.

One mistake that companies make is to focus too much on costs and too little on nurturing and investing in the brand. This has been perhaps one of the greatest weaknesses of companies in the region. Many Hong Kong companies do not place sufficient emphasis on brand-building. Instead, they focus on tangible things like cost and product function. To many Hong Kong companies 'brands' are intangible; they do not yield immediate results, and hence people, being pragmatic by nature, do not pay much attention to them. But as markets become bigger and competition gets fiercer, the company that develops its branding will be a winner.

We have recognized the importance of our brand as a competitive advantage for a number of years. In this respect, VTech has been atypical in Hong Kong. We may not have done it in as coordinated a way as we would have liked, but we are now assigning a very high priority to branding as a factor for future competitive advantage.

This has to be done without actually losing sight of innovation, reliability and value, of products exceeding customer expectation – those things that comprise our vision and core values. It goes without saying that we need good products in order to compete. No matter how great our brand is, if our products are inferior they don't stand a chance.

Another strong rationale for our branding thrust is the fact that we are competing in more mature markets such as Europe and the USA. In these regions, we have an excellent opportunity to build our presence the way companies like Fisher Price have. We are much younger than Fisher Price and some of the other major names in the toy business, but our market outlook is very positive, so building our brand strength will be an important way to beat our competitors, which we are determined to do over the next few years.

The role of the corporate brand

In tandem with our focus on brand-building is the strategic positioning of our corporate brand. In the past we did not exploit the strength of the corporate brand and had in its place what could be called a multiple brand strategy. For example, we believed that different product ranges in telecommunications and computers would be better off with different brand-names, because we felt

that VTech was strongly associated with more 'low-tech' toy products. We felt that using the VTech name on sophisticated personal
computers or telecommunication products might affect customers'
perceptions.

However, five years ago we began to rethink this and changed
our strategy, focusing on VTech as a monolithic brand. At the crux
of our change of mind lay the growing realization that our brand
values – innovation, quality, reliability – do not actually have to be
product-related. In fact, these characteristics are 'givens' even
before an idea reaches a VTech drawing-board; they are part of
the fabric of the organization. These qualities therefore can be
applied to any product, whether it is high-tech or low-tech.

If our brand represented only one product type, then we couldn't
have made VTech monolithic. By having a range of products and
investing in strengthening the core values of the brand, however,
we have greater brand elasticity and are able to transfer the VTech
name across our full range. We have therefore shifted what were
distinct product brand-names to the corporate brand.

However, we intend to keep using product line-names. For
instance, under the VTech category of educational toys we have
four basic line-names – Pre-computer, Talking Whiz Kid, Smart
Start and Alphabet Desk – although there could be more over time.
There are a number of benefits to this structure of corporate brand-
and line-names. First, there are strong commercial benefits to be
reaped from leveraging the corporate brand-name across all individual line product promotions. This tactic also lessens confusion
in the market. Previously, when we used product brand-names
alongside VTech, it meant that we had to try much harder to
explain the relationship. Using VTech as the main brand now makes
things much simpler, especially at the trade level. On the end-user
level, this approach strengthens the brand-name in the minds of
opinion-makers. Parents may read about us in the business pages,
and then go home and see their children using VTech products.
It leaves a solid impression.

Finally, there is another potentially long-term benefit for putting
the VTech brand centre stage, so to speak. There are currently

around 15 million children playing with VTech products. Those who are aged between six and twelve will be growing up with VTech. As they become teenagers, we will have an opportunity to create products that will appeal to them, in part through brand recognition. One of the reasons why a company like Fisher Price, for example, has better brand recognition is that several generations have grown up with its products – when children become parents themselves, buying Fisher Price is a natural choice. Since VTech is a younger company, we cannot make as large a claim but, given our market dominance, looking ahead we can see where we want to be. We have already come a long way: in the USA, for instance, results from focus group studies of people with children in the target age group for our toys give VTech 70 per cent brand recognition compared to 96 per cent for Fisher Price. We have an excellent opportunity to enjoy the same high level of brand recognition in a few years' time.

In our major markets we promote the brand and the products quite heavily. In terms of print advertising, the magazines people read have not changed much. However, there have been tremendous changes in television, which is why we are reconfiguring our strategy so that we can use this medium most effectively, facing the challenges of cable and satellite, the Internet and so on. Having said this, however, the importance of word-of-mouth as one of the most effective means for brand promotion cannot be underestimated. For example, the Little Tikes company has a very low promotional budget, and yet it has a name that is almost as well recognized as Fisher Price. It comes full circle, then, essentially to product substance and customer satisfaction. In view of this, the 14 million people who buy our products every year are our best brand promoters, ambassadors and advocates.

Developing the design

Visual branding is also something that speaks to the customer. At VTech, we try to make sure products are inviting and user-friendly. In fact, our products are designed in such a way to encourage interaction between the parent and child. In this way, parents use the toy to play with their children to the greater enjoyment of both.

Designing electronic toys so that they attract parents as well as children is perhaps one of our greatest challenges in this sector. Ninety per cent of purchase decisions are made by parents, so they also have to like and understand what they see. This also holds true for our promotions – box designs and in-store displays are essential components of the success of a product. Our research shows that 60 per cent of purchase decisions are made in-store. The customer will come in wanting something educational – a traditional toy or an electronic-type product – or they may initially decide to buy a Nintendo. They see our product and decide to buy it as well. Point-of-sale impact of our designs is therefore crucial and we always keep in mind that the person who chooses is not necessarily the child.

Currently, we are considering another aspect of our visual branding: how similar a design should be across the various product lines. For instance, there is a 'family' resemblance across three particular lines: the electronic learning aids (age six to twelve years), electronic preschool (age two to six years) and the electronic infant–toddler products. At the same time, the three lines are still distinct from each other. The debate is about how far to go in giving the products a similar appearance. We have to be careful not to stifle the creative spirit of our designers by imposing strict guidelines.

We are now making a major effort to impose our corporate identity on all our products as we have not done this enough in the past. Based on our thinking at the time, our aim was to sell products and this basically meant promoting what the product did. For example, the name of a product like Talking Whiz Kid was more prominently displayed and better promoted than the name

VTech. As a result, Talking Whiz Kid became the better known name.

This situation is not that harmful in the short term, but in the long term it is no way to build a corporate identity. We have amended this by having more distinct brand positioning on packaging and on products. And in our television advertisements we show the VTech logo for the final five seconds.

We have found that the brand equity we do have is a valuable foundation upon which to build. We have a good twenty-year track record and a following of customers and business partners who have confidence in our brand and what it stands for. While we have made inroads into brand awareness and recognition, the essence of the matter is that VTech is competing against high-growth and very competitive industries. Our branding efforts must continue to augment and leverage our strengths for the group's future growth and continued success.

Translating vision to culture

Our brand values are not just associated with our products; they are also contiguous with our corporate culture. If we were to describe VTech as a person, it would be someone with these qualities: creativity, possessing high integrity and reliability, with more substance than meets the eye. You might say that our corporate personality fosters our corporate culture internally and externally; it imbues all our enterprises and our conduct in business and society.

Perhaps because of this, VTech is involved in advising, mentoring and educating through schools, universities, business and industry organizations, and government agencies. We like to undertake joint projects with Hong Kong's institutions of higher learning, helping students to understand the industry. We participate in government and industry panels and organizations, offering what knowledge we can to help policy-makers make decisions for the continued vitality of Hong Kong's business environment. Our support of education also extends to other countries in which we do business. We donate our products to schools and are committed to educational charity work.

We see our involvement and activities in these areas as good business practice and good corporate citizenship. Our role in working with the university exposes us to students who might consider working for an organization like VTech when they graduate. When we donate products to schools there is a business incentive, but we also have a sense of social responsibility and feel it is simply the right thing to do.

This responsibility is something we feel very strongly when it comes to our employees. We feel that our success is attributable to the high quality of our staff. We put a great deal of effort into human resources development and ensuring the well-being of our employees, including those at our prime manufacturing facility in Dongguan in southern China. We strongly believe that if our employees are happy, they will do a better job. In our Dongguan manufacturing complex, we have invested in providing standard conditions in terms of the quality of the working environment, living standards, dining and recreational facilities, and training. We continue to offer comprehensive development programmes and training courses, covering topics such as computers, languages, accounting and technology. To outstanding performers we offer a Hong Kong training programme so that, over time, our staff in China will acquire Hong Kong management style and methodology. We decided when we moved our manufacturing operations to China to use the resources there that we were also going to give something back.

We don't want to give the impression that we are not profit-driven. We are a company where the bottom line is still the most important thing, but we feel that it is equally important to do all other things correctly. The people who work for us benefit, our products benefit, and the company as a whole advances. While our Chinese employees are making 14 million toys a year to help educate children in the USA and Europe, at the same time we also offer venues to educate themselves. Quality begins with the people in an organization and successful organizations nurture the culture that enables them to succeed. Our attitude is that, within our capability and adhering to the highest ethical standards and business practices, we seek to achieve success for ourselves and this success can also be used to benefit society. With this approach, we are consistent in our corporate values, within and without, which is as it should be.

A passion for R & D

We are still growing and learning. We try to learn from our mistakes and take each of our successes to a new height. In the evolution of VTech, we study the successes of other players in the industry and learn from them. Look at a company like Hewlett-Packard. It stands for innovation, integrity, performing beyond people's expectations; everything we also strive to stand for. Hewlett-Packard has put a lot of emphasis on hiring good people. When the company was set up it established itself near Stanford University and was built around hiring Stanford's brightest graduates. Its emphasis on good research and development has been instrumental to its success.

We are also deeply committed to research and development, and our R & D department is one of the strongest in the region. We have not needed to locate our R & D facility right next to a university as Hewlett-Packard did in order to get the best people, because nothing in Hong Kong is that far away. We do, however, have a product development group of 100 people in Kowloon Tong in Hong Kong next to the City University. We also have a group in China of about 300 people from Chinese universities which provides support to the Hong Kong group.

We work on the basis that some regions have particular technological strengths and offer the best fresh ideas, so we recruit people from individual markets and technology clusters to provide us with the latest market information, technologies, and what's going on in general. Sourcing the best talent from areas with expertise and excellence results in a world-class, world-quality team of experts – the best minds working for us in one of our most vital areas, contributing to the organization's growth. We have our telecommunications R & D team in the UK and Canada, our computer people are in Silicon Valley in the USA, our educational electronics are in Europe and the USA. We have also recruited engineers from China's top universities. In our industry, product cycles are getting shorter and shorter, so we need good engineering teams to turn out new products and ideas quickly. We have found that recruiting from China has been a very good solution to rounding out our teams of engineers. The way our R & D departments are structured enables VTech to tap ideas from all over the world and bring state-of-the-art innovations back to Hong Kong.

R & D is the life-blood of innovation and creativity. It has been through R & D that we have been able to be pioneers, helping our company gain overseas market share and recognition. One of our earlier successes, introducing voice synthesizers into our line of electronic, interactive educational toys, set a new trend in the marketplace and placed us at the cutting edge of this technology.

Building the brand

If you put together our emphasis on research and development, our vision, our values, and our culture, we feel we are in a strong position to benefit from the tremendous growth potential in this dynamic industry. We have set our sights on what we should tackle over the next few years. High on our list of priorities is to strengthen our brand – it is still not as developed as we would like. Strong focus on technology and products is on-going. The product is still key – quality is the number one objective. We need to have better products than anyone else. However, for the time being we will stay with our core businesses; product extensions are something we can consider longer term. At this point in time VTech is not like Coca-Cola where you can apply your brand to other products and people will still buy them. We are still at an earlier stage in development.

As the chief executive and chairman of VTech, I have the ultimate responsibility for guardianship of the brand. I also have the advantage of having been one of the company's founders, so I see the corporate brand and what it stands for from the point of view of someone who has seen a vision realized and embodied successively in our products.

Basically, one question needs to be answered in all corporate promotion or corporate identity development – does it represent the company's vision? Will it further the themes of quality, integrity, high technology, innovation and creativity that the company was built on from inception? In VTech, as with any organization, issues must be managed at both macro- and micro-level to be effective, including brand management. Individual marketing departments are responsible for promoting products in their market segments and within brand guidelines. My responsibility is to see that the overall integrity of the corporate brand and all our orchestrated efforts stay true to the vision.

12 | London International Group: The Benefits of Globalizing a Brand in a Fragmented Marketplace

NICK HODGES, *chief executive*

London International Group plc (LIG) makes around one-fifth of the 3.6 billion condoms sold each year. Today, LIG continues to re-name and re-package local products which are added to its portfolio through acquisition, and it is entering developing markets. It has approximately a 22 per cent share of the world branded condoms market; its nearest rival, Ansell, stands at 12 per cent. Durex condoms represents around one-third of LIG's business – the group's other core brands include Regent medical gloves and Marigold household and industrial gloves.

Latest financial figures show a steady improvement in profits. Much will depend, however, on the success of LIG's attempts to raise its condom profile in America, where it trails in second position, and the sustained growth of Regent medical gloves. The company's recent acquisition of Aladan, a leading US examination glove and condom manufacturer, coupled with its focus on a single condom brand, Durex, and continued technological innovation are expected to boost earnings and market share.

Brand – or bust

The day I was appointed chief executive of LIG, in September 1993, we posted a profits warning. We were in trouble and needed time to assess what to do. Three months later, we came back with our plan: to concentrate on core parts of the business and refocus on the Durex brand. We refinanced the business with a one-for-one disaster rights issue in July 1994. Those who bought then have so far more than doubled their money. Today, we have a very profitable business which is cash positive. We set a three-year term for recovery of the business and, in the third year of that, we are on track.

The origin of the Durex brand-name is Du-rability, Re-liability and Ex-cellence. It was registered in 1929 by the London Rubber Company. LRC was founded in 1915 selling barbers' sundries and 'protectives' imported from Germany and sold from the back room. Until comparatively recently, Durex has been a British brand with some exports – and I put the stress on 'exports' rather than saying we were a 'multinational business'. The brand was distributed by export managers and developed a presence in quite a few territories, mostly in colonial countries. Only since we actively started acquiring international businesses – from 1987 onwards – did we truly start to 'go international'. Even then, we didn't immediately brand the products Durex. In some countries we had Durex products, in others we had acquired local brands. Only since 1994 have we actively worked to globalize Durex as a single brand.

The change in strategy was a result of the state of group business. LIG had diversified throughout the 1980s. The then management was convinced that growth in condoms was minimal, as the business had been in decline before the AIDS crisis. The Pill was gaining market share, and our traditional surgical gloves business was still to develop. Diversification was a 1980's vogue, so we moved into areas many at the time thought surprising (and they were subsequently proven right): photoprocessing and fine china. We bought Royal Worcester and Spode, which bore little relationship to our core business. Eventually, we got out of china – but only after we tried to buy Wedgwood and were stopped by the Monopolies Commission.

However, LIG continued to invest extensively in photoprocessing. By 1989, we were one of the largest photoprocessors in the UK with a substantial mail-order presence in Europe. Photoprocessing, however, was a cash-eater, requiring new technology every year. And from 1989 to 1993, the business progressively declined from being profitable to haemorrhaging cash. Management tried to protect the business by squeezing core activities to the limit. In 1993, not only was photoprocessing losing money but all our other businesses were being stretched – in profit terms – to the very limit. We were considerably in debt. If we hadn't taken action, we wouldn't have been able to refinance the company and we would certainly have gone bankrupt. Diversification had led to management losing sight of the core business – the Durex brand and Biogel surgical gloves – and the heritage of the company. It was clear to me that we had two superb businesses: condoms and surgical gloves. They were interlinked because the technology was basically the same, but they were very different markets. I was always convinced both could provide long-term growth for the company and profit growth for our shareholders. The question was: how?

Before 1994, LIG's condom business had a very fragmented range – with different names in different territories for the same product, and different packaging for the same product, and even different products for the same sub-brand name. The net result was a diluted effect on the brand because while Durex was recognizable in a number of countries, there was cross-over, confusion and duplication. With no opportunity for global advertising and marketing, there was no opportunity for enhancing the brand.

During 1993 and 1994, we put together a plan to globalize the Durex brand, cutting costs by closing smaller factories, moving production to the East and automating production in the West. In May 1994 we agreed our goals: to increase our share of the world condom market; to be the quality leader; to achieve a single brand-name which was instantly recognized in all trade sectors, globally; to have common advertising and PR messages, lower costs, central control of logistics; to improve margins and profitability in the major cash contributors of the group. It was a single-minded strategy: to focus on the Durex brand and make it global.

World ambitions, local sensitivities

At the time, while we were in most territories, we had not adequately supported the Durex brand. LIG's markets were being run by local barons, with no thought to global strategy. We decided to globalize by expanding geographically, and by acquiring other brands such as Mister in Malaysia and Androtex in Spain.

Internally, a number of people had loyalties to existing local brand-names, so they had to be convinced of our strategy. We had to adopt a whole new system: instead of local factories supplying only local products, we had to globalize sourcing and streamline packaging, so that while we might have different artwork on local packs, Durex was instantly recognizable on all of them. We also had to rationalize our sub-brands to make them as comparable as possible in all the countries. Fetherlite, for instance, must be the same product variant around the world, not thin in one territory and ribbed in another.

Although LIG had a central marketing department pre-dating my appointment, it was somewhat toothless. From the time we said we would globalize the brand we gave it the power to ensure that all marketing strategies from every country were centrally approved. Today we have a situation of global-led strategy and local interpretation and implementation.

To ensure visual consistency and consistency of tone and message, we produced branding guidelines for internal use and for use by external suppliers. The Durex brand has rational and emotional values; our positioning is designed to communicate quality, reliability and safety and the brand's unique selling proposition: sensitivity *and* protection. The emphasis varies by market: in developed countries we talk more about the sensual experience; in less developed, stricter countries, we address the need for protection. The tone in all communication has to be positive. Consumer research underlines the fact that people do not respond positively to AIDS-driven gloom and doom.

We also specify what information and guidance should be carried on all packs and on leaflets within, so as to educate consumers on the benefits and limitations of the product and comply fully with local regulations. We give local managers full details and back-up information to support product and corporate claims.

Another important element of the globalization process was the introduction of the Durex Seal of Quality – a trademark used for external branding although use varies by market. When re-branding local brands – such as Hatu in Italy, Sheik in the United States or London in Germany – we implement a three-step plan. Step one sees the Durex Seal of Quality on the front of all non-Durex branded packs. Step two links the local brand to Durex on the front of the pack. Step three positions Durex as the parent brand, Durex Sheik, for example.

Considerable efforts have been made to ensure the Durex brand does not become a generic; for example, we refer not to sales of 'Durex', but 'Durex condoms'.

However, we can't decide to roll out a brand globally and just do it. Local attitudes, approaches and sensitivities must all be taken into account. While eventually all our brands will have the Durex name, they will retain different external designs; for instance, in Middle East markets we're not allowed to show women on pack. In some countries birth control is taboo. Other companies face similar challenges. You always see the corny expression, 'Think globally, act locally'; well, even big brands must take local action.

Then there are the attitudes of local managers. We are moving as fast as possible but are very aware of the danger of damaging a strong, local brand. Frequently the biggest resistance is from our own territory managers rather than members of the public who, if the re-branding is conducted properly, don't even notice. Take Rowntree's Smarties: the packs are now clearly branded Nestlé with no sign of Rowntree at all.

Italy is one of the world's largest branded condom markets. In Hatu we already have the leading brand, with approximately 55 per cent market share, and a brand heritage older than Durex. Over the last eighteen months, through working with MTV Europe and global PR initiatives, and the launch of a new premium sub-brand,

Tutto, the first branded condom to carry Durex in the Italian market, we have moved subtly to link Durex with Hatu.

One aspect of the Durex brand positioning is that sex is fun. Of course, we have to judge how much to play this up (or down) depending on the particular territory. In Western countries we can promote the safer-sex message through humour, but Eastern cultures are more restrained. Malaysia forbids condom advertising, for example. Indonesia, the world's largest Muslim population outside the Middle East, allows advertising, but cautiously. With a population of 200 million, AIDS has the potential to become a major problem in Indonesia. So, with government agreement, US-funded AIDS education and condom distribution programmes are now being implemented by LIG and local non-governmental organizations, initially in the high-risk areas of Java and Surabaya, now elsewhere as well. It is a blend of both commercial initiative and social marketing.

The impact of AIDS

AIDS really came into the public arena in the UK between 1987 and 1988. It was being talked about before then, but it was not until the government's high-profile AIDS-awareness advertising that it became a national issue. We realized from the start that we needed to understand what was going on; how the HIV virus was spread and how its spread could be reduced. We therefore invested in our own clinical research to get the support data which would enable us to say, 'Use condoms because they are effective barriers for disease control'.

A significant hurdle was the ban on condom advertising on UK television, although this ban was quickly lifted. The first major education initiative came from the government with its 'Iceberg' and 'Tombstone' advertisements in newspapers. Although they involved a 'use a condom' message, these early advertisements focused on doom-laden imagery and scare tactics – an approach we were not keen to take. Our first TV campaign ran in 1987 using the theme song 'The Power of Love'. In 1989/90, we cooperated with the Health Education Authority which made the 'Mrs Dawson' campaign featuring a female worker in our condom factory. This coincided with visits by MPs to condom production lines. The aim was to familiarize the public with the condom and to become used to discussing safer sex.

We also moved quickly to participate in the government's All-Party Parliamentary Group on AIDS, set up in 1986, and we have sponsored the committee's activities ever since. The committee ensures that HIV remains on Parliament's agenda, bridging the gap between statutory and voluntary sectors and providing a forum for the exchange of information.

Our strategy towards AIDS was honed in the UK and rolled out in other markets as the Durex brand was developed internationally. While education has always been a part of our branding and marketing activity, AIDS forced us to place an increased emphasis on gathering data and disseminating facts. Our educational materials and pamphlets became more sophisticated.

We have used clinical trials to clarify our protection message. We have to be able to discuss the respective risks and benefits of condoms when used in different ways. There are often restrictions on what we can say in our advertising, but we are addressing it now in our in-pack literature. We have also developed our own globally applicable pack health warning. Although we can't spell it all out, we can offer best-use advice. It's a difficult, highly sensitive issue.

Cashing in on corporate conscience

From the corporate perspective, we are trying to grow LIG's share of the condom market and grow condoms' share of the entire birth control market. We see ourselves as one of the major educators with an obligation to inform people of the limitations of the product, as well as to explain the product's benefits and correct usage throughout the world. We have enhanced our brand-name considerably by spending money on education programmes, literature, sponsorship and so on. The whole methodology is to educate people that a condom is a life-saving device, and a healthcare product.

We work with local GPs and healthcare workers to get across the message of why, when and how condoms should be used. In the UK we produce 'Practice Makes Perfect', a sexual health resource for medical professionals. In other markets, we rely on third-party endorsement and work with external experts to offer best practice guidelines and information. Another example is 'Condoms across the Curriculum' which is 'supported by an education grant from LIG'. The book suggests schools projects and exercises which can familiarize pupils with the existence and importance of condoms – rubber production in Malaysia in a geography class, for example; advertising jingles for condoms in a music or marketing class. We also produce a booklet called 'The Ins and Outs of Sex Teaching' for those who teach healthcare professionals.

International initiatives range from sponsorship participation at international conferences on AIDS, including the biannual World AIDS Conference, and campaigns such as the 'Europe Against AIDS' programme, to more practical activities in developing markets. With MTV, we have promoted safer sex in over seventy-seven countries worldwide, addressing key issues of importance to the young: sexually-transmitted diseases and unwanted pregnancy.

India is potentially the single biggest condom market in the world. The spread of HIV is alarming, and if population growth is unchecked, estimates suggest it will exceed China in the early twenty-first century. There has been no active promotion of family planning or use of condoms for healthcare for years. Our response is proactive marketing and the promotion of healthcare and condoms. We have a joint venture in India where our local brand, Kohinoor, dominates the relatively small market. Since the 1980s, when TV controls were relaxed, we have been able to market our product more aggressively, but we are up against religious beliefs, lack of education and overwhelming economic factors. Eighty per cent of India's population is rural and so, during the past two years, we have started to take the safer-sex message to them, employing professionals to go into small villages to advise on birth control, AIDS and sexually-transmitted diseases. We hope the success of such initiatives will persuade the government to invest further in family welfare and AIDS programmes.

Inevitably, these activities have a benefit to us and to our share-holders; however, I believe we still have a corporate responsibility to become involved in education programmes. There is clearly a major problem in many countries where birth control is still unavailable or condoms are yet to be accepted. I'd tell any govern-ment minister it is his or her duty to promote products like ours. The more education campaigning we put in, the more people we can convert to using our product.

Quality is the key issue, here. Durex must be seen as the highest quality condom in the world. We make significant investment in research to ensure all our products are made to the highest regulat-ory standards and are acceptable anywhere. We work closely with regulators to advise on quality guidelines and are actively involved in revising international condom quality through our representation on national, pan-national and international standards committees. All of this gives us an advantage over our competitors. As we have said in a number of recent publicity campaigns: 'If it doesn't have Durex in the pack, it's not Durex in the box.' We don't produce own label.

During the last two years we have also begun to supply unbranded product to government and non-government agencies for distribution in developing countries. The fact remains, once we get people using condoms, whether free or not, they will start to demand branded products.

Staying ahead of the game

Of course, there will be a growth of own brands in other markets, as markets develop – where you have a credible pharmacy chain, for example. Boots launched own brand condoms in the UK in 1996, and at the same time we re-launched Durex. The facelift involved dynamic new products and packs designed to be more modern and up to date. We identified three distinct stages of condom usage in the market, and targeted each accordingly. We created sub-brands for each, for example, Safe Play for younger adults and Select, a variety pack including ribbed, coloured condoms and flavoured condoms (such as 'Ice Mint' and 'Tangerine Dream') and square foil packaging to enhance quality.

Own brands will be the ultimate test for the Durex brand and I'm very comfortable about that. They may take a small share of the market, but they may help expand the market, too. The worldwide condom market continues to grow at around 2 to 3 per cent a year – quite slowly when you think the Pill is probably in decline and you still have a large number of people at risk, having casual sex without using a condom. This is because the condom is still not widely seen as the preferred product to use: it has to be at hand, at the right time. And that's where I think a good brand-name and wider acceptance is going to help.

Our advertising is designed to create new usage; in other words, to make the sexual act with a condom more exciting than it is without one. Achieving this is always going to be a challenge, because using condoms you start from second base, so to speak. The new products we are bringing into the market (the polyurethane condom, for example) should help tempt new users and expand the market.

Rival brands have always posed a threat in certain markets, but the greatest threat came when Durex was seen as a tired brand, and when newer brands, such as Mates, were seen as more fashionable. Durex is now positioned as the upbeat brand, and we feel prepared to fight anyone. Since 1993, we have tried to make Durex appeal more to younger users while still remaining relevant to and trusted by older users. We have achieved this by segmenting the market. Evidence suggests that if we can pick up the young, we keep them as they age. Our strength used to be in the older age bracket: twenty-five and upwards. What I'm hoping is that our new marketing and positioning will ensure we are seen as the right choice when people start out, and that we also get endorsement from mother to daughter, father to son in later years. The ability to pick and choose different products in the range as users get older – for greater sensitivity, for more security and so on – is essential. To encourage people to move through the range we use leaflets, packaging, advertising and PR to explain the differences.

The positioning of the product has shifted. In the early days, condoms were only ever bought at the barber or pharmacy. But throughout the 1980s, in developed markets, condoms shifted towards being a fast-moving consumer good (FMCG) as increasingly they were sold in grocery stores and supermarkets. Because of the importance of research to all our activities, and partly in response to AIDS, we felt it was important to position condoms as a rational purchase. Our approach was to position them as a clinical product. This also moved Durex away, once and for all, from condoms' once seedy image. Despite the increased public debate, many people still had a little smirk about them, and advertisements still showed people embarrassed by the product. We started saying, 'This is just a standard medical product'; in the most extreme case it might save your life; it can stop you catching a sexually-transmitted disease; it can prevent unwanted pregnancy; and it's for sale over the counter.

Clearly, condoms are now under intense regulatory controls around the world. At the same time, business is being driven by clinical endorsement of the product. In the past, doctors and nurses rarely endorsed condoms, instead they advised people to use the Pill. Today, however, we are seeing increased endorsement from GPs and healthcare professionals around the world. In addition, in-store promotional activities related to new products communicate that using a condom is more acceptable – we have to encourage people to think of using condoms as second nature. As fun.

Room for growth

At an international level, competition has altered very little – the market remains fragmented; there is no other global branded player. There is tremendous advantage in having a global brand-name in a deeply fragmented market. In Italy and Spain Durex is up against Artsana; in Germany – Mappa; in France – Prophyltex; in Scandinavia – RFSU; and in North America – Carter Wallace and Ansell. A single brand-name and a single message communicated across all markets poses a significant problem for local brands. They face the weight of our local advertising and international campaigns, too. This is important for us. Unlike other global brands – such as the big Proctor & Gamble brands – our market remains relatively small worldwide, so we can't possibly afford to advertise in every single country. We therefore have a broad swathe of PR and advertising which covers a single brand. I am confident it will work well.

In the past, well before my time, there were widespread ventures which tried using the Durex brand-name. We still have Durex-branded spermicidal lubricants. My personal opinion, however, is that I see a very clear message for condoms and closely-related products. I would be very wary of trying to make it a wider range. There may be obvious possibilities for brand extension – such as pregnancy-testing kits – but I believe the time is not yet right. We must ensure there is absolutely no confusion or dilution of the Durex name. Durex must be synonymous with being the best condom in the world. Besides, there are other more immediate challenges.

The biggest conversation about brands today is no longer about taking on local labels and own brands. It's about what to do when we have a low-price product and a high-price brand and whether we can put Durex on the low-price product. Or, when there are pharmacy and mass market differentials, whether we can sell the same brand at different prices in those two outlets. In that situation, we have kept the Durex name, but have used different sub-brands. This is a feature in many markets – especially larger and more developed ones where our traditional sector remains pharmacy. But mass market grocery outlets are growing in most cases, taking up to a quarter of the market, often at a much lower price.

I won't be satisfied until we have good awareness of the brand in as many countries as possible. We are already a leader in forty countries and in another twenty or thirty we are number two. We are on an aggressive acquisitions strategy and I am determined Durex will be the sole condom brand for the group. I will be happy when I have achieved good brand recognition in every country where we sell. But product innovation and sustained investment in research and development is also important. By ensuring our product gets better and better, we raise the standards for everyone else. This gives us an edge.

Also, we continue to develop new products. We launched the polyurethane condom because it has a number of attractions, being non-latex, odourless, colourless and made from a material that is twice as strong, allowing a much thinner film to be used to increase sensitivity. It is another way of bringing new users into the market. We think it will be a niche, certainly for the foreseeable future, although I think non-latex condoms will have 10 per cent of the market in ten years' time, which is why we are continuing to work to improve it.

I am a great believer in single brands where you are a single distributor. I admire Coca-Cola. I think Procter & Gamble still does a magnificent job. I admire these companies both because of their confidence – it's not misplaced, but correct – which leads them to do more for branding and sales of product, and because they are strong enough to withstand the retail pressure which comes from own brands. Wherever there are very strong brands, the retail own brand has tremendous trouble trying to take them on. Kellogg is another strong company which defends its brands and basically says, 'Nothing else is as good'. That's my position on Durex for condoms. I want the world to hear the message: 'Durex is the best – you can go and buy a cheaper one, but it isn't as good.'*

* Durex, Durex Seal of Quality, Regent, Biogel, Marigold, Fetherlite, Mister, Androtex, London, Hatu, Tutto, Kohinoor, Safe Play, Sheik and Select are all trademarks of London International Group plc and are registered in the countries of use.

13 | Mandarin Oriental Hotel Group: Delivering the Eastern Promise Worldwide

ROBERT E. RILEY, *managing director*

Mandarin Oriental Hotel Group is an international hotel investment and management group which operates a dozen deluxe and first-class hotels, principally in the Asia Pacific region, employing 6,600 staff in twelve countries. The business generates most of its income from the Hong Kong hotel market which has enjoyed a significant recovery since mid-1995 following a period of static growth. Its flagship hotel is Mandarin Oriental, Hong Kong, which opened in 1963 – originally as 'The Mandarin' – as a deluxe hotel catering for the growing number of business and leisure travellers visiting the island.

In the early 1970s, additional Mandarin Hotels were built in Jakarta and Manila, the Excelsior Hotel was built in Hong Kong and the Oriental, Bangkok, was acquired. In 1974, to accommodate this expansion, Mandarin International Hotels Ltd was formed as an umbrella hotel management company. In 1985, in anticipation of further expansion, the company restructured its management company under the brand Mandarin Oriental and adopted the fan logo. During that decade a further three deluxe hotels were added in Macau, Singapore and San Francisco. Thus far during the 1990s, a further four deluxe hotels have been added in Indonesia, Hawaii, London and Kuala Lumpur. Mandarin Oriental International Ltd is now a publicly listed company with net assets of $1.3 billion.

The group's focus is to continue to expand its deluxe hotel portfolio while meeting the interests of guests, staff and shareholders. Mandarin Oriental defines its mission as 'to completely delight and satisfy' its guests. Near obsession with building and maintaining a corporate culture to achieve this mission significantly contributes to the reinforcement on a daily basis of the Mandarin Oriental brand.

Aiming above customers' expectations

Mandarin Oriental had a wonderful brand long before I came to the group in 1988. As is often the case with a business like ours, a group of core individuals was committed to deliver a service, as opposed simply to satisfy customers – there is a difference. They delivered a service that rapidly became recognized as something extraordinary. Mandarin Oriental, Hong Kong, was rated the 'Best Hotel in the World' by *Forbes* magazine in 1967. And from then on it enjoyed growing recognition. A brand is a promise, and our promise is never to say 'no' to a guest. Guests can rely on the fact that if they ask for something that's humanly possible to deliver, we'll do it, and that we do not have regimented parameters beyond which we will not step.

There are many good companies represented in our markets. Our total commitment to our guests distinguishes us and keeps us competitive. All of our training programmes are designed to ensure everyone takes personal responsibility for whatever a guest needs. Our Mandarin Oriental mission is not only to give guests a great service, but also to delight them with our ability to anticipate their needs. And it's a surprise for them: we aim to do something for them that they need, before they even know that they need it.

This mission is underpinned by some basic guiding principles. We strive to understand client and guest needs by listening to their requirements and responding appropriately. We are committed to working together as colleagues – with an emphasis on sharing responsibility, accountability and recognition through teamwork. By treating each other with mutual respect and trust, every employee contributes to the group's overall success more productively than if each worked in isolation. We actively promote a climate of enthusiasm, working to create a caring, motivating and rewarding environment. We work hard to be the best – an innovative leader in the hotel industry – and, as a result, we seek the same standards from our suppliers. We are committed to growth and delivering shareholder value, to internal and external relationships that match our high service standards in terms of integrity and fair play, and to act responsibly, for example, in environmental improvement.

There are some simple illustrations of this which are duplicated day in, day out, as a matter of course. When a guest asks for an international newspaper, somebody will go out and get it, instead of saying where it can be bought down the street. If a guest arrives with a broken piece of luggage, it's repaired without anybody making a big deal out of it. Even if a passer-by is having a problem, our staff respond. In one particular case, a lady was struggling outside with a sick child, the doorman jumped into a cab and took them to hospital. These things continue to surprise guests. Recently, a housekeeper in Thailand found $40,000 in cash and turned it in. This value system filters down to all areas of interaction between staff and non-staff: it's a basic response to human beings whether they are our paying guests, or not. Because, often, you just can't tell the difference.

The Mandarin Oriental brand is all about human values – people who really care. It's more than being a caring company. Like British Airways, it's about personal interaction. This is a difference that really matters – it's about care, concern and delight.

Learn to live the brand

To ensure we live the brand, one of the first things we must do is to attract the best people.

We are committed to 'modelling' – leading by example. If I see a piece of rubbish lying on the hotel floor, I will pick it up, put it in my pocket and keep right on going, rather than pick it up and hand it to somebody, or tell somebody else to do it. When a member of management sees an ashtray in an elevator bank overloaded, he cleans it, and takes it out with him. We do it because we want the staff to see the importance attached to even the smallest matter. Of course I could tell somebody to sort it out, but doing it myself adds to the modelling effect and stresses the fact that we all should take responsibility for anything that needs doing.

Senior managers try to get all management – everyone, in fact – to appreciate that often the folks with the lowest job in the hierarchy have the most important job. They're the ones who are with the guests continually. Housekeepers, doormen, waiters are constantly with guests, they certainly see more of them than I do. The doorman probably has 3,000 interactions with guests every day.

So, although they are trained to do a specific function, our people are trained beyond that, too. Again, we use this word 'delight' a lot. Because it's a better word than 'serve'. 'Isn't it wonderful to see a guest squeal with delight?', someone once said and that's how we came up with the word. We all have our specific functions, but the central issue is that the guests are there for an experience. They will come back because of a real, positive, personal interaction with our staff. All of us are the people that they look to for security and comfort.

Building pride in the brand through recognition and development

Mandarin Oriental operates a highly visible modulized staff training programme. Whenever employees complete a module, a star goes up by their name on the training board.

It's a creative development programme. If someone wants to move from being a waiter to a head waiter, say, he has to complete a certain number of modules before he is eligible for promotion. When people get gold stars by their names, it's a highly visible way for us to acknowledge their achievement.

Building on this, we're introducing a 'you made a difference' campaign. Whenever somebody does something important, we give them a certificate straight away. Instant, personal recognition is extremely important. I write at least half a dozen letters a week to individual staff members, thanking them for doing something special for a guest.

Being a laundry attendant is a pretty tough job, and so is washing dishes. How do we keep these people motivated when they've been doing the same job for the past thirty years, so that they really get their tableware clean and out there in time for the other staff to get them back on the tables? We must recognize their efforts. We must pay them well (we offer among the highest rates in the industry). And then, for appropriate positions, we must find ways of making them reach upwards – through incentive compensation. We all respond positively to stroking. We're fortunate in that we have different hotels and different cultures, therefore we can use a lot of what we call 'cross exposure' – motivational trips. For instance, Giovanni Valenti, an Italian concierge at Mandarin Oriental, Hong Kong, who's been with us for twenty years, recently spent time at the Mandarin Oriental Hyde Park in London. We had inherited a lot of Italian business there, and we did it because we wanted to show Hyde Park's Italian guests that they were important, and so is Giovanni Valenti. He had a wonderful time sharing experiences with his new London colleagues.

Also, we send people to night schools and summer schools for further education and career development. We also send a number of staff on courses at Cornell or INSEAD, and each year we try to have at least one general manager go on either Stanford's or Harvard's executive business program. In the past many of our general managers did not have university degrees, and it was quite difficult for us to get them in the program. However, because of their past performances in the program, these universities now welcome our people.

World standards, local needs

Many Western guests – particularly Americans – are very comfortable with service staff being personally familiar with them. In contrast, European guests and, to a greater extent, people in Asia, prefer to be recognized for their status and position. So you have to find the right balance. I was at Mandarin Oriental, San Francisco, recently, having lunch with the general manager, and a waiter that I knew came up and said, 'Hello, Mr Riley, how are you?' He then reached across the table and shook my hand, adding, 'Good to see you back.' The general manager turned to me and remarked that this behaviour is typical in America. And I love it. But a senior waiter wouldn't be comfortable behaving the same way with many of the guests at Mandarin Oriental, Hong Kong.

It's not always easy in Eastern cultures to ensure people get the right balance of personal interaction. So we devote time to helping our people understand the effect of eye contact, and that sometimes it doesn't hurt to touch a guest affectionately. At the same time, cultural differences have an impact. Eastern guests have different expectations from Western guests which must be respected.

Back in the mid-1980s it was easy to talk about the service levels of Asian hotels. There weren't many international groups operating in Asia. Labour was inexpensive, therefore staff were plentiful and so was service. But now it's different. Labour costs are no longer so inexpensive. We experience a lot of competition for good staff from white-collar industries such as insurance and banking. In these white-collar service industries, young people don't have to work shifts or weekends. So we have more challenges with recruitment, training and retention than we used to. We still attract dedicated and talented people, but there's just much more competition for them.

Then, of course, there are many other hotel companies here, who are also doing a fine job. Standards are very high everywhere. There are lots of good hotels in American cities, too. We have to approach the market differently. We try to focus our activities. Using the word 'delight' helps us concentrate on personal interaction. It's now the core theme of our marketing and advertising activities. The mission to delight is our brand. That's the Mandarin Oriental promise.

Meeting changing service needs

We've been going through a transition. When we first started here in Hong Kong, we knew exactly what we needed to do; we based this knowledge on past experience in other markets, primarily the UK and Europe. But the increasing numbers of people travelling here and the rise of affluence in Asia means that Asians had their own ideas about what they were looking for in hotels. We have to accept that 'the traveller' is changing, which is why we continually update our image.

In the late 1980s, we asked customers (and non-customers) what they thought of us. They thought we offered excellent services. However, they also thought that we were 'formal', and if you wanted to take that over to the negative, 'stuffy'. We've had to recognize that the travelling public has become younger, and that more Asians are travelling. We've had to adapt to this. Again the word 'delight' came up. We've worked very hard to overcome what was perceived as a stuffy image. We've tried to engage and interact and never to say 'no', to present ourselves as offering everything you want. The consistent offer is essential.

Today, the challenge is to become more accessible, while at the same time preserving our traditional customer base. And we're doing it with considerable success. In the past three years we have totally revamped eighteen of our restaurants to compete with free-standing restaurants in the local marketplace. We don't want them to be seen only as 'hotel restaurants'. And we've done that, at times, without the total enthusiasm of our more traditional loyalists. I'm pleased to report, however, that in most cases we have been able to keep these loyalists, who now acknowledge that some of the changes were the right thing for us to have done in the current market environment.

Our guests are made up of a variety of different groups, from 'traditionalists', older more conservative travellers, to 'achievers' who are younger, assertive and ambitious. Our customer mix depends on where our hotels are located, so we constantly have to balance the interests of each group.

In the late 1980s, we dropped the requirement for jacket and tie in several of our restaurants and bars. Before then, we had Europeans walking in wearing expensive designer casual outfits and Asians with open-neck shirts and we couldn't serve them. So dropping the jacket and tie requirement made sense. When you come down to it, very few Asians wear a jacket and tie when they're travelling. They live in hot climates. It was important therefore to modify the code while at the same time maintaining the degree of decorum our clientele expected.

Also, we've refitted our restaurants and bars to appeal to a younger clientele. In Asia, the image and the positioning of your hotel is highly dependent upon the perceptions of the local market. The recommendations of local people are vital for customers deciding where to stay. If you have younger achievers coming into your hotel for food and entertainment and they find it fun, they'll recommend your hotel. If they find us stiff, there's a whole market that's not going to be recommended to us. All of these were profound changes for a very traditional European-influenced hotel company.

Sometimes, we've made mistakes in promoting our brand. When I arrived at Mandarin Oriental, our advertising campaign was based on 'the legend'. If you think about it, calling something a legend today seems rather old-fashioned and arrogant. Also, we had an advertising campaign where we focused on the negative side of travel: restless flights, long days of meetings. The idea we wanted to portray was that, after all this hassle, it's always lovely to come home to the warmth of Mandarin Oriental. The problem was that we weren't really promoting the reasons why you should choose Mandarin Oriental first, or what it was that made Mandarin Oriental really special.

Today, the creative strategy is about moments of personal delight based on customers' experiences. Customers regularly contact us and recount details of their stay. 'I found paradise at the Oriental Spa, Bangkok. I never thought I'd feel this good,' one wrote. 'We now understand why your hotel has received all these awards. Your staff are like angels,' another said. We came to realize we should be proud of what we are doing, and that what we talked about should have real consumer appeal. The refocusing on our mission to delight placed the emphasis on interaction and involvement with our customers. That is what we believe to be our unique selling point.

Our latest advertising campaign is much cleaner, fresher and more vibrant than previous attempts: it reflects the vibrancy of all the new things that we're doing with our hotels.

A monolithic approach to branding

Mandarin Oriental is our brand for our deluxe hotels. Our symbol – the fan – is always accompanied by our name. The fan encapsulates service in an elegant, incredibly refined way. It is about achieving the right temperature – being comfortable. It can be either a basic comfort or the height of indulgence. The eleven-point fan symbol is particularly effective because many Asian cultures have an interest in symbols. That's why all of our hotels around the world adopt it. The fan logo links all of our hotels, even if they all, for one reason or another, cannot carry the Mandarin Oriental name. However, for decorative purposes, each hotel has the flexibility to design a variation on the symbol that's relevant to them. Some have been based on locally produced antiques. In London, for example, we worked with Sotheby's and Christie's to find the right design. In Hawaii, where their bamboo fans did not convey the required image, a local florist designed one for us using local flowers. This kind of originality gives life to our identity – it's not a rigid, static thing.

If it were possible, every luxury hotel we operate would carry the Mandarin Oriental name. It's not surprising that there are a number of hotels throughout Asia named either 'Mandarin' or 'Oriental'. In the mid-1980s, we joined the two names for two reasons. The first was to link our two flagship properties, The Mandarin in Hong Kong and The Oriental, Bangkok, both then and now recognized as among the best in the world. The second reason was that the joint name, together with the fan logo, is a separately identifiable brand-name which could be protected. And we legally protect the brand aggressively.

So now, whenever it's legally permissible, our hotels will be called 'Mandarin Oriental'. And where for historical purposes, such as The Oriental, Bangkok, and Hotel Majapahit, Surabaya, we use the historical name, the use of the fan logo and other references to Mandarin Oriental make it clear that the hotel is part of our group.

In some cases, we've been able to combine both the strength of our brand and the benefit of the historical name. In Hawaii we now have Kahala Mandarin Oriental, Hawaii. Actually, if we had our way it would be called Mandarin Oriental Kahala. Our partner, who initiated the purchase and invited us in has a sentimental attachment to the name 'Kahala'. Since we did not want to lose the deal over the name, we agreed to have Kahala precede Mandarin Oriental. Also, since the local community and many frequent guests knew the hotel as 'the Kahala', substantial benefit was gained by keeping that reference.

In 1996, we bought the Hyde Park Hotel in London, now known as The Mandarin Oriental Hyde Park. Again, combining the strength of the brand with the benefits of past associations. Because we own it, one hundred per cent, Mandarin Oriental is the most important name it could have. We will always put the Mandarin Oriental name on a hotel if it's at all possible. If we bought the Ritz in Paris, I'd call it the Mandarin Oriental Ritz Paris because I think it's important for the brand.

However, wherever we put the brand-name we have to assume that we are able to deliver on the promises the brand stands for: to delight and never to say 'no'. Although, because of differences in local cultures, a guest will get a different style of service in San Francisco, Hong Kong and London, we can still focus on the important areas to make sure we delight our guests in those areas. What we have found is that, as long as you're within the luxury segment, your guests will understand that there's a difference in style in different parts of the world. Their loyalty to the brand is solid, and they are prepared to adapt their expectations depending on the local culture of the place in which they are staying.

This becomes particularly challenging when we make an acquisition like the Hyde Park Hotel. With such an established hotel, you can't expect regular guests to understand your brand offering overnight, but you can gear up the hotel to act immediately on the change. We closed the Hyde Park deal very quickly and, within thirty-five minutes of signing, we were in the hotel introducing ourselves to the staff and assuming its management. That was on a Friday and I came back the following Tuesday to present our mission statement to them. I presented the concept to all the staff and personally gave each a personal copy of the statement and our fan pin. As a result, I have been able to meet each one of them. It takes time, but it is vital if they are to buy into the new concept.

Interestingly, the general manager at the Hyde Park recently told me of a guest's letter of complaint. This guest had been staying at the Hyde Park for many years, and he wrote with a long list of things that were wrong with his latest visit. In the last paragraph he said: 'I've been putting up with all these things for many years, but now that Mandarin Oriental is managing it, I expect better.' He said it tongue-in-cheek, but our involvement immediately raised his expectations.

Learning by example

You cannot help but admire and try to emulate those organizations which know how to develop really motivated staff. Take a company like General Electric, which is consistently recognized as one of the best performing companies in the world. GE attracts good people, keeps them and makes sure they're motivated, and they are aggressive and gung-ho for each other. At the same time, they're tough businessmen and they understand their brands, too.

Then there are those who successfully change or improve their brand, like British Airways. What's encouraging there is that there's hope for everyone – that you can change if you've got sufficient belief and will. We're close to British Airways and we've invited their training company to talk to us about what they do; it's all about putting people first, because you have to. People talk about satisfying the customer, but what this invariably stems from is satisfying your staff. As senior management, that's our job – we must ensure that our staff have the resources, the training, the motivation and the appreciation, so that when they're out there, on the front line, it flows through to the guest.

The brand starts from within and then moves outwards. As part of our induction programme, along with the presentation of the mission statement, we give everybody a fan-shaped pin to wear. It's a symbol of our commitment to our mission. It's not compulsory to wear it, but most people do.

Avoid the pitfalls of uncontrolled growth

We have to be very deliberate when planning for growth. We are a niche player, but there are a number of ways in which the company can build profit without necessarily having to dilute brand. I don't think there are many hotels that can carry our brand-name. Mandarin Oriental is more than just a five-star brand; we would be devaluing ourselves if we were using the name on a typical business hotel in Cleveland or Houston or Mobile, Alabama. You cannot compromise on the promise. In the fashion business, certain exclusive brand-names have widened their appeal and you now see them everywhere. This certainly devalues the positioning. Some fashion brands have tried to become mass market, and it may be that they limit their life-cycles by doing so.

If you want to remain competitive and broaden your appeal, you need to adapt. There is a danger in assuming that in protecting the brand you cannot broaden the promises it makes. We cannot be the same Mandarin Oriental that we were in 1963. Then, eighty per cent of our business was from the UK, compared to the twenty-five per cent British business today. So, even if we're prepared to stay a niche player, we keep reminding ourselves that our customer changes every day and that we have to continue to broaden our base because there's more competition. Therefore your customer base, by its every nature, is always getting diluted. You're forced to broaden your base, but hopefully there are more people moving up: the achievers and the people who want to achieve – those who are on the cusp of achievement but aren't quite there yet. They are all part of our customer base.

Therefore, we must be selective with each new hotel. Or, if an acquisition could not carry the Mandarin Oriental brand, consider an alternative, such as our Excelsior brand for our first-class hotel in Hong Kong. Of utmost importance is not diluting the value of the brand by using it for properties which don't meet the standards. We must always be able to fulfil the promise and our customers' expectations. At the same time, we must understand the changes that are taking place with expectations so we can fine-tune our services to met the new expectations of tomorrow's customers.

A further danger is misjudging the attitudes of your market. Another Mandarin Oriental campaign was not totally effective with our Asian guests. It featured guests chatting and joking around informally with staff. It was strong in the sense that it was all about personal interaction. We started using photography featuring staff interacting with guests, which seemed perfectly natural for someone with an American bias. But we were so focused on shifting away from being stuffy to having personal interaction that we overstated the case. The research feedback six months on revealed it was not going down well with Asian consumers. Asians have a strong sense of politeness and it wasn't credible to them to sit in a restaurant and be over-familiar with a staff member. It wasn't something that warmed them. We were trying to tear down the stuffy image but went so far to the other extreme that they shrugged their shoulders and said 'who would want to do that anyway?'

As managing director, I take ultimate responsibility – for the brand – as any CEO must. Sometimes that requires hard decisions that may not be popular. A few years ago, for cost considerations, someone in our organization came up with a less expensive customer magazine. It was less expensive – and it looked it. So I cancelled it. The employee who suggested it had good motivation – we could have saved $100,000 a year by printing it on cheaper paper with lower quality editorial – but from a branding standpoint it's better not to have a magazine than to have one that doesn't match your standards. Recently, there was a hotel for sale in Los Angeles that many of our colleagues thought would be an appropriate acquisition for us. But I made the decision that it couldn't carry the Mandarin Oriental brand. It was a good financial deal, but it was only a four-star hotel: it just couldn't carry it off. In every organization, ultimately the CEO must decide on the final balance between short-term financial objectives and the requirement to build the brand with a long-term perspective.

14 | Mazda: The Journey towards Harmony

SHIGEHARU HIRAIWA, *director*
and president, Mazda Motor (Europe) and
DAVID HESLOP, *chairman and managing*
director, Mazda Cars (UK) Ltd

Today marks a critical point in Mazda Motor Corporation's seventy-six-year history. In 1996, long-time partner Ford, the US car giant, took a controlling 33 per cent stake in Mazda, resulting in a management shake-up, with Ford's Henry Wallace appointed Mazda president – the first Westerner to head a leading Japanese car company. The past eighteen months had been a period of fundamental yet welcome change for Mazda. Despite a long-standing reputation for innovation – Mazda has developed some highly acclaimed technologies, such as the rotary engine, and its cars are widely recognized for their superior engineering – the company suffered falling profits in the early 1990s.

In 1994, vehicle production in Japan fell 22 per cent to 773,000 units, or nearly half the peak level of 1.4 million units just five years before. The reason was a lack of clear focus on branding, Mazda's management now concedes, that had a significant effect on the bottom line. Mazda is now working with Ford to harmonize product development strategies and marketing communications. Just how Mazda's traditionally individualistic approach will fit within a coordinated group strategy that aims to set Mazda alongside the Ford and Jaguar portfolios will become apparent in coming months.

A unique heritage

Mazda Motor Corporation, based in Hiroshima, Japan, makes a diverse range of passenger cars and commercial vehicles and is one of the largest employers in western Japan. In developed markets it has become synonymous with the revitalization of the sports car market following the launch of its successful two-seater convertible, the MX5. Mazda trucks and cars are exported to 153 countries and in each the same guiding principle prevails: the customer comes first. Customer service standards are set high and maintained by a 5,200-strong network of Mazda dealerships around the world and 2,700 sales and service outlets in Japan.

The company's Japanese heritage has been central in shaping the Mazda brand, at the heart of which lies customer friendliness. Research shows Mazda is a highly desirable and user-friendly vehicle brand. A recent German 'Customer Barometer' study (conducted by the Emnid Institute of Bielefeld in 1996, polled 32,000 members of the public on attitudes to 700 companies), for example, shows Mazda and Honda ranked ahead of Mercedes and Toyota. Another study carried out in Germany, by ADAC (General German Auto Club) shows Japanese cars are consistently at the top of the list in terms of reliability. The ADAC study, carried out in 1995, shows the Mazda 121 to be the most reliable small car in the German market, ahead of the best German car, the VW Polo, and the Seat Ibiza, Fiat Uno and Citroën AX. In the lower-middle-class category, the Mazda 323 came first, ahead of the Toyota Corolla, Suzuki Vitara and Nissan Sunny. In the middle-class section, the Mazda 626 beat the Mercedes 190 Diesel; the Citroën BX came in last. In 1995, Mazda's series 121, 323 and 626 won in three out of four categories for reliable engineering.

In one sense, the Mazda philosophy is a product of Japan – a country renowned for high-quality, high-standard products and modern technology. In another sense, it's a product of Hiroshima. Hiroshima is a mid-size, local city with a population of approximately 700,000. The people working there maintain a strong work ethic. Every single worker is dedicated to his or her job and committed to building the best quality vehicles. By contrast, Tokyo is a cosmopolitan city. In local cities in Japan, however, people move less frequently and stay there longer – they maintain values more easily than those living in cosmopolitan cities. Mazda cars are the most reliable and user-friendly. Customer satisfaction has become a core value and it must now be a key message because, historically, we have established and focused on product quality. This has been inherently at the core of Mazda. Sometimes we may emphasize sport, sometimes easy-to-drive features, sometimes fun – but always value.

This is a different approach to other Japanese car brands. And it has created a particular corporate culture. Mazda people have certain ways of working, of talking, of communicating. Certain values – a distinct sense of integrity – are the essence of how we live. We have open-plan offices. Our people communicate. They are cross-functionally linked in terms of seating arrangements and work groups. They take pride in developing themselves in order to develop Mazda.

The company has another guiding philosophy. It is committed to cooperating, wherever possible, with the needs of the international community. Mazda takes seriously the need to contribute to the further growth of the global automotive industry and the world economy. It is increasing its commitment to environmental research and development programmes to promote new levels of harmony among cars, society and the environment. To this end, it has developed hydrogen-fuelled vehicles, and pioneered a number of technological breakthroughs including a new plastic composite that can be recycled at least eleven times for structural material, and a decomposing catalyst for recovering gasoline and kerosene from all types of plastics.

However, a further aspect of Japanese culture – a belief that you do not need to shout – has had a less positive effect. For too long we have been product- rather than market- and marketing-led. This is now changing. And this change is being fuelled by the closer relationship with Ford.

East meets West

Mazda and Ford have had a long relationship. In 1969, Mazda, Ford and Nissan formed Japan Automatic Transmission Company – a joint venture to manufacture automatic transmissions (Ford subsequently withdrew in 1981). In 1979, Ford acquired a 25 per cent stake in Mazda, and in 1996, increased this stake to 33.4 per cent. Nineteen ninety-six was a year of restructuring for Mazda which involved a refocusing on customer satisfaction and a reassessment of the quality of our dealer network. In the light of fundamental changes associated with the Ford deal, one might have hoped, at best, for the business to plateau. In fact, year on year, European performance was up. In the USA, a major new advertising and marketing strategy got underway to boost image and stabilize segment performance. In Japan, volume share finally stabilized, after a seventeen-year decline.

The coming together of Ford and Mazda presents significant potential for culture clash. The power and dominant nature of American Ford is being linked to the incredibly cultured and structured society of Japan. In one sense, they are two opposites: the ying and the yang; East and West; formal and informal. However, branding is about people and, for a brand to work, the people within the organization have to have some purpose to drive consistency. That purpose is the vision and aspirations of the corporate body, where endeavour drives harmony. There are differences between the two organizations, but the corporation is a living, changing thing: the summation of every individual in the system.

Of course, when American culture is linked to Japanese culture, the result could be a confused mess, but there is another possible outcome. Through an organization's focus and willingness to talk and learn, such a union can become a building process – a way of developing a new and refined language. Brands are not static things, they have to evolve. This is our aim. Ford has its language, Mazda has another. All the time, we are talking and listening and out of this is coming a new understanding for the future. The process is forcing us to express ourselves better and, in turn, to develop a stronger understanding of our brand.

Global corporations transcend religion and culture. They drive their own consistency and actually create the corporate brand. Mazda UK isn't just 'Mazda Cars UK'. It is a group of people driving the success of the Mazda product and brand. The real structure is much more inclusive; it includes suppliers, agencies, customers, shareholders, bankers. And all the stakeholders must understand the Mazda culture.

Corporate harmony

The Double Concerto for Saxophone and Cello commissioned, in 1997, by Mazda for John Harle and Julian Lloyd Webber and composed by Michael Nyman has a harmonic plot. The subtext relates to the location of Mazda's headquarters, Hiroshima. The source of inspiration was a photograph displayed at the Hiroshima Peace Memorial Museum which simply and horrifyingly represents presence and absence simultaneously. The photograph depicts the entrance to a bank only 260 metres from the hypocentre of the atomic bomb dropped in August 1945. A person was sitting on some steps waiting for the bank to open. It is believed that they were facing the direction of the blast at the moment of the explosion and, without any chance to escape, died on the spot after being completely burned. The space where the person had been sitting remained dark, while the surrounding surface of the stone steps turned white due to the heat rays.

In the Concerto, the saxophone and cello soloists shadow each other and the jagged sound of the first section evolves into a more harmonic language at the conclusion. Kansei means harmony, the resolution by human intervention of the many conflicts of life into ultimate concord. It's a philosophy which has led to the design of some beautiful and practical cars. This philosophy is reflected in the Concerto's composition.

The attraction of opposites

Ford is a volume player and Mazda, while it wants to become more mainstream, is a distinctive player. Ford's brand positioning doesn't complement Mazda's, but it doesn't interfere with it either, which is what is needed in a portfolio of manufacturing brands. Jaguar, Ford and Mazda will be maintained in distinct and differentiated brand positions. There is collaboration in terms of technology and new product development, to avoid duplication. But there is also differentiation, distinctiveness and differences in branding and positioning. Through collaboration, we can also make sure we each remain distinctive.

There are obvious marketing and branding benefits from the Ford–Mazda union. Until now, our operations have been product-led. Our own people engineer and distribute our products. All our people love the cars and understand the differences between them and other products, ourselves and other companies. They in turn try to communicate this to the consumer. That is why there is such a close relationship between other countries' operations and Hiroshima. Everyone must understand the core philosophy, the core values, so importers and dealers are carefully selected and monitored. We encourage everyone to take pride in understanding the core values of the brand and, where applicable, to develop their own ways of communicating it.

Due to the structure of Mazda worldwide – with Mazda HQ at the centre, and regional Mazda executives, national Mazda offices and local dealerships representing business in each country – there is what we call a 'communications cascade'. It's like a waterfall. So, when we have a whisper in Hiroshima, it multiplies through the cascade until one whisper becomes a million shouts: a million customer experiences. This multiplier effect is the same for many global organizations. And it presents the same problem: how to make the whisper from Hiroshima live as an experience which is consistent with every customer, every dealer, every national office, every regional office.

There has been a breakdown in communication in recent years.

We have had misinterpretation and other weaknesses in the communications cascade. Historically, the difficulties have been with translating our understanding of the Mazda culture at regional and national levels. It meant there was an unclear understanding of the culture between Hiroshima and different continents. We had consistency of product, but not consistency in positioning.

To overcome this, the company must have a single, central vision. What a lot of marketers don't understand is the difference between the role of global strategies and the local experiences of customers. Global strategies are about economies of scale. Local issues are about flexibility and pace and consistency of experience. What we try to do in our organizations around the world is channel global visions, global manufacturing and all the economies of scale into local experiences. We drive this through global to local (you might say 'glocal') marketing, which gains the economies of scale of central manufacturing, while allowing for the local experiences of the brand. Certain cost and marketing mechanisms create efficiencies at different levels within the cascade: from Japan, Europe, UK, England, London, Swiss Cottage, the dealer to the customer. So, for example, customer databases exist most efficiently and effectively at a national level. Motor show stands are better developed and designed at a regional level – pan-European, for example – for the Paris, Frankfurt and Birmingham shows. One of the skills of 'glocal' understanding is knowing what is best done in a factory in Hiroshima and what is best left to the dealership in Harrogate.

The communications cascade is not a one-way process. Service is as important an element within it as product and marketing communication, and efficiency of service. We have a system where we go from the customer direct to the managing director to Japan, cutting out all the bits in between. The actual act of communication is critical to the brand, not just in the sense of marketing the consistency, but because we are listening. Our listening organization is a healthy one and we have to have a mechanism to get the critical point back fast. So, if the brakes aren't working properly on a car in the UK, our colleagues in Japan would know within minutes.

Think laterally

Traditionally, Mazda is strong in product and weak in marketing, whereas Ford is very definitely a marketing-led company. There is much more accumulation of know-how today, which is one great benefit of our closer cooperation with Ford.

Last year we created a marketing division at our headquarters in Hiroshima. Although there were some marketing activities in place, there was no dedicated strategic division. The aim is to coordinate brand messages around the world and control communication of our values. Real brand marketing is not about fabricated slogans, it's a total approach; which is why conventional above-the-line advertising has its limitations. We are now looking more seriously at communicating through the line and at other ways in which the brand interfaces with the driver. These other 'real' contexts will become more influential in the future. That's why we now believe we are no longer selling cars – we're selling customer experiences.

Our approach goes beyond traditional definitions of marketing. With the Double Concerto, for example, we wanted to highlight a debate in a way that no one else has ever done it before: it's a lateral step. What we try to do is write advertising to communicate our brand, product and message. We translate the language we've learned. That's what our agencies must do: to get the essence of the position, of the product, so they can translate this creatively into communication. We want people to talk about what we do. We want staff to talk about the brand and understand.

Branding is critical for Mazda. Immediate market concerns inevitably pose the challenge of tactical necessity against longer-term, strategic needs. It's chicken and egg. But we must communicate our brand values which, in turn, become part of the commodity price to the user so that when we are in the pricing game we can be a better player. It is dislocating if the brand image is not clear and may dilute reasons for a consumer to buy. We must ensure we do not jeopardize our brand values by tactical activities, such as price-cuts and discounting, while remaining highly competitive in value-for-money terms.

If we expect people to spend £20,000 on our product, we must get them to trust us. A relationship with the brand (and consumer) is essential. All the more so if you are Sainsbury and you want to be accepted as a bank. To be a bank in the old days, you had to have pillars and a bank manager who was difficult to get to see. Technology changed all that, and First Direct proved it could work. Emotional values give a brand stretch, because of trust. The battle-ground is choice rather than selling: that you *choose* to buy Mazda, rather than do so out of habit. Brand extension is the future of brands – it's about emotional commitment, the summation of the experience of a consumer with all the products and services and elements operating within our brand. It is an area we are now starting to explore.

The brand is also the language of a corporation. It offers the ability to communicate consistency. Mazda brand values are every-where around us, on a daily basis. We built out UK headquarters in 1983, with a garden, a pond with koi carp, and a car park sunk into the side of the hill – it's all part of the culture of how we relate to the material world. This affects every aspect of our communi-cation. At motor shows, we give our staff the opportunity to design their own clothes – it allows them to express their understanding of Mazda-ness through their own creativity. Our motor show stands are built from recycled bumpers. Environmental issues and recyc-ling are becoming an increasingly important part of how the car industry will survive, if it survives at all.

We spend a lot of time trying to communicate all this. People who create our insurance products, our warranties, our sunroofs, have to understand what it is that ties them together as a brand. The brand needs to be a communication mechanism to ensure disparate parts of the organization are united. We always think of end-user customers as the recipients of communication. But actu-ally, staff, suppliers, shareholders, bankers, all of these people are stakeholders and get the same message. If the brand is a chain of inclusive stakeholders – from manufacturer through distributor and retailer to the ultimate link: the consumer – it lives through each stakeholder's participation in that product and service. The way the chain holds together is a brand statement. The best brands work where the inclusion of every stakeholder is strongest.

Our current method of using advertising is also very much influenced by Ford. The Japanese traditionally assume an agency is 'only' an agency; they have a strategy devised by themselves, and the agency is called upon only to develop the creative work. We are now working to change our relationship with agencies to encourage closer cooperation and implement collaborative efforts, treating advertising agencies as if they were part of the marketing department. Agency staff become more innovative, stimulated and better motivated that way and come up with better creative ideas. We had already got to this point with all our other suppliers, but not in terms of marketing and brand development.

Mazda is starting a number of aggressive marketing strategies in Europe. One crucial decision was to retain the advertising agency JWT to support marketing communication throughout the region. This is a very sensitive area for us. For although we now have a pan-European strategy, Europe comprises regions and local communities, and each local market has its own character. I don't think we will ever be able to rely on just one standard strategy. We need happy harmonization between local and regional cultures.

Listen, and learn

As well as being more marketing-focused, we are becoming more market-led. In the past, we were not listening to the demands of our consumers. We are now asking whether we have done enough and where we have gone wrong. This involves talking to each other within the organization and talking with our consumers at length. We are making use of a broad range of research, from JD Power Customer Satisfaction data to tailored studies. All of this now shapes marketing and product planning, which it did not before. This is of course a time-consuming process, and we are still only one-third of the way there. But we are moving in the right direction. We encourage our employees to be aware of competitor initiatives and learn from their successes.

Engineers will traditionally lean towards making the top quality, whereas customers care about good value, the best quality for a certain price. There are a number of examples of where we have gone wrong. Mazda created many sports cars and speciality vehicles in the early 1990s. We thought the market demand was shifting and actually we ended up producing too many cars. This is one reason why Mazda has recently found itself in such a difficult financial situation. Also, we have developed many innovations that have been copied by others, such as a design to maximize interior space by folding down the back rest of the rear seat. We invented this in 1980. We also pioneered the wind deflector on the convertible, now a standard feature on rival models.

However, we were very poor at communicating the exclusivity of our products and features to our consumer. Part of the Japanese culture is that silence is golden and that the product speaks for itself. In modern Western culture, however, this is not sufficient. We must communicate loudly and we shall. Once the user experiences one of our cars, he or she will come to love it. But growth will be limited if only a small number of consumers know about our cars. That's the problem we must now overcome.

Our conclusion is that we didn't listen deeply enough. We must be more careful, more attentive. We have streamlined many product lines, focusing on core areas and growing segments in the market. For example, in the sports segment, we have the MX3, MX5 and MX6. No other company has such a wide range, and we could probably live with just one or two. Growing sectors include speciality vehicles, such as station wagons. We have a focus now on these growing segments and are shifting our emphasis accordingly. However, while Mazda must increase volume, it must not move away from its market positioning. Ford is a volume player, while Mazda has a distinct customer appeal: a feeling of distinction and exclusivity. Take the Ford Fiesta and the Mazda 121 – both are now made at the same Ford plant in Dagenham and basically share the same engineering platform. However, each is clearly and distinctively positioned.

If we refer niche back to product, from developing a broader range of model types, we could have around 90 per cent of the potential market. If we develop only a limited range, we're cracking only 10 per cent in product terms and, as we've discovered, we can't run a top ten manufacturer with that strategy. So what we have now is a shift in strategy. With a 2 per cent share of sales we're still a distinctive player, but we will attack mainstream opportunities in Mazda's unique and branded ways. Rather than building cars to attack only 10 per cent of the car market, we will build cars to attack 90 per cent, and yet appeal to this broader footprint with our unique interpretation of customer needs, expectations and experiences.

In order to grow Mazda's share we must coordinate activities with Ford, matching production cycle plans to avoid clashing with new product development. There will also be a clearer international strategy for the Mazda brand. This will be a major advantage, enabling manufacturer, distributors and dealers to be more sensitive to local needs. That is our longer-term goal: to produce a variety of products, satisfying a range of needs. At the core of this business will be the 323 and 626. We will also develop new models to diversify the range – recreational vehicles, wagons and diesels. Continued production and a widening range will ensure that Mazda is never relegated to being just another car at the back of a Ford showroom.

In late 1996 we launched a new speciality vehicle – the Demio – available only in Japan. We are ensuring it adheres to our core values of quality, style, user friendliness and excitement, and that the presentation of it to, and interaction with, the consumer communicate these core values. It's not so much a question of what we hope our brand will be in five years time. Our plans are clear: we must communicate our brand proposition to the consumer more effectively.

The road towards perfection

Another element to the Mazda brand is the Japanese concept of Kaizen. Kaizen is the concept of continuous improvement, without ever accepting that you will actually reach or achieve perfection. Instead, life is about the journey towards perfection. People may talk about the Mazda brand but, in fact, the Mazda brand today is slightly different from what it was yesterday. Because in just twenty-four hours, millions of people – employees and customers – have interacted with it. Let's say the sunroof fails on a car at twelve o'clock today, then that customer's experience of Mazda will dramatically change. And the experiences of consistency and value, structure and directive will change. We will then have to try and re-create a sense of harmony from that unfortunate event.

If we are good managers this happens in an evolutionary way, as it has over the many years it has taken for Mazda's business to evolve. During the twenty-five years Mazda has operated in Europe, we have been partially restricted by quotas, partially restricted by the model range, partially restricted by our ability as managers, funding, the commercial pressures and the currencies. All these factors have affected how well we have communicated, as have changes of government and fragmentation of media. In the old days, if you advertised on TV, the communication was very focused. Big brands such as Heinz, Unilever and P & G were built through being able to communicate with their end-users more effectively through the impact and focus of terrestrial television. Now, marketers are struggling. Suddenly you can hear radio messages locally, get cable TV and communicate using the Internet. Media fragmentation and new media make for a more difficult, complex world.

Such triggers can rock a brand. What we must do is learn and continually react to external factors better than our competitors by being more flexible, competitive, consistent. A healthy brand is one which can adapt quickly in the modern world. That is why this is a continuous process. The worst brand in the world is one which has arrived, because it if has arrived, it's dead.

15 | Federal Express: The Supremely Packaged Warehouse in the Sky

FREDERICK W. SMITH, *founder,*
chairman, president and CEO

In April 1973, the first night of Federal Express Corporation's operation, we had fourteen jets at our disposal and managed to deliver 186 parcels overnight to twenty-five North American cities. Today, our fleet of more than 560 aircraft – the largest all-cargo fleet in the world – travels nearly half a million miles every twenty-four hours, carrying nearly 3 million packages and documents to 211 countries every night. FedEx couriers log 2.5 million miles a day, the equivalent of 100 trips around the world.

We invented the concept of overnight delivery, creating a whole new market where previously there was none. But now, after nearly twenty-five years of rapid growth – we were the first US company to reach $1 billion revenues without mergers or acquisitions – our prospects are, if anything, even brighter. We started out in documents and small packages in the USA. Today, as the largest express transportation company in the world, we can ship virtually any package of virtually any size to virtually anywhere in the world.

For a growing number of major corporations, our air fleet has become their 500 mile-an-hour warehouse: we take over their logistics functions, allowing them to minimize their investment in stock and warehouses, and maximize the speed and flexibility of their service to their customers. And now, FedEx is ready to provide the distribution infrastructure Internet commerce needs. What the clipper ship and railroads did for nineteenth- and twentieth-century trade, we are ready to do for the twenty-first century.

The FedEx brand lies at the heart of the organization's success

– and its future potential. Many companies just wouldn't feel comfortable entrusting the management of their inventory, logistics and order fulfilment to an outsider. The FexEx name offers them peace of mind and quality service. So what makes the FedEx brand tick and how is it changing?

Anticipate customers' needs, innovate to meet them . . . and do it again

The biggest business opportunities rarely come from serving a need that has already been identified. The greatest opportunities arise when you spot the things that your customers didn't have a clue they needed until you offered it to them. That is what FedEx did with overnight delivery. When we launched, the idea of overnight parcel delivery as a viable, profitable business didn't exist. Yet we could see that moving small high-tech, high-value items such as computer and electronic components was becoming very important to the economy. And that skill – the ability to meet the needs customers don't know they have – is what continues to drive our business forward, as we open up new markets in logistics and electronic commerce.

The ability to identify an unidentified need, however, is nothing unless you can also come up with a way of meeting it. To be able to deliver a new service you have to innovate. The hub-and-spoke distribution system that lies at the heart of the FedEx network is one example of that sort of innovation. Another was the way we integrated ground and air systems from the very start. Up until that time people had operated surface vehicles or they operated aeroplanes, and the two were seen to be separate. We never felt that way.

Perhaps even more important was our recognition that, along with time-sensitivity, the ability to track the status of every item at every stage on its journey, from sender to recipient, would be crucial to customer satisfaction. We understood this even before we had the technological means to do it. As we have developed the means to do it, so information and information technology have become central to the FedEx offer, next to our fleet of planes and trucks.

Right from the very beginning we understood that FedEx stood apart from traditional postal carriers in two key ways. First we offer fast, time-definite delivery, whereas most postal services are non-time-sensitive. Second, our service is information intensive whereas theirs is non-information intensive – and we have worked non-stop to extend, deepen and innovate in the information side of our business. For example, our introduction of SuperTracker bar code readers in 1985 has helped to revolutionize the transport industry: a FedEx courier collecting a shipment scans it with a hand-held scanner identifying critical shipment information. Each item is typically scanned at least six times during its journey.

Also, we have continually developed each of our core competencies. For example, we have migrated our tracking system, from something which is internal to FedEx, into our customer shipping docks and into our customers' offices. To begin with customers had our own proprietary terminals, but increasingly the information is coming through their own computer terminals – so we have created an integral, on-line, real-time management system which is at our customers' fingertips.

At the centre of the FedEx information network is FedEx COSMOS®, which stands for Customer Operations Service Master On-line System. This is the central component of FedEx's strategic computer systems, allowing us to keep track of the status of every item as its bar code is scanned, from the moment it enters our hands until delivery. COSMOS currently tracks in the region of 45 million transactions a day.

Another essential part of the system is DADS (Digitally Assisted Dispatch System) which we launched in its original form back in 1980. When a package is picked up, the information gleaned by the scanner goes into a DADS transmitter which uploads the data into COSMOS via radio waves and telecommunications devices. We have a radio network linking our 35,000 couriers worldwide, to enable us to respond rapidly to customers' requests for tracking information.

This information is not only for internal consumption and use. Indeed, parallel to the development of our information infrastructure, we have always looked for ways to help customers access that information in the most convenient way possible. Back in 1978, we were one of the first transportation companies to introduce automated call centres to handle customer queries. In 1984 we introduced Powership, a dedicated desktop computer system that connects directly with the COSMOS network and allows customer to generate shipment documentation, streamline billing and track the status of their shipments virtually in real time. The next extension of this was FedEx Ship® software, which allows ordinary PCs to do the same. Both are offered free of charge to most customers, and now 60 per cent of all FedEx US transactions start electronically rather than starting on paper and having to be digitized later. We hope the Internet will help us automate the remaining 40 per cent.

In 1994 we became the first express transportation company to offer Internet connectivity for tracking and service availability transactions on the World Wide Web. Initially customers could use our Internet site to track the progress of their parcels simply by tapping straight into FedEx systems: no need to call customer service. The next step was to enable them to use it to initiate a transaction with FedEx InterNetShip^{SM} on-line shipping application – in a sense, making the Internet a seamless extension of COSMOS.

At the same time, we have always tried to innovate at the tactical level too. United Parcel Service (UPS) was at one point eight times bigger than us and began operations in the traditional post and parcel business – routine packages that were not necessarily fast, not time definite and with no information content. When UPS grafted an express system on top of their parcel post network, in response to FedEx's early success, we moved the goal posts. We went from next-day delivery to offering a money-back guarantee that we would deliver on time.

To defend your position, when competitors are coming in and narrowing the market, you have constantly to innovate and improve in order to maintain a leadership position. The focus of that quest to stay at the top currently fall into three areas: global capability, logistics and electronic commerce.

Offering 500-mile-an-hour warehousing across the globe

FedEx started out as a domestic US operator, but we soon realized that many of the items we were shipping, such as computer and aircraft parts, were essential to the operation of global businesses. So we started seeing ourselves as the clipper ships of the information age. Once, world trade depended on majestic sailing boats. Today, if you look at a news programme talking about world trade, you are likely to see some pictures of container ships in Long Beach, Liverpool or Le Havre. But in fact, the movement of goods by air, especially express carriers such as ourselves, is taking an increasing proportion of the value of the world's trade. We might be moving only 1 per cent of the items traded, but because they are high-tech and value-added items, they account for 40 per cent of the value of worldwide commerce. By 2020, it will be closer to two-thirds.

The expansion of our global network hasn't always been plain sailing. When we entered the European market we began by offering many intra-country and intra-Europe services, where the barriers to entry were low and where there were already many local competitors providing good services. We stuck to it for about seven years, and finally in 1992 we decided to restructure our operations there.

Our transportation infrastructure continues to expand rapidly. We now have eight hubs in America, three in Europe and two in Asia. In the last few years we have opened a new Asian hub in Subic Bay, in the Philippines. We have launched a new intra-Asia overnight delivery service and become the only US express transportation company to offer direct flights to China. We have created a new Latin American and Caribbean division reflecting our focus on the second fastest-growing economies of the world. Now we are the only transportation company that can connect 90 per cent of the world's GDP using our own aircraft and equipment.

This global transportation and the information infrastructure are the vital ingredients of major new developments for FedEx. The first of these is full logistics on a global scale. As part of our 'V3' (Vision, Value, Virtual) strategy, we are helping customers who manage complex logistics and transportation operations to reduce inventory, speed up their processes and improve customer satisfaction. In other words, to substitute information for mass. What we are saying is that we can speed up our customers' processes to such an extent that they can invest far less in warehousing and inventory; at the same time we are improving customer satisfaction, increasing their flexibility and their ability to respond to changing markets, thereby reducing the risks of obsolescence.

For example, in the past, if a company made aircraft parts in Arizona and wanted to sell those parts to people in Germany, it would have had a warehouse in Germany. Nowadays we can deliver to Germany within short time frames, so that a warehouse is no longer needed. That's why we sometimes say that FedEx planes are our customers' 500-miles-an-hour warehouse – or that our trucks are their 50 miles-an-hour warehouse. One of our customers used to have warehouses in twenty different locations, now it has three, and its inventory order-to-fulfilment cycle has been reduced from three weeks to three days.

We are using the same transportation and IT capabilities to position ourselves as a key part of the infrastructure in the emergence of Internet shopping, and in doing so we are providing a very powerful engine of commerce. The Internet should probably be compared to developments like the jet engine and submarine telephone cables: it will change the way the world does business. In particular, it will make time, place and infrastructure irrelevant in terms of selling and sourcing around the world – especially in business-to-business contexts. Another way of seeing it is to look at the link between the telegraph and the development of the rail system. The telegraph created the connections and the railroad allowed fulfilment. In the same way, where the Internet creates the connections we hope to provide the fulfilment.

In business-to-business transactions particularly, we believe there will be an enormous explosion of demand for products bought from catalogues over the Internet, and we have already developed the software to facilitate it. Called FedEx VirtualOrder^{SM}, this highly sophisticated system integrates order placement, billing, invoicing and inventory management to allow any company to sell on the Web. It lets our customers publish their business catalogues on the Internet and enables their customers to say which products and which of several FedEx delivery options they want. It helps the person shipping the item to know that there is a tariff of x per cent for products of that description, say, for Italy or Indonesia. It also notifies them electronically of the delivery. That means that a payment must take place, and we help facilitate that as well. Thus, you can sit in Leeds, Memphis or Wo Han in China and make it easy for someone on the other side of the world to order your goods and have them delivered and paid for, without the expense or hassle of finding a representative or a sales person or a partner there.

Build a service culture

Our goal is perfection, but we live in an imperfect world. It is probably beyond our grasp, given that we have to deal with hurricanes and snow, flying machines and trucks and traffic accidents. Nevertheless, we do our best. Every night an empty jet freighter leaves Portland, Oregon, for Memphis, tracking close to other FedEx airports on the way - just in case another FedEx jet can't fly that evening. If we do have a service problem we act promptly to try to make amends and make it right for people. Every day we make a huge effort to take what are already very high service levels towards perfection. In 1990, we were the first company in the service category to win the Malcolm Baldrige National Quality Award.

What makes FedEx stand out from most companies is our philosophy of People, Service, Profit (PSP). These three words are the very foundation of FedEx. They represent our belief that if you take care of people, they, in turn, will deliver the impeccable service

demanded by our customers, who will reward us with the profitability necessary to secure our future.

This has been a core part of FedEx since its inception and it's
been a very powerful business combination. We make it absolutely
clear to everyone who draws a FedEx pay cheque that job number
one is to create a 100 per cent satisfied customer, by 100 per cent
on time deliveries and 100 per cent information accuracy. We want
to make sure that customers understand that, in a sense, service is
the only thing we sell. But the key is this: you cannot deliver the
kind of impeccable service that is expected of FedEx unless you
have satisfied and committed people working for the company.
They've got to think that it's a good deal for them, they've got to
be committed to the organization, and the organization has to be
committed to them.

So how does this actually translate into action? First, every manager has to undertake a week-long training programme to learn
the basics of PSP – at FedEx managers work for employees; it is
a manager's job to help employees get their work done. Part of
that training says that managers must seek to elevate human dignity
and to reinforce a relationship of trust and respect with our
employees.

Second, there are a number of programmes to make sure that
employees feel they are fairly treated. We have a Guaranteed Fair
Treatment Procedure that allows employees to raise grievances and
have those grievances judged by their peers. We also have something called Survey Feedback, where we not only conduct annual
employee surveys, but employee groups explore ways to improve
on areas of concern.

Third, we have avoided layoffs when at all possible. This is good
business sense for an operation like ours, where we are continually
driving for, and need employee ideas on, extra efficiency through
the use of new technologies.

Fourth, if the business is facing a tough time, the top people
bleed first. Between 1990 and 1992, when many airline businesses
in the USA were making substantial losses, executive salaries were
cut before employees' merit increases.

Whether or not every sort of business needs to have a set of values like ours is a moot point. But, from the very beginning, I felt strongly that PSP was the way you need to treat people if we were going to have a high-performance organization. It reflects what I think is necessary to run this kind of business – and this is the kind of business I would like to run.

Building the FedEx brand

When I first started out with this business I didn't particularly consider branding issues. My mind was focused on filling a business need for moving the computer and electronic parts that were becoming so important to the economy. However, branding soon became a major issue. Initially, as we developed more front-office services, and now, as we move into Internet commerce, the FedEx reputation becomes invaluable. The fact that it is the FedEx world-wide express delivery system offering the opportunity of Internet commerce gives customers greater confidence than software coming from some other company.

Still, the core of the brand goes back to the idea of express networks that first emerged 150 to 200 years ago; they were networks through which you moved something very important under someone's custodial control and delivered it within a specific time frame. That is the heart of our business. Anything which falls under that umbrella fits the FedEx brand – transportation, logistics, the movement of goods – and everything we have done was a logical step for FedEx.

At the same time, because we are dealing with a service where expectations are extremely high, management of the brand becomes tantamount to providing customers with a degree of security. It's comparable to what American Express did in the early years of travellers' cheques. Our brand is utterly focused on what it identifies: express networks. At the same time it is selling something very general: peace of mind.

We are also broadening our offer into a wider range of services:

carrying different types of document, packages, freight for a range of customers from the very small to the very large. In a sense we are a bit like IBM. In its early days, IBM was many different things to many different people, making mainframes, mid-level computers, PCs, copiers, electric typewriters and so on. But it wasn't really important for the secretary who was very fond of his or her electric typewriter to know that IBM did all those things.

In many ways, competitors are able to come on the scene and close the gap on some of the transportation services we offer. So we have to look at where the battleground of the future lies, which is in information services. That is where all the added value is, and we're not going to let it be taken away.

We want to use our information expertise to strengthen and deepen the brand. Thus, as we broaden these services, we are deliberately using FedEx as a master branding device. We have, for instance, FedEx VirtualOrder, FedEx Powership® and FedEx Inter-NetShip. One of the main reasons we revised our corporate identity in 1994 to emphasize the FedEx brand was to develop the capacity to connote this panoply of services. We needed a better umbrella to deal with all these discrete segments.

Another very important reason was that 80 per cent of people had started calling us FedEx rather than Federal Express. There was a big parade out there and we needed to jump in front of it.

Working out the actual business value of making a change like that is difficult, but we do know that the new logo is much more efficient in terms of use of space. We have calculated that the impression that we will deliver would be worth about $60 million a year to us, simply because the letters are bigger and clearer. In other words, if we had to go out and buy the incremental impressions from the more efficient use of the same space on the side of the truck, the sign was worth about $60 million a year to us. It was also cheaper to maintain because of the amount of paint used; the extra time that the paint lasts on the aircraft and the trucks was also worth several million dollars a year to us. So it was a good business decision as well as a good marketing decision.

Communicating the brand

The nature of business determines the way we approach our sales and marketing. We use all the advertising and promotion techniques available to us, but when you are talking to Fortune 500 companies about redesigning their logistics, creating virtual companies with seamless technological access where your warehouse becomes a FedEx plane, a thirty-second advertising spot on TV is not going to convince them to change the way they do business.

Today, we have shifted our brand management and advertising focus away from time-sensitive delivery problems, to emphasizing our worldwide business capabilities. The brand management challenge is helping people understand that FedEx is much more than a document company. Many people don't know about the vast network we have in place and what its potential is. Also, while we have a twenty-year heritage in the United States, building the brand equity in Europe and Asia, where we are younger, is more of a challenge.

Today's advertising revolves around the slogan 'The Way the World Works'® in an attempt to address these challenges. We hope it provides a level of customer trust. It stresses our global capabilities, while providing an umbrella for more targeted marketing activities directed at different types of customer. And it's a big enough umbrella to cover the wide range of customers we now have: the way the world works *is* very different if you are shipping semi-conductor components from Malaysia to fifty different locations around the world, to moving manuscripts within the same city.

The next level of marketing reflects our intensive study of different customer segments' shipping needs: what type of shipments do they make, and how often? This also drives our automation strategy. For example, if our customer is a multinational company shipping 300 to 400 times a day from many locations, it may require EDI links, mainframe to mainframe. If it is a single location company making ten shipments a week, mainly paper-based, all it needs might be a bit of software on its PC. If a customer is shipping packages weighing 15 to 20 lb, he won't want to walk down the street looking for a FedEx retail outlet or drop box. But if it's just a document, he might be very receptive. For that reason, we actually have three sales forces: one for electronic commerce, one for freight, and one for the document and package business.

One of the best channels of communication we have is our own operations. By integrating our information systems and our transportation systems so closely with those of our customers, it becomes very difficult for them to think of an alternative. They have a symbiotic relationship with FedEx: when they turn on their PC, one of the first things they see on the screen is FedEx. To this degree, when we say we want to get close to our customers, we don't mean it in a metaphorical way. That phrase has become a cliché because there is no physical manifestation. We *do* mean it physically. We mean getting our systems integrated with our customers' systems. There is an interesting aspect to this. What started out as part of an offer of excellent service has become the ultimate sales channel. We have now got over half a million people using it to interface with us every day.

All these communications – advertising, direct mail, corporate identity sales force, couriers, information systems – play a part in developing the FedEx reputation. Maintaining this reputation and its brand image is a top priority for me, since it is one of the most valuable things the company has. Clearly therefore, acting as the brand guardian is part of my job as CEO. But that could be said of almost everything. You could say I am the safety officer too, because I have to make sure that everybody understands that safety comes above all else. So the operational responsibility for the brand lies with our senior vice-president for marketing worldwide, Mike Glenn.

At the end of the day, FedEx is not its logo or its advertising or its sales force. To the customer, FedEx is the person who comes to your door and doesn't let you down.

Index

Co-opetition

Two leading business thinkers use game theory to rewrite business strategy

BARRY J. NALEBUFF AND
ADAM M. BRANDENBURGER

The game of business changes constantly. So should your business strategy.

This is the first book to adapt game theory to the needs of CEOs, managers and entrepreneurs. *Co-opetition* offers a new mindset for business: a strategic way of thinking that combines competition and cooperation.

Though often compared to games like chess or poker, business is different – people are free to change the rules, the players, the boundaries, even the game itself. The essence of business success lies in making sure you are in the *right* game. Actively shaping which game you play, and how you play it, is the core of the innovative business strategy laid out in *Co-opetition*.

Barry Nalebuff and Adam Brandenburger, professors at Yale and Harvard, are pioneers in the practice of applying the science of game theory to the art of corporate strategy. They have devised a practice-oriented model to help you break out of the traditional win-lose or lose-lose situations, and dozens of companies – including Intel, Nintendo, American Express and Nutrasweet – have been using the strategies of co-opetition to change their game to enjoy the benefits of win-win opportunities.

Co-opetition will revolutionize the way you play the game of business.

'Seize on *Co-opetition*'   *Economist*

'A terrific book'   TOM PETERS

0 00 638724 1

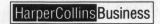

The Fish Rots from the Head

The Crisis in Our Boardrooms:
Developing the Crucial Skills of the Competent Director

BOB GARRATT

An organization's success or failure depends on the performance of its board – an ancient Chinese saying is that 'the fish rots from the head'. Yet the vast majority of directors admit that they have had no training for their role and are not sure what it entails.

As boards' activities are made more and more transparent under national and international law, there is an urgent need for a transformation in the way directors' competencies are developed.

Bob Garratt argues that directors need to learn new thinking skills to apply to the intellectual activities of direction-giving and implementing strategy. They need to develop a broader mindset to deal with the uncertainty of higher-level issues such as policy formulation, strategic thinking, supervision of management and accountability.

The Fish Rots from the Head is the first book to clarify and integrate the roles and tasks of the director and provide a programme of learning. As the tide of regulation swells, no board director can afford to ignore it.

'An important contribution to the corporate governance debate and clear and intelligent advice on how to improve the performance of a board'
TIM MELVILLE-ROSS, INSITUTE OF DIRECTORS, London

'This clear, very readable book should ensure that many more fish swim rather than rot'
SIR MICHAEL BETT, CHAIRMAN, Cellnet plc

0 00 638670 9

HarperCollins Business

Jamming

The Art and Discipline of Business Creativity

JOHN KAO

No corporate asset is at once so prized and yet so poorly managed as the imagination and creativity of a company's people. In today's competitive environment, companies who understand how to manage creativity, how to organize for creative results and who willingly implement new ideas will triumph.

John Kao, who teaches creativity at the Harvard Business School, offers an approach that demystifies a topic traditionally confounding to business people everywhere. Drawing an analogy, Kao illustrates that creativity, like the musical discipline of jazz, has a vocabulary and a grammar. He explains how creativity needs a particular environment in which to blossom and grow. Like musicians in a jam session, a group of business people can take an idea, challenge one another's imagination, and produce an entirely new set of possibilities.

Jamming reveals how managers can stimulate creativity in their employees, free them of constraints and preconceptions, and guide them instead to a chosen goal where imagination is transformed into competitive supremacy. Using specific examples from a wide range of companies – including Coca-Cola, DreamWorks SKG and Sony – *Jamming* is a fascinating study of the shape and relevance of this most valued commodity in the workplace of the future.

'No matter how much you've downsized, or reengineered your company, all those efforts don't mean a thing if you ain't got that zing . . . *Jamming* serves as a primer on how to nurture talented workers . . . Kao's message is sound'   *Fortune*

0 00 638682 2

Microsoft Secrets

How the World's Most Powerful Software Company Creates Technology,
Shapes Markets and Manages People

MICHAEL A. CUSUMANO & RICHARD W. SELBY

Beyond the unquestioned genius and vision of CEO Bill Gates, what accounts for Microsoft's astounding success?

Microsoft commands the high ground of the information superhighway by owning the operating systems and basic applications programs that run on the world's 170 million computers.

Drawing on two years of unrestricted access to confidential documents and project data, eminent technology-scientists Cusumano and Selby reveal, for the first time, many of Microsoft's innermost secrets.

Forty in-depth interviews with employees enabled the authors to identify seven key strategies which demonstrate exactly how Microsoft competes and operates. They reveal a style of leadership, organization, competition and product development which is both consistent with the company's loosely structured 'programmer' culture and remarkably effective for mass-market production of software.

Managers in many different industries will discover hundreds of invaluable lessons in this superbly readable book.

'A fascinating book about a fascinating company'
PETER SENGE, author of *The Fifth Discipline*

'Anyone intending to approach their bank manager to fund their own software company should make this book the centre of their business plan'   *Computer Weekly*

'A unique glimpse into the company's inner workings'   *Daily Telegraph*

0 00 638778 0